The Cuban Counterrevolution

Jesús Arboleya
Translated by Rafael Betancourt

Ohio University Center for International Studies
Research in International Studies
Latin America Series No. 33
Athens

The books in the Ohio University Research in International Studies Series
are printed on acid-free paper ♾

08 07 06 05 04 03 02 01 00   5 4 3 2 1

La contrarrevolución cubana by Jesús Arboleya
first published by Editorial Ciencias Sociales, La Habana, 1997

Library of Congress Cataloging-in-Publication

Arboleya, Jesús.
[Contrarrevolución cubana. English]
The Cuban counterrevolution / Jesús Arboleya ; translated by Rafael Betancourt.
p. cm. — (Research in international studies. Latin America series ; no. 33)
Includes bibliographical references (p. -) and index.
ISBN 0-89680-214-0 (pbk. : alk. paper)
1. Cuba—Politics and government—1895- 2. Revolutions—Cuba—History—20th century. 3. Counterrevolutions—Cuba—History—20th century. 4. Cuba—Relations—United States. 5. United States—Relations—Cuba. I. Title. II. Monographs in international studies. Latin America series ; no. 33.

F1787.A6613 2000
303.48'27291073—dc21   00-032688

Contents

Introduction vii
Abbreviations xv

1. Background: Revolutions and Counterrevolutions 1
2. Counterrevolution within the Revolution 37
3. From Uprising to Invasion 75
4. The Counterrevolutionary Revolution 99
5. The War over the Roads of the World 136
6. Immigration and Counterrevolution 177
7. The Counterrevolution Renewed 218
8. The Counterrevolution after the Cold War 257

Abbreviations in Notes and Bibliography 301
Notes 303
Bibliography 337
Index 357

Introduction

We Cubans appreciate our history. This is not surprising, considering that since the colonization of the Americas our island, because of its location, has been one of the most coveted territories in the world and our national identity has necessarily been forged in the struggles to achieve and defend our independence.

For two centuries we have been known mostly for the sugar and tobacco grown on our soil, and from the beginning of time for the exuberance of our tropical environment, where Alejo Carpentier's "real-marvelous" is manifested daily. But, above all, we are known for our nineteenth-century epic of independence, for the notable radicalism of our political struggles of the early twentieth century, and, in particular, for the 1959 revolution that brought socialism for the first time to the Western Hemisphere and enhanced this small country's influence on world affairs to a level beyond its economic or military weight.

Yet, less is spoken about another angle of Cuban history, the fact that the Creole was, to a large extent, the fruit of the extermination of the indigenous population. That the Cuban nationality was founded on the basis of slavery and that the Creole elite defended that institution, contravening the most advanced and universal ideas of their era, all of which determined that we were the last country in Latin America to gain its independence. That the Cuban oligarchy became a natural ally of Spanish colonialism, with which the Latin American emancipation processes had to contend, and the basis of political support for an annexation current that dreamed of a Cuba integrated into the slave states of the American South. That we became the first of the U.S. neocolonies due, in part, to the fact that the native bourgeoisie[1] facilitated and joined in this effort.

The tenacity of the Cuban people in their struggles for national independence has earned them a special place in the history of modern revolutionary processes. Precisely because of this, an organic and integrated counterrevolutionary reaction has always been present in this scenario, a reaction that has been representative, like few others, of the domestic dimension that the implantation of the patterns of capitalist domination has had on dependent lands. A high degree of class polarization, inserted into international conflicts that project onto the national scene, has been a constant in Cuban political processes. Insularity and universality have marked Cuba's destiny, forcing it to assume the costs of a protagonism that on occasions has completely consumed the physical and emotional resources of the country.

Karl Marx warned that every revolution arises by confronting a counterrevolution that it itself generated: "a tight and potent counterrevolution, engendering an adversary."[2] Viewed from this perspective, counterrevolution is the inevitable result of every revolutionary process. It does not have an independent origin or identity; rather it is defined by the project it confronts. Its source of legitimacy is its denial of the revolutionary proposal. As a result, to undertake the study of the counterrevolutionary phenomenon it is imperative to first understand the nature of the revolutionary event that gave it birth.

The Cuban Revolution is a project of social justice that found its viability in anti-imperialist nationalism. It could be no other way, since the fundamental contradiction of the nation is to be found in the neocolonial condition imposed on it by the United States. That was Cuba: a neocolony. Transforming this reality—the objective of every revolution—meant radically modifying the system of domination that reigned in the country. Whether another option existed to reform the relation of dependence is open to discussion, but to "revolutionize" that relation there was no other alternative but to establish a new order.

Anti-imperialist nationalism in Cuba found its traditions in the preaching of José Martí. To this it added the doctrine of socialism, which rationalized the project of social equality and guaranteed the insertion of the Cuban Revolution into an international context that rendered its development—and in certain instances, its survival—valid until the collapse of the USSR and the European socialist camp. Nationalism, anti-imperialism, and socialism became the theoretical body of Cuban revolutionary ideology. The counterrevolution has been, therefore, the antithesis of this ideological proposition.

This revolutionary foundation is the result of a historical process that has its origins in the conflicts inherent in the formation of the Cuban nationality under specific colonial conditions. Those conditions were determined by the role that the country assumed in the emergent industrial capitalism of the nineteenth century, by the attempt to create a national identity from fiercely contradictory class perspectives, by the consequences of asserting independence against the grain of the dominant interests in each period, and, above all, by the ongoing historical dispute with the United States.

That dispute is the fruit of a class structure inherited from the colonial system, a structure that is transformed when the United States imposes new patterns of submission on the country and integrates the native elite into a dominant bloc with multinational bases, promoter of an ideology of dependency that is expressed in multiple ways. The study of the Cuban counterrevolution cannot overlook this supranational character of the conflict. "Ours is a counterpunch revolution," Che Guevara told Jean Paul Sartre, with which he described, maybe without meaning to, not only the origin of the tactical movements of the process, but also its strategic conditions.[3]

The stimulus to and the organization of the native counterrevolution have been essential components of U.S. policy toward Cuba, even before the revolutionary victory of 1959. The difference between this historical moment and previous revolutionary-counterrevolutionary processes is that for the first time the counterrevolution had to form and operate alienated from political power, and was forced to establish its principal social bases of support outside national territory. This transformed, at the same time, the composition and traditional political-ideological orientation of the Cuban migration processes, to the degree that this new emigration was assigned a counterrevolutionary function from which derives the preferential treatment it has received and the benefits that the U.S. system has bestowed upon it.

Due to the nationalist and anti-imperialist orientation adopted by the Revolution, its popular character and the deep structural transformations that occurred at all levels of the Cuban society, the native oligarchy—and the rest of the social strata integrated or identified with the neocolonial model, for economic or ideological reasons—emigrated early, and the core of opposition to the revolutionary project concentrated on U.S. soil. Presently, over a million persons of Cuban origin—nearly 10 percent of the island's population—live in the United States. Although that country has been the final destination of most Cuban immigrants since the early nineteenth century, currently that community is comprised mostly of persons that left the country after the revolutionary victory of 1959. This becomes a relevant fact for the nation's history given its economic, demographic, and cultural implications but, above all, because it reflects a political environment where one of its features is precisely immigration.

As a result, the counterrevolution has evolved not only in light of constraints imposed by the Cuban domestic political system, but also as a function of the relations between Cuba and the United States, of the nature of its links with the North American system and the degree of maturity which has been achieved in the process of integration of the Cuban immigrants into the host society. Therefore, the counterrevolutionary phenomenon within the immigration has two components. One, more far reaching and clearly in the majority, reflects the multiple and complex reactions of those sectors of the Cuban population dissatisfied with the revolutionary process which decide to emigrate, and which reinforce this position in accordance with the demands and benefits imposed by U.S. policy toward Cuba. The other constitutes a militant political movement, in the minority, tightly linked to the U.S. government, which has become a professional subversive structure whose continuity bears upon the personal well-being and the political status of those involved.

At first, the counterrevolution referred to the restoration of the structure and essential values of the prerevolutionary society, thus its main leaders were primarily figures that had played an active role in traditional Cuban politics. But later it became the expression of the political plans of a Cuban bourgeoisie consolidated as a result of its links with the U.S. power structure. It considered itself capable of participating organically in the system in alliance with other forces, in order to impose a Cuba policy which, if successful, would enable them to reap the benefits resulting from the role they hoped to play in the new mechanisms of domination which the United States would impose on the country. This new nature of the counterrevolution is related to the degree of integration of the Cuban immigrants into North American society and to the specific weight of the Cuban-American community in the whole of that society.

The counterrevolutionary function that the U.S. system has assigned to the Cuban immigration has conditioned its political activity, even its participation in that nation's domestic policy. This explains the persistence of an attitude that, defying the logic of time and of social transformations, continues to focus on Cuba from extremely hostile positions, which exert a negative influence not only on the possible options to resolve the differences between the two countries but also on an eventual normalization of relations between the immigrant community and the rest of Cuban society.

In contrast with the other Latin-American communities in the United States, and thanks to the preferential treatment received, the Cuban-American community has achieved in a relatively short time levels of economic and social development that make it one of the most successful immigrant groups ever established in this country. Much has been said about its participation in the mechanisms of penetration and domination of the United States in Latin America and its alliances with sectors of the extreme right in that continent. This, together with the counterrevolutionary function assigned to it by the system, has determined the clearly conservative political tendencies of the majority. This constitutes a break with the political tradition of prerevolutionary Cuban immigration and with the predominant historical characteristics of the Cuban political debate prior to 1959.

It is impossible to understand the way in which the Cuban counterrevolution was structured and has evolved, nor the role that the immigration has played in it, without reviewing the history and the role of the social classes in Cuba and, particularly, the relations of the island with its northern neighbor, the scenario in which the main contradictions of the Cuban postcolonial society have been played. The particular nature of the Cuban counterrevolutionary phenomenon, the role of the émigrés in it, and their interrelation with political processes that transcend Cuban reality oblige us, when approaching its study, to delve into the analysis of the ideological, political, and economic premises of the North American system of hegemony and the impact that the Cuban Revolution has had on this model of domination.

Counterrevolution in Cuba constitutes a historically inevitable phenomenon, because it reflects the struggles of the Cuban people for their independence and social development, always under adverse conditions, and which have placed us in the two extremes of the political spectrum in the continent. This explains the intensity of the rivalries that even today characterize the conflict between revolution and counterrevolution in the Cuban case.

This book describes the evolution of this process, beginning with its fundamental tendencies, comments on its constraints, and characterizes the context in which these have developed. The first chapter covers, in synthesis, the history of the political struggles in Cuba prior to 1959. Its objective is to provide the reader with useful background for understanding the events that take place after that date. Chapters 2, 3, and 4 cover the first stage of the counterrevolution, a process that culminates with the assassination of John F. Kennedy. Chapter 5 deals with a transition period, characterized by the bankruptcy of the traditional counterrevolutionary organizations, the strengthening of certain forms of terrorism, and the rise of alternative political groups within the Cuban immigration. Chapter 6 reviews the migration processes in Cuba and explains the relationship between immigration and counterrevolution in recent Cuban history. Chapters 7 and 8 analyze the new nature of the counterrevolution, its expression after the Cold War, and the variables that should influence its future behavior.

I am aware that I am not dealing with a linear process or one that is historically concluded. On the contrary, today more than ever the Cuban Revolution faces the challenge of demonstrating its viability, in opposition to forces revitalized by an international climate particularly favorable to their positions. As in any synthesis, we cannot escape the limitations inherent in generalizations, nor can we pretend to capture all the angles of the human drama, a phenomenon that resists being pigeonholed. My most evident purpose is to characterize, as objectively as possible, the "other option" proposed for the political future of the Cuban people.

A more ambitious objective—because it would last longer—would be to contribute elements to the already essential study of the Cuban Revolution, the most transcendental political phenomenon of the twentieth century in Latin America. Thus, this work is not, at least in my conception, limited to Cuba. Rather it pretends to advance the understanding of a wider context, to contribute an indispensable reference to the study of recent relations between Latin America and the United States, and to discern the logic that inspires North American strategy toward the continent. This policy is as old as our nations.

Under the aegis of a national security that has never been truly threatened and democratic aspirations very rarely achieved, it conceals a desire for hegemony that can only be realized through maintaining an unjust world order, in which we are expected to be not just peaceful observers but also grateful victims.

Abbreviations

ACU	Agrupación Católica Universitaria
ADR	Acción Democrática Revolucionaria
BAM	Brigada Antonio Maceo
CANF	Cuban-American National Foundation
CCD	Comité Cubano para la Democracia
CDR	Comité de Defensa de la Revolución (Committee for the Defense of the Revolution)
CORU	Comando de Organizaciones Revolucionarias Unidas
CRC	Consejo Revolucionario Cubano
CTC	Central de Trabajadores de Cuba
DEU	Directorio Estudiantil Universitario
DIER	Departamento de Investigaciones del Ejército Rebelde (Department of Investigations of the Rebel Army)
DRE	Directorio Revolucionario Estudiantil
ELN	Ejército de Liberación Nacional
FAR	Fuerzas Armadas Revolucionarias (Revolutionary Armed Forces)
FAL	Frente Anticomunista de Liberación
FEU	Federación Estudiantil Universitaria
FLNC	Frente de Liberación Nacional Cubano
FRD	Frente Revolucionario Democrático
FUO	Frente Unido Occidental
FUR	Frente de Unidad Revolucionaria
IEC	Instituto de Estudios Cubanos
INRA	Instituto Nacional de Reforma Agraria
JAC	Juventud de Acción Católica
JCS	Juventud Cubana Socialista

JEC	Juventud Estudiantil Católica
JOC	Juventud Obrera Católica
JURE	Junta Revolucionaria Cubana
MDC	Movimiento Demócrata Cristiano
MININT	Ministerio del Interior
MIRR	Movimiento Insurreccional de Recuperación Revolucionaria
MNRC	Movimiento Nacionalista Cubano
MRC	Movimiento de Resistencia Cívica
MRP	Movimiento Revolucionario del Pueblo
MRR	Movimiento de Recuperación Revolucionaria
M-30-11	Movimiento Treinta de Noviembre
NCCA	National Coalition of Cuban-Americans
NED	National Endowment for Democracy
OA	Organización Auténtica
OAS	Organization of American States
PCC	Partido Comunista de Cuba (Cuban Communist Party)
PDC	Plataforma Democrática Cubana
PPC	Partido del Pueblo Cubano (Ortodoxo)
PRC	Partido Revolucionario Cubano (Cuban Revolutionary Party)
PSP	Partido Socialista Popular
RCA	Resistencia Cívica Anticomunista
RECE	Representación Cubana en el Exilio
SGA	Special Group (Augmented)
UR	Unidad Revolucionaria

The Cuban Counterrevolution

Chapter 1

Background: Revolutions and Counterrevolutions

During the first few centuries of colonization, Spain's interest in Cuba was a result almost exclusively of the position of the island in the center of the Caribbean Sea. Lacking significant mineral resources and a native population sufficiently numerous or prepared to survive the rigors of the exploitation to which it was subjected, Cuba was utilized above all as a base of operations to exploit and colonize other American territories and, later, as a Spanish factory.

During this period, domestic production was limited to satisfying the needs of local consumption, the requirements of the ocean fleets, and the demand of a regional contraband market that came to be of some importance. The rise of the Cuban Creole was based on this economy. The Creole was a complex and unique product of transculturalization. The fruit of diverse ethnic, racial, and class roots, when Creoles recognized themselves as different from their ancestors they established a new relation of identity and belonging with the land where they were born and where they and their descendants would live. That moment marked the beginning of the formation of what would become Cuban nationality.

The bourgeois revolutions of the late eighteenth century, the emergence of industrial capitalism, the European wars, and the beginning of the independence movements in the Americas created the conditions for Cuba to begin to play a prominent role in the world market through the production of sugar with slave labor, paving the way for the consolidation of a native or Creole oligarchy organically integrated with the world capitalist market.

The extermination of the native population opened the way to the introduction of African slaves since the sixteenth century. But this occurrence did not achieve true relevance until the late seventeenth century, when the economy was oriented toward production for the world market. At that time, slave labor achieved such economic, political, and social importance that when they considered the question of slavery the Creole planters rejected independence as an option. Instead, the majority embarked on a search for reforms within the colonial system or sought separation through annexation to the United States.

On one hand, the plantation system favored Cuba's integration into the world market, allowed access to new technologies, and created sources of wealth that enabled cultural development and the rise of a very advanced intellectual core that would become the architects of the national ideology. But on the other, it led to deep social divisions that delayed independence, left an aftermath of racism, hampered integration of nationality, and limited Cuba's links with the rest of Latin America. Above all, the plantation system determined the dependence of the country on emerging systems of domination that set the conditions for chronic underdevelopment and prevented the powerful native oligarchy from leading the movement toward independence.

The autonomy movement—or its variant, assimilation—became impractical because of the very nature of the Spanish Empire and the decadence that had overtaken it by the nineteenth century. On the other hand, the annexation option did not succeed due to a combination of factors, evidence of the complex environment in which Cuban politics evolved in this period.

From an economic point of view, annexation to the United States had, for the Cuban planters, the attractions of preserving slavery and enabling full integration into what constituted their natural market. This project fit perfectly into the doctrine of North American expansionism and contributed an area of strategic value for its economic interests and the development of its military might. The doctrine of Manifest Destiny guided U.S. policy. In 1856, barely eight years after occupying half the territory of Mexico, the United States offered to buy Cuba from Spain for $130 million, an offer the Spaniards refused. The annexation of Cuba implied, nevertheless, a possible conflict with the European powers—England, in particular—that the United States was not willing to risk. It also would have favored the Southern slave states, at a time when the contradictions that led to the Civil War were already emerging. These factors thwarted a consensus in favor of annexation within the U.S. power elite.

In response to this situation, Washington initiated the theory of political gravitation: sooner or later, the weakness of the Spanish empire would drag Cuba inexorably into the hands of its northern neighbor. In fact, that was precisely the tendency on the economic front: by 1840 the United States had replaced Spain as Cuba's main trading partner. U.S. policy was aimed at preventing any other European power from taking over the island, or allowing Cuba to gain its independence and join the family of Latin American nations. The Cuban case was one of the causes that led to the pronouncement of the Monroe Doctrine in 1823, a philosophy that even today guides U.S. policy toward Cuba and the rest of Latin America.

Another source of early opposition to the annexation of Cuba was the cultural barrier, expressed in the birth of a national identity that resisted assimilation. Félix Varela and José Antonio Saco, two of the most important Creole political figures of the first half of the nineteenth century, rejected this option outright, based on strictly patriotic arguments. For Saco, annexation would have entailed the "disappearance of the Cuban nationality, the collective suicide of a people . . . to which a true patriot could never resign himself."[1]

The idea of annexation permeated the revolutionary sectors of the period due to the influence of these liberating ideas and the example of emancipation that the North American Revolution represented. But essentially this current had its basis in the interest of the Creole oligarchy in maintaining a system of slavery that was no longer defensible. The abolition of slavery and the victory of the Union in the U.S. Civil War sealed the destiny of slavery in Cuba. Nevertheless, the tendency toward annexation was revitalized, for other reasons, when the second great independence movement surged at the end of the century.

The Struggle for Independence

The revolution for Cuban independence, an unusual and unexpected event that began in 1968, occurred against the grain of the most powerful interests of the period. It began without a sufficiently mature national unity, it lacked resources or outside aid, and it challenged an army far superior in weapons and training. It reflected the will of a selected group of eastern Creole planters, organically less committed to the structures of slavery and imbued with the most advanced ideas of the time, of transforming the colonial reality of the country and bringing it to life as an independent and democratic nation. The Cuban historian Ramiro Guerra described this episode: "The Eastern insurrection was . . . an uprising of free peoples—white, mestizo, and black, and a great majority of a rural population. This insurrection was joined from the beginning . . . by all the slaves that were freed from their chains. . . . In dashing to war, the white insurgents assumed, because of their superior position, the direction of the war and took upon themselves an immense weight of responsibilities. All was sacrificed—family, social status, material goods, life itself—with the greatest resoluteness . . . in a war that the history of the ex-Spanish colonies shows, was possibly the bloodiest of the American wars of independence."[2]

The revolutionary sector of the Creole bourgeoisie was practically consumed in the war and thus the conflict took on a popular character that decisively confronted the interests of the slave oligarchy. The first insurrection for independence was frustrated after ten years of war. One of the main causes of this failure was the counterrevolutionary role played by the Creole oligarchy, in a context characterized by a high degree of ideological heterogeneity within the revolutionary ranks and regional conflicts resulting from an insufficiently mature national unity. Nevertheless, this war gave the Cuban people a sense of identity and consolidated a consciousness of Cuban nationality, a process that had begun long before.

Notwithstanding the class differences associated with racial diversity—at least as it relates to the generalized predominance of whites over blacks and mestizos—the process of the formation of Cuban nationality was facilitated by ethnic homogeneity. That homogeneity was formulated on the basis of unity of language, culture, character, and a sentiment of territorial belonging that were forged in the summons to the anticolonial war.[3]

Even as the slavery question alienated the majority of the national bourgeoisie from the independence struggle, that class played a decisive role in the formation of an identity that served as the basis for the nationalizing process in the prerevolutionary period of the nineteenth century.[4] But toward the end of that century the conditions in Cuba had changed radically. Slavery was abolished in 1886, followed by a significant concentration of wealth as well as a notable increase in U.S. control over the economy of the island. In contrast, the war consolidated an ideology and tradition of struggle that popularized the leadership of the revolution and radicalized its objectives. "The bourgeoisie did not participate in the War of Independence. Far from that, they harassed [the war] as much as possible from the ranks of the Autonomist Party. . . . If the antirevolutionary reformists of the era of Arango y Parreño, Saco, and Morales Lemus indirectly favored the development of the Cuban nationality, those of the Montoro period betray them without any excuses. Those were antirevolutionary attitudes. This one is counterrevolutionary."[5]

On the other hand, toward the end of the century the United States had become one of the world's principal economic powers and required secure markets for its products. The monopolization of its industry, finance, and commerce rolled forward with crushing force. And, having concluded its territorial expansion toward the west and south of the continent, the United States intended to connect both coasts by means of a interoceanic canal, which in turn required the protection of military bases located in the Caribbean and the Pacific. By that time Europe was in no condition to slow the expansionist impetus of the United States in Latin America. Such is the situation José Martí foresaw and tried to avoid with the independence of Cuba, incorporating a unique and advanced sense of anti-imperialism into the Cuban independence movement of the late nineteenth century. If the Monroe Doctrine constituted the theory of the expansion of U.S. "vital space" in Latin America, the Cuban Independence Revolution—in its most radical sense, consistent with the teachings of José Martí—was launched with the aim of preventing that expansion: "The free Antilles will save the independence of our America, and the honor, already doubtful and injured, of English America, and will possibly accelerate and secure the equilibrium of the world. . . [That is, it will] prevent, with the independence of Cuba, the expansion of the United States over the Antilles and their falling with that extra force over our American lands."[6]

U.S. Intervention

The intervention of the United States in the second Cuban War of Independence in 1898 frustrated once more the revolutionary aspirations of the Cuban nationalist movement and consolidated a system of dependence that employed the native bourgeoisie as its basic guarantor. According to André Gunder Frank, "Dependence should not nor cannot be considered a purely 'external' relationship imposed on all Latin Americans from outside and against their will. Rather dependence is also an 'internal' and integral condition of Latin American society, which defines the dominant bourgeoisie in Latin America, but at the same time is consciously and gladly accepted by them."[7]

Dependence determined the nature of the Cuban bourgeoisie, conditioned its interests in relation to the rest of the population, and established its attitude toward the nation. "When you speak in Cuba about a national bourgeoisie, the concept must refer not to criteria of nationality, generically speaking, but to the positions derived from the national interest. From that perspective the sugar planters cannot be considered national bourgeoisie, though they may be a native bourgeoisie, because their historical interest essentially contradicted the interests of the nation and their actions opposed those interests. In contrast, the nonsugar bourgeoisie could have played a progressive historical role in the presocialist period, which, nevertheless, it did not do, even timidly."[8] Later I shall analyze the objective limitations that this nonsugar sector of the Cuban bourgeoisie also faced in order to play the role described by Carlos Rafael Rodríguez. For now it is sufficient to point out the influence that that intervention had on the formation and definition of the interests of this class in the Cuban neocolonial context.

The United States did not decide to undertake the annexation of Cuba because internal and external factors prevented it—among them the existence in Cuba of a consciousness of independence that could not be ignored. But there was also the presence of powerful domestic sugar interests in that nation that feared Cuban competition for the U.S. domestic market under conditions of equality. In addition there was the pressure against annexation exerted by a strong anticolonial ideological current in the United States, which for many years sympathized with the Cuban cause and only accepted North American intervention in the war on that basis.

In any case, U.S. intervention imposed a government of occupation that dismantled the military and political institutions of the revolution and created the conditions that guaranteed the imposition of the neocolonial domination of the country. U.S. investments and loans enabled the recovery of the battered Cuban sugar industry, but that was in exchange for customs preferences that subordinated national trade to exports originating in the United States. It also consolidated the structural dependence of the Cuban economy on the United States to a degree that no other country had experienced at the time. This was the culmination, in its fundamental aspects, of a process of penetration of U.S. capital into Cuba that began after the end of the first War of Independence in 1887. By 1886, U.S. investments amounted to $45 million and trade between the two countries totaled $100 million, ranking Cuba as the fourth largest U.S. trading partner.[9] These interests carried significant weight in the decision to intervene in the Spanish-Cuban War and meant, moreover, that, in the Cuban case, the nucleus of the exploitive class was comprised principally of foreigners, a key element to understanding the nature of Cuban political struggles.[10]

The war and occupation produced profound changes in the structure of agrarian property holdings. Over 70 percent of the land was mortgaged and in many cases the land titles were not recognized by the occupation forces. U.S. companies purchased another portion for the construction of railroads. Large U.S. plantation companies became firmly entrenched, so that by 1906 they had accumulated 20 percent of all land and 75 percent of cattle ranches. Besides the great landholdings, U.S. corporations came to dominate in a brief time the railroads, telephone service, electric power, urban transportation, construction, mining, and banking. Only those Cubans with large sugar plantations and mills were able to maintain or increase their holdings.[11]

Political subordination to the United States was the inevitable result of this situation. Nevertheless, the U.S. government wanted to give dependence legal basis and thus imposed the Platt Amendment to the constitution of the new republic.[12] "Plattism" was above all an expression of "Monroeism,"[13] that is, a measure meant to check European interests in the Caribbean, establishing in unequivocal terms the U.S. desire for hegemony in the area. The Platt Amendment became, in the final analysis, a "property deed" over Cuba, which, in light of the contradictions among the superpowers, was tantamount to establishing a colony. President McKinley viewed it as such when in 1899 he said that "the new Cuba . . . shall, necessarily, be united to us by strong ties of unique intimacy and strength. . . . the binds of union shall be organic or conventional, but the destinies of Cuba are, in a legitimate form and manner, irrevocably united to ours. How and to what degree is to be determined in the future."[14]

The chosen option was the establishment of a neocolonial model, the first of its kind in Latin America, sustained on the domestic side by an ideology of dependence that accepted Plattism as a "natural condition," rooted in the supposed incapacity of the Cuban people to govern themselves. This endeavor was complemented by the educational policy imposed by the government of occupation: public schools were to teach English, and knowledge of that language became a cultural prerequisite for the Creole elite. Moreover, the occupation government established a training program for Cuban teachers that by 1920 had sent 90 percent of them to the United States to study English. Protestant churches, the great majority of which were financed by U.S. companies, established their houses of worship and some of the most exclusive private schools in the country. North

American newspapers, culture, products, and tastes invaded the island, and Cuba also became one of the principal destinations for U.S. tourism.[15] The nature of this relationship conditioned the Cuban economy and established the class structure as well as the main parameters of the social and political struggles in the country until the 1959 revolution.

This neocolonial state demanded the existence of a dominant bloc that would legitimize and orchestrate the system of dependence. For that reason, U.S. intervention left the social structure intact, protected the native oligarchy and assured it a predominant role in the future administration of the country, integrating it in this manner into the new scheme of domination. The resulting class structure of the neocolonial model was configured on the basis of a dominant Creole bloc comprising the sugar producers, the planters, and the importer-merchants[16]—to which should be added what has come to be known as the bureaucratic bourgeoisie. This latter group constitutes a social category that found in the public sector an accessible source of capital, in exchange for guaranteeing the stability of the regime. These sectors traded functions, related to one another in various ways, and were organically integrated for historically determined economic and ideological reasons. "The neocolonial oligarchy was obliged to accept and defend—we consider that historically it had no other choice—the role of supplier of sugar to the U.S. market and importer of products of North American origin. . . . The historical and structural limitations of the neocolonial oligarchy increased incessantly the vicious circle of underdevelopment."[17]

The nonsugar industrial bourgeoisie reflected the other alternative of Cuban capitalist development. Its origins tended to place it in opposition to the interests of the neocolonial system, but the incapacity of this sector to lead a structural reform of the Cuban capitalist model was determined by the nature of the system itself and the way that system functioned in the country. Not even the relative boom in national industry driven by the Second World War was able to modify significantly this state of affairs.

Between 1946 and 1958, although U.S. investment in the manufacturing sector constituted only 7.8 percent of total investment in Cuba, it doubled the capital in this sector of the economy to date,[18] marking a tendency that favored a modest growth of the domestic industry. Rather than helping, this process restricted even more the possibilities of the development of an independent national bourgeoisie. Nearly all the principal nonsugar Cuban industries that originated in this period were in fact subsidiaries of U.S. corporations or were associated with U.S. capital. Only the various small industries that supplied the less competitive areas of the market were spared this process.[19]

The connections between the nonsugar bourgeoisie and foreign capital that ensued, together with the financial, business, and family ties arising between the various native capitalist groups, determined that, by the middle of the century, there no longer existed clear boundaries between the different strata of the national bourgeoisie. The bourgeoisie would end up organically incorporated into the neocolonial system, not only in economic but also in cultural terms. "What evolved throughout the twentieth century was the rise of a Cuban wealthy class that had been educated in American schools and that was usually bilingual in English and Spanish, Protestant or nominally Catholic in religion, conservative in political and economic views, intimately linked by investment and employment to the American corporate world, and familiar or addicted to the products of the American consumer society and to the symbols of the American popular culture."[20] This tendency to assimilate in order to survive as a class within the neocolonial system limited, perhaps more than any other factor, the possibilities of the nonsugar industrial bourgeoisie of leading the country's political process. After 1959 this tendency became a decisive element in the massive incorporation of this sector into the counterrevolution.

This conflict was sharpened by the specific factors that influenced the evolution of class relations in Cuba as a result of the progressive development of the labor movement. Two contemporary analyses of the Cuban economy, the *Conference for the Progress of the National Economy* (1948) and the study carried out by the Reconstruction and Development Bank (1951), agreed that the single most important obstacle to investment in Cuban nonsugar industry was the relatively high salaries obtained by the working class and its degree of unionization.[21]

The increase in North American investment in Cuban nonsugar industrial sectors created areas of coincidence between foreign capital and the nonsugar industrial elite in topics such as reduction of labor costs and expanding the opportunities for domestic industry. This last aspect was detrimental to the interests of the native importer-merchants, but not to the sugar producers, whose antidevelopment attitude was more political than economic: the obligatory North American reciprocity. This phenomenon had to do with the advancement of the globalization of U.S. capital, whose control over Latin-American domestic markets reversed to a great degree the effects of protectionism. In the Cuban case, U.S. capital became one of its advocates, thus increasing the dependence of the bourgeoisie as a whole.

In many countries of Latin America the bourgeois populist movements had as their foundation the emergence and development of a sector of the bourgeoisie linked to the domestic market. Yet in Cuba, because of the factors noted above, when these movements arose they were headed by the petite bourgeoisie, a class that played a very significant role in Cuban political struggles. By the standards of underdeveloped countries, Cuba had a very large petite bourgeoisie.[22] Functionally, this class comprises small artisans, merchants, employees, professionals, tradesmen, and the majority of the students in middle and higher education, which together have come to be known as the middle class.[23] "With a degree of intellectual enlightenment and understandable ambitions for progress, the urban petite bourgeoisie constituted from the beginning a very sensitive area, capable of embracing the ferment of revolutionary restlessness every time historical conditions fostered it."[24]

Although this tendency could, in fact, be perceived in important sectors of the middle class, it should be remembered, nevertheless, that the majority of this social stratum was allied in a special way with the dominant bloc, whether as managers and top technicians in the nation's businesses, as government officials, or as officers in the military and security services. The conservative intellectual sector was also drawn from the middle class. On the other hand, the middle class, determined on the basis of a more or less arbitrary average income level, reflected an absolute heterogeneity of economic interests and ideological beliefs that limited their ability to band together on a given political project.

In 1958 farmers were a social class of some 200,000 persons, of which 140,000 were peasants or semiproletarians and less than 25 percent owned the land they tilled.[25] Although in areas adjacent to the main cities the small farmer was a supplier to the local market, the single-crop nature of agriculture determined that, in the 1950s, the country imported 41 per cent of the food it consumed.[26] The medium and small farmer was linked to sugar production, mostly as a sugarcane grower, whether owner or tenant of the land, and his interests were mostly tied to the economic structure that depended on the North American market for sugar. Because of this, a good part of the agrarian middle class, made up of some 25,000 persons,[27] resembled the nonsugar industrial bourgeoisie in their relation to the dominant sectors of the neocolonial system.

The Cuban working class toward the end of the 1950s was made up of some 500,000 industrial workers—including sugar industry workers—and another 600,000 farmworkers.[28] The cardinal problem for this sector of the population was unemployment, which hovered around 25 percent during much of the republican period,[29] as well as underemployment, which also remained very high. The structural problems of the economy raised few hopes for a solution to this situation. The sugar industry employed half of the labor force, occupied 82 percent of the land (although it cultivated only 22 percent),[30] and utilized 70 percent of the installed industrial capacity.[31] Similarly, the sugar export quota system and the limitations imposed by the market on other production alternatives also tended to perpetuate unemployment.

U.S. companies generated a significant labor aristocracy comprised of some 150,000 workers,[32] who, besides enjoying better salaries and guarantees, made up the strongest sectors of the organized urban proletariat. Despite the differences between rural and urban workers and the destabilizing factor of mass unemployment, by the 1930s the labor movement had achieved a high degree of organization and their influence over the political life of the country was significant.

The Revolution of 1930

Neocolonialism reproduced, under a new label, the corruption of the Cuban institutions and political ways characteristic of the colonial period. In the first twenty years of the twentieth century the United States intervened militarily in Cuba another three times. The sugar crisis of 1920 bankrupted a good portion of the national landholders and concentrated even more the agrarian and industrial property, services, and banking in the hands of North American capital, making the Cuban economy one of the most subordinate in the world.

This crisis was followed by a period of political tensions whose principal manifestations were the establishment of the Machado dictatorship in 1925, the general economic crisis of 1929, the 1930–34 revolution against Gerardo Machado y Morales, and the counterrevolutionary counteroffensive that followed. This was a period in which the voracity of the North American monopolies harmed even their domestic allies and provoked the temporary reaction of the native oligarchy. Nevertheless, the most relevant aspect of this period was the formation of a popular movement that had as its principal protagonists the working and middle classes. Cuban political history would be indelibly marked by these years, which saw the rise of the principal groups and many of the individuals that were to be protagonists of the processes of revolution, counterrevolution, and reforms that took place in the country until the victory of the 1959 Revolution. And their impact extended even later, since some of the principal counterrevolutionary groups had their origins in the organizations that arose at this time.

Since 1923, when Communist leader Julio Antonio Mella founded the Federación Estudiantil Universitaria (FEU), a current of opposition began to converge in many forms and expressions. The Protesta de los Trece, the struggle for sovereignty over the Isle of Pines, and the Movimiento de Veteranos y Patriotas intensified the internal political debate. The creation of the Central Nacional Obrera de Cuba and of the first Communist Party radicalized the process and laid the organizational bases for a labor movement that would play a leading role in later events. Machado was able to forge an alliance with the principal groups comprising the oligarchy that assured the continuity of the dictatorship, but also sparked the reaction of other sectors. In 1927 a group of important intellectuals expressed their opposition through the Grupo Minorista, and the Directorio Estudiantil Universitario (DEU) was founded. Its membership included such figures as Gabriel Barceló, Eduardo Chibás, Antonio Guiteras, and others who became important protagonists in the political battles of the nation from that time on. Mella, exiled in Mexico, was struggling to organize an armed insurrection when he was assassinated by order of Machado in 1929. He was replaced in the leadership of the Communists—if not officially, at least morally and practically—by Rubén Martínez Villena. The student and labor strikes of 1930 launched the anti-Machado revolutionary process. That same year the DEU was reorganized and its leadership fell into the hands of the group that years later would form the leadership of the Auténticos, among them Carlos Prío Socarrás and Manuel Antonio "Tony" de Varona. In the midst of the revolutionary fervor—expressed through strikes, urban terrorism, and revolts of various groups—the Ala Izquierda Estudiantil was founded under the leadership of men like Pablo de la Torriente Brau and Raúl Roa, uniting the most radical student sectors. On the other extreme of the political spectrum, the ABC, headed by Jorge Mañach, represented a sector that, assuming national-socialist positions, opposed the dictatorship from an extreme-right perspective. It was also during this period that the Agrupación Católica Universitaria (ACU) was created, with the aim of uniting the Catholic right wing and projecting it ideologically. The ACU would later become the bedrock of the Falangist and the Christian Democracy movements in Cuba.

By 1933 it was becoming evident that the dictatorship was incapable of resisting popular pressure. The Cuban case became a problem for the Good Neighbor policy of Franklin D. Roosevelt, and he sent Ambassador Sumner Wells to Havana to forge a mediated solution that would avoid intervention yet be favorable to U.S. interests. The ABC and the traditional parties backed this effort but it was rejected by the rest of the political forces and by Machado himself, who, through his intransigence, succeeded in temporarily aborting the mediation. Nevertheless, in August, events unfolded with another and this time definitive general strike. The army command withdrew their support of Machado, which led him to seek exile in the United States. The U.S. government tried to impose the figurehead Carlos Manuel de Céspedes, but most of the opposition groups refused to accept him. Inspired by the DEU, a revolt of army sergeants and soldiers took place that resulted in the dismissal of the principal chiefs of the armed forces and the appointment of a military junta headed in the end by Sgt. Fulgencio Batista Zaldívar. The government then passed into the hands of the *pentarquía,* or five-man junta, that governed barely five days, followed by the appointment as president of the republic of Ramón Grau San Martín, a university professor backed by the DEU. The designated minister of government, war, and navy was Antonio Guiteras, the most radical revolutionary of the period.

The Grau government refused to swear allegiance to the Constitution because it still contained the Platt Amendment. The United States countered by refusing to recognize the new government and threatening to intervene militarily. Guiteras dissolved the traditional parties, confiscated properties obtained through corruption, enacted the eight-hour workweek and the minimum wage, established the protection of native workers against those born abroad, and nationalized the U.S.-owned electric company. The conflicts continued: in October a group of former army officers revolted, and were massacred by Batista's troops; the same occurred with an attempted uprising by the ABC. In the end, as a result of North American maneuvers and the inability of the Grau government to form a united front against the reaction, the Government of 100 Days fell and the presidency was left to Carlos Mendieta. This proved that the right wing had reorganized and that true power was in the hands of Fulgencio Batista, subordinate in body and soul to U.S. interests. It marked the beginning of the counterrevolutionary counteroffensive. Raúl Roa described the brief Grau presidency:

> The apolitical, technocratic, and academic government did not know where to begin, nor what to do, nor where to go. Bewildered, it twisted and turned. The thin line broke. The spirit of *Pubillones* was installed at the palace. From a competent physiologist, Grau changed into a marvelous juggler. He graciously flirted with the left and winked conspicuously at the intimidated bourgeoisie. He uttered affronts to Wells and paid the foreign debt. He was anxious to be recognized by Washington and permitted anti-imperialist meetings. He launched a virulent manifesto against Business and Corporations and secretly sent emissaries to seek their support. There was never a funnier and,

at the same time, more tragic spectacle. Thus was born the "Mongonato,"[33] between anxiety and mockery.[34]

The Counterrevolutionary Counteroffensive

The repression resulting from the counterrevolutionary counteroffensive was fierce and generalized, although the government tried to assuage it with popular measures such as the abolition of the already anachronistic Platt Amendment and promises of economic concessions for various sectors of the population. The majority of the leaders of the DEU, under the leadership of Ramón Grau, formed the Partido Revolucionario Cubano (PRC), popularly known as the Auténticos, due to the existence of a dissident faction that also pretended to capitalize on the name of the party founded by José Martí. Joven Cuba was also created under the leadership of Antonio Guiteras, who planned for armed insurrection. Just one year later Guiteras was betrayed and died combating Batista's troops. Rubén Martínez Villena had also died some months before, a victim of tuberculosis, thus bringing an end to the revolutionary cycle that began in 1930.

The Revolution of 1930 represented a break with a primitive neocolonial order that had not yet been able to reconcile the expansion of North American capital with the need to maintain a dependent bourgeoisie that would guarantee the stability of the system. The multiplicity of conflicts generated by this situation permitted the anti-Machado revolution to mobilize diverse sectors of Cuban society, but also imposed organic limitations on the opposition forces that hindered its unity and thwarted the success of the revolutionary project. Rubén Martínez Villena characterized the crisis of the Cuban neocolonial model: "The principal problem for Yankee imperialism in Cuba is the conflict of its own internal difficulties, difficulties that a regime of exploitation and domination already consolidated in the nearly exclusive penetration of the basic sectors of the economy of a country, but that has come to be unbearable for the masses at the same time as it begins to show signs of internal decay.... Cuba constitutes at present the weakest link of the imperialist chain in the Caribbean."[35]

Despite its failure, the Revolution of 1930 was significant in that it identified the neocolonial condition as Cuba's principal problem, revitalized the sense of civic duty of the popular forces, and consolidated the labor movement, which was to become one of the most powerful of its times. Besides, the revolution transformed the system of alliances by which the country had been governed, and centered the focus of the struggles around the agrarian issue and workers' rights. The native oligarchy supported as much as possible the Machado dictatorship, but its situation was affected by a decade of economic crisis and by displacement at the hands of foreign capital. The balance in favor of counterrevolution was tilted by the support of the army for U.S. mediation, thereby converting the armed forces into a decisive element in the political life of the nation.

The victory of the counterrevolutionary counteroffensive provided guarantees and stability to the restructured dominant groups, which reflected a greater degree of organic maturity of the neocolonial system. Once the revolutionary moment was overcome, efforts were made to perfect the mechanisms of that system and reform the political machinery, but the country's economic structure left little room for building a consensus. The dependence on the North American market was reaffirmed with the signing of a new treaty of "trade reciprocity" in 1934 that established quotas for sugar exports to the United States, regulated sugar prices, and established a system of import preferences disproportionately favorable to U.S. products. This made it even more difficult to develop alternative domestic production and aggravated the structural problems of the economy. In this manner, domination, and not hegemony—understood from a Gramscian perspective—characterized the Cuban neocolonial system before and after the revolutionary process of 1930.

The PRC became the main opposition force. Its program represented essentially the reformist aspirations and interests of the nonsugar industrial bourgeoisie and the petite bourgeoisie. The PRC took advantage of the revolutionary mystique—in particular of Guiteras's radicalism in the Government of 100 Days—to reap significant popular support. The political crossroads created by Roosevelt's New Deal and the international antifascist movement's so-called popular front favored the reformist theses of this current, packaged within a nationalist rhetoric that included a loosely defined anti-imperialism. "The PRC's scheme of changes proposes to . . . harmonize the relations between capital and labor by means of state intervention, and generate, through state control, the means necessary to distribute the social wealth. . . . Although the program refers to the need for agrarian reform, its contents do not alter the oligarchy's relations and command. On the other hand, they do not propose measures to promote primary industrialization. And although it denounces the harmful economic domination of the United States . . . it proposes no concrete project of anti-imperialist liberation."[36]

The revolutionary opportunity aborted, what ensued was a period of relative political opening. Political parties, including that of the Communists, were legalized, the labor movement was institutionally strengthened, and a Constitutional Assembly convoked. The resulting Constitution of 1940 turned out to be, doctrinally, one of the most advanced of the times, yet it never benefited from the complementary legislation that would have enabled it to be effective in practice. This was the period of greatest stability for representative democracy in Cuba and, after Fulgencio Batista completed his presidential term, the Auténticos went on to win the electoral contests of 1944 and 1948.

The first Auténtico president was Ramón Grau. He enjoyed wide popular support and governed in a climate of economic bonanza that enabled a relative increase in social spending, improvements in domestic industry, and record sugar harvests. The Auténticos, nonetheless, were charged with imposing on Cuba the doctrines of the Cold

War. Their administrations, particularly that of Carlos Prío Socarrás, Grau's successor to the presidency, were characterized by repression of the labor movement and persecution of the Communists. Political corruption and gangland battles became official practice during this period.

The dependent nature of the Cuban political system inverts the roles of the opposing political groups; thus the Batista administration of the 1940s ended up adopting a "tropical version" of Roosevelt's New Deal, while the "populist Auténticos" some years later turned out to be frenzied McCarthy crusaders. Germán Sánchez summarizes the results of the Auténtico reformist experiment:

> Autenticismo and the charismatic figure of Grau obtained control of the government after a strong mass movement without precedent in neocolonial history. The absence of an emerging industrial bourgeoisie, with aspirations and possibilities for controlling the populist movement, caused the PRC, which did not have the strength to overcome or resist the national oligarchy, to weaken in its exercise of government until it became an instrument of the most reactionary sectors. The crisis of reformism provoked the frustration of the masses, who, having been cheated by the Auténtico experiment, began to question more emphatically the entire neocolonial political system.[37]

The last reformist effort in prerevolutionary Cuban politics was the creation, in 1947, of the Partido del Pueblo Cubano (Ortodoxo) (PPC), under the leadership of Eduardo Chibás, until then one of the principal leaders of the Auténticos. The PPC did not arise with the political support of the United States; on the contrary, the Cold War had ended the period of reforms that constituted the foundation of Ortodoxo philosophy and confronted the party with the situation that existed in the country. The organization was thus created from a heterogeneous and complex system of alliances. The right wing was comprised of a group of traditional politicians that saw the party as a new electoral option. The center—its fundamental political nucleus

—represented the sectors that reflected the interests and aspirations of the reformist middle class. Meanwhile, the left was composed of very radical revolutionary elements who were not yet capable of forming an independent organization, nor of totally breaking with the rules of play of national politics. Fidel Castro succeeded in becoming the principal leader of this last current.

The PCC centered its program on cleaning up corruption in government and respecting democratic order, based, according to Eduardo Chibás, on the following conditions: "Rescue the Auténtico program and doctrine—nationalism, socialism, and anti-imperialism—carrying out the activities within the democratic system established by the Constitution of 1940. Create with this objective a party truly revolutionary in its functional structure that will bring together the elements interested in national liberation—that is, professionals, farmers, workers, young people, and women. Fight ceaselessly against corruption, privilege, bribery, abuse of power, and other vices of traditional politics. Against the politics of alliances without ideology, firmly maintain ideology without mystification of the authentic Cuban Revolution. Adopt forms of organization and leadership that will generate the discipline and militancy essential for a revolutionary party. Launch a process of dialogue with the people in order to form the party."[38]

Chibás was no communist—on the contrary. Throughout his life he was an ardent enemy of that movement and its ideology. Despite a radical rhetoric very much in tune with the times, he did not exceed the limits of bourgeois liberalism, which explains how at the same time that he fought foreign monopolies and Cuba's dependence on them, he could defend the political-ideological structures that covered up this pattern of domination. The tragedy of Chibás was his awareness of the problems and his incapacity to supply viable alternatives within the limits imposed by his class interests and his ideological development. His principal historical merit lies in having made decency a political banner and in transporting this sense of ethics to those who honestly came to believe in him. As in the case of the Auténticos years before, the Ortodoxos reflected the existence of a political climate and a popular conscience that conditioned the radicalism of the domestic political debate and demanded reforms unattainable within the context of the neocolonial system. Such was the dilemma of the Cuban political movement when, on March 10, 1952, Fulgencio Batista once again appeared on the scene and led the coup d'état that would sharpen these contradictions and accelerate the Revolution.

The Batista Dictatorship

In the decade of the 1950s, Cuba was a country of striking contrasts. If on the one hand, according to some indicators, it ranked as one of the most economically and culturally developed countries in the hemisphere, the social imbalances were so acute that the political situation was constantly under tension. According to a report by the Truslow Commission for the Bank for Reconstruction and Development in 1951,[39] since 1924 the Cuban economy had lost its dynamism and become unstable, not only because of high chronic unemployment, but also because of the insecurity of salaried workers and investors. Confirming this view, Thomas G. Paterson argues that in the 1950s, despite an increase in U.S. investments, the Cuban economy grew at a rate not greater than 1 percent annually.[40] Furthermore, a study by the U.S. Department of Commerce covering the period from 1950 through 1954 revealed that the annual per capita income of Cubans was $312, one-third that of the poorest states of the union at that time. Nevertheless, they said, this average could be overstated and a figure closer to reality could be 180 pesos annually, or even less, if one considered the large inequalities that existed in the country.

In 1956 the ACU carried out a study that analyzed the differences between urban and rural sectors in Cuba. The study concluded that

75 percent of rural dwellings were *bohíos,* or shacks with dirt floors, palm-board walls, and palm-thatched roofs. Half these dwellings lacked any kind of sanitary installation, 91 percent lacked electricity, 97 percent had no refrigeration, and 85 percent were without running water. Only 4 percent of the peasants ate meat as a regular part of their diet, less than 1 percent ate fish, less than 2 percent consumed eggs, only 3 percent ate bread, 11 percent drank milk, and they rarely ate vegetables. This same study revealed that 60 percent of the country's doctors practiced in Havana province. Thus, while in the capital and surrounding area there was one doctor for every 420 inhabitants, in Pinar del Río, to the west, the ratio was one for every 2,100, while in the extreme east it fell to one doctor for every 2,550 inhabitants. Half the children of school age did not attend school, and of the population above six years, one-third was illiterate and another third had no schooling beyond the third grade, which made them functional illiterates.

The rigidity of the economic structure had become a disincentive to investment, thus the bourgeoisie tended to invest in real estate or expatriate their wealth, particularly to the United States. According to the aforementioned studies of the Truslow Commission and the U.S. Department of Commerce, in 1950 there were more than $100 million of Cuban origin invested in Florida real estate, and deposits in U.S. banks totaled $260 million. We can assume that the tendency toward capital flight increased during the 1950s as a result of the improvement in the economy, explosion in political corruption, and increased political instability. For example, it is estimated that in 1957 alone Cuban "tourists" spent $400 million in Miami,[41] that Carlos Prío took with him some $90 million in public funds when he left power in 1952, and that Fulgencio Batista fled with another $350 million in 1959.[42]

By 1958 U.S. investment in Cuba topped $1 billion and controlled 40 percent of sugar production, owned 90 percent of electric and telephone utilities, and dominated transportation and mining; 25

percent of all deposits were held by U.S. banks. In addition, the taxes paid by these companies contributed only one-fifth of the revenue financing the national budget. On the contrary, it was quite common for the Batista government to assume part of the costs, and therefore the risks, of new investments, which became one of the main techniques for embezzlement of public funds and made the U.S. Mafia one of the great beneficiaries of these arrangements. Through investments and government guarantees, 28 hotels with gambling casinos were built between 1952 and 1958, and the Batista government even named the notorious gangster Meyer Lansky as advisor for tourism.[43] The level of control acquired by the U.S. Mafia over various sectors of the Cuban economy and the resulting political connections developed at all levels in the country help to explain the future participation of North American organized crime in counterrevolutionary activity.

In Cuba neocolonialism was incapable of consolidating a hegemonic bloc that stabilized national political life. This period was characterized by the absence of stable leadership, which helps to explain the cyclical convulsions of the political system and the sharpening of the contradictions. These take on an anti-imperialist character once the problem of overcoming the state of dependence becomes the dividing line between classes, as well as the patriotic premise and precondition for achieving ethics in public life. As in 1925, the dictatorship accelerated the corrosion of political structures and blocked the structural adjustments that were necessary to stem increasing popular dissatisfaction. The revolutionary opportunity did not arise in Cuba as a result of the absolute deterioration of the economy. On the contrary, compared to other periods, these were relatively good times for the national economy as a whole. Possibly due to this, the revolution did not take the form of uncontrolled social explosions. Rather, it was the result of the conscious will of those sectors interested in transforming the imposed modus vivendi, and the inability of the dominant group to create a consensus capable of neutralizing their intentions. It was, in fact, a reflection of a crisis of power that found in the Revolution the only realistic opportunity for a solution.

Since the 1930s, Batista was the United States' man of trust in Cuba. His 1952 coup fit in with the trend of U.S. politics in Latin America. This was despite, or perhaps precisely because, the military takeover radically altered the rules of the system of representative democracy that had been functioning in the country. "Containing the Soviet threat" had become the dominant theme of U.S. foreign policy, in part as a reaction to the new challenges that were posed by the advances of socialism and also as an excuse to create a consensus to justify the interventionist actions of the United States. Noam Chomsky writes that this strategy of world domination, resulting from the position of hegemony gained by this country after the war, considers chronic political instability in the Third World as one of the main threats to the new world order. It opts in favor of the repressive control that the dependent governments are able to impose on these countries.[44] Therefore, whatever their participation in the Batista coup, the event was well received by the North American power structure. It corresponded with the desire for hegemony that required continental stability, understood as the firm control over the governments of Latin America.

The revolutionary phenomenon in the Cuban case was precisely the rise of new and prevailing forces within the opposition that represented a political project which, even though it was moderate in its program, proposed objectives contrary to the very essence of the neocolonial model. The attack on Moncada Barracks on July 26, 1953, led by Fidel Castro, evidenced the rise of this new generation of revolutionaries who, in their aims and methods, broke strategically with the traditional political forces and set their sights on transforming the dependence of Cuban society on the United States. This project could not be implemented without affecting North American interests and those of the native oligarchy, upholders of the neocolonial regime. But it also posed in the medium run the dilemma of the real possibility of structuring a system of alliances headed by the nationalist sectors of the bourgeoisie and the petite bourgeoisie, capable of launching an alternative model of independent capitalist development for Cuba. The fundamental ideological differences in the anti-Batista movement centered on the strategic objectives of the Revolution, and these contradictions can later be found among the causes for the break of many of the participants with the revolutionary process after 1959.

Analyzing this historical moment, Fidel Castro said:

> The traditional parties and leaders were absolutely incapable of organizing any resistance to the reactionary military dictatorship.... The Marxist-Leninist Party, on its own, had neither the means, forces, nor national and international conditions to carry out armed insurrection against a modern army. Some maintained the reactionary theory that you can make revolution with the army or without the army, but never against the army.... That was and had to be the work of new communists.... If, in fact, this was not the generalized thinking of all of us who took the path of revolutionary armed struggle in our country, it was the thinking of the principal leaders.... The attack on Moncada Barracks did not bring about the victory of the Revolution at the time, but it signaled the way and outlined the program of national liberation that would open for our country the doors of socialism.[45]

The 26th of July Movement was originally made up of individuals from the more radical sectors of the Ortodoxo youth wing. They were, for the most part, humble men without any commitment to the political past of the republic and convinced that armed struggle was the only alternative against the dictatorship. The conscious aim of Fidel Castro to insure that this remain the social composition of the vanguard of the revolutionary movement is evident in the selection of the men who would attack Moncada Barracks in 1953. As its influence grew, the movement assimilated elements from all social classes and the struggle was extended to many fronts and sectors.

The most significant strategic contribution of the 26th of July

Movement was the formation of the Rebel Army. In recognizing the "guerrilla focus" as the catalyst of the revolutionary struggle, the Rebel Army not only obtained tactical military advantages that facilitated the survival of the revolutionary forces, but it was also able to constitute a mass movement, which the urban warfare groups, because of their vulnerability, could hardly organize. In this manner, the peasantry, which was the principal productive force in the country, was recruited into the revolutionary movement, and the struggle was aimed at confronting, defeating, and demoralizing the military apparatus, the backbone of the regime. The Rebel Army also filled the power vacuum caused by the collapse of the dictatorship; the revolutionary forces assumed control of the country, completely replacing the old repressive instruments.

The bourgeoisie and middle-class sectors, to date the principal protagonists in the Cuban political arena, were basically urban. Therefore, the capital was the traditional stage for these contests. But the economic bases for the neocolonial system were in the countryside; thus the formation of a guerrilla army affected the regime at its foundation and increased the rebels' influence beyond the weight of its military might alone. The urban fighters did not always comprehend the strategic value of the guerrillas, sparking debate over the method of struggle, both within the 26th of July Movement and between that organization and the other revolutionary groups.

In the early stages of the anti-Batista struggle, one such group was the Directorio Revolucionario Estudiantil 13 de Marzo—a spin-off of the Federación Estudiantil Universitaria—a group of valiant young men and women that adopted urban conflict as their principal method of struggle. In 1956 the student leader and head of the Directorio, José Antonio Echeverría, met with Fidel Castro in Mexico and, even though the unification of the two organizations was not achieved, they agreed to collaborate in the struggle to overthrow the dictatorship. On March 13, 1957, in conjunction with a group of radical young Auténticos led by Carlos Gutiérrez Menoyo, the Directorio carried out an attack on the presidential palace with the objective of assassinating Batista. The action failed and many of the principal leaders, including Gutiérrez Menoyo and Echeverría—who fell in a parallel encounter—died in the effort. The rest were persecuted ruthlessly by the Batista police, and the organization had to be practically dismantled. It was reorganized with the aim of opening a new guerrilla front in the Escambray Mountains, under the leadership of Eloy Gutiérrez Menoyo, younger brother of Carlos. Eloy subsequently separated from the organization and formed his own group, the Second National Front of the Escambray. Faure Chomón assumed the leadership of the Directorio and established an alliance with the troops of the 26th of July Movement when in 1958 they arrived in the region under the command of Che Guevara and Camilo Cienfuegos. After the victory of the Revolution, the Directorio formed part of the triad of organizations—together with the 26th of July Movement and the Partido Socialista Popular (PSP)—that took over the government and eventually fused to create the present-day Partido Comunista de Cuba.

The differences within the anti-Batista movement transcended, nevertheless, the tactical domain. The Auténticos and the majority of the Ortodoxo hierarchy did not oppose the tyranny from a revolutionary perspective; rather they conceived armed struggle as one more element of pressure to achieve a return to the political status in existence prior to the military coup. Thus they tried, particularly through their leaders in exile, to implement formulas of mediation acceptable to the United States and the national oligarchy. This strategy led to their support of the Civic Dialogue proposed by the Sociedad de Amigos de la República in 1955, and their role in the Junta de Liberación de Miami, which in mid-1957 endeavored to control the revolutionary movement and limit the advancement of the Rebel Army. About that time and also with the aim of counteracting the influence of the 26th of July Movement, the Second National Front of the Escambray became the guerrilla alternative to the Auténticos and the right-wing Ortodoxos. From exile, Carlos Prío also financed various expeditionary projects and the purchase of arms to send to Cuba. The North American authorities generally harassed these activities, an action that stemmed from their desire to support the Batista regime as long as possible and their fear of the chaos that could ensue from the return of the Aunténticos to power.

Once the dictatorship was overthrown, the Aunténticos were discretely rebuffed from participation in the government. Thus, they opposed the Revolution from the start and played a key role in the formation of some of the early counterrevolutionary groups. The conservative sectors of the Ortodoxos had a greater influence in the first government institutions, but in most cases they also eventually broke with the Revolution. Yet their participation in the counterrevolutionary movement was less organic and decisive than that of the Auténticos.

Within the 26th of July Movement two sectors turned out to be particularly antagonistic and most of their principal leaders later joined the counterrevolution. One of these sectors was the Movimiento de Resistencia Cívica (MRC), a semiautonomous civic group sponsored by the 26th of July Movement to mobilize support among the liberal bourgeoisie, the middle class, and the intellectuals. The MRC, which finally was integrated into the Movimiento 26 de Julio (26th of July Movement), was mainly comprised of persons of bourgeois and petit bourgeois origin who, under the leadership of prestigious professionals such as Manuel Ray, Felipe Pazos, and Rufo López Fresquet, represented its "moderate" wing. The majority reflected a bourgeois nationalist thinking that became relatively popular in the 1950s and yearned to consolidate an independent national bourgeoisie, a dubious task in Cuba at that time. Between joining the counterrevolution, which they truly abhorred, or committing class suicide and joining the revolutionary popular movement that surged after 1959, this group chose to break with the Revolution. The reasons had more to do with class instincts, anticommunist prejudices, and personal aims than with differences with a program of reforms that the revolutionary government initially implemented, and that formed part of an agenda that they themselves had defended and helped to create as an alternative for the country.

> A similar evolution took place within the leadership of the labor movement that formed part of the 26th of July Movement. The failure of the call for a general strike on April 9, 1958, demonstrated the conceptual and structural limitations of this sector of the anti-Batista movement. In reality, their influence in the labor movement was more moral than organic, insofar as they represented the organization that was heading the Revolution. This, together with the sectarianism of their actions, limited their capacity to rally for their cause. Moreover, the participation of the working class in the movement against the dictatorship was a politically complex process. According to Carlos Rafael Rodríguez, some students of the Cuban Revolution ask themselves if the behavior of the urban proletariat between 1952 and 1958 did not show signs of passivity. It did. Not only due to disunity, but also to objective causes that arose from characteristics of the Cuban economic situation already described. . . . We have said that the main sectors of the urban proletariat, principally those in Havana . . . had salary levels that surpassed the best in Latin America and compared with those of certain capitalist nations. These workers were also secure in their jobs through the strength of the unions. . . . This condition meant that the urban workers . . . demanded guarantees of security and organization before joining a strike that, if insufficiently organized, would have culminated with an easy defeat for them and irreversible misery. . . . The lack of these minimum conditions for proletarian action until after April 1958 paralyzed the potential force of a proletariat that was one of the most active and conscious of any in the world.[46]

One explanation for this process of integration and division among the revolutionary ranks lies in the fragile cohesion that always characterized the anti-Batista movement. The unity of this movement was forged almost exclusively on the basis of opposition to the dictatorship. Thus, the class composition and the conditions inherent in this coalition appear clearly only after the regime is overthrown, when the question is precisely what to do with the newly seized power. The political and military support that the U.S. government bestowed on the dictatorship also contributed to maintaining this precarious unity, to the degree that other options were not endorsed. U.S. cooperation with the Batista regime included advising the repressive forces, keeping tabs on exile groups, and providing intelligence to the armed forces. Only when the fall of the dictatorship became probable did the U.S. government decide to look for alternatives that would moderate in its favor the political events about to take place.[47]

By late 1958 the CIA created the Cuba Project and focused its interests on the analysis of the Cuban reality and on penetrating the revolutionary movement.[48] As in 1933, the primary objective lay in finding allies within the anti-Batista movement that would guide the revolutionary process toward aims compatible with U.S. interests. Logically, the main target of their initial efforts was the Rebel Army itself. One of the most illustrative actions was the meeting held between Lyman Kirkpatrick, then CIA inspector general, and Dr. Luis María Buch Rodríguez, a member of the national directorate of the 26th of July Movement, on August 18, 1958, at the Tamanaco Hotel in Caracas.

According to Buch's own testimony, William E. Patterson, political attaché of the U.S. embassy in Venezuela, arranged the interview. Kirkpatrick introduced himself as a representative of the U.S. National Security Council and said that the meeting formed part of an "exploratory" trip that included a visit to Cuba. The top CIA chief expressed displeasure with his government's policy toward Batista and made a number of inquiries. These included the movement's position toward U.S. aid, the possibility of a compromise through a military junta, the relations between Fidel and his brother Raúl, the role of the Communists, and the guarantees of political and social stability in the country once the dictatorship was overthrown. Buch answered,

"We do not allow, nor will allow at any time, any aid nor any intervention in our favor, since the only thing we demand of your government is the most absolute neutrality in our domestic affairs. That if they had maintained neutrality in the Cuban case, the tyrannical Batista regime would have fallen long ago." He also said that they would not accept a coup d'état that would lead to a military junta and that the Rebel Army would guarantee peace and security once the dictatorship was overthrown.[49]

A fortnight later, Patterson informed Buch that, with the aim of establishing an exchange of opinions, his government was willing to answer twelve written questions. Some of the answers to the questionnaire were truly significant. The U.S. government considered that there was no possibility of solution without the surrender of one of the contending parts and that only when that occurred could they carry out a "friendly intervention." They were aware of preparations for a military coup but, in the opinion of the U.S. government, this could be undertaken only by low-ranking personnel or officers who had maintained a "special" attitude, such as Martín Díaz Tamayo and Eulogio Cantillo. In any case they would have to deliver the government to the revolutionaries in less than seventy-two hours because they lacked the forces to resist any longer. They gave assurances of recognizing a government headed by Manuel Urrutia within forty-eight to seventy-two hours, if it was established in the capital and fulfilled the requirements of maintaining order and recognizing the "international commitments" of the republic. They promised that Ambassador Earl T. Smith would be replaced as soon as Eisenhower died, "which could happen at any time," or immediately after the fall of Batista. They further promised that the U.S. government understood that the elections—slated for November of that year—were a farce but, if they were carried out, the elected government would be recognized.[50]

The interviews continued and Patterson went on to offer, in the name of his government, 1,000 M-1 carbines with the corresponding ammunition, which would be delivered to the Rebel Army through Guantánamo Naval Base, a proposition that Buch flatly refused. Patterson also raised the possibility that an emissary of his government—possibly he himself—would visit the Sierra Maestra, to which Buch agreed because it meant the recognition of a state of belligerency on the island. But he refused to accept the plan that they leave together on a U.S. plane from Miami or Guantánamo Naval Base, and proposed instead traveling from Venezuela on an aircraft supplied by the 26th of July Movement.[51]

According to Buch himself, the approaches of the U.S. government to the 26th of July Movement took place in other directions as well, but each time that the leadership responded it only served to ratify their noninterventionist position. To that effect, he quotes statements made by Raúl Castro on November 22 to a North American journalist in the middle of the guerrilla zone: "We do not desire for the U.S. government to aid the rebels. What we demand is the end of all aid that the U.S. government is indisputably lending to the Batista tyranny. . . . Our people, jealous of their national sovereignty, obtained by our elders after a century of arduous struggle, reject any form of foreign intervention in the affairs that only pertain to them, the Cuban people."[52]

The positions taken by the leadership of the 26th of July Movement troubled the U.S. government in a number of ways. They reflected a clear attitude of avoiding commitments that could hamper the nationalist sentiment of the Revolution. This, together with the leaders' refusal to accept any compromise with the forces of the dictatorship—in particular to bargain with sectors of the army—forecast their willingness to promote radical changes in the system of neocolonial dependence. Beyond other considerations—including the real presence of a Cold War psychology obsessed with the fear of communist penetration in this hemisphere—the immediate practical concern of the United States turned out to be the predicted dismantling of the structures of domination. This became the fundamental reason for U.S. opposition to the revolutionary current headed by the Rebel Army. Thus, beginning in the second half of 1958, U.S. policy centered on the search for a "third force" that would guarantee the continuity of the vital elements needed for the perpetuation of the system. The historian Thomas G. Paterson, who recently researched these connections, describes the existence of at least four U.S. government plans aimed at favoring, in their quest for power in Cuba, those groups they deemed less radical and more amenable to their influence.[53]

In December 1958 the U.S. government proposed to Batista a way out of the situation through the establishment of a provisional junta headed by Colonel Ramón Barquín, former military attaché of the Cuban embassy in Washington. Barquín belonged to a group of military men known as the pure ones, ("los puros") who, due to their opposition to the regime, were imprisoned on the Isle of Pines. Barquín also had the support of a group that represented the Agrupación Montecristi, which, under the leadership of Justo Carrillo, former president of the Bank of Agricultural Development, maintained contacts with the U.S. government in order to find alternatives to the dictatorship. Carrillo had even planned, with financial and political backing from the CIA, to liberate Barquín by bribing his prison guards. Finding out about the junta proposal made to Batista, the head of the army, General Francisco Tabernilla, suggested including in the junta his chief of staff, General Eulogio Cantillo. It was he who was entrusted with the mission of negotiating the transfer of power with Fidel Castro, to whom he admitted having the support of the North Americans. Later, Cantillo orchestrated a coup that was rejected by the 26th of July Movement, leading to the revolutionary general strike of January 1959. That same officer liberated Barquín on January 1, 1959, and made him head of the army, desperately seeking to save the regime. But, as the CIA had predicted, the arrangement lasted barely seventy-two hours.

Another option organized by the CIA, according to Paterson, was strengthening the Second National Front of the Escambray so that that organization could serve as a military and political counterweight to the Rebel Army. With this aim the CIA organized the shipment of a considerable quantity of arms, but they did not reach the Escambray until late in the year, when the victory was already sealed. The last attempt of the CIA was to coordinate with Tony de Varona and José Miró Cardona for the purpose of sending Varona with an expedition to Cuba. Varona was to get in touch with a group of dissident military officers in Camagüey and assume the command of the province. But he also arrived too late, failed to find any of his contacts, and calmly watched the fall of Batista from his mother's home.

These links of the U.S. government to various anti-Batista groups in search of a "third force" that would prevent the ascent to power of the movement led by Fidel Castro constitute important background material for understanding the future organization of the counterrevolution and the implicit conflict of these groups with the nationalist ideology that inspired the more radical revolutionary sectors. This would be more so when the policy objective of the United States toward Cuba became the overthrow of the Revolution.

Contemporary counterrevolution in Cuba, therefore, manifests the result of the contradictions inherent to an imperfect neocolonial system, where the predominance of foreign capital and political intervention limited the authority and capacity of influence of the native dominant bloc, and their possibilities of resisting the transforming force of the Revolution. The balance of these forces, at a specific historical moment, explain the way in which the Cuban revolutionary event takes place, and the organic dependence of the counterrevolutionary movement on the North American system and its policy toward Cuba. This subordination characterizes the political nature of the counterrevolution from the beginning, a tendency that was strengthened to the degree that immigration became the social base of the counterrevolution.

Chapter 2

Counterrevolution within the Revolution

THE VICTORY OF the Cuban Revolution in January 1959 took place at a unique moment during the Cold War. The postulates that sustained the doctrine of U.S. hegemony, an expansionist logic rooted in the birth of the United States itself, reflected an adaptation to the new realities of the world after World War II. "The fundamental assumption is that the American system of power and social organization, and the ideology that accompanies it, should be universal. Anything less is unacceptable. No challenge can be tolerated, even the belief in the historical inevitability of something different. . . . [Thus] each action carried out by the United States to extend its system and ideology is defensive."[1]

The existence of the USSR was not only an obstacle to the construction of a global system based on relative freedom to trade but an obstacle in the quest for unlimited access to raw materials, markets, investments, and cheap labor in the Third World. The Cold War thus fulfilled a utilitarian function insofar as it justified the expansionist purposes of the North American hegemony. Based on this logic, the Cuban Revolution challenged not only the geopolitical and ideological assumptions that guided U.S. global politics after the Second World War, it also threatened the old continental order established on the basis of the Monroe Doctrine an order that reached its apogee during this period, but which for Cuba had begun much earlier. Breaking the laws of gravitational politics, a force unknown to the U.S. system had taken the apple that, as expected, had so easily fallen into its hands and made it levitate.

The success of the Cuban revolutionaries against the dominant native bloc on which the neocolonial system was based, and the subsequent organization of the general population into an armed militia, established a dangerous precedent for the U.S. system. The impact of the Cuban Revolution transcended the domestic context, and, indeed, bilateral relations, and produced international repercussions. In this sense, the Cuban revolutionary phenomenon constituted a challenge to the system as a whole, far beyond the concrete political, economic, or military capabilities of Cuba itself. Thus, the customary pragmatism of U.S. politics was not applied in the case of Cuba, not even after it won the Cold War.

According to Ernesto "Che" Guevara, the truly exceptional condition of the Cuban revolutionary phenomenon was the fact that in the beginning it disoriented the U.S. government, which was unable to gauge its true reach.[2] No doubt this surprise influenced U.S. policy in the early moments of the Revolution. It may even have averted armed intervention during the anti-Batista struggle or immediately after the victory, as was the case in the Dominican Republic some years later. But the U.S. attitude was never complacent and the counterrevolutionary option constituted, at all times, the compass of this policy. Tad Szulc writes that in the beginning the United States decided to appear "friendly" toward the new Cuban government. But even before truly ascertaining what was going on, as early as March 10, 1959, the National Security Council, contradicting estimates of the CIA station in Havana, arrived at the conclusion that it was necessary to replace the revolutionary government with one more amenable to U.S.

interests. The interview between Fidel Castro and Richard Nixon one month later confirmed this perception.[3]

Several factors influenced the failure of this policy, including the global correlation of forces and the international solidarity generated by the Cuban Revolution. But this was determined, in the first place, by the unity reached within the revolutionary forces and the incorporation of the general population into this current. In that sense, the capacity for resistance of the revolution in Cuba has been an essentially domestic circumstance, favored or not by international junctures at any given time. Unity and popular support were to be the two constants in the articulation of the resistance to U.S. policy. Therefore, the conflict between revolution and counterrevolution in Cuba was characterized by U.S. efforts at eroding this front and the revolutionary determination to maintain it at all costs, knowing that it was the key to its survival. Fidel Castro's personality, his capacity for governing the country, and his demonstrated ability at managing the tactics of the dispute played a determinant role in this effort. This explains why his physical elimination became an important ingredient in U.S. plans.

Nine successive U.S. administrations have maintained essentially unaltered the premises by which Eisenhower and Kennedy confronted the Cuban revolutionary phenomenon. The key ingredients of this policy have been economic strangulation, political discredit, internal destabilization, and promotion of counterrevolutionary activities. Counterrevolution has constituted an integral part of U.S. policy toward the island. Other priorities have been subordinated to this aim. The principal political institutions of the United States have been involved in its planning and execution, giving the Cuban counterrevolutionary movement a transnational quality that has influenced its conduct and ideology.

The victory of the Revolution against the Batista dictatorship was possible, among other reasons, due to the erosion of the dominant bloc and the absence of viable alternatives that could serve to reconstruct it. This dilemma was intensified by the popularity of the revolutionary government when the counterrevolutionary thesis was proposed as an option for the restoration of the groups displaced from power. From the beginning the counterrevolution had to accept a U.S. tutelage that was historically conditioned and that was the only factor that could give it the cohesion and power that it did not possess on its own. No counterrevolutionary group escaped this destiny. Organizations and ideological currents, until then very diverse and apparently contradictory, operated together on this basis.

The Batistiano Reaction

Most of the main figures of the Batista regime fled the country in disorder when the Revolution came to power. A group of them accompanied the dictator in his escape to the Dominican Republic. Rafael Leonidas Trujillo, the Dominican ruler, did not appreciate them but was determined to use them. Nevertheless, the majority fled to the United States by diverse means. U.S. government refusal to extradite some of the principal thugs of the dictatorship and its criticism of the execution of those captured in Cuba constituted the first confrontation with the newly installed revolutionary government.

Many lower-level collaborators of the Batista regime remained in Cuba and, indeed, the military personnel not accused of crimes or abuses against the population continued serving in the armed forces, until escalation of the conflicts and increased involvement of these persons in counterrevolutionary activity brought about their discharge. In the United States and the Dominican Republic the Batistianos immediately formed two related counterrevolutionary groups: the Rosa Blanca and the Legión Anticomunista del Caribe. These groups, sponsored by the Dominican dictator, organized in 1959 the first armed invasion against the Cuban Revolution.

Most researchers claim that the Eisenhower and Kennedy administrations tried to distance themselves from the Batistianos, and CIA participation in the Dominican adventure has not been demonstrated. Nevertheless, it is noteworthy that the strategy—creating a beachhead in order to receive outside aid—as well as the selected site corresponded to what would later become the invasion plan of the Bay of Pigs.[4] In addition to this, according to research by Fabián Escalante, in February 1959, Trujillo met with CIA officer Gerry Doller and explained his plan against Cuba. Doller turned out to be Frank Bender, one of the future organizers of the invasion.[5]

The Rosa Blanca was the first of the counterrevolutionary organizations. It was short-lived and its impact in Cuba and abroad was slight. It was founded in New York on January 28, 1959, under the leadership of Rafael Díaz-Balart, an old collaborator of the dictator who had occupied, among other positions, the post of minister of government, the institution in charge of controlling the repressive forces.[6] The Rosa Blanca represented, in some ways, the civil wing of the Batistianos, although many ex-military men joined it and by definition its objectives were subversive. Various small-scale actions were carried out within Cuba in the name of this organization. But it is hard to determine whether they came in response to a coordinated effort or resulted from the spontaneous inspiration of the Batistianos that remained in the country—some sought for crimes committed during the dictatorship. In the United States the organization clashed with the majority of the émigrés, most of whom still supported the revolutionary process. In fact, the organization is best known for its brawls with other immigrant groups.

The Legión Anticomunista was organized in the Dominican Republic for the purpose of arming and preparing a force to invade Cuba. Trujillo representatives tried to recruit the leaders of the Second National Front of the Escambray for the venture but the project was exposed by one of them, Eloy Gutiérrez Menoyo. Some of the conspirators were captured in August 1959 while attempting to land in Cuba and the operation was a failure with a comical side. Gutiérrez

Menoyo himself described the events to the media: "Some four months ago William[7] called me to tell me that he had been invited to join the conspiracy by landowners and ex-military men that maintained contacts with Trujillo. I authorized him to join and asked for an appointment with Fidel to explain to him my plans."[8]

Lázaro Artola, another one of the protagonists, added: "Fidel and Camilo, hidden in a shack 200 meters from the airport, watched as the plane landed. A priest, a trusted associate of Trujillo, was aboard. Our troops were dressed in peasant clothes to suggest that the common farmers supported us. The landing was met with shouts of 'Viva Trujillo' and 'Down with Fidel' . . . . The priest promised gifts from the *Generalísimo* and a new shipment of arms for the following night. Three hours later the plane returned to Santo Domingo. . . . And the next day . . . we observed the plane that attested to our plan and constituted the best proof of the Trujillista aggression."[9]

The flop of the Trujillista undertaking did not keep the Batistianos from getting involved in other conspiracy plans, attempting to reorganize its forces in Cuba, or winning the support of the North Americans. The coordinator of these efforts on the island was Luis Taconal, who turned out to be an agent of Cuban security. In a report dated March 17, 1960, Taconal described the results of a recent trip to Miami: The morning after arriving in Miami I met with Rolando Masferrer, who explained to me his plans for a landing.[10] They think that with the support of the State Department they can get all the material and moral support necessary. . . . Colonel King of the Central Intelligence Agency, Head of the Latin American division, is in charge of appraising and proposing the plans of the different groups, who are also called to Washington to confer about them. The day before I left Miami, Colonel King called Masferrer and told him that he was considering approving his plan. . . . During my first meeting with Masferrer, Yito del Valle, the ex-congressman . . . arrived. Masferrer explained to me that he was going to Washington to meet with Carlos Marquez-Sterling.[11] He asked me to accompany him to Washington to talk to Carlos Marquez and take the opportunity to go on to Larchmont, New York, to talk to Rafael Díaz Balart. My trip was to be financed by Dr. Anselmo Alliegro.[12]

Dozens of people were detained when the conspiracy was dismantled in December 1960. In spite of these failures, the Batistianos later occupied many of the top military positions in the Bay of Pigs invasion and were systematically supported by the CIA, which considered them a particularly trustworthy group. This allowed them to maintain an active presence within the counterrevolution and win greater influence despite the initial rejection they inspired. They were particularly active in the press, from their ranks rose many of the current counterrevolutionary leaders, and they achieved relevance within what would become the Cuban-American elite. Nonetheless, at that time the notion that the Batistiano groups had any possibility of regaining power in Cuba was unthinkable. The U.S. government had in mind cultivating other sectors to interpose in the revolutionary process and steering them in their interests.

A New Attempt at Mediation

In February 1959 a survey by *Bohemia* magazine indicated that 95 percent of the population supported the revolutionary government.[13] Six months later, after some radical measures had been taken and the dispute with the United States could be discerned, this support still hovered above 90 percent.[14] Maintaining this level of cohesion required satisfying popular expectations while at the same time avoiding the alienation of those who did not have irreconcilable conflicts with the revolutionary process. Fidel Castro's attention to this issue can be observed in his words to the Council of Ministers in March 1959: "Comrades, we must live with the constant concern that the Revolution cannot foster extra enemies. We have enough already without having to look for more. . . . I know that any just and revolutionary measure we take will necessarily hurt certain interests, but just the same we must affect as few as possible. . . . Currently we can count on 95 percent of public opinion and we can maintain that if we cease mass layoffs, close the door on nepotism, get agrarian reform rolling, promote industrial development, lower rents, and implement the housing plan."[15]

The opposition to the dictatorship had been extensive. All sectors of the country viewed positively the possibility of honest government management as well as attaining a state of peace and national stability. New contradictions, determined by the scope of the revolutionary social project, would define the political scenario once victory was achieved. The conflict between reform and revolution would be the essence of the first stage of the Revolution; thus the political struggles were expressed within the revolutionary process itself, which was understood in different ways by the various actors, in the midst of the logical confusion of its first moments. The popular support enjoyed by the Revolution discouraged the rise of openly confrontational positions. In the words of Fidel Castro, "In those days each wanted a revolution according to his beliefs; that is, some wanted a false revolution, as always, and others wanted a true revolution, as never before."[16]

Although the sectors representative of the traditional order were alienated from power, they behaved at first with the certainty that, in the final analysis, they might control the process and guide it to their advantage. Thus, the political game was one of gaining position starting from a discourse that did not sway theoretically from the revolutionary process. Even at year's end, although the first conspiracies were already being hatched, Carlos Prío, speaking on behalf of the Auténticos, said: "We fully and unconditionally support the foreign policy and the revolutionary laws passed by the government. The Organización Auténtica [OA] champions the measures taken, and those that the government may take, against foreign aggression, reactionary intrigues, and treason against the Revolution. The OA applauds the revival of the revolutionary tribunals to judge those guilty of treason or aggression against the Revolution and the Cuban people."[17]

The U.S. administration followed this process closely, helped those it considered closest to its interests, and in general adopted the policy of encouraging any sign of division within the revolutionary bloc. In truth, this strategy was not misguided. The Revolution had a long string of difficulties to overcome, the revolutionary forces were heterogeneous and inexperienced, and its internal unity was not consolidated. The means of mass communication continued to be fundamentally in the hands of the elite. The Catholic Church—which during the dictatorship had upheld a vehemently apolitical course—advanced rapidly toward opposition to the revolutionary regime. And, with the exception of the Batistianos, all the political parties continued operating in the country.

Lowering rents and electricity and telephone rates, increasing minimum salary, and other measures benefiting the working sectors openly clashed with the interests of the privileged few and the North American consortiums established in the country. Nevertheless, the definitive step in the process of radicalization was the enactment of the Agrarian Reform Law in May 1959, despite its relative moderation and its correspondence with the Constitution of 1940,[18] the basis for the program of the anti-Batista movement. All groups approved this decision at first sight, but there were significant differences between the type of agrarian reform that one or the other wanted to make. The right proposed agrarian reform based on the granting of untilled lands and the voluntary and compensated concession of a portion of the large plantations, thereby maintaining unaltered the essence of the agrarian property structure, where the power of the rural oligarchy and the U.S. corporations had its roots. The more radical sectors proposed instead to demolish the basis of the system, dismantling the great landed estates and socializing most of the land, through the creation of cooperatives and state farms. In the form that it was passed, this law proposed a substantial change in the country's economic system, the foundation for the projected political transformations.

The reaction of the oligarchy did not take long. The planters, who until then had spoken of donating 10,000 pregnant heifers to the peasants that lacked "milk for their children,"[19] were now intransigent. "The ranchers will fight to the death if they [the government] try to enact into law the current draft," said Armando Caíñas Milanés, president of the Asociación de Ganaderos de Cuba.[20] The conflict became a struggle and the mass media became its principal battleground.[21] The U.S. government lodged a formal protest. In a diplomatic note it recognized that "under international law a State has the right to take for public ends the properties subject to its jurisdiction." But the government complained not only about the system of gradual compensation contemplated for foreign enterprises—in fact, five large U.S. corporations that possessed the majority of the land[22]—but also about the effects that this could have on the Cuban planters. This was, by all accounts, interference in the country's domestic affairs, duly protested by the Cuban side.[23]

Among all political considerations, the question of unity takes priority. Therefore, in the beginning the revolutionary government did not confront all the elite indiscriminately. On the contrary, it sought to comply with the industrial sectors and preserve its interests, through a policy designed to protect domestic production. In February, Fidel Castro asked the people to support three slogans: complete the sugar harvest without interruption, consume domestic goods, and carry out agrarian reform.[24] In fact, according to Cuban-American sociologist Marifeli Pérez-Stable, the Revolution's economic program reflected, in the beginning, the strategy that had long been advocated by the reformist sectors of the Cuban elite.[25] One of its principal theoreticians, Rufo López Fresquet, the minister of finance, defended the principle that the basis of economic development rested on increasing demand—that is, improving the purchasing power of the population. This could be achieved by reducing the costs of certain basic needs, like housing, increasing minimum salaries, and controlling prices—measures that the Revolution actually implemented.[26]

In spite of this intention, the aim of achieving greater autonomy from foreign capital through the class conciliation proposed by the liberal sectors of the elite met with objective obstacles. Under conditions of underdevelopment, the growth of an independent national bourgeoisie—in competition with the more efficient foreign industry—could be achieved only at the cost of the extensive exploitation of the working class, whether by reducing salaries or, indirectly, by increasing prices and establishing a strict protectionist system.

In the months following the revolutionary victory, if measures were actually taken to stimulate domestic production, their application necessarily had to adapt to the logical priority of increasing the standard of living of the population, an objective that could be achieved only by reducing, in one way or another, the capitalist profit rate. These alternatives confronted the reformists with their own proposals and impaired the nonsugar industrial capitalists from establishing alliances with the workers and thereby forming a national resistance bloc. This explains why the nonsugar industrial bourgeoisie solidly supported the laws favoring domestic industry yet opposed, in unison with the oligarchy, the policies of employment and salary benefits to which the Revolution adhered at this stage.

In its first ten months the revolutionary government decreed salary increases of 66 million pesos for the sugar industry and 20 million for other sectors, thereby increasing workers' earnings 14.3 percent that year, compared to a 4.2 percent increase during the Batista period. Labor conflicts became common in 1959 and the government was forced to mediate in more that 5,000 labor-management disputes.[27] In many cases business ignored the governmental decisions, which favored the workers, and sabotaged production in different ways, which led to an escalation of the conflict. The government used its influence to reduce the number of strikes, but it reacted strongly against the resistance of the business sector and increasingly resorted to nationalizing the businesses that contested its authority. Thus the conflicts with the capitalists escalated and thereby the middle class gradually broke with the Revolution. This rift had an impact on many of the institutions of Cuban civil society, including the press, and would be reflected both in the composition of the migration as well as in the formation of the first counterrevolutionary groups.

> From an ideological perspective, the problem of communism becomes the center of the political debate in this period. Some used communism as an excuse to justify a counterrevolutionary attitude that had its true foundation in the loss of benefits and privileges. But its general impact on Cuban society at the time should not be underrated. Fidel Castro pointed out: "To many of our citizens, including persons of humble origin and status, the word *socialism* instilled fear and the term *communism* aroused much more terror. . . . If we were an economic colony of the United States, we were also an ideological colony. An old social order is not maintained solely through the force of arms, the power of the state, and the economic power of its privileged classes, but also to a great degree by the reactionary ideas and political prejudices that the politicians instill in the people. . . . Every revolutionary social change implies, therefore, the eradication of the old political culture and the victory of new ideas. In our country ideas battled side by side with events.[28]

The Cuban Revolution upheld the doctrine of socialism, popularized it, and enlarged its foothold in the ideology of the Latin American left. But in 1959 political ideas were different, and anticommunism constituted the central core of the dominant ideology. Almost fifteen years of Cuban McCarthyism—under the Auténticos and Batista—reaffirmed this rejection of communism. This was aggravated by the consequences for the Cuban Communists of their incorporation during World War II into the "antifascist common front," which included a circumstantial alliance with Batista. The image of communism was related to the repudiation of God, persecution of the faithful, and rejection of the values of Christian civilization, beliefs that greatly influenced people's affiliation with the counterrevolutionary movement. To accept the socialist option also implied an inevitable confrontation with the United States, an alternative many considered suicidal. The ideological component was, thus, an important factor in the constitution of the counterrevolution and a resource that the U.S. government and the opposition groups widely capitalized on. The Catholic Church, in particular, employed it to attract new followers within the population, beyond the narrow confines of the elite and the other privileged strata of Cuban society.

The anticommunism issue realized its concrete political expression in the refusal to accept that the Communists could form part of the political life of the country and participate in the government. At that time all political forces, save those that openly collaborated with the dictatorship, operated freely. The attitude of the emerging opposition was not one of widening democracy, but restricting it, limiting or prohibiting the participation of the Communists. Aside from the ideological prejudices already noted, at the root of this attitude was the struggle to occupy positions of power, a characteristic that was to mark the political conflicts at this stage.

The issue had particular impact within the labor movement. The reorganization of the labor unions faced a complex political situation. On the one hand, it required substituting the union machinery that appeased the dictatorship and controlled the labor movement. On the other, it had to avoid new divisions and mobilize workers to support the general aims of the Revolution, an agenda that at times would clash with the immediate interests of particular sectors of labor. As in other cases, the policy of the Revolution was to support unity. During the tenth congress of the Central de Trabajadores de Cuba (CTC) in 1959, Fidel Castro declared: "The enemy, who is uniting, forces us to unite, because therein lies our true force. The spectacle that would please our enemies most is that of any division within this congress."[29] The lack of comprehension of the strategic importance of unity, aggravated by anticommunist prejudices and internal power struggles, led a sector of the labor movement, headed by the Catholics and some anti-Batista labor leaders, to break with the Revolution some time later.

These clashes were mirrored within the revolutionary government itself. The cabinet, which served as a basis for the provisional government organized in 1959, was composed mainly of representatives of a reformist technocracy that claimed greater space for the development of the domestic business sector, allowing it to be less dependent on the United States but without altering the fundamental premises of the system. Men that, before the revolutionary victory, had flirted with U.S. approaches to create a "third force" in order to moderate the process, occupied many of the leading posts. Once the revolutionary government was established, the United States tried to arrange for a new "mediation" that, as in 1933, would alter the course of the Revolution from within its own structures of power. It was precisely their relative loss of power, or their inability to achieve it that determined the early break of these individuals with the Revolution. The contradictions were marked by the conflict with the United States and the wavering attitude of some ministers. In March, Fidel Castro called for the Urrutia administration to show cohesion and a will to carry out the transformations promised by the Revolution. His words provide a glimpse into the existing situation: "One fact is indisputable: the government appears shackled, delayed in implementing the Revolutionary program. You know that this was what determined my presence in the Council of Ministers. . . . The state apparatus has to move forward, has to normalize its functions. . . . All factors have to work in unison so that the people can quickly realize the fruits of the Revolution."[30]

Barely a month before, Castro had assumed the post of prime minister, replacing Jose Miró Cardona. May 1959 marks the creation of the Instituto Nacional de Reforma Agraria (INRA), which would eventually become an alternative government and which would bring together the more radical revolutionary elements headed by Fidel Castro himself. An institutional crisis took place in July that culminated in the resignation of President Manuel Urrutia and the dismissal of other ministers, such as Roberto Agramonte, Humberto Sorí Marín, and Elena Mederos, representatives of the most conservative sector of the government. The Ministry of the Armed Forces was created in October and Raúl Castro was named to head it. In December, Che Guevara was named president of the Banco Nacional, a post formerly held by Felipe Pazos, possibly the most relevant figure of the reformist group.

Nor was the Rebel Army free of these contradictions. The desertion of Major Pedro Luis Díaz Lanz in June and the insubordination of Comandante Húber Matos in October 1959 introduced a new element to the political clashes of the early period.

Cracks in Revolutionary Power

Pedro Luis Díaz Lanz, pilot for the North American company that operated the mines in Nicaro, Oriente, rendered a vital service to the insurrection by transporting arms to the eastern guerrillas from Miami. In recognition of this he was named chief of the air force after the victory of the Revolution and occupied that post until his replacement in June. Díaz Lanz probably made contact with the CIA before the victory. His principal associate was Frank Fiorini, better known as Frank Sturgis, agent for the U.S. espionage services, who later became one of the infamous "plumbers" in the Watergate scandal. Pedro's brother, Marcos, whom he named major of the air force, had been accused of being a U.S. police informant while in exile, and since that time some of the revolutionaries were puzzled at the unusual freedom with which Díaz Lanz operated on U.S. soil.[31]

Immediately after his dismissal, Díaz Lanz left for the United States and asked for political asylum. He based his decision on the participation of Communists in the revolutionary government. In a letter to then president Manuel Urrutia, he said, "all these actions taken against me are due exclusively to the fact that I have always been opposed to the attitude of allowing the Communists to occupy prominent positions in the Rebel Army and in government agencies."[32]

Díaz Lanz's desertion earned him considerable coverage in the U.S. media. He was invited to appear as a witness at hearings held by the Senate Sub-Committee on Intelligence, where he made statements against the Revolution. Some prominent figures of the Batista regime also appeared at these hearings, which led some to interpret the Díaz Lanz statements as a deliberate provocation of the U.S. government, a reflection of the already sorry state of relations between the two countries. Almost immediately, Díaz Lanz went on to head one of the first counterrevolutionary organizations, the Cruzada Cubana Constitucional, whose second in command was none other than Frank Sturgis, and which carried out some air raids against Cuban territory. One of the attacks coincided with the attempted mutiny of Húber Matos and cost a number of lives in Havana.

Húber Matos used the same argument as Díaz Lanz to break with the Revolutionary government. Matos came from a rural, middle-class family associated with rice plantations in the Manzanillo region of the old province of Oriente. He had been a teacher in the area and after limited participation in the previous political struggles he joined the anti-Batista insurrection. He stood out for his role in transporting a shipment of arms into rebel territory toward the beginning of the military offensive by the dictatorship in 1958. After the defeat of this drive, he was promoted to comandante and awarded the command of one of the new guerrilla columns. He was assigned a group of fighters with an outstanding record in the column personally led by Fidel Castro, many of whom had more combat experience and merits than Matos.

According to testimony by then Captain Duney Pérez Alamo, Matos obtained this appointment because, when faced with the decision of creating a new column, the captains who were to form part of the troop proposed Matos to Castro. The fact that Matos was the oldest and most educated of the group had influenced this proposal, affirmed Pérez Alamo.[33] Once he assumed command, Matos had serious conflicts with Fidel Castro. Nevertheless, in early 1959 he was named military commander of Camagüey province, a region that included some of the largest plantations in the country and whose social composition made it one of the most politically complex.

In the beginning Matos applied the revolutionary laws with inflexible rigor. Few anticipated the impending conflicts between him and the revolutionary leadership, although a number of events hinted at that possibility, or they calculated that there would be time enough to find a solution that would reduce the political cost, as Fidel Castro's testimony at Matos's trial on December 14, 1959, suggests:

> They were preparing conditions for the 21st [of October], they were preparing a crisis for the revolutionary government. And we had already faced two crises: the crisis of the traitor, Pedro Luis Díaz Lanz, with whom we took the initiative—that is, we removed him from his post. There was another crisis, the crisis of the executive, with Mr. Urrutia, where we also took the initiative against the maneuver. Yet this was not the case with Mr. Hubert [*sic*] Matos; it was he who offered his resignation, he presents it under conditions that leave us no other way out. . . . The court must understand and the people must understand that for the revolutionary government and the Revolution any other way out would have been much more useful and much more convenient. . . . It would have been preferable even to have been tolerant. Anything would have been preferable to this scandal, which has been a delight for the reactionaries, a delight to the plotters against our country and against our Revolution.[34]

Events unraveled on October 19th, coinciding with the appointment of Raúl Castro as minister of the armed forces, who, along with Che Guevara, was one of the revolutionary leaders most attacked by the right. That day, Matos wrote a letter to Fidel Castro in which he announced his resignation because, he argued, persons with communist leanings were gaining power in the government. Although he claimed that it was a private letter, that he wanted to avoid a confrontation, and that his only intention was to retire from the political arena, the officers under his command were aware of this move, as were opposition groups and the media in Camagüey. They were all ready to make public their rejection of his resignation, to themselves resign in mass and support Matos against the leadership of the country.

Apprised of the situation, Fidel Castro ordered his loyal forces to take the initiative and occupy the province. He sent Comandante Camilo Cienfuegos, chief of the army, to halt the insurrection, while he himself traveled to Camagüey and mobilized the people toward the base where Matos and his men were located. Minutes before, Camilo Cienfuegos, accompanied merely by his personal bodyguards, had taken over the base without resistance. Comandante Arsenio García, police chief of Camagüey at the time, described the events:

> At the time many people were surprised, even though later it [Matos's arrest] was associated with other events. Subsequently his links with Díaz Lanz and Urrutia were revealed, but that was not well known at that time. What was evident was that Matos was interested in political protagonism and used it opportunistically in Camagüey. He distributed countless copies of the letter he sent Fidel. I personally seized some of these letters. The sedition was demonstrated. Moreover, we later confiscated a tape recording of Matos in which he sought support for his positions. After Matos was detained, two of his men tried to play the tape over the radio in Camagüey and a small shoot-out broke out, the only incident of its kind.
>
> I was in Ciego de Avila confiscating arms from the counterrevolution, when I learned of the conflict and I left immediately for Camagüey. That dawn I spoke with Fidel and informed him that the predicament was, in fact, popular knowledge and that Mendoza had denounced it over the radio, but that the situation was calm and under control and that there was no uprising nor sign of armed resis-

> tance. Minutes later I receive a call from Matos in which he places himself at my disposal. I tell him that he will have to answer for his actions, but that at that time I lacked instructions for what to do with him, and for him to sit tight in his home, that I would find out what would be done. I gathered that Matos was chicken, that he did not expect events to unfold the way they did, and this I communicated to Fidel, who ordered me to wait for Camilo's arrival in the early morning hours.
>
> Camilo arrived very early, accompanied by four or five comrades, and we set out with this small group to detain Matos. We entered the regiment without incident, arrived at Matos's house, asked for him, and were told he was in his room. Camilo and I found him in his pajamas reading a book. Camilo pulled out of his pocket some handwritten pages and threw them on the bed, telling him that it was Fidel's response to his position. Matos read them and said only that he already knew. Camilo ordered him to dress and told him that he was under arrest.
>
> Camilo summoned all the personnel and, in the presence of Matos, a meeting was held with the principal officers of the regiment. There was much confusion; some complained of being falsely accused. One even said that if a conspiracy were proved he would commit suicide, which, in fact, he did only days later. In the middle of this we get word of Fidel's arrival and we race for the airport. We find him en route to the base, leading a popular demonstration, and we join him. At the base Fidel spoke to the people from a balcony and we later transferred the detainees to Havana.[35]

According to Duney Pérez Alamo, Matos had been traveling to Havana for months to meet with some ministers, among them Manuel Ray and Manuel Fernández.[36] "[Matos] did not speak clearly, he did not openly oppose Fidel because that would have been rejected by the majority. But generally when he returned from these trips he shared his concern about communist infiltration and the need to make this known to Fidel, which had influence over a group that was politically very ignorant and had little education."[37]

A day or two before events unfolded, continues Pérez Alamo, Matos met with a group of officers and talked about the letter and of his intentions to resign. Pérez Alamo suggested he send the letter to Camilo, his immediate superior, but Matos refused, claiming that he had the support of various ministers. A part of the group said that they would also resign—on the twentieth, before the problem became public, fourteen officers resigned—but some of the main commanders, including Pérez Alamo himself and Francisco Cabrera, refused to adopt that position and tried to dissuade Matos.[38] Félix Duque, who commanded an important troop in eastern Cuba and who was one of the principal chiefs of the column that Matos headed, was also approached by him and invited to join the conspiracy. Duque communicated this to Fidel Castro before events unfolded, despite recognizing that at the time Matos had convinced him.[39]

> Húber Matos was an ambitious man who wanted to be named minister. I am convinced that since then he has been an agent of the CIA or another U.S. government agency. His chauffeur at the time, who now lives in Miami, told me later that Matos had two or three meetings a week with the British consul in Camagüey. The officer who served as translator was Lt. Romagoza, a character that I don't know where he came from or where he's gone to. This suspicion, about his links with the CIA, has been confirmed to me by facts I learned later. When he left Cuba he was met in Costa Rica by an individual who was a CIA officer. While he was in prison the CIA provided for his sister, who lives in Puerto Rico. When he arrived in Miami he made use of funds whose origin nobody knew, brushed off his old comrades, and created an organization with new people who were unaware of his old schemes.[40]

The Matos affair took on dramatic consequences when Comandante Camilo Cienfuegos, one of the most popular guerrilla chiefs, lost his life on one of the many trips he made between Camagüey and Havana. In his investigation into these events, Fabián Escalante Font indicates that Matos's plan called for declaring a general strike in the region, and that he counted on the support of most of the officers in his regiment, government officials, and student leaders in the province, as well as control over the mass media of the territory. Escalante also points out that, one month before, Matos participated in a meeting in Havana that included Edward C. Wilson, first secretary of the U.S. embassy in Havana, and Humberto Sorí Marín and Manuel Artime, who were already conspiring and would play a significant role in future counterrevolutionary activities.[41]

According to information contained in the files of the Ministry of the Interior, Artime corresponded with Húber Matos and ordered these letters destroyed when he found out that Matos had been arrested.[42] One of the arguments used by Artime when he publicly broke with the Revolution is the treatment given the Húber Matos affair. Among the individuals implicated in the conspiracy, according to information of the Directorate of Intelligence of the Rebel Army at the time, was the former comandante Higinio "Nino" Díaz, who, together with Artime, would organize one of the first counterrevolutionary groups some months later.[43]

The possible linkages between these events, pending investigation by historians and as yet unconfirmed, may well indicate participation of the U.S. government. A report by the Ministry of the Interior dated November 28, 1961, states that since September 1959 the Departamento de Investigaciones del Ejército Rebelde (DIER) had been investigating in Camagüey the connections between Rogelio Cisneros Díaz and officers linked to Húber Matos.[44] Cisneros had connections to the 26th of July Movement in Camagüey and was a trusted associate of Manuel Ray, who became an important counterrevolutionary leader. Among the closest collaborators of Cisneros was a certain engineer named Romaguera,[45] who could be the "Romagoza" whom Pérez Alamo mentions as Matos's translator in his contacts with the British consul.

The Húber Matos failure was the last of the attempts aimed at transforming the revolutionary regime from within. After this the confrontation would take on a violent character, the bourgeoisie would decidedly join the counterrevolution and would lead the formation of the first clandestine groups. The objective will become to revert the revolutionary process, not to transform it, and the U.S. government will convert counterrevolution in its official policy toward Cuba. On the other hand, the leadership of the Revolution realized also that there was no other alternative but to confront the reaction that loomed, thereby the political process became even more radicalized. Measures such as accelerating agrarian reform, insuring the control of the economy in other fronts, military training of the population, restructuring the state apparatus to place it in charge of trustworthy personnel, appropriation of the major means of mass communication, and reconvening the revolutionary courts to combat the counterrevolution constituted means of survival that set the tone for the Cuban political future and its relations with the United States.

For Che Guevara this meant the culmination of a stage of purification of the revolutionary process. In evaluating what he considered "a sin of the Revolution," he later said, "Let us not balk at calling a thief a thief, because we ourselves, in honor of what we call 'revolutionary tactics,' called the thief 'ex-president' when the 'ex-president' did not call us 'despicable communists' like now, but 'saviors' of Cuba. . . . There they are together, those that thrashed our conscience. . . . They point out our sin, the sin of the Revolution, not to be repeated, the lesson to be learned. . . . Revolutionary conduct is a mirror of revolutionary faith and when one who calls himself a revolutionary does not behave as such, he is nothing other than shameless."[46]

The Rift

Although the CIA had been working for months on agent selection and intelligence operations, all indications are that, beginning in late 1959, the U.S. government decided to stimulate the formation of a counterrevolutionary movement and place it under its control. In December 1959, the CIA began to discuss the implementation of an integrated plan to subvert the Cuban Revolution, which it presented to the administration on January 13, 1960. The main objective was to build opposition to the Cuban regime. In what was apparently the first meeting of the National Security Council to discuss the agency's proposal, Allen Dulles "emphasized that we do not have in mind a quick elimination of Castro, but rather actions designed to enable responsible opposition leaders to get a foothold."[47] These decisions were taken before Cuba restored diplomatic relations with the USSR—suspended by Batista in 1952—and before it unleashed the process of nationalization of U.S. companies, in response to that government's refusal to allow U.S. refineries to process Soviet oil. This served as the excuse for the United States to suspend the Cuban sugar quota and escalate the crisis until relations were finally broken off in January 1961.

The formation of the first counterrevolutionary groups in early 1960 was not fortuitous. They were structured on the basis of the Catholic organizations and the traditional political parties. But the North American subversive plan overrated both groups' capacity for mobilization. The traditional political parties were in disrepute and the Catholic Church, although an important organization within the prerevolutionary civil society, was established mostly in the urban centers. Its connection with the colonial regime first, and the native oligarchy later,[48] had conferred on it a particularly conservative and elitist ideological profile that distanced it from the popular masses.

The dominant sector of the clergy was composed of Spanish priests affiliated with various religious orders. More educated and economically better off than the rest, this sector had political ideas that revealed strong Falangist inclinations. These priests controlled an educational system that included the most exclusive and prestigious schools in the country. In 1959 the Catholic Church had one cardinal, two archbishops, six bishops, 753 priests and nuns, 200 churches, 209 convents, 360 schools, and 101 charitable organizations.[49] There was one priest for every 8,500 persons and one church for every 30,000, less than half the access that the institution offered in the rest of the Latin American countries.[50] For these reasons Cubans never stood out as devotees of Catholicism; rather, while defining themselves as believers of that religion, they practiced it privately or through popular cults. "The presumption of Catholic supremacy in Cuban religiousness has been a fiction that today has little validity. At the popular level the most widespread beliefs are those born of the historical convergence between Catholicism and the African cults, associated with Yoruba and Bantu cultures, together with the spiritisms and primary religious manifestations that, strictly speaking, cannot be typified as tributaries of these roots. This syncretism, which gives birth to an autonomous popular religiousness, originated and was consolidated on the fringes of the ecclesiastic institutions, and even under their severe censure."[51]

The position of the Catholic Church concerning the Revolution was ambivalent at first. The first significant skirmish took place with the summons to a Catholic congress in 1959. The revolutionary government maneuvered to avoid a conflict and, in fact, Fidel Castro participated in the closing ceremony. In August 1960 a pastoral letter from the Cuban bishops marked the confrontational position of the church, and after the Bay of Pigs invasion came the culminating moment of crisis, when nearly 600 foreign priests were expelled from the country.

The lay Catholics congregated in branch organizations of the Agrupación Católica Cubana, among them Juventud de Acción Católica (JAC), Juventud Obrera Católica (JOC), and Juventud Estudiantil Católica (JEC). But the religious orders—in particular, the Jesuits—controlled the organizations that contained the elite of the national bourgeoisie. Chief among them was the ACU, first the birthplace of the Falangist movement and later of various groups that situated themselves at the far right of the counterrevolution.

The ACU was the primary source of the counterrevolutionary movement. It did not confront the Batista dictatorship, yet it provided the movement's principal leaders and many young people who joined the ranks of the counterrevolutionary groups. Its class composition, its predominant ideological tendencies, and the role played by its leader, Father Armando Llorente—with clear Falangist leanings—determined this conduct. In particular the ACU served as the basis for the Movimiento de Recuperación Revolucionaria (MRR), the first and most important of the organizations of the Catholic right wing. The ACU also spawned the Movimiento Demócrata Cristiano (MDC), which brought together the most conservative and economically most powerful sector of the Catholic right, and the Directorio Revolucionario Estudiantil (DRE), which claimed to represent the counterrevolutionary Catholic student body. Reynol González, who went on to become one of the principal leaders of the counterrevolution, declared in 1961: "The clergy has participated actively in the counterrevolution, the hierarchy [acting] through the priests. In fact, the two movements with which it has collaborated are the MRR and the MDC. The Catholic organizations have served to prop up various movements. The ACU shored up the MRR; the Catholic Knights of Columbus and Catholic Ladies supported the MDC. . . . The facilities of the JOC served at various times to clandestinely print propaganda and store paper, money, etc. . . . Before they were nationalized, many of the religious schools were used to hold meetings, print propaganda, etc. . . . In the early stages of development of our activities we were aided by the Franciscan priest Father Julián de Bastarrica, the undersigned not knowing the origin of the funds."[52]

The announcement of the creation of the MRR was made in Costa Rica on June 8, 1960.[53] In reality it was being structured long before. Only a few months after the revolutionary victory, the Catholic right probably took the first steps toward creating a clandestine organization. According to statements by Manuel Reyes García, since mid-1959 Manuel Artime had explored the possibility of forming a secret group from among the members of the ACU.[54] Artime's own evolution is representative of the process of construction of that organization.

Artime was born in Camagüey to a family of wealthy sugarcane planters. He studied to be a psychiatrist. At an early age he joined the ACU and other political organizations of the Catholic right, and he was a member of the National Constitutional Committee of the Partido de Liberación Radical, founded by Amalio Fiallo in October 1957.[55] Although he did not participate in the fight against Batista, barely a few hours before the fall of the dictator he joined the Rebel Army. Favored by the grace of Comandante Humberto Sorí Marín,[56] Artime was awarded the rank of lieutenant without participating in any battle. Both ex-CIA officer Howard Hunt[57]—who became a personal friend of Artime—and Justo Carrillo maintain that Artime was sent to the Sierra Maestra by the Jesuits,[58] but it has not been possible to establish the connection between them and Sorí, giving rise to the hypothesis that the CIA was the coordinating force behind this arrangement. A review of the press during this period reveals the strong links between Sorí and the U.S. embassy, and his ties to the ACU continue into 1959.

Artime was appointed second in command of an agricultural development zone in the Sierra Maestra. With the political and economic support of the Ministry of Agriculture, headed by Sorí, the Comandos Rurales were established in the region, an organization sponsored by the ACU that probably served as a foundation for the creation of the MRR. The professed objectives of the Comandos Rurales were to explore alternatives for agrarian reform, to train the peasants in new agricultural techniques, and to teach them reading and writing as well as norms of hygiene and social relations.[59] Only members of the ACU participated in this organization, and the project had the additional political ingredient of sponsoring farmers' associations independent of the wide-base groups that the Revolution was creating and that Artime accused of being communist. Artime also had at his disposal a radio hour financed by the Manzanillo clergy and was a frequent orator at political acts organized by them. In June 1959, scarcely five months after the victory, someone who was supposed to be a young and inexperienced revolutionary, recently named delegate of the Manzanillo Agrarian Bureau, wrote a detailed report of the activities of the Comandos Rurales and concluded with these prophetic warnings:

> It has been proven that what they have introduced here in the Sierra Maestra is a very positive component of counterrevolution, of division. They were sent to the Sierra Maestra with a purpose, and the facts show us that they are playing their counterrevolutionary role quite well. They have a radio hour here in Manzanillo, paid for by the clergy. They tell the peasants that they have come here voluntarily to the Sierra Maestra to serve the farmers, and I am surely not mistaken that each of them receives a pension from the clergy. And who are the clergy? The established interests. And what do the established interests seek but counterrevolution. And how do they achieve it but by dividing the masses? And that is what the Comandos and Lt. Manuel Artime are doing, creating the conditions for the counterrevolution. Why did they choose the Sierra Maestra for their maneuver? Because when they saw that Fidel and his men put ashore near the Sierra and that the mountainous terrain is what made possible to a great degree the victory of the Revolution, the established interests thought, We have to prepare because we will surely have to take to the hills. And they thought, We will march to the Sierra early on and we will win the sympathy of the peasants, and when it comes time to revolt we will have broken the ground. Therefore, when I came here to Manzanillo and heard Lt. Artime's speech and [saw] the letter that the farmer Rosales brought and the one that I saw written for May Day and the peasant organization they were creating, and I saw the desperate state of the peasants in the Sierra Maestra, I thought, This is bad; these people are preparing the ground for the counterrevolution, and I immediately sent off a report to the Bureau of Investigation of Moncada Barracks. If more information is needed about these people I am

> willing to gather it because the sooner this focus of counterrevolution is eliminated the better. That way we will spare our fatherland many sad days.[60]

In November 1959, a search and seizure order was issued against Manuel Artime for the embezzlement of some 100,000 pesos from La Sierra cattle cooperative. The investigation of the case fell into the hands of none other than Sorí Marín, who confirmed the crime,[61] but probably facilitated his escape and that of his collaborators. According to declarations of Artime himself, the MRR was formed that December. The original plan called for organizing two uprisings in Oriente province, for which Artime was to gather arms and support abroad. With the support of the CIA he fled Cuba hidden in a ship flying the Honduran flag and landed in Florida. There he held further meetings with CIA officers and began a tour of various Latin American countries.[62]

A source with direct access to this information but who has asked to remain anonymous[63] claims that in February 1960, while Artime was in Argentina, he received a call from Angel Fernández Varela, who summoned him urgently to New York. According to his own statements, Fernández Varela had been a professor at Belén Jesuit School, ex-president of the ACU, former editor of the newspaper *Información,* leader of the Cuban Falangists, and an agent of the CIA from late 1959 until 1968.[64] According to the anonymous source, Fernández Varela introduced Artime to Frank Bender and arranged for the incorporation of the MRR into the counterrevolutionary coalition that was soon to be created.

Various accounts exist concerning the original composition of the MRR. Nevertheless, the majority agree that it came together in late 1959 with the incorporation of some members of the ACU and a small group composed of representatives of a sector of the eastern landholding elite that had participated in the anti-Batista struggle.

Some of the principal figures of the group were the ex-comandantes of the Rebel Army—Ricardo Lorié, Antonio Michel Yabor, and Nino Díaz—who, together with Artime, signed the press release announcing the creation of the organization in Costa Rica in June 1960.[65] Some time later they split with Artime and formed the so-called MRR de los Comandantes.

The Central Intelligence Agency was not oblivious to the formation of the MRR. Its rise coincided with the CIA's initial efforts at creating a counterrevolutionary front, and both the exit of Artime from Cuba as well as his subsequent tour of Latin America are evidence of the existence of operational ties before his reported meeting with Bender. Thanks to this support, the MRR went on to become one of the principal organizations of the national oligarchy and one of the most active counterrevolutionary groups in its first stages. In fact it constituted one of the original cores of the counterrevolution, insofar as many persons who later formed other organizations began their conspiratorial activities in this group. This protagonism would not have been possible without the significant participation of the clergy and the principal organizations connected with the Catholic Church.

The Movimiento Demócrata Cristiano had other characteristics. Founded legally in late 1959 by a group of young, conservative Catholics headed by José Ignacio Rasco, the MDC at the time followed the model of the Partido de Liberación Radical, a Christian-Democrat reformist group that participated in various schemes aimed at finding a peaceful way out of the Batista dictatorship. For a while the MDC took part in the public political debate following the revolutionary victory. Its message at this time reflected the eclecticism of its positions:

> The Christian-Democratic formula seeks in the social arena the reform of the economic structure as an integral whole, where the common good prevails over class or group interests. . . . We do not preach struggle against capital nor against the proletariat . . . not even hate for

> the Communists—Children of God, even though they consider themselves atheist orphans—and, therefore, brothers of the Christians, capable of being redeemed from the deception and treason that the red beast signifies. . . [We do not side with] the imperialism of either the dollar or the ruble. But in case of political conflict, if we had to chose between Washington and Moscow—between Lincoln and Lenin—we would have to assume the risks and side with the world in which liberty does not die. . . . In sum, we seek a Christian humanism, not under the slogan of "proletarians all" but rather, "proprietors all."[66]

In April 1960 the MDC pronounced itself against the Revolution in a document whose content Rasco previously vetted with prominent figures of the COPEI Party of Venezuela as well as with various Cubans that had already settled abroad.[67] Perhaps he had even consulted with the CIA, since, according to the anonymous source previously cited, in late February Rasco met with agency officers who proposed that the MDC join the counterrevolutionary coalition then being formed. The MDC thus became the first legal political organization that openly broke with the revolutionary process. Rasco returned to Cuba and with the sole aim of gaining publicity—since he was not being persecuted—he sought asylum in the embassy of Ecuador, returning to the United States in mid-April. One month later, again with little conspiratorial logic—because its members were known and continued to live normally—the MDC announced the dissolution of its public wing and the decision to go underground. With few members and composed primarily of conservative Catholic bourgeois intellectuals, in truth the MDC never stood out for its violent activity. The majority of its members emigrated early on and the party dedicated itself, above all, to disseminating propaganda abroad.

The Directorio Revolucionario Estudiantil, the third group in the triad of organizations of the Catholic right, originated as a splinter group of the MRR. Its origins go back to late 1959, when the Catholic student sector lost the elections for the control of the Federación Estudiantil Universitaria (FEU). Some months later, in February 1960, they provoked a clash at an activity held in the context of the visit of Soviet vice premier Anastas Mikoyan to Havana. In March, Alberto Muller, Juán Manuel Salvat, and Ernesto Fernández Travieso, all leaders of the ACU, formed the Frente Estudiantil Universitario Democrático, which a few weeks later became the Frente Revolucionario Democrático Estudiantil, and in December, after having left Cuba, its principal leaders launched the DRE.

Although the DRE participated in some armed attacks, it was created with the principal aim of playing a propaganda role within the CIA plans of that period, since the nationalization of private education—particularly the Catholic schools—prevented it from becoming a significant force within the Cuban student movement. The rise of the DRE coincided with the moment in which the counterrevolutionary coalition that served as the civilian front for the Bay of Pigs invasion was being restructured. Thus their participation was also used to augment the representation of the Catholic right in this alliance. Its membership was similarly comprised of young people from the ACU and the majority of its constituents had previously been affiliated with the MRR and had maintained tight relations with that organization. Although it pretended to capitalize on the prestige and authority of the homonymous organization that brought together an important sector of the Cuban youth in the struggle against the Batista tyranny, this association had no organic relation to, nor was it the continuation of, the Directorio Revolucionario Estudiantil 13 de Marzo.

In the beginning, the organizations of the Catholic right acted with a high degree of cohesion, notwithstanding the differences that would later appear. In fact there seemed to be few clear boundaries between them, which indicates the presence of a governing entity—not necessarily one that governed in a formal manner, but one that acted on the basis of its authority over the different groups. Originally certain sectors of the Catholic hierarchy and clergy played that role, but the influence of the U.S. government increased to the point of becoming the dominant force in a brief time.

The other tributary for the formation of the first counterrevolutionary groups was the Auténticos. The traditional party of Grau and Prío had been overlooked in the composition of the revolutionary government. Their substantial economic power and the requirements of unity against the dictatorship impelled most anti-Batista organizations to reach a compromise with them. Yet the party was rejected by both the right and the left because of the corruption in their administrations. They also had been displaced from the labor movement, not only because of their unscrupulous conduct against the Communists in the 1940s but also because the Auténtico labor leadership caved in to the dictatorship; in fact, the Mujalismo became Batista's labor union.[68]

In 1959 the Auténticos were grouped around three organizations: the PRC, headed by Ramón Grau until the 1958 elections and afterward by Manuel Antonio "Tony" de Varona; the Organización Auténtica (OA), led by Carlos Prío; and the Frente Nacional Democrático Triple A, under the direction of Aureliano Sánchez Arango. The first Auténtico leader that openly broke with the Revolution was Tony de Varona, former prime minister in the Prío administration. Since Carlos Prío still lived in Cuba and pronounced himself in favor of the revolutionary process, in May 1960 the Auténticos close to Varona decided to form a new organization, giving rise to Rescate Revolucionario Democrático. In reality, Rescate already existed a month before. The idea took form when the CIA convinced Varona to remain in the United States, organize the Auténtico counterrevolutionary faction, and join the coalition they had conceived. In his declarations, Artime described what happened: "I spoke to Tony and he said that he was considering returning to Cuba but that Justo, Rasco, and Martínez Fraga convinced him to stay. He told me that he had not left anything organized behind but that from there he could organize it in a month."[69]

Rescate went on to become the most important of the Auténtico organizations and one of the preeminent counterrevolutionary groups.

Outside Cuba they enjoyed the funding and political contacts derived from their experience in government and the subsequent exile of many of their principal leaders. The importance of Rescate at this stage was related to its contacts with the Mafia inside and outside Cuba. These links, confirmed by FBI reports in late 1960,[70] provided Rescate with operational capabilities not enjoyed by other groups. In Cuba they could count on a machine formed during years of activity on the domestic political scene. Many of these men shared the experience of the political gangster wars and possessed a conspiratorial training that would prove quite useful in making counterrevolution. Rescate would stand out for its active role in the attempts to assassinate Fidel Castro. The most notorious of these were organized in conjunction with the CIA and the Mafia between 1960 and 1962.

The Triple A represented a minority sector of the Auténticos linked to Latin American social democracy. It was led by the controversial former minister of education and state under the Prío government, Aureliano Sánchez Arango. Founder of the DEU in 1927 and the Ala Izquierda Estudiantil, Sánchez Arango stood out in the struggles against Machado for his leftist positions, which placed him close to the Communists, but later, as part of the Auténtico administration, he often clashed with the leftist student movement. Triple A was formed to combat the Batista dictatorship and it was joined by numerous Auténtico personalities with a background in the gangster wars. It represented a leftist faction of the Auténticos, unlike the more conservative sector headed by Tony de Varona. When the Revolution came to power they participated in the political debate as one more group until early 1960 when, encouraged by the CIA, who also invited them to form part of the counterrevolutionary coalition, Sánchez Arango broke publicly with the revolution and left the country. This organization was never very consequential for its actions inside or outside Cuba. In reality, the controversial figure of Sánchez Arango was never very well regarded by the agency, because of both his background and his personality, and he was progressively driven away from the counterrevolutionary leadership.

Also around that time, a group of ex-Auténtico persons living outside Cuba organized Unidad Revolucionaria (UR), led by the powerful landowner Alberto Fernández, who had settled in the United States in 1959. The UR, using a boat owned by Fernández, specialized in the infiltration and exfiltration of CIA agents and personnel of the different organizations, placing it at the center of conspiratorial activity and in a privileged position of trust vis-à-vis the North American espionage services. In Cuba it would later be headed by Rafael Díaz Hanscom, who had been head of intelligence of the MRR until he gravitated away from that organization and joined the UR, receiving in the process CIA support and training.[71] Humberto Sorí Marín joined this organization, where he occupied the post of military chief.

Sorí had been conspiring since 1959 and enjoyed the support of the CIA, who, according to various sources, recruited him in mid-1959 through Robert Weicha, a U.S. diplomat stationed in Havana.[72] According to statements by CIA agent Alfredo Izaguirre, in early 1960 Sorí proposed to him a plan to establish a beachhead in the eastern region of the country and from there request the military support of the United States. On two occasions Izaguirre presented the plan to the CIA station in Havana and, even though they told him it was "trash," they expressed their willingness to support him. Subsequently Sorí told him that he had made contact with Guantánamo Naval Base and that they would back him. Toward the end of that year, continues Izaguirre, CIA officer Arthur Avignon, attaché to the U.S. embassy, communicated to him that the station had found out that Sorí was to be detained and urged Izaguirre to warn him. Izaguirre did not believe Avignon and Sorí was captured.[73]

Other organizations of lesser membership and relevance joined the counterrevolution in the first half of 1960, among them the Agrupación Montecristi. This group was practically a family clan, designed to serve as cover for the political maneuverings of Justo Carrillo.[74] His contacts with the anti-Batista military officers and other political sectors gave him a following that won him a space within the counterrevolutionary movement.

The first semester of 1960 was a crucial period in the formation of the first counterrevolutionary groups. The intervention of the U.S. government was a determining factor in this process. These first groups were clearly conservative in their political orientation and essentially bourgeois in social composition, representative of sectors that did not confront Batista or did so—as in the case of the Auténticos—with opportunistic and demagogic aims. In May these organizations, encouraged by the United States, began to integrate a front that was politically divided yet more or less ideologically homogenous that was to head the counterrevolutionary movement. In the second half of the year three new organizations, of different backgrounds and origins, joined the domestic political conflict. The rise of the Movimiento Revolucionario del Pueblo (MRP), the Movimiento 30 de Noviembre (M-30-11), and the Segundo Frente Nacional del Escambray further complicated the possible integration of the various counterrevolutionary groups.

A MININT (Ministerio del Interior) report dated September 1961 revealed that the MRP was created between July and August 1960,[75] as a result of the fusion of three groups. The first was called Movimiento 30 de Julio and included Manuel Ray, Felipe Pazos, and other former members of the first cabinet of the revolutionary government, who for the most part were veterans of the Movimiento de Resistencia Cívica. The second group was Verde Olivo, of similar origins, led by Rufo López Fresquet and Raúl Chibás, and the third was Acción Democrática Revolucionaria (ADR), made up of Catholic leaders, among them Reynold González, Andrés Valdespino, Antonio Fernández Nuevo, and Amalio Fiallo. Ray was named national coordinator and he designated his second-in-command, Rogelio Cisneros —the above-named alleged contact between Húber Matos and the CIA—as liaison between the organization and the U.S. embassy.[76]

Nevertheless, the majority of the provincial commands came under the control of the ADR, who eventually came to dominate the MRP.

For the rest of the counterrevolutionary groups the MRP espoused a sort of "Fidelism without Fidel"—that is, they proposed reforms that were equally unacceptable to their interests and ideology. Notwithstanding their criticism of "Communist totalitarianism," on appearance the MRP program did not differ substantially from what the Revolution had been carrying out. They recognized the need for state intervention in the economy, agrarian reform, social justice, and free access to education and health care.[77] Their conflict with the Revolution had a strategic sense and, above all, it reflected an alternative of the liberal bourgeoisie, which, after being dislodged from the government, lost relevance in a conflict characterized from that moment on, not by the dichotomy between reform and revolution, but by the collision between revolution and counterrevolution.

The MRP adopted a nationalist and populist line alien to the rest of the counterrevolutionary groups, but its legitimacy was questioned from the moment its leadership established organized contacts with the U.S. government and submitted to their policy. The argument that it was just a tactical alliance would only serve to demonstrate a naiveté that did not correspond to the political experience of the men who commanded the organization. In reality, whatever their feelings, the MRP allied with the United States because there was no other alternative if one wanted to make counterrevolution. Thus, like no other group, they embodied the drama of the liberal bourgeoisie overcome by events. Even with the circumstantial support of the president of the United States, they found little room within the conservative standards that characterized the counterrevolutionary coalition.

Something similar occurred with the Movimiento 30 de Noviembre. Originating in the labor union sectors of the 26th of July Movement and spurred by anticommunist prejudices, the M-30-11 came in conflict with the Revolution when the unification of the labor movement was proposed in 1959. Its principal leader was David Salvador, secretary-general of the Central de Trabajadores de Cuba in 1959. Although the positions of Salvador were consistently to the left of the main currents of the counterrevolution, his detention meant that the leadership of the organization passed into the hands of more conservative elements, who submitted to the CIA and went on to convert it into a very reactionary group.

The MRP and the M-30-11 competed to win followers from among the dissident sectors of the revolutionary ranks, as well as for the favor of the less conservative groups of the U.S. government. Perhaps this competition determined that both Ray and Salvador would attempt to leave the country on the eve of the 1960 presidential elections. On November 7, Ray succeeded in escaping, with the support of the CIA station in Havana, but David Salvador was detained that very day.[78] As Reynold González later stated, Ray fled to the United States without prior warning, which was viewed as an act of cowardice, since an established rule of the MRP was that its leaders should remain in Cuba.[79] Whether or not this was true, the fact is that Ray left for the United States in search of support that turned out to be essential for the survival of the organization within the counterrevolutionary movement. Perhaps the CIA may have even encouraged this trip, in accord with their pattern of removing counterrevolutionary leaders from the country.

Barely two months later Eloy Gutiérrez Menoyo also arrived in the United States. Accompanied by twenty of his men, he announced his intentions to join the plans in process. Although Menoyo's prior links were with the Auténticos, he now spoke of an alliance with Manuel Ray. Until then Menoyo had maintained a public posture of support for the Revolution. Nonetheless, the capture and conviction a few months before of some rebels formerly connected with the Segundo Frente and of two of his principal associates, the comandantes William Morgan and Jesús Cabrera, possibly hastened his decision to leave. John Maples Spiritus, a former CIA officer captured in Cuba, affirms that this was a plan on which the agency had been working for some time.[80] Nevertheless, Menoyo was not well received. According to Howard Hunt, there were doubts as to his loyalty and in the training camps he was rejected for his role in the discovery of the Batista conspiracy. As a result he was confined, together with this men, in an Immigration Service prison until after the Bay of Pigs invasion.[81]

All through 1960, therefore, the Cuban political spectrum was being defined, and a head-on struggle ensued between the revolutionary and counterrevolutionary sectors that would set the stage for future political struggle in Cuba. Nevertheless, for structural reasons, the problem was not confined to domestic class conflict, but rather found its true dimension in the realm of bilateral U.S.-Cuba relations. For their part, Cuba, conscious of these implications, assumed the risks and costs. The revolutionary discourse did not evade the anti-imperialist angle of the project; on the contrary, it emphasized it and mobilized most of the population on the basis of its premises.

Chapter 3

From Uprising to Invasion

On March 17, 1960, President Eisenhower approved the implementation of the plans to overthrow the Cuban Revolution. Although the president's approval represented a quantitative and qualitative change, this policy was in fact already in effect. Since 1958 the U.S. government had been following the Cuban situation closely[1] and had every intention of influencing it. They intervened in the domestic political conflicts in one way or another throughout 1959, and toward the end of the year Washington had already drafted a policy of subversion that led to the rise of the first counterrevolutionary organizations not linked to Batistianos.

The plan that the Central Intelligence Agency originally proposed to Eisenhower consisted of a covert operation with four elements.[2] First, it called for creating a political organization outside Cuba that would spark the formation of counterrevolutionary groups and provide the necessary legitimacy to the U.S. plan. Second, it proposed organizing a counterrevolutionary front on the island, formally subordinate to the exile organization but in fact under the leadership of the CIA. Third was the need to develop a strong propaganda offensive that would include establishing radio stations directed at Cuba. Finally, a paramilitary force was to be trained for infiltrating the island in order to develop clandestine and guerrilla operations. Eisenhower approved the project and indicated that his only concern was the possibility of leaks compromising U.S. participation: "Everyone has to be ready to swear that they never heard of this." In the final analysis, the plan depended on the counterrevolution's capacity for mobilization inside the country.[3]

The Uprising

In order to access the potentially counterrevolutionary sectors of Cuban society and organize them on behalf of the U.S. plans, the CIA sponsored the creation of the Frente Revolucionario Democrático (FRD). Its function was to provide legitimacy to U.S. policy and a catalyst for the development of the counterrevolutionary movement, but at no time was it conceived as the instrument assigned to truly head this process. Most of the organizations formed so far were conceived and organized from abroad and their principal leaders remained at all times outside Cuba. The creation of the FRD accelerated the formation of these organizations. As Manuel Artime later recalled, at the moment the CIA proposed the creation of this coalition, he ignored the existence of other groups.[4] In other words, in early 1960 there was no organized counterrevolutionary movement in Cuba.

Despite the diversity that the CIA was supposedly looking for, the FRD represented the most conservative tendencies in Cuban political thinking of the period. The testimony of Justo Carrillo demonstrates the political line that prevailed in the coalition: "From the first meetings of the FRD, I concluded that, despite some interventions by Aureliano Sánchez Arango, the predominant style fit the old Cuban political mold, without any understanding of the sociological phenomenon that was taking place in Cuba and that was typically counterrevolutionary—meaning by that the mental attitude of revoking as soon as possible all the revolutionary legislation that was being passed in Cuba."[5]

The first meeting called to organize the FRD was held in late February in Arlington, Virginia. It was hosted by CIA officer Frank Bender, and was attended by Angel Fernández Varela, Oscar Echevarría, and José Ignacio Rasco. At the meeting the participants chose the potential members of the front, discussed the creation of a radio station aimed at Cuba, and planned the organization of a paramilitary force. Fernández Varela was charged with contacting some of the potential constituents of the coalition and returning to Cuba to select a group of young men that were to receive military training in the United States. In the following days he contacted Artime, Tony de Varona, and Justo Carrillo.[6]

The first meetings of the selected group took place in May 1960 in Miami. The first joint session was held at the New York Bar Association, again presided over by Frank Bender, this time assisted by Willard Carr, who spoke fluent Spanish. At these meetings, which lasted days, the participants set the conditions that were to guide the relations between the U.S. government and the counterrevolutionary organizations. The agency delegates made it clear that they were empowered to represent their government and to carry out the promised cooperation.[7] The front finally consisted of Manuel Artime, Manuel Antonio de Varona, Aureliano Sánchez Arango, José Ignacio Rasco, and Justo Carrillo. Rafael Sardiñas was later included, representing a group of extreme right-wing organizations of the Cuban bourgeoisie. The final composition of the FRD was made public in Mexico City on June 22, 1960.[8]

Hunt affirms that Varona requested $754,000 per month for the operation of the front, and received an average of $115,000.[9] Hunt himself remarked that his impression of the members of the front was disappointing since, with the exception of Rasco and Artime, "all were professional politicians whose business was public demagoguery and private intrigue. . . . I considered them superficial opportunists who were greatly indebted—for their lives—to the U.S. government and specifically to the CIA."[10] Frank Bender, on the other hand, used to boast that he "carried the counterrevolution in his checkbook."[11]

To promote and control the activity of the groups that comprised the FRD within Cuba, the CIA used a wide network of agents and the contacts provided by the members of the front. According to Enrique Ros, on May 13 he traveled to Miami to meet Rasco and was told of the incorporation of the Movimiento Demócrata Crisitiano into the FRD. He then met with Artime and later with Varona and Carrillo, who encouraged him to contact his followers and incorporate them into the front. On May 31, before the official announcement in Mexico of the creation of the front, the first meeting of the national coordinators of the organizations making up the FRD in Cuba was held.[12]

During June and July they worked on structuring the front's clandestine arm. Although Rogelio González Corzo—chief of the Movimiento de Recuperación Revolucionaria (MRR) in Cuba—was named military coordinator, by the end of the year Ramón Ruisánchez—Tony de Varona's brother-in-law—controlled the main operations, particularly those related to the organization and supply of the rebels in the mountains and the plans to assassinate Fidel Castro. Ruisánchez spent millions of dollars, coordinated the principal arms shipments, and communicated directly with the CIA.

The selection of the officers to command the new guerrilla groups was made primarily among former military men and MRR militants coming from the Agrupación Católica Universitaria.[13] A portion was recruited among the immigrants, but a significant number were signed up in Cuba. Angel Fernández Varela, recruited by the CIA in December 1959, managed to select and send to the United States a substantial group of young Catholic men who enlisted in the first camps.[14] This group's training began in the summer of 1960. Nevertheless, it quickly became evident that the possibilities for the counterrevolution in Cuba had been exaggerated; thus the decision was made in November to adopt the idea of an invasion.[15] In summary, the evolution of the tactical concept of uprising to that of invasion was determined by the inability of the internal counterrevolution to create a generalized rebellion on the island. According the Taylor Report, by the summer of 1960 it became evident that there was "diminishing confidence in the effectiveness of the guerrillas to solely overthrow Castro."[16]

The newly elected U.S. president was informed of these plans on November 18. By that time the original project had been modified and substituted by a massive landing of amphibious forces on the shores near Trinidad, in the southern part of the former province of Las Villas. The provisional government would land as soon as a beachhead was secured "adjoining a territory favorable to guerrilla operations." A factor to be taken into account at the time of the escalation of the operation, according to the report, would be evidence of the genuine existence of "generalized opposition to the Castro regime."[17]

The Invasion

John F. Kennedy's victory in the 1960 elections changed the political climate in which the invasion project had been conceived. The Kennedy policy of modernizing the U.S. system of hegemony increased concern over the potential negative consequences of the project and the political composition of the counterrevolutionaries involved. Better excuses and greater participation of the countries of the region were required. Nevertheless, it was very hard to reverse the decision. The rhetoric of the electoral campaign had compromised the president's hand and the bilateral confrontation had advanced to the point that, only days before leaving office, Eisenhower had severed diplomatic relations with Cuba. In any event, on January 28, immediately after assuming office, Kennedy was again informed of the development of these plans and he authorized proceeding with them.[18]

Kennedy harbored doubts as to the planning and political assumptions on which the invasion was based, but in fact assumed the CIA project practically without any changes. One month before the invasion, the State Department, concerned about evidence of U.S. involvement in the operation, substituted the Trinidad landing site with one less populated, the Bay of Pigs, and reiterated that no U.S. troops would participate. Even so, it is practically impossible for the president and his team of advisors not to have understood the logic of the plan. It was clear by just looking at the map that the invaders could not survive without external support, which would inevitably lead to the intervention of U.S. troops. The change in the landing zone completely ruled out the guerrilla option, an alternative that had been rejected de facto from the moment guerrilla training was suspended in November 1960. Another aspect has been overlooked in the analysis of the plan: the invasion brigade had no reserves. Once the beachhead was secured and the guerrilla option ruled out, there were no more troops to send but the U.S. military. This hypothesis is confirmed by the fact that the CIA did not believe in the possibility of an immediate popular uprising, according to testimony by its director, Allen Dulles, and therefore did not take this prospect into account in its plans.[19]

The differences between the CIA position and that of the president was that Kennedy considered as prerequisite to greater U.S. involvement that the Cuban counterrevolution demonstrate a degree of popular support that legitimized these actions and justified other countries of the region in lending their support to U.S. policy. Barely three days before the start of the air raids that served as prelude to the invasion, Kennedy declared at a press conference: "First, I want to state that under no circumstances will there be an intervention in Cuba by the armed forces of the United States. This Government will do all in its power, and I believe it can fulfill its responsibilities, to make sure that no American will be involved in any action within Cuba. . . . The basic problem in Cuba is not between the United States and Cuba. It is among the Cubans themselves. I want to see us comply with this principle and, as I understand it, that is the attitude of the Administration and it is shared by the Cuban exiles in this country."[20]

According to Howard Hunt, the Central Intelligence Agency did not assign a significant role to internal clandestine operations: their mission was, at best, to create confusion in the cities.[21] Nevertheless, fearing cancellation of the project, the agency avoided debate on the capabilities of the internal front. Instead they pressed for a decision on the basis of the accelerated build-up of the Cuban armed forces, and the problems that would result from demobilizing a brigade of more than a thousand military-trained men and reinserting them into an acutely dissatisfied and aggressive community living within U.S. borders. Nor did they believe the presidential promise not to invade Cuba, says Hunt. Everything was ready and they were so certain of victory that they regarded the president's words as disinformation and did not take them seriously.[22] In summary, the CIA trusted that in the event of a possible failure, Kennedy would opt for intervention. This was the key element in the plan of the U.S. "hawks" and the certain expectation of the counterrevolutionary groups involved.

> Something is lost in Bissell's plan. It appears that the feeling—and maybe the heart of the plan—was that the climax of the operation would force Kennedy to abandon his official neutrality and intervene with U.S. forces, despite Kennedy's oath not to do so. The pressures of that situation would certainly have been great. It is possible that Bissell and Dulles thought that Kennedy's hand would be forced by the transparency of U.S. involvement and the difficulty in abandoning

the exiles, once they secured what the CIA always called an "entrenchment." Bisell claims that he and Dulles did not have this plan, but it is difficult to see what else could have shifted a balance so disproportionately against the trapped and isolated exiles. Even with total air superiority the exiles' B-26 could not have conquered the island alone, and the exiles were too few in number. The best that the entrenchment could offer to the Cuban people was a civil war, a bitter gift indeed.[23]

The 2506th Brigade was the paramilitary group entrusted with carrying out the invasion. The CIA organized the paramilitary arm independently of the FRD and established direct channels to communicate with and supply the internal clandestine groups. The FRD participated in these operations only on demand.[25] This explains the apparent irrationality of removing from the country the alleged chiefs of the main counterrevolutionary organizations. In other words, although they encouraged the participation of its militants and pressed for a larger presence in the invasion force, these groups had no say in the selection process nor did they intervene directly in the military structure of the invasion. The counterrevolutionary organizations, therefore, played a subordinate and collateral role in the invasion project, which was wholly directed by the U.S. government.

Although the principal military officers and more than 10 percent of the brigade members were former soldiers in the Batista armed forces, the main component of this military force were young men from the Cuban upper middle class, matching the characteristics of the migration at this stage, as well as the individuals recruited in Cuba and sent to train abroad. The Catholic right—particularly the MRR—provided the majority of these recruits. The class composition of the brigade is unique in the history of Cuban political struggles. Neither before nor after did the bourgeoisie act in such a concerted manner nor play the protagonist in the development of armed struggle.[26]

At the brigade's trial in Cuba following the defeat of the invasion, the defense attorney stressed the importance of class: "It is a fact—as the prosecutor emphasized and we discussed yesterday when questioning some of the witnesses—that class composition plays an extraordinarily important role in all of this. The historical conditions that reign, the composition of the majority of those who made up the brigade, as well as [the composition] of the persons who are judging them, and who will sentence them in the name of the People, who defeated them at Girón, are undoubtedly antagonistic."[27]

According to the transcripts of the trial, "the invasion brigade included: 100 large landowners, 24 large property holders, 67 major landlords, 112 large merchants, 194 former soldiers and goons of the dictatorship, 179 well-to-do, 35 industrial tycoons, 112 bums, and others. Among them they pretended to recover the following: 852,000 acres of land, 9,666 houses and apartment buildings, 70 factories, 10 sugar mills, 3 commercial banks, 5 mines, 12 nightclubs, bars, and various other properties."[28]

The training of the 2506th Brigade took place primarily in Guatemala. A force initially numbering 300 intended for guerrilla operations was in the end made up of 1,200 officers and men trained for regular combat as amphibious forces. The first commanders had been high ranking officers in the former Cuban army, led by ex-Colonel Eduardo Martín Elena. But these leaders played merely a symbolic role and never participated in the planning of the operation, nor in the training of the men. In January 1961 they were replaced by younger officers, most previously trained in the United States, who were more trusted by the CIA and not committed to any of the existing counterrevolutionary groups.

Another ingredient in the operation was the infiltration, or "gray teams." Its members, primarily young Catholics, had been among the first to join the training camps and their mission was to infiltrate into Cuba before the invasion and organize the counterrevolution from within. After rigorous training, forty-seven men were designated for this task[29]—"the best possible men," according to Howard Hunt. The mission of these teams consisted in "creating massive armed resistance simultaneously in various areas of Cuba."[30] In reality, they essentially took care of communications, training, and supply for the domestic front.

Although by means of these groups a great deal of arms and explosives were introduced into the country, the system failed in its essential aspects. The air operations meant to supply arms to the rebel groups were ineffective and thus from the beginning of the year the operatives requested that they be revised. The sea operation did not fare much better. According to Félix Rodríguez, one of its participants, just seven groups succeeded in infiltrating and only fifteen men survived the experience.[31] This figure is consistent with the investigations of Fabián Escalante, who states that of the thirty-five men who infiltrated, twenty-three were captured (although three later escaped). At the time of the invasion, says Hunt, the internal clandestine front was not taken into account, simply because nothing had been organized that inspired the trust of the agency.[32]

The invasion project included accomplishing previous diversionary attacks in the former province of Oriente. A group led by the ex-comandante Nino Díaz was to carry out, some days before the invasion, a landing on the extreme southwest coast of this province. This group was trained in New Orleans and although the most widespread version insists that that Díaz's objective was limited to diverting attention from the main thrust at the Bay of Pigs, other hypotheses cannot be discarded—among them that the operation included a staged attack on Guantánamo Naval Base. Díaz himself had been involved in this provocation project on various occasions and it was a constant in the U.S. plans.

The operation headed by Nino Díaz is still an unknown in the invasion project. Before the Revolution, Díaz had been linked to the Organización Auténtica and later joined the Rebel Army, where he achieved the rank of comandante. Toward the end of 1958 he joined the conspiracy lead by Eulogio Cantillo—the general in the Batista army who was preparing a negotiated settlement for the regime—who offered him the post of mayor of Santiago de Cuba. He was discovered, tried publicly, stripped of his rank, and placed under arrest until the end of the war. He later participated in the Húber Matos conspiracy, and still later became one of the founders of the MRR.[33]

Díaz has stated that in the summer of 1960 he fell out of grace of the CIA, and thus was excluded from the invasion plans. He was not called until March 1961, when he was assigned with creating the special force that would land at Oriente. The training took place in Louisiana, on an abandoned military base near the Mississippi River. Díaz recalls that one day they were told that they were leaving for Cuba: they were 158 men and some had not received a full week of training. They were not told of their landing site until they were at sea, their armament was in bad condition, and no one was waiting for them upon arrival. "I sent a reconnaissance patrol ashore and we realized that the area was occupied by a great force. We retreated. We asked the Americans for an alternative landing site. They did not have one because they had sent us to the scaffold. They did not need alternative sites. It was complete treason."[34] In the opinion of the Taylor Commission, "the landing did not take place probably due to deficient leadership of the Cuban officer responsible for the same."[35]

One of the most unusual diversionary operations of the invasion plan consisted of an attempted landing of some fifty men west of Baracoa—also in the former eastern province—under the command of José Ignacio Rasco and Laureano Batista, both leaders of the Movimiento Demócrata Cristiano. This landing group was made up of individuals from various organizations who barely knew each other. According to their own testimony, the ships left Miami on April 4, and the men were similarly told of the destination on the high seas: a coral reef–lined coast that was practically inaccessible. They were detected by Cuban gunboats and the operation resulted in complete disaster. In the ensuing retreat the would-be invaders threw overboard some ten tons of arms.[36] In Ros's opinion, "Very probably [the CIA] took advantage of that plan [the diversionary landing] to arm on their own another diversionary force, which, at the same time, would allow them to get rid of some elements that had become undesirable to the agency."[37] Maybe Ros is partly right, although it has not been proven that this group had had substantial conflict with the CIA. On the contrary, the group included the main leaders of the MDC, noted figures of the MRR and the Auténticos, as well as various known CIA agents. Nevertheless, it is logical to suppose that this operation formed part of the diversionary plans and that the CIA, willing to sacrifice its participants, did not warn them of the risks they were taking.

The invasion components were completed with a specialized counterintelligence corps that participated in the investigation of the recruits and was slated to constitute the police force in the zones eventually occupied during the invasion. This group, led by Joaquín Sanjenís, remained active until 1972, when it was disbanded once Sanjenís's connections to drug trafficking were made public.

The struggles for leadership plagued the unity of the FRD. The resignation of Sánchez Arango and his subsequent attacks on the front, as well as the extensive role played by the Batistianos in the invasion corps, created the first schisms within the coalition. Other battles ensued as a result of the replacement of Edgardo Martín Elena and the generation gap that pitted the younger members of the FRD against the traditional politicians. But the most serious problem occurred in the camps when a part of the brigade threatened mutiny and Varona was obliged to travel to Guatemala and support the CIA decisions.

On the other hand, President Kennedy began to call for the front to espouse a political line more consistent with the program of reforms proposed for Latin America by his government. The Administration was promoting precisely what the right-wing hawks within the CIA and the counterrevolutionary groups in the FRD were unwilling to accept: a reformist program that admitted the need for change in Cuba, and a new image, which would include the incorporation of the Movimiento Revolucionario del Pueblo. Hunt warned the agency's directors that neither the FRD nor the groups that were training for the invasion supported the inclusion of this organization.[38] Nevertheless, the MRP enjoyed the support of important presidential advisors and of Latin American leaders such as Luis Muñóz Marín, Rómulo Betancourt, and José Figueres. These reformers were as concerned with the influence of the Revolution on the left in their countries as they were with a solution to the Cuban problem that would revitalize the most reactionary forces in the continent.

The pressures exerted by the administration to change the ideological and political composition of the FRD, coupled with the inability of its members to maintain cohesion, led to the decision in March 1961 to disband the front and replace it with a new entity named Consejo Revolucionario Cubano (CRC). Years later, Justo Carrillo stated that at the time Bender began to insist on the expansion of the FRD, which meant the inclusion of various persons and organizations. He also proposed that the front ally with the MRP. Meetings were held between the FRD and the MRP, with Artime, Miró, and Carrillo representing the former, and Ray, Pazos, and Fresquet the latter. After debate on the program, a very conservative agreement was reached, but it was not accepted by the body of the FRD and thus was not implemented. The U.S. government in the person of Willard Carr pressed for an accord, making clear that without unity there would be no support. During these meetings Miró Cardona was chosen as the front's new president. In early April, only days before the invasion, the proposed future government of Cuba, to be installed at the conquered beachhead, was finally established. It was comprised of Miró, Varona, Artime, Carlos Hevia, Antonio Maceo, Ray, and Carrillo.

Miró was the choice of the CIA. They had contacted him in Argentina and arranged for his transfer in October to Miami,[39] where, according to Ros, he was received as a pariah due to his past service in the ranks of the Revolution.[40] Howard Hunt proposed that Miró take over as president of the FRD and offered him financial aid, which Miró accepted.[41] Varona was opposed to naming Miró because of his links with Ray, and he was not far from the truth. Although he was allegedly not committed to any existing organization, a source associated with the formation of the MRP asserts that Miró was a member, and that he adopted an apparently neutral posture because of the organization's interest in gaining stature within the representative organs of the counterrevolutionary movement.[42] The source in question cannot say whether the U.S. government was aware of this ploy.

The agreement between Hunt and Miró included naming Artime as the civilian head of the invasion brigade. This was apparently a post of little importance, since it did not entail assuming command of the troops nor imply that he would enjoy any special authority once the CRC landed in Cuba. It is safe to assume that the CIA was creating conditions for the political future of Artime on the island. That is the interpretation of Varona, Carrillo, and others who complained that the decision constituted a "coup" against them by the agency. Carrillo characterized Artime as a political opportunist, without ideological foundation or solid principles, whose only merit consisted of being the CIA's "golden boy."[43]

The process of expanding the civilian structure of the invasion could not, however, transform the essential nature and political agenda of the operation. According to Arthur Schlesinger Jr., one of President Kennedy's principal associates, the dependence of the CRC on the agency was complete. It embraced not only operational questions, but also included a political agenda so reactionary that the president's advisors were obliged to personally draft the organization's communiqués, often without the previous knowledge of the members of the council. Schlesinger recalls that its leaders tended to espouse positions "full of incentives for foreign investors, private bankers, displaced property holders, but had little to say to the workers, the farmers and the blacks."[44]

The CRC turned out to be an artificially created superstructure without any political authority of its own. What power they had was consumed in disputes over a protagonism that depended on the favor of the North Americans and confrontations where the personal ambitions of professional politicians predominated. The role of the counterrevolutionary organizations within the CRC was even more diffuse because, unlike the front, in which each member represented his group, council members were selected primarily on the basis of personality, whether or not the individuals were connected with specific counterrevolutionary structures. Nevertheless, the CRC played a vital role in the invasion project because it was the legitimizing factor for an eventual direct intervention by the United States. If the FRD was originally conceived as the catalyst for the counterrevolutionary movement, in the evolution that culminated with the founding of the council, the civilian body of the invasion became the "government" that would open the way to the intervention. All its members were fully aware of this objective.

Beginning April 8, the CRC became a virtual hostage of the CIA at the Lexington Hotel in New York. On the 12th or 13th a now famous meeting was held between Miró, Schlesinger, and Adolf Berle. The two North Americans claim they told Miró that U.S. forces would not intervene, which Miró denied until his death. The council was not advised of the moment of the invasion; thus the supposed Cuban leadership learned of the event on the radio in the early hours of April 17 while in reclusion in one of the barracks at a military base in Opa-Locka, Florida.[45]

Awaiting the Invaders

Although it never acted as a truly cohesive political movement, before the invasion the counterrevolution within Cuba was possibly stronger than at any other time during the revolutionary process and it was perfectly defined along class lines. According to CIA estimates, the counterrevolutionary groups at that time had some 3,000 members supported by approximately 20,000 sympathizers.[46] Its principal organizations were active within the country and in many cases were led by young men that acted decisively and were inspired by strong religious convictions and a great trust in U.S. support. Nevertheless, despite these favorable conditions and the ample resources invested by the United States in its organization, the domestic counterrevolutionary movement was clearly vulnerable to a defensive system that involved the great majority of the Cuban population.

In the days before the invasion the CIA made a new effort at unification through the creation of the Frente de Unidad Revolucionaria (FUR). Its mission was to establish sole command of the counterrevolution in Cuba, create conditions for the support of the invasion through the assassination of Fidel Castro, intensify sabotage and urban terrorism, and create two guerrilla fronts. Chosen to head the FUR were Rafael Díaz Hanscom as civilian coordinator and Humberto Sorí Marín as military chief. Also included were CIA agent Manuel Puig Miyar and MRR chief in Cuba Rogelio González Corzo, the only member of the FUR in the country at the time.

In December 1960, Sorí Marín escaped home detention and in early 1961 succeeded in fleeing to the United States. Once there, Alberto Fernández arranged a meeting for him with Miró, Varona, and the CIA, from which Sorí emerged "appalled" by the divisions existing among the counterrevolutionary groups and the way the agency was handling the situation.[47] Sorí himself later confirmed that while in the United States he met with Miró Cardona and Ramón Ruisánchez.[48] According to Escalante, Sorí also met with Howard Hunt and from that meeting emerged the idea of creating the FUR.[49] With that purpose in mind, in March 1961 one of the agency's paramilitary groups carried Sorí, Díaz Hanscom, and Manuel Puig back to Cuban shores. On March 18, Cuban authorities arrested Sorí, Díaz Hanscom, González Corzo and the bulk of the FUR leadership.[50] Cuban security also controlled the two guerrilla parties they were attempting to create; thus the operation failed in all aspects.

Alberto Muller, one of the main leaders of the Directorio Revolucionario Estudiantil, sought to organize another guerrilla front before the invasion, this time in the Sierra Maestra. Muller later declared that he coordinated that effort with Artime and enjoyed the support of the CRC, and by extension of the CIA. He arrived at the Sierra Maestra in early April and succeeded in organizing four insurgent camps, but he was detected and captured, together with all his men. While in prison, Muller sent a document abroad in which he accused the CIA and Artime of having betrayed him.[51] All indications are that the Muller insurgency was also related to the diversionary plans in Oriente and that he was treated like the other expendable forces.

At the moment the invasion took place, Cuban authorities carried out an extraordinary mobilization of forces and people to detain hundreds of persons suspected of having links with the counterrevolution. Most of those arrested were released shortly afterward; thus many individuals active in the counterrevolutionary movement eluded the authorities and continued their antigovernment activities. But the operation charged with supporting the invasion was totally dismantled and incapacitated, a factor that turned out to be decisive for the later course of events. The rest is well known: in less than seventy-two hours the invasion troops were defeated and the diversionary action in the eastern region failed when its participants decided not to land. The speed with which the invaders were defeated was fundamental in avoiding escalation of hostilities that would have allowed U.S. troops to be committed.

The Kennedy administration evaluated the defeat from the perspective of strictly operational causes. The CIA was blamed for the fiasco, and it was decided that the plans should be revised, this time with the technocratic input of the men of the New Frontier. But the plans were not the problem. The agency did all in its power to encourage the internal counterrevolution as a function of the invasion plan. It capitalized to the utmost the capabilities of the counterrevolutionary groups established abroad and succeeded in enrolling practically all of them in the project. In addition, millions of dollars and hundreds of men were employed in the effort. The error did not lie in the military tactics or in the conduct of the clandestine machinery, but rather in the political evaluation of the Cuban reality.

Kennedy could not avoid the Bay of Pigs appearing to be what it really was, "an American invasion," and he was forced to assume personal responsibility. This event had a negative effect on the recently inaugurated administration and conditioned, to a large degree, its future policy toward Cuba. Projects of the scope of Operation Mongoose (see chapter 4) and actions such as the economic embargo are among the results of the failure of the invasion. The defeat at Playa Girón also influenced the strategies of the United States toward the rest of Latin America and the former socialist camp. In addition, it inspired substantial changes in the criteria that guided the operations of the U.S. intelligence services, which helped bring about a profound restructuring of the agency.

For Cuba, the victory proved a decisive step toward the consolidation and radicalization of the revolutionary process, defined the socialist character of the Cuban political project,[52] and intensified the already strong nationalist sentiment in the populace. National defense became the country's main concern, which accelerated the process of its integration into the socialist camp from a perspective of collective security, an aspect that would influence events leading up to the 1962 Cuban missile crisis.

In the period before the Bay of Pigs invasion the main counterrevolutionary organizations were structured and organic ties were established between them and the CIA. The participation of these groups in the invasion invalidated them as patriotic organizations in the eyes of most of the Cuban people and polarized the political battlegrounds to this date. The Cuban counterrevolution assumed the defeat as a betrayal of the U.S. government, to the point that many analysts link this attitude with the subsequent assassination of President Kennedy (see chapter 4).

Reaction to the Failure

The defeat at Playa Girón disintegrated the internal counterrevolution. Many militants were detained and most of those remaining chose to emigrate. The CIA lost contact with most of its agents. U.S. intervention was assumed to guarantee success; thus the defeat destroyed the myth of U.S. invincibility and darkened the perspectives for ultimate victory within the counterrevolutionary movement. The counterrevolutionary groups felt betrayed and the demoralization became quite generalized. José San Román, the military chief of the invasion brigade, noted sometime later: "Most of the Cubans were there because they knew that the whole operation was going to be directed by the Americans, not by me or anyone else. They did not trust me or anyone else. They simply trusted the Americans; they went to fight because the United States backed them."[53]

Assassinating Fidel Castro was viewed as the only realistic option left to the counterrevolution to reverse the Cuban revolutionary process. In some cases cold political calculation teamed with arrogance (in some cases, desperation) to thrust this objective to the core of the counterrevolutionary plans. Assassination turned out to be the mission that brought Alfredo Izaguirre de la Riva to Cuba after meeting with important figures of the U.S. government. An heir of one of the most aristocratic families of the national oligarchy, and a former editor of the newspaper *El Crisol,* Izaguirre's ties to the CIA went back to 1959, when he had approached the U.S. embassy with the intention of taking money out of Cuba illegally. He traveled to the United States for training in September 1960 and again in February 1961, and went on to become one of the principal CIA agents in Cuba. Izaguirre was fortunate enough not to have attended the meeting where Sorí Marín, Díaz Hanscom, and González Corzo were captured. A few days after the Bay of Pigs fiasco he again traveled to the United States. There he met with some of the main agency officers in charge of actions against Cuba, and they arranged for him to meet

General Maxwell Taylor, who at the time was drafting the famous evaluation of the Bay of Pigs operation.

As Izaguirre himself later declared, the meeting was held in June in Washington and lasted forty-five minutes. Taylor explored the situation of the counterrevolutionary groups within the country—in particular, the potential of Manuel Ray. Izaguirre responded that the situation was very bad and that all the organizations together were incapable of defeating Fidel Castro. Taylor agreed with that evaluation but said that the United States could not act "out of the cold" and therefore depended on the groups inside the island to create a political situation that justified North American "aid." Taylor indicated that the objective at that time was to improve communications, and he was amenable to the idea of uniting the organizations. Finally, Taylor gave assurances that the Cuban question would have an adequate solution and that he would do all in his power to achieve it.[54]

By late May, Izaguirre returned to Cuba entrusted with unifying the main counterrevolutionary groups. In early June he met with representatives of the principal counterrevolutionary organizations in an apartment at the Focsa Building, located in the exclusive Havana neighborhood of Vedado. According to a Cuban counterespionage agent present at the meeting, Izaguirre told of his conversations with Taylor and the CIA, and emphasized the need to assassinate Fidel and Raúl Castro and to carry out a wave of terrorist actions that would serve as a basis for a general uprising. He also said that one of the CIA plans included organizing a counterfeit attack on Guantánamo Naval Base, which would justify a direct military invasion.[55] At this meeting the Frente de Unidad Revolucionaria was reactivated. Carlos Bandín, national coordinator of the MRR, was designated to head the FUR, and the M-30-11, MDC, MRP, UR, and other organizations joined the coalition. Izaguirre and another agent, José Pujals Mederos, were entrusted with maintaining contact with the CIA.[56]

Foreseeing that Fidel and Raul would participate in the celebrations commemorating the anniversary of the 26th of July, a plan named

Operation Patty was drafted that called for simultaneous assassinations in the cities of Havana and Santiago, an attack on the Santiago oil refinery, sabotage throughout the country, and a staged attack on Guantánamo Naval Base. The details of the plan were transmitted by radio to the agency and Pujals Mederos traveled to the United States on July 12 to personally report on the operation. Despite security measures, on July 22 the main plotters were arrested.[57]

Other assassination attempts had also been planned for the 26th of July, but they failed as well. In addition, Luis Torroella, another of the principal agents established on the island, was also captured.[58] These fiascoes further increased the bewilderment already present among the counterrevolutionary groups. Nevertheless, the agency stuck to its plans and sent Pujals Mederos once again to Cuba. This time his mission was to explore the possibilities of the MRP, the organization that had apparently suffered the fewest blows at the hands of Cuban counterintelligence.

Following the Bay of Pigs disaster, Manuel Ray was ousted as head of the MRP, Reynold González was appointed its head in Cuba, and Ignacio Mendoza designated as his delegate in the United States. This decision must have been influenced by the fact that, by that time, the majority of the leaders of the Movimiento 30 de Julio—the organization that Ray had united with the MRP—had left Cuba and thus Ray had lost authority among the members who operated within the country. It could also have been influenced by the CIA's interest in reducing Ray's sway over the Kennedy administration and putting the MRP in the hands of a more conservative group that had also emerged from the Catholic ranks. In any case, the MRP never had the strength in Cuba that the Kennedy administration supposed, neither before nor after Ray's leadership. In that sense the agency was right. The MRP had distinguished itself for carrying out a terrorist offensive that included burning down some of the principal department stores in Havana as well as factories and other civilian objectives. Yet its membership was sparse and its capacity for mobilization fell far short of the expectations they attempted to spark in the United States.

At the time of the Bay of Pigs invasion the MRP ordered the dispersion of its men and the suspension of its activities, allowing it to survive the revolutionary counteroffensive with few losses. Also, it was less dependent on outside help. They obtained most of their arms and explosives by either buying them or seizing shipments that the CIA had destined for other organizations. They counted on their own sources of funds—basically the donations of members who had fled the country and the embezzlement of some 300,000 pesos from the Banco Financiero de Cuba by one of the group's militants, Antonio Veciana. In addition, the organization had benefited, paradoxically, from the relative isolation to which the other counterrevolutionary groups had submitted them, and from the mistrust of the CIA because of their liberal positions.

This did not mean that it acted independently of the U.S. government. From its inception the MRP had maintained contacts with the CIA, and the agency had recruited or infiltrated agents within its structure. One of these was the same Antonio Veciana, a public accountant and a trusted associate of the sugar tycoon Julio Lobo. Veciana had been recruited by the agency in mid 1960 and he went on to become the military chief of the MRP.[59] Within Operation Patty, Veciana had been in charge of an alternative plan to shooting a bazooka from a balcony across from the presidential palace. This was the plan that the CIA hoped to reactivate and for which it sent Pujals Mederos to Cuba.

A source who has requested anonymity recalls that toward the end of May 1961, González gathered the leadership of the MRP to analyze Ray's replacement and the status of the counterrevolution after the defeat at Playa Girón. It was González's opinion that the U.S. government had betrayed them and thereby frustrated any possibility of success, and he therefore proposed that he disband the organization and then leave the country. A group of leaders opposed this option, arguing that they possessed a significant amount of armament, nearly two tons, that had originally been sent to the UR and that the MRP had recovered on April 23 and shared with the Directorio Revolucionario Estudiantil. The leaders approved the proposal to study the possibility of opening a guerrilla front in the Escambray Mountains. Roberto Jiménez traveled to that area and met with Osvaldo Ramírez. In the middle of June, González, under pressure from the more radical sector, agreed to the launching of Operación Liborio, a terrorist offensive aimed at provoking chaos in the city by the end of September. The plan was to burn five stores, two tobacco warehouses, some factories, and four movie houses, as well as to attack with grenades various police stations and offices of the Comité de Defensa de la Revolución (CDR).[60]

As Reynold González later declared, the purpose of these attacks was to provoke Fidel Castro to appear at a mass rally,[61] but the majority of the leadership ignored Veciana's assassination plans. In fact, González was to be the only participant from the MRP in the attempted assassination, as the rest of the team came from the ranks of the Auténticos. The plan took shape in August at a meeting held with the assistance of Pujals Mederos, Reynold González, Antonio Veciana, and Octavio Barroso. The arrest of Pujals and Barroso on August 8 delayed the plans, but the opportunity presented itself on October 4, at a rally marking the return of President Osvaldo Dorticós from a trip to Eastern Europe. However, on September 29, Dalia Jorge Díaz, a member of the MRP, was captured while attempting to place an incendiary device in one of Havana's large department stores. Frightened that he had been detected, Veciana left the country on October 3, the day before the operation, and thus it was never executed. Later the rest of the conspirators were arrested, including Reynold González, who was captured October 11.

The MRP was practically dismantled as a result of this fiasco. By the end of 1961 the counterrevolution in Cuba had been almost totally destroyed. Most of the leaders were either under arrest or had fled the country. The level of penetration by the Cuban security services was intense, the Revolution enjoyed immense popular support, and the morale of the counterrevolutionary groups had deteriorated so much that most spoke of dissolution. Even so, Operation Mongoose was designed on the supposed potential of these groups to spark a general insurrection. But the original fault of that plan lay precisely in this misconception, totally akin to the real political situation of the country. The CIA knew this. When asked by Richard Helms, at the time the agency's assistant director, to investigate the scope of the operation, one of the officers in charge of the anti-Cuba program asked: "With what? We don't have the resources. We don't even know what's going on in Cuba."[62]

Chapter 4

The Counterrevolutionary Revolution

THE BAY OF PIGS invasion ran counter to the principles that inspired the foreign policy of the Kennedy administration. The New Frontier was a concept of political renovation that attempted to accommodate the United States to the profound changes taking place in the postwar world. The advances achieved by the USSR in the areas of space exploration and nuclear energy generated new fears and challenges for the United States. The emergence of the European Common Market established a new competitive scenario for which U.S. industry was not totally prepared. The dismantling of the old colonial empires opened up an extraordinary space to the North American market, but the nationalist sentiments of the decolonization processes and the influence of socialist ideology on most of them required a new course and widened the scenario of the Cold War.

In Latin America, the impact of the Cuban Revolution found fertile ground in the economic situation of that region. The boom originated by the two world wars and the Korean conflict passed Latin America by without leaving any enduring effects. The dictatorial regimes, a basis for the relative political stability of the 1950s, were typically no longer capable of sustaining themselves, and the reformist bourgeois governments that ensued staggered under the convergent pressures of the oligarchy on the right and the revolutionary forces on the left. A strongly anti–North American nationalism characterized the political situation of the subcontinent.

The U.S. economy was going through a period of recession, and racial discrimination and civil rights for blacks were becoming explosive issues. The conservative sectors held firm to their positions and gained ground, especially in the South, which had been until then one of the bastions of the Democratic Party coalition. Possibly more than any other politician of his time, Kennedy understood the need for profound changes in the design of U.S. policy. His principles did not differ from those postulated by the Truman Doctrine—the doctrinal basis for the Cold War—but in their application he proposed innovative concepts that demanded profound structural and ideological reforms.

The Kennedy administration turned out to be a technocracy that assumed the task of designing a new model for exercising North American hegemony. On one hand, it advocated a policy of development aid and the need for structural reforms in poor nations. On the other, it defended the need to modernize the capacity for U.S. intervention, openly or covertly, in those local conflicts that were deemed detrimental to U.S. interests, a kind of retaining wall against emerging Third World revolutionary movements. For Kennedy, the main scenario of the Cold War had shifted to the underdeveloped countries and his strategy was to articulate a consensus among the United States and its allies in order to face up to this challenge. "Non-nuclear wars, and sub-limited or guerrilla warfare, have since 1945 constituted the most active and constant threat to Free World security. . . . The Free World's security can be endangered not only by a nuclear attack, but also by being slowly nibbled away at the periphery, regardless of our strategic power, by forces of subversion, infiltration, intimidation, indirect or non-overt aggression, internal revolution, diplomatic blackmail, guerrilla warfare or a series of limited wars. In this area of local wars, we must inevitably count on the cooperative efforts of other peoples and nations who share our concern."[1]

Kennedy's approach to this problem contrasted with the simplistic notions predominant during the Truman and Eisenhower administrations. "It is easy to dismiss as Communist-inspired every anti-government or anti-American riot, every overthrow of a corrupt regime, or every mass protest against misery and despair. These are all not Communist-inspired. The Communists move in to exploit them, to infiltrate their leadership, to ride their crest to victory. But the Communists did not create the conditions which caused them."[2]

As part of this renovated policy, Kennedy launched the Alliance for Progress, the most ambitious economic plan for Latin America ever proposed by a U.S. president. Kennedy himself equated the Alliance for Progress to the Marshall Plan. It proposed an economic assistance package of $500 million to $1 billion annually for ten years, and encouraged significant economic and social reforms in the countries that were to receive the aid. It proposed the economic integration of the countries in the region and the establishment of bilateral treaties with the United States. It included food aid, scientific exchange and technical assistance, the creation of a system of collective defense through the Organization of American States (OAS), the rationalization of national armies, as well as an increase in cultural and educational interchange. The project eventually failed because, as Kennedy himself had foreseen, it inevitably collided with the resistance of the Latin American oligarchies and the narrow interests of some large North American corporations. "This political freedom must be accompanied by social change. For unless necessary social reforms, including land and tax reform, are freely made—unless we broaden the opportunity for all our people—unless the great mass of Americans share in increasing prosperity—then our alliance, our revolution, our dream, and our freedom will fail."[3]

Nevertheless, the Kennedy Doctrine did not veer from that of his predecessor James Monroe. For him, U.S. intervention in Latin American affairs was not an ethical, but rather a tactical problem. It had to do with the adaptation of the system of hegemony, in the Gramscian sense of the term. This required exporting a better image of the United States and implementing a flexible foreign policy, capable of employing a variety of resources in order to impose itself morally and physically. What was necessary to achieve this were economic and political reforms, strengthening the Atlantic Alliance and the mechanisms of hemispheric cooperation, increasing efforts to improve living conditions in underdeveloped countries, and better utilization of international organizations.

"We must reject over-simplified theories of international life—the theory that American power is unlimited, or that the American mission is to remake the world in the American image. We must seize the vision of a free and diverse world—and shape our policies to speed progress toward a more flexible world order."[4] Flexibility had its limits on the frontiers of the Cold War, which explains the administration's attitude toward events in the Congo, southeast Asia, and Cuba. In the Cuban case, Kennedy inherited a policy of confrontation that allowed little room for maneuvering and that he himself exacerbated during the presidential campaign. Lacking room for criticism in light of the reforms he recommended for other parts of the world, his position on the Cuban Revolution had no other justification beyond its role within the East-West conflict. As in the case of Vietnam, Kennedy lacked an understanding of the nature of the nationalist sentiment that, for historical reasons, inevitably clashed with traditional U.S. policy—as Robert McNamara recently admitted.

The capacity for U.S. interference in Cuban affairs was limited by the popular support of the Revolution and the sympathy that the Cuban political process evoked in the rest of the world. In his famous speech before the American Society of Newspaper Editors, days after the U.S. defeat at the Bay of Pigs, Kennedy said, "Any unilateral American intervention, in the absence of an external attack upon ourselves or an ally, would have been contrary to our traditions and to our international obligations. But let the record show that our restraint is not inexhaustible. Should it ever appear that the inter-American doctrine of non-interference merely conceals or excuses a policy of nonaction —if the nations of this Hemisphere should fail to meet their commitments against outside Communist penetration—then I want it clearly understood that this government will not hesitate in meeting its primary obligations, which are the security of our Nation."[5]

In order to intervene militarily and openly against the Cuban Revolution without sensibly affecting the credibility of his foreign policy, Kennedy required the fulfillment of at least three conditions: (1) a climate of political instability in Cuba to contrast with the massive popular support enjoyed by the Revolution; (2) international conditions that would allow the Cuban problem to be presented within the ideological and geopolitical context of the Cold War, depriving it of its nationalist and Third World character; and (3) the regionalization of the conflict through the support of the rest of the continent. He also required that his policy be cloaked in the progressive attributes of U.S. revolutionary heritage, regaining for his country the concept of revolution, so vigorous in those times, in order to bestow on it a counterrevolutionary meaning. To fulfill those aims, measures were taken that today continue to characterize U.S. policy toward Cuba. Paradoxically, the most liberal and creative president since Franklin D. Roosevelt assumed the historic responsibility for justifying and taking the first steps in what would turn out to be two of the most notable failures in the history of U.S. foreign policy: Vietnam and Cuba.

The Counterrevolutionary Experiment

On June 13, 1961, General Maxwell Taylor presented to President Kennedy the evaluation he had requested of the experiences of the

Bay of Pigs operation. The Taylor Report argued that coexistence with the Cuban Revolution was impossible for the United States; thus he proposed devising an integral program capable of reversing the revolutionary process.[6] Following this logic, Kennedy approved the start of Project Cuba. The covert war plan contained in Project Cuba was named Operation Mongoose.

On January 18, 1962, General Edward Lansdale presented to the Special Group (Augmented) (SGA) a project comprised of thirty-three tasks, whose objective was "to help the Cubans defeat the Communist regime in Cuba and establish a new government with which the United States can live in peace."[7] The logic of Project Cuba was to orchestrate the international isolation of the island, strangling the economy and orienting the counterrevolutionary efforts toward the encouragement of internal revolts that would justify direct military intervention by the United States.[8]

In one of the first meetings of this group, Robert Kennedy informed the participants that the president felt the last chapter of the Cuba issue had yet to be written, that the overthrow of Castro was possible, and that achieving this objective had the highest priority in his administration.[9]

As a result of U.S. pressures, Cuba was expelled from the OAS at the end of January, which served as an excuse for the United States to decree an economic blockade on February 3, 1962.[10] The principal elements of Operation Mongoose were approved on March 14. They included the maximum utilization of "native resources" but recognized that the final success of the operation required "a decisive military intervention by the United States." The native resources would be employed in preparing and justifying the invasion. Operation Mongoose reiterated the premise of domestic insurrection as a catalyst for the counterrevolutionary escalation and assigned the CIA an even more instrumental role in the leadership of the counterrevolutionary movement. Finally, the SGA instructed the Joint Chiefs of Staff to continue elaborating plans for a decisive military invasion of

Cuba.[11] Operation Mongoose included the continuation of joint efforts with the Mafia to assassinate Fidel Castro. According to the Church Committee Report, this operation—begun during the Bay of Pigs period—was reactivated in late 1961 and continued until March 1963.[12]

In late July, Lansdale evaluated the results achieved in the first phase of the operation. In his opinion, there had been progress in the gathering of intelligence and in the application of the economic blockade, but few advances were evident in the efforts to increase guerrilla activity, diplomatic actions were met with resistance on the part of Latin American nations, and the psychological operations, centered on radio transmissions to Cuba, had been similarly ineffective. He reported that eleven teams of agents had infiltrated into Cuba, but that nineteen sea operations had aborted. By that time, plans for a military invasion were ready and were continually updated.

The report gave special attention to the Cuban counterrevolutionary groups, considering that they still exhibited limited participation in covert operations, and that their potential could be more fully exploited in military and political actions. The key to incorporating Cubans into the operation was, in Lansdale's opinion, that the United States demonstrate a clear intention to overthrow the government of Fidel Castro. He would say that the will of the anti-Castro Cubans depended on North American inspiration. Lansdale believed that the efforts to develop the guerrilla potential within Cuba were affected by the same moral factors whereby infiltrated agents felt isolated and were incapable of recruiting new fighters. The report concluded that if in April 1961 there were few possibilities the Cuban people would join the active resistance, now there were even fewer.[13]

At that time, as a result of conflicting interpretations of the Cuban reality, the administration and the CIA were often in contradiction, just as they had been during the execution of the Bay of Pigs project. Key administration officials accused the CIA of ignoring the more liberal—and supposedly more effective—opposition groups in favor of groups more loyal and easy to manipulate. The agency, for their part, argued that they were working with what they had and that the administration's favorite groups did not enjoy the support they claimed. The infiltrated agents insisted on the limited possibilities for an insurrection, so that the plan, without discarding efforts to encourage revolt, gradually concentrated on carrying out sabotage and terrorist actions. These were activities more in tune with the true capacity of the domestic counterrevolution and the groups operating from abroad.[14] According to a chronology assembled by Fabian Escalante, during this period 5,780 terrorist acts were carried out in Cuba, of which 716 were significant acts of sabotage against industrial sites.[15]

In August, Taylor informed the president that he saw no possibility that the Cuban government could be defeated without direct U.S. military intervention, therefore the SGA recommended a more aggressive course for Operation Mongoose. Kennedy authorized putting these plans into effect but again resisted approval of his country's open military involvement.[16] Toward the end of the month, the planners at Operation Mongoose were in for a surprise: according to CIA reports, a group of counterrevolutionary organizations was preparing a generalized uprising in Cuba.[17] This possibility led the SGA, with the president's approval, to direct the Joint Chiefs of Staff to prepare a contingency plan to aid and abet the rebellion.[18]

But there would be other decisive events for the evolution of Project Cuba. Since late May, the Soviet and Cuban governments had been holding talks on the possibility of installing nuclear missiles on the island. In August, U.S. intelligence services began receiving information that these weapons were possibly being installed. This suspicion increased their concern and measures were taken to corroborate the information and prepare a response.[19] On October 4, Robert Kennedy made known to the SGA the president's dissatisfaction with the way the plans against Cuba were being conducted and the need to increase the campaign of sabotage. On the 15th, they were urged to make every effort to develop new and more imaginative initiatives.[20] One day after this meeting, U.S. intelligence received the first photographs that demonstrated the presence of Soviet missiles in Cuba.[21]

The Cuban missile crisis began on October 22. Immediately, an evaluation was carried out to determine if covert operations should be suspended and the activities of the Cuban counterrevolutionary groups halted. Nevertheless, Operation Mongoose was not officially canceled until October 30. On the 25th, Cuban authorities captured a group that intended to dynamite the Matahambre copper mines in Pinar del Río. As late as November 8, after the operation had been canceled, another group of CIA agents penetrated into Cuba with the intention of carrying out sabotage operations.[22]

The missile crisis concluded with the USSR agreeing to withdraw the missiles and other weapons that the United States considered offensive, in exchange for which the USSR obtained the apparent commitment of the United States not to invade Cuba, which in itself is a contradiction of international law. The government of Cuba was not consulted and it did not sanction this agreement, nor did it permit the inspection of its territory. The U.S. commitment, therefore, was never acknowledged in any official document and, in fact, its validity has been questioned by Cuba's leaders.

The Reorganization of the Domestic Clandestine Front

In the Bay of Pigs project, direct contact with the CIA was quite generalized due to the formation of camps with North American instructors and the participation of officers in political activities. By contrast, in Operation Mongoose, for functional reasons determined by the conception of the project, most of the persons involved had no personal contact with agency officers; rather it was with Cuban agents that acted as intermediaries. Nevertheless, it would be difficult for any of the participants to claim that he/she ignored the role of the

United States in the management of the counterrevolution. This involvement was widely discussed; it had to do with the specific weight of each group and was evident in each detail of the political and operational activities.

In fact, the use of the domestic front in Operation Mongoose restricted even more any possible autonomy and political authority of the counterrevolutionary groups. All were considered, in one way or another, CIA "resources." The CIA attempted to forge a political movement the way they would organize an intelligence operation, ignoring the functional and organic differences between the objectives. The work of the agency, despite its intentions to the contrary, had a notable influence in increasing the already existing divisions within the domestic front and between it and the representatives in exile. They also played a role in dissolving many organizations that lost their identity and cohesion when they were organized as intelligence networks. In consequence, the dependence of the counterrevolution on the U.S. government was absolute, and expressed itself on both the ideological and practical levels. This affected the self-image and the morale of the counterrevolutionary movement and generated strong conflict among those men and women who felt manipulated by a foreign power that did not respect their lives, idiosyncrasies, and perceptions of what was taking place in their country. The bond with the United States was never viewed as an alliance, but rather as a voluntary or even painful submission that, for many participants, left wounds that never healed.

In correspondence with the objectives of the first phase of Operation Mongoose, the initial task of the CIA was to create or revive intelligence networks to gather the information necessary for the formulation of their plans. Since these networks were also designed to eventually carry out acts of subversion, they did not fit the typical pattern for espionage activity. These structures were vulnerable due to their size, composition, and variety of functions. The most successful effort—as described in the Lansdale Report of July 1962—was the creation of the Frente Unido Occidental (FUO), which operated in Pinar del Río province and eventually comprised hundreds of men. Under the leadership of Esteban Márquez Novo, a former officer in the Batista military trained by the CIA in the United States, the FUO became a huge, atypical, and precarious espionage network that was basically engaged in gathering information until its disbanding in 1964.[23] Another example was the network created in collusion with the Belgian embassy in the central region of the country. Besides obtaining information, this group was to guarantee supplies for various bands of rebels operating in the mountains. Headed by a former prosecutor, Mariano Pinto Rodríguez, and the Belgian consul in Cienfuegos, Luis Puig Tabares, the network came to have some 100 members and operated until late 1963, although most of the time it was penetrated at the highest level by Cuban State Security.[24]

The main efforts were directed at infiltrating agents capable of restructuring the domestic clandestine front along new operational criteria. While this reorganization improved security, it also created serious political problems. That entailed dismembering existing organizations, isolating their leaders, forming groups that did not always operate harmoniously, and imposing the leadership of persons selected by the CIA. The agency infiltrated Juan Manuel Guillot in January 1962 to carry out these directives, reorganize the domestic clandestine front, and integrate it with the guerrilla groups. Guillot had begun to conspire against the government in 1959 and participated in the formation of the Movimiento de Recuperación Revolucionaria. After the Bay of Pigs invasion he fled to the United States, where he underwent training. The Guillot plan consisted of restructuring the MRR in order for it to head the projected reorganization of the counterrevolution movement within Cuba.

The problem was that the MRR faced the same crisis as the other organizations. It was the group that had contributed the most men to the invasion project, therefore many of its members, including Manuel Artime, were in prison. Rogelio González Corzo had been captured and sentenced to death before the invasion, and Carlos Bandín, who had replaced him, had fled to the United States. Juan Falcón Zammar, national coordinator at the time of Guillot's return, described the situation:

> If one stopped to analyze at that instant what we had done, what we had achieved, and what our prospects were, he would be convinced that we were risking our lives for something that had no possibility of success. . . . Any aspect of the movement that could be analyzed at that time, whether it be action and sabotage, propaganda, financing, this or that province. . . . In everything, absolutely everything, we had fallen back instead of advancing. . . . Consequently, practically all of us lost faith in the struggle, and despair spread among the ranks of the MRR militants. Plans were made to remove from Cuba all the MRR militants that were exposed, and those that were not received permission to leave legally. A complete cessation of activities was decreed and everyone was ordered to avoid meetings and shun places where we were accustomed to meet.[25]

Nevertheless, Guillot assumed the task of reorganizing the clandestine front, contacting the heads of the Directorio Revolucionario Estudiantil, Movimiento Demócrata Cristiano, Movimiento 30 de Noviembre, and Movimiento Revolucionario del Pueblo. The plan included establishing ties with the guerrilla groups and incorporating them into the alliance. He held meetings with some band leaders that operated under the shadow of the MRR and returned to the United States on March 29 to report on his actions.[26] He later stated that in Miami he met with his commanding CIA officers. They "authorized" him to create a front with the organizations contacted, but he had to restructure them with a greater degree of secrecy. He was advised, once he had achieved unity, to remove the leaders of each organization from the country.[27] The objective was to dissolve the national leadership of the respective groups, select and recruit the most capable men, and establish agency control by inserting its agents in the different regions.

Guillot returned to Cuba on May Day. He immediately met with the leaders of the organizations and they decided to form a coalition named the Frente de Unidad. But it was short-lived. Only days later most of the top leadership was arrested, among them Falcón and the radio operator who was to make the contacts between Guillot and the CIA. Guillot himself was captured on May 20.[28] Falcón Zammar would later relate the CIA instructions that Guillot brought to Cuba:

> He told me that unity was based on the military aspect. The national coordinators were to form a sort of "advisory council" and we were to establish ourselves outside Cuba, in a U.S. city but not in Miami itself. He did not clarify the reach of the term *advisory council*. . . . Consolidation was to be conducted by province, and among the five provincial coordinators—that is, among the five coordinators of the five movements in question—the most capable was to be chosen, the one with the best qualifications, and sent to the United States to undergo training. . . . Each province was to work totally independently of the others and there was to be no national leadership to unite them. . . . The national military coordinators would also be located outside Cuba. . . . He also told me that in the future, for each shipment of supplies to be received in Cuba, we had to advise our "friends" in advance who was to receive it, how it was to be transported, where it was to be stored, who was going to guard it, etc. . . . With this system, each province was to have its own telegraph and would function as a unit, totally independent from the others.[29]

The capture of most of the principal CIA agents and counterrevolutionary leaders in mid-1962 led to significant changes in the social composition of the counterrevolutionary domestic front and diminished the capacity of the agency to control it. From now on the breach also widened between the groups operating inside Cuba and those established abroad. It was no longer simply a question of differing perspectives on the process, but of an organic separation, defined inclusively by the loss of the interpersonal relationships that originally existed. Precisely because of the metamorphosis, the CIA was surprised by the projected uprising by the Frente Anticomunista de Liberación (FAL), an organization created primarily by former Batista military officers that established contact with the rest of the more important groups. The planned insurrection included carrying out sabotage and assassinating revolutionary leaders, attacking militia garrisons and police stations, and promoting the uprising of most of the groups operating in Havana and Santiago de Cuba. The date initially set for the operation was August 30, but the day before most of the conspirators were captured.

Around that same date, Luis David Rodríguez González became coordinator of the MRR. For the first time, the organization was not being led by someone of bourgeois origin but rather by an individual with a criminal background who—in the absence of other options—practically took over the MRR, transforming its composition and the way it had been operating. Rodríguez González infused the organization with greater aggressiveness as well as the methods learned from his criminal experience. He plotted new assassination attempts on Fidel Castro and embarked upon the task of once again consolidating the counterrevolutionary groups into a united front, now called the Resistencia Cívica Anticomunista (RCA). Created in the second semester of 1962, among its first plans was a feigned attack on Guantánamo Naval Base. Ricardo Lorié, one of the former comandantes of the Rebel Army that formed the MRR, was to lead this assault.[30]

The plans for a staged attack on the naval base deserve a separate analysis. Despite their continued presence in the conspiracies hatched since 1960 and being the object of frequent denunciations by the Cuban government, these schemes have received scant attention from studies of the period. I have demonstrated that the idea for such an attack was present in the original plans of the MRR, in those of Sorí Marín in 1960, in the Bay of Pigs invasion, in the instructions received by Alfredo Izaguirre after the defeat of the invasion, in the context of Operation Mongoose, and in the plans outlined above. In most cases, the Office of Naval Intelligence at the base was involved, along with the group of former comandantes that created the MRR. We can presume that behind this idea was a group whose intentions were to force the U.S. government to intervene militarily, but it is also possible that this was one of the options consciously planned by U.S. authorities to justify an invasion. Coinciding with the development of the last of the aforementioned plans, President Kennedy warned: "Unilateral military intervention on the part of the United States cannot currently be either required or justified, and it is regrettable that loose talk about such action in this country might serve to give a thin color of legitimacy to the Communist pretense that such a threat exists. But let me make this clear once again: If at any time the Communist buildup in Cuba were to endanger or interfere with our security in any way, including our base in Guantánamo . . . then this country will do whatever must be done to protect its own security and that of its allies."[31]

The missile crisis determined that this plan not be carried out. In November, Rodríguez González held a meeting with the leader of the guerrillas, Tomás San Gil, with the participation of all the chiefs-of-staff of the bands operating in the Escambray Mountains. This meeting served to plan anew for the desired national insurrection. But on February 28, San Gil died in combat and a few days later, while preparing a new attempt on the life of Fidel Castro at the University of Havana, Rodríguez was captured and killed while trying to escape, after killing one of his guards. By the end of 1962, the domestic clandestine front, which Operation Mongoose tried to revitalize by all possible means, was irreparably dismembered.

The Counterrevolutionary Guerrillas

The first guerrilla bands began to form immediately after the victory of the Revolution and were comprised of former Batista military officers, who in many cases were running away from the law. The most common location for these uprisings was Pinar del Río, the westernmost province, although they also occurred in other parts of the country. These bands constituted a remnant of the Batista dictatorship and thus their military and political impact was minimal.

The counterrevolutionary guerrilla pattern as such appeared in mid-1960 with the formation of bands generally comprised of campesinos, natives of the area where they operated. These bands were made up of persons of various political persuasions, although by this time a significant number of insurgents were coming from the ranks of the Second National Front of the Escambray. In the beginning, then, the Escambray region became the principal site of the uprisings. The region's location in the center of the country, the mountainous terrain, the structure of agrarian property in this area, and the operations of the Second Front there during the struggle against Batista all favored this tendency. The guerrilla bands were characterized by their organization into "columns," relatively numerous units that followed the structural pattern adopted by the Rebel Army in the Sierra Maestra. The background of most of their members facilitated their adaptation to the rigors of guerrilla life, provided them with a good knowledge of the zone of operations, and guaranteed them a degree of support from relatives and friends. Their source of encouragement and aid was a sector of the rural bourgeoisie largely unaffected by agrarian reform.

Until mid-1960 the insurgents posed little military threat, even though some bands already numbered a few dozen men. In this period the Fuerzas Armadas Revolucionarias (FAR) did not pursue them with much tenacity, either. In September of that year the first steps were taken to organize troops with the purpose of confronting the insurgent groups, which resulted in the dismantling of some bands and the capture of their leaders, some of them prominent figures in the Second National Front of the Escambray.

Toward the end of 1960, Ramón Ruisánchez, acting on behalf of the Frente Revolucionario Democrático, tried to organize the guerrilla groups and place them under a unified command. The purpose was to act in a coordinated manner in support of the landing of the invasion force, conceived at that time to be in the Trinidad region, an area practically surrounded by the Escambray mountain range, where the majority of the bands operated. On December 10, Ruisánchez met with most of the band leaders and formed the Ejército de Liberación Nacional (ELN). Evelio Duque was designated its leader and Osvaldo Ramírez as second-in-command, both natives of the region who had fought against the dictatorship. But due to conflict between the two, Duque's leadership lasted barely a month, and by early January 1961, Ramírez replaced him.[32]

The arrangement with Ruisánchez included the supply of considerable quantities of arms that were to be dropped from planes hired by the CIA. Between January and March 1961, five important drops were made, which included bazookas, antitank guns, rifles, explosives, and communications equipment.[33] This obviously did not correspond to the needs of a guerrilla force, but rather was destined for support missions on behalf of the invaders. These arms fell primarily into the hands of the revolutionary forces, who since December 1960 had been carrying out an offensive dubbed the First Cleanup of the Escambray. As a result, some 50,000 urban militiamen were mobilized to the mountains. The Escambray thus became a huge training ground for the recently organized popular forces. The First Cleanup lasted until March 1961, resulting in 39 insurgents killed and 381 taken prisoner.[34] The main achievement of this offensive was to break up the bands and make them incapable of playing a supporting role for the invasion.

Nevertheless, nearly 200 guerrillas survived the First Cleanup, among them Osvaldo Ramírez. They then organized into small groups, discarding the idea of a structure based on columns, to better elude the pursuing army and militia. In mid-June the leadership of the ELN was restructured, Osvaldo Ramírez was sworn in as its commander, and the region was divided into five zones commanded by the other surviving leaders. According to Ciro Vera Catalá, leader of one of the bands, between mid-1961 and April 1962, the tactic was to grow both in numbers and organization, without carrying out attacks or letting themselves be seen in the areas where they operated.[35] The battalions of militia had been relocated outside the Escambray awaiting the invasion. Beginning then, the pursuit of these guerilla bands was entrusted primarily to the army reserves. The soldiers spent only brief periods in operations and had scanty knowledge of the terrain and of the singularities of this type of war, which allowed for the proliferation of the insurgent groups. By early 1962, some 500 men had organized into forty-one bands operating in the former province of Las Villas and another thirty groups across the rest of the country.[36]

In 1961 the revolutionary government implemented a number of measures that significantly changed the sociopolitical context in which these bands operated. An intense program of political and cultural development was launched in the mountain regions, supported by a mass media campaign, as a result of which, in the Escambray alone, almost 24,000 illiterates were taught to read and write. The reaction of the bands to the literacy campaign was violent. In fact, the literacy brigades throughout the country were named after a volunteer teacher killed by the Escambray guerrillas. Later, the assassination in this same area of a second volunteer and of the peasant who housed him led to the passage of a law that decreed the summary execution of any armed insurgent. In addition, the government carried out a currency exchange that deprived the insurgents and their collaborators of previously accumulated capital, and launched a program that focused on the mountains—in particular, the Escambray—that included setting up state farms and cooperatives and repopulating these regions.[37] Between January and March 1962, ninety-eight skirmishes were fought in the Escambray resulting in the death of 150 insurgents and the capture of many more.[38] In mid-April, Osvaldo Ramírez and "Congo" Pacheco, two of the principal leaders, also fell, shredding the fragile unity of the insurgent front that had been forged since late 1960. This incident occurred just when Operation Mongoose aimed to bolster the role of the guerrilla foci in U.S. plans against Cuba, and when the agency sent Manuel Guillot to Cuba to reorganize the bands and consolidate them with the domestic clandestine front, overlooking that they constituted two radically different tendencies of the counterrevolution.

The urban front was composed mainly of middle-class persons, politically cultured and with social and ideological ties to sectors historically influential on the national scene. Although the class composition of these groups tended to shift as time passed and the leading sectors of prerevolutionary society emigrated,the upper middle class continued to predominate in the composition of the urban counterrevolutionary movement. The guerrilla groups had their origins in the farming sectors. An important component of the guerrilla bands were adventurers and outlaws with little or no education or political savvy. The authority of their leaders did not transcend the boundaries of their territory; thus their support was meager and local, based on family or social ties within their zones of operation. At best, their support networks extended as far as the population centers adjoining the mountains. There were cases of relations between the urban groups and the mountain guerrillas, even coalitions of mutual convenience, but in practice those contacts were few, coordination nearly nonexistent, and political integration a virtual impossibility. These diverse groups shared little cultural or ideological affinity and operated in their respective environments alienated from society and constantly besieged by the populace. Kennedy was incapable of understanding these limitations when he tried to reproduce the experience of the anti-Batista guerrilla struggle, this time to combat Castro.

In mid-June 1962 the chiefs of the guerrilla bands met to name a substitute for Ramírez and they chose Tomás David Pérez Díaz, also known as San Gil, a young merchant who had also been manager of a plantation belonging to an important landholding company in the region. This restructuring of the ELN coincided with the launch of a new offensive by the revolutionary government called the Second Escambray Cleanup. In contrast to the first, this operation was based on the participation of elite troops recruited from among the region's campesinos. Their tactic was to surround each band and harass them incessantly. The peasants that collaborated with the guerrillas were removed from the area and relocated in other zones. Counterintelligence activity was highly improved and ingenious means were devised to locate and capture the insurgents, all of which served as inspiration for numerous works that found their way into Cuban literature and film. Under these conditions, the bands had no other choice but to try merely to survive, hiding in caves and remote mountain sanctuaries. Their combats were limited to attempts at escaping encirclement and carrying out small ambushes. They led a virtual nomadic life and degenerated into robbing and terrorizing the rural population. Their crimes escalated in direct proportion to their desperation, brought on by the unending siege. Participation in these crimes became, in fact, the bands' strongest force for cohesion and will to fight, insofar as it served to verify the loyalty of the members and obliged them to fight to the death.

By the end of 1962, despite all the efforts of Operation Mongoose, the bands were in crisis and the majority of the chiefs were only interested in saving their lives and abandoning the country. San Gil died in combat in March 1963 and was replaced by Emilio Carretero, a former Batista supporter who took up arms in 1960 but was taken prisoner only months later when attempting to flee to the United States. In October of that year the population sectors that supported these counterrevolutionary foci received a crushing blow when the Second Agrarian Reform Law was passed. This statute limited landholdings to a maximum of 168 acres, radically affecting the rural bourgeoisie. The political reasoning behind the measure is clear in one of its clauses: "Yankee imperialism increases its activity against the Revolution and the Fatherland, based on the classes that are the enemies of the workers and peasants and particularly on the rural bourgeoisie;

thus it becomes imperative to deprive them of their economic and social influence."[39]

The insurgent groups endured until 1965 but they were never able to develop beyond mere bands. The guerrillas disappeared from the Cuban highlands because, even though they at first enjoyed a measure of local support that allowed them to subsist, it was insufficient to satisfy the political and infrastructure requirements demanded by this type of warfare. Their destruction had also a symbolic value for the revolutionaries, who had come to power through this form of combat. Fidel Castro later said, "the imperialists received an unforgettable lesson; the imperialists received a lesson no less important than the one they got at Playa Girón; the imperialists learned that the counterrevolutionary guerrillas could not prosper. . . . Guerrilla struggle is a formidable weapon, but only as a revolutionary weapon."[40]

The CIA's Army

The approach of Operation Mongoose was in itself contradictory. Theoretically it assigned the main role in the operations to the domestic front, but in practice the CIA put its trust in resources outside Cuba. The agents who were to infiltrate the island to reorganize the domestic clandestine front and supply the guerrilla bands were chosen and trained abroad. José Miró Cardona was designated as the leader of the counterrevolution. Having been received by Kennedy in April 1962, he returned to Miami certain of U.S. government support for the counterrevolutionary cause. But in this phase the Consejo Revolucionario Cubano would play an even less relevant role than it did in the Bay of Pigs invasion. Taylor had foreseen that in his interview with Alfredo Izaguirre. The counterrevolution, he said, needed international legitimacy. Therefore, although he was conscious that the persons who comprised the CRC were discredited within Cuba, they enjoyed a certain amount of support abroad, hence their usefulness. But, he emphasized, the U.S. government had no intention of granting them the participation they requested.[41]

Miró encouraged the incorporation of Cubans into the U.S. armed forces,[42] as well as the creation of special units for invading Cuba. He went so far as requesting mandatory military service for all Cuban exiles under the age of fifty and proposing that the U.S. government invest $50 million to implement that effort. Nevertheless, the priority for the CIA lay in the paramilitary groups and in the agents that were to be infiltrated into Cuba. Those teams were initially merged with the remnants of the 2506th Brigade and put under the direct command of the agency, without any organic ties to the counterrevolutionary organizations.

To satisfy the requirements of Operation Mongoose, the CIA initiated the largest clandestine operation ever launched to date. Task Force W was the special unit designated to carry it out, subject to the oversight of the Special Group (Augmented), and included the creation of a CIA station in Miami, identified by the code name JM/WAVE. Located in a building belonging to the University of Miami, it is the only CIA station known to have operated within U.S. territory. Its staff included approximately 600 officers, some 3,000 Cuban agents residing in the United States and as many as it was possible to recruit inside Cuba, a private navy of ships and speed boats, and an annual budget of millions of dollars. Each CIA station around the world was assigned at least one officer in charge of the Cuban cases. This operation is calculated to have cost U.S. taxpayers upwards of a billion dollars.[43]

The navy created by the CIA was composed of six "mother ships"—entrusted with transporting the groups as near as possible to Cuban shores—and 122 smaller craft that could operate in conjunction with or independently of the mother ships. The sailors on these ships, most of whom were former members of the Batista armed forces, received a monthly salary of $300.[44] Initially conceived for the infiltration of agents and supplies for the groups operating within the country, the domestic front proved unable to handle the task and the sea route thus became the principal means for carrying out sabotage and attacks against the Cuban coastline as well. Some counterrevolutionary organizations under the control of the CIA also increased their naval capabilities, and the Caribbean Sea, as if victim of an inescapable destiny, became an anachronistic stage for international piracy. In 1962 alone, ninety-seven such operations were carried out, making a total of 291 since the Revolution came to power.[45]

These activities were hardly undercover: the ships, docked at Miami's principal piers, went to sea and returned undisturbed by the Coast Guard or customs authorities. It was common for counterrevolutionary groups to broadcast real or imaginary attacks and brag about their outcomes. When a DRE commando attacked a hotel and theater on the Havana coast on August 24, 1962, from two CIA vessels, the participants held a press conference on their return to Miami and the principal North American news media reported the event in great detail. The naval operations continued even at the height of the Cuban missile crisis. Before the end of the year, still in the midst of the negotiations, armed ships based in the United States carried out at least five more attacks against Cuban shores.[46] Miguel Orozco Crespo, chief of the CIA Special Missions Group, was captured November 5. He had been infiltrated October 20 with the objective of carrying out espionage activities and supporting the sabotage on the Matahambre mines in Pinar del Río. In the ensuing interrogation, he admitted having personally carried out twenty-five missions against Cuba in that year alone. He also declared that these groups pretended to recruit another 150 men and that they were training a new organization called Alpha 66.[47]

With the aim of covering up its activities, JM/WAVE formed some fifty-five companies in Florida, which encompassed activities as diverse as fishing, arms sales, private investigation, stores, and real estate. Various banks and law firms were placed at the service of the agency. A number of radio stations were purchased, and area newspapers willingly submitted to censure and were manipulated for the purpose of disinformation and propaganda.[48] In summary, the execution of Operation Mongoose inevitably entailed: violating statutes governing the work of the CIA; ignoring the Neutrality Act; evading customs, immigration, and tax laws; covering up criminal acts; corrupting government and nongovernment officials and agencies; and silencing the press. The infrastructure created by the CIA in Miami and the resulting injection of capital and resources into the region had—as we will later see—significant impact on the process of settlement and integration of the Cuban community into North American society and in the recomposition of what would later become the Cuban-American bourgeoisie. It also gave rise to the formation of a subversive network that would gain a life of its own, going beyond its original functions in time and space and reappearing repeatedly in the recent history of covert activities and organized crime in and out of the United States.

The settlement of the missile crisis meant the cancellation of Operation Mongoose, but not the end of covert activities against Cuba. Nevertheless, important qualitative changes in the objectives and design of these activities were introduced from that moment on. In truth, the Cuban Revolution was now assumed to be a political fait accompli, inextricably intertwined with relations between the world powers. From now on subversive activities against Cuba would have more limited objectives (in the context of a war of attrition), would have to fulfill the condition of being "plausibly deniable," and would depend essentially on the success of the counterrevolutionary groups abroad.

Autonomous Operations

For Kennedy the results of the missile crisis marked a definite turning point in the international balance of power: "Future historians, looking back at 1962, may well mark this year as the time when the tide of international politics began at last to flow strongly toward the world of diversity and freedom. Following the launching of Sputnik in 1957, the Soviet Union began to intensify its pressures against the noncommunist world. . . . People in many countries began to accept the notion that communism was mankind's inevitable destiny. . . . 1962 stopped this process—and nothing was more important in deflating the notion of communist invincibility than the American response to the Soviets' provocations in Cuba."[49]

The outcome of the crisis strengthened U.S. confidence in its military superiority and bolstered the strategy of preserving this balance of power, negotiating with the USSR from advantageous positions. Nevertheless, contrary to the prophesies of the most orthodox premises of the Cold War, the evident military inferiority of the Soviets did not lead to bonanza of hegemony for the United States. Nor did Kennedy's prediction of Third World rejection of communism come to pass. On the contrary, the war in Vietnam thrust the U.S. system into crisis, shook Europe, and raised nationalist expectations among dependent nations to a peak. Latin America experienced a decade of revolutions for which Cuba was the center of inspiration and support. This evolution constitutes a case study of the true nature of the Cold War, insofar as it demonstrated that bipolar military balance was not the basis for international stability, nor U.S. predominance in this area any guarantee that its dominion could be imposed.

The outcome of the crisis demanded a revision of some of the premises that had guided U.S. policy toward Cuba. Although formal agreements were never signed regarding the U.S. commitment not to invade the island, it was implicit that such a guarantee formed part of the understanding between the two powers. Similarly, the failure of Operation Mongoose demonstrated how unrealistic was the strategy aimed at provoking an internal insurrection. An additional factor to consider is the emergence of dissension between the Cuban and Soviet governments as a result of the way the latter handled the crisis, encouraging the North American side to embark on a new course of action directed at heightening these differences and promoting conflicts within the Cuban revolutionary forces.

Following this logic, in January, McGeorge Bundy floated before the Special Group[50] the idea of somehow coming to a gradual understanding with the Cuban government, leading to a greater influence of the United States over Cuba and facilitating the reversal of the revolutionary process by peaceful means. Orders were given in early April to temporarily halt sabotage operations, and some days later Bundy submitted for discussion a document entitled "Alternatives for Cuba." It outlined three options: look for a noncommunist solution by any means necessary; continue the harassment, but with more limited objectives; or move in the direction of peaceful subversion, which implied seeking some sort of accommodation.[51] Although the majority leaned in favor of the violent overthrow of the Cuban government and its replacement with one "completely compatible with U.S. interests"—despite the fact that most forecasts agreed this was highly improbable—the second option was chosen, but the others were not discarded. Therefore, U.S. policy toward Cuba was defined as a "program of multiple means" that in all cases sought to overturn, or at least subvert, the Cuban Revolutionary process.[52]

This was the beginning of a new phase of counterrevolutionary activity, characterized by the concentration of the counterrevolutionary movement in the United States and other foreign countries as a result of the nearly complete dismantling of the clandestine front and the guerrilla groups inside Cuba. This dismantling, in turn, strengthened the role of the Cuban exile community as a social base and legitimizing factor for the opposition to the revolutionary regime. The strategy of the Kennedy administration consisted of encouraging, financing, and supplying counterrevolutionary groups outside Cuba, allowing them to operate with a certain degree of autonomy from bases outside U.S. territory. Robert Kennedy summarized the logic of the administration when he said, at one of the meetings of the Special Group, that the United States had to do something against Castro even though these actions could not overthrow him.[53]

This policy, nevertheless, set limits on counterrevolutionary activity. Various attacks on Soviet ships in the first quarter of the year forced President Kennedy to publicly denounce this terrorist practice and demand greater control over the actions of those groups operating from U.S. territory. The counterrevolutionary groups criticized this decision. The "Bay of Pigs syndrome" once again characterized the relations between the U.S. government and the counterrevolutionary organizations, and this marked the end of Miró Cardona's romance with the Kennedy administration. Miró accused the White House of breaking their commitments and he withdrew from the Consejo Revolucionario Cubano. The U.S. government responded by suspending the CRC's monthly stipend of $200,000, and by May 1963 the council had disintegrated.[54] Despite the council's lack of authority, its dissolution shattered the symbolic unity of the counterrevolution and left a void that would be filled by no other group or coalition.

Nevertheless, only days later, on June 19, a new sabotage plan against Cuba was approved. According to its sponsors, it had the objective of "encouraging the spirit of resistance and dissatisfaction which could lead to significant desertions or other results."[55] On this basis, the work of the CIA was reorganized, Task Force W was replaced by the Special Tasks Group, covert activities plans were revised, and the Miami CIA station was kept in operation. The counterrevolutionary groups were reorganized on the principle of operating from bases located outside U.S. territory, so as not to compromise the image of the U.S. government. The resulting autonomy was, nonetheless, restrained, insofar as these groups continued to depend on the financial support and political backing of the United States, who, through the CIA, set the rules and made sure they were carried out. In any case, this situation increased the room for maneuvering and made it possible for some groups to act behind the agency's back, and even to violate its orders. This was a tendency that increased in proportion to dissatisfaction with the official policy, prompting the authorities to repress, occasionally and selectively, the more docile counterrevolutionary elements.

As had taken place earlier in Cuba, beginning in 1963 there were significant changes in the social composition of counterrevolutionary groups established abroad, at least with respect to those persons involved in operations. The moral and organizational decay of the counterrevolution, together with the characteristics of the new operations, determined that the bourgeoisie, up to then direct participants in paramilitary and terrorist actions, increasingly turned to remaking their lives in the United States or to developing as counterrevolutionary political activists against the Revolution. They left the battleground to those less suited for settling in the U.S. but, at the same time, better prepared to carry out naval raids and endure the rigors of the camps. For such persons, counterrevolution became a way of life. The tendency for many was to degenerate into criminal activities—to the extent that administration support declined. And Latin American governments and bands of drug traffickers sought increased contact with these groups, in order to take advantage of their training and as political cover for their activities.

Although the participation of the exiles in counterrevolutionary activity diminished daily, anti-Cuban belligerence was well rewarded by the U.S. government: it was the basis for a preferential treatment received by no other immigrant group to that nation. In this manner counterrevolution, both in its political and military manifestations, became a lucrative business, and constituted one of the original sources of capital for the economic development of the Cuban community in the United States and for its future insertion into the U.S. political system. Hundreds of groups began to compete for the representation of the exiles and the favor of the United States. In 1962 the CIA reported to the FBI the existence of 371 counterrevolutionary organizations operating on U.S. soil.[56] Nonetheless, in analyzing this period the House Select Committee for the Investigation of Assassinations concluded in 1979 that only eleven of those groups carried out activities sufficient to merit scrutiny.[57]

The Bay of Pigs invaders returned to the United States in December 1962. Their liberation was possible thanks to negotiations held between the Cuban government and a private North American group supported by the Kennedy administration. The final agreement included the payment of an indemnity demanded by Cuba. The invaders were honored at a rally held at Miami's Orange Bowl on December 29, in the presence of the president and first lady. Kennedy was handed a Cuban flag that supposedly had accompanied the brigade during the invasion. With visible emotion he called for counterrevolutionary unity and said, "I want to express my great appreciation for making the United States the custodian of this flag. I can assure you that this flag will be returned to this brigade in a free Havana," which was interpreted as a commitment to a new invasion.[58]

Immediately afterward, over half the brigade members were inducted into the U.S. Army and some three hundred were selected for training in special operations at Fort Benning, Georgia. This decision is consistent with the argument that the culmination of the Bay of Pigs and Operation Mongoose would be an invasion of Cuba by U.S. troops. Nevertheless, another plausible hypothesis is that induction into the army was the plan chosen to disperse the brigade and control its members. In fact, except for those assigned to Fort Benning—many of whom remained attached to the CIA and participated in its operations in various parts of the world—no special "Cuban unit" was ever created, the brigade's top officers were dispersed, and, as far as is known, never again participated in Cuba-related operations. As a result most of these officers left the ranks.

Once again Manuel Artime was chosen to lead the principal CIA operations. He met with Robert Kennedy and received the necessary political and economic backing to reorganize the MRR forces. The officers and men would all be Cuban and operate from bases located in Nicaragua, but the CIA would control plans and provide logistical support, intelligence, and training. Some three hundred men joined the MRR, which operated two bases and one communications center in Nicaragua, an arms depot in Costa Rica, and offices in Miami, the site of their headquarters. Eventually they had at their disposal two 250-foot mother ships, two speed landing craft with silent-running engines, a C-47 aircraft, two Cessna airplanes and a hydroplane, two hundred tons of weapons, and a sophisticated communications system that included links with the agency.[59] Artime's MRR cost the CIA some $7 million in two and a half years of operation, and only carried out a few minor attacks against Cuban ships and coastline.[60] In truth, the operation was an organizational turmoil that ended in virtual disaster when, on September 1964, they mistakenly attacked a Spanish ship, murdering the captain and wounding several sailors. Months later the CIA suspended support for the bases, although Artime continued to receive a monthly subsidy of $15,000 to continue his political activities.[61]

At first, the enlistees to the camps were members of the MRR that had participated in the Bay of Pigs invasion or trained at Fort Benning and other bases, but as expectations for the project diminished, other persons from diverse origins joined up, especially Batistianos. Many would later become mercenaries—particularly pilots—in service to the CIA in the conflicts in the Belgian Congo, Portuguese Angola, and Mozambique. Others turned to drug trafficking; some did both. In 1988 convicted drug dealer Ramón Milián Rodríguez declared before a subcommittee of the U.S. Senate that he had been trained in his illegal activities by persons associated with Artime in the mid-1970s, and that after the latter's death in 1976, he dedicated himself to laundering money for this group.[62] Artime lived out his life as a trusted associate of the Somoza family in Nicaragua and an important figure in Miami local politics.

Another group that gained the financial support of the CIA for carrying out operations against Cuba was the Junta Revolucionaria

Cubana (JURE), led by Manuel Ray. Despite their reluctance to associate with Ray, administration pressures impelled the CIA in June 1963 to once again back him on terms similar to those agreed on with Artime. The JURE had been created in September 1962 in Río Cañas, Puerto Rico, almost a year after Ray had been expelled from the MRP.[63] His participation in Operation Mongoose was very limited, but he was able to structure a political organization that constituted one of the options of the Kennedy administration after the CRC was dissolved. The JURE argued in favor of developing the struggle within the island, for which they proposed restructuring the internal counterrevolutionary movement based on the return of its principal leaders.

In the autumn of 1963, Ray communicated to the CIA his intention to infiltrate into Cuba and his request that they plant arms and explosives in the country for him. The agency fulfilled its part, but Ray's vessel never reached the Cuban coast because, according to him, it ran out of fuel.[64] Months later, he publicly announced his intention to land in Cuba before May 20, 1964. Five days before that date, accompanied by two reporters from *Time* magazine,[65] a CIA mother ship transported Ray and seven of his followers near Cuban shores, but this time, by his account, bad weather and pursuit by Cuban gunboats prevented the landing. The would-be infiltrators hid on the island of Anguila, in the Bahamas, where they were arrested, fined fourteen dollars each, and deported to the United States.[66] They made a new attempt on July 14, but failed when the U.S. Coast Guard captured them, although, according to Ray, U.S. customs had authorized their departure and obviously the CIA was privy to the operation.[67]

After these miscarriages—interpreted by most of the exiles as a hoax perpetrated by JURE—Ray, never well accepted in counterrevolutionary circles, was totally discredited. The junta accused "the gangsters of exile politics" of intentionally slandering them, and the CIA, whose role in JURE's misadventures was never clarified, decided to end the association by paying Ray a "consolation prize" of $75,000.[68] The extreme right were not the only ones that considered JURE activities a farce. According to Duney Pérez Alamo, one of the organizers of their Tampa camp, the drills were an excuse to raise money. He attests that Rogelio Cisneros, who insisted on being addressed as Mr. President, became a millionaire through these operations.[69] For all these reasons, JURE's influence on the counterrevolutionary movement was drastically reduced, even though it lasted until the late sixties.

One of the most active organizations of this period was Alpha 66. Its appearance in mid-1962 stemmed from Antonio Veciana's ties to the CIA. The subsequent incorporation of Eloy Gutiérrez Menoyo as military chief marked the union of Alpha 66 with the Second National Front of the Escambray. Alpha 66 specialized in carrying out naval raids, organizing into commandos known during this period for their hostility. Its attacks against Soviet ships in March 1963 forced Kennedy to prohibit such assaults for a time. The organization also received financial support and political backing from North American ultraconservative businessmen, right-wing paramilitary groups, and a sector of the agency in downright opposition to the option of reaching an accommodation with Cuba. Therefore, it is not far-fetched to assume that the actions of Alpha 66 during the missile crisis constituted a provocation by those who wanted to escalate the conflict behind the back of the Kennedy administration. More so, when various operations carried out by that organization during 1963 were encouraged and financed by the ultraconservative Henry Robinson Luce, owner of the Time-Life publishing consortium, who openly criticized President Kennedy's Cuba policy.[70] Both Veciana and the officer who supposedly "managed" him, David Phillips, were later implicated in the president's assassination.[71]

In one way or another Alpha 66 joined the scheme of "autonomous operations" and began to create bases of operations in the Bahamas and the Dominican Republic. According to Warren Hinckle and

William Turner, the idea of installing a base in the Dominican Republic was approved by Robert Kennedy on the basis of a proposal presented by Enrique "Harry" Ruíz Williams, one of the Bay of Pigs invaders and a friend of Gutiérrez Menoyo. Besides serving as a launching point for naval operations, this base was conceived for training some forty men that were slated to establish a new guerrilla front on the eastern end of the island, near Guantánamo Naval Base. With that aim, Gutiérrez Menoyo landed in Cuba in late December 1964, but among his men was a Cuban security agent, and he was captured scarcely a month later.[72]

The Miami CIA station was pleased with the presidential decision of June 1963 that authorized the continuation of sabotage organized by their own personnel. This despite the conclusion, a few days earlier, by the agency itself that it was unlikely that political opposition or economic difficulties would lead to the collapse of the Cuban regime.[73] The station was not comfortable with the restrictions imposed on them by the "autonomous operations" project, trusted neither the capacity nor the integrity of the counterrevolutionary leaders, and preferred to act with its own resources, even though this had not in itself proven to be any guarantee of success. The list of CIA objectives in Cuba included power plants, oil refineries, warehouses, highways, railroad tracks, and factories. For the first time, attacks were authorized on former U.S. companies. The agency also proposed increasing efforts to recruit personnel from within the Cuban armed forces, with the aim of provoking a coup d'état from within the apparatus of the revolutionary government.

To this end, the CIA created a phantom organization that took the name Comandos Mambises. Manuel Villafaña, who had been head of the air force during the Bay of Pigs invasion, was chosen to lead it. The Comandos in reality consisted of an elite paramilitary group trained in New Orleans that was to operate with the support of the agency's fleet. Possibly, the agency's plans included converting the organization into the center of counterrevolutionary activity and through it control the rest of the anti-Castro movement. In August 1963 the Comandos went public by means of a communiqué released in Guatemala. Only days before they had carried out a raid against the port of Casilda, on Cuba's southern coast, and destroyed an 8,000-gallon oil tank. In October, while carrying out an operation on the north coast of Pinar del Río, Cuban authorities captured Clemente Inclán Werner, a former yachtsman at a private Havana club, who described on Cuban television the origin of his organization and the way in which the CIA fleet operated. The Comandos Mambises quickly disappeared from the scene.[74]

Some of the CIA instructors involved in the preparation of these operations were officers of the U.S. armed forces, specialists in commando attacks, infiltration, and demolition. Many of the operations that the different counterrevolutionary groups took credit for were really carried out by teams of agents trained by U.S. military officers. In October, U.S. authorities even authorized the use of minisubmarines for infiltrating Cuban shores and specialized training of sabotage groups that were to destroy the country's most important industries.[75] Among those that made use of the CIA naval resources and training grounds were the Mafiosi still intent on assassinating Fidel Castro. John Rosselli, after the failure of his plans with Tony de Varona, attempted at least twice to infiltrate sharpshooters financed by organized crime groups. Rosselli had personally piloted agency boats on these missions.[76]

The Mafia came to have its own counterrevolutionary organization, led by Paulino Sierra Martínez, a lawyer previously unknown in Cuban political circles. Sierra, who lived in Chicago, appeared in Miami in the spring of 1963 claiming to represent important North American business interests willing to support the counterrevolutionary cause. In fact, the businessmen were organized crime figures determined to control gambling on the island when the Cuban government was overthrown. He proposed constituting a government in exile led by ex-president Carlos Prío Socarrás and forming a coalition dubbed the Junta de Gobierno de Cuba en el Exilio, which the principal counterrevolutionary organizations at the time immediately joined.[77]

Sierra embarked on the task of gathering arms and coordinating training with INTERPEN, an extreme right-wing U.S. paramilitary group. Although there is no evidence of links between Sierra and the U.S. government, his unparalleled rise within the counterrevolutionary movement and similarities between his project and the patterns of the "autonomous operations" program suggests a connection. Sierra has even been quoted as saying that, even though an independent operation, his project had the support of high-ranking U.S. military officers through the supply of arms and the establishment of bases in Latin American countries.[78] By the end of the year nothing concrete had been achieved and Sierra returned to the anonymity of his business ventures. His name did not come up again until the House Select Committee, which in 1979 investigated the assassination of President Kennedy, considered him among those involved. By a strange coincidence, the Junta de Gobierno had an unexplained office in Dallas that was deactivated one day after the assassination.[79]

The "program of multiple ways" ranged from assassination to normalization of relations. That year, 137 actions were recorded against Cuban shore installations and vessels, the highest figure in all the years of the Revolution.[80] Plans for the assassination of Fidel Castro once again had the highest priority, and were now graced with the boundless imagination of Desmond Fitzgerald, the new chief of the CIA Special Tasks Group, who did not rule out such weapons as exploding seashells and poisoned scuba diving suits. In the fall of 1963 he reestablished contacts with the agent Rolando Cubelas and put into action a plan to inject Fidel Castro with a hypodermic needle camouflaged inside a fountain pen, a plan Cubelas himself considered foolish, preferring to kill Castro simply with a rifle fitted with a telescopic sight. Some analysts propose that this plan in reality sought to serve as an excuse to involve Cuba in the Kennedy assassination.[81]

The CIA also worked at creating dissension within the Cuban armed forces and encouraging disagreements with the Soviet Union. In early 1963 the agency put in motion Project AMTRUNK, designed to recruit persons within the revolutionary leadership. The plan was in operation for a number of years, until the capture of José Rabel, one of the agents charged with contacting those persons considered vulnerable. Rabel had also been connected with JURE.

Bundy's proposal to explore the possibility of a more conciliatory policy had no concrete expression until the end of September. Then, Ambassador William Attwood, with the knowledge of the Kennedy brothers, initiated a rapprochement that included the use of emissaries, meetings with Cuban UN ambassador Carlos Lechuga, and telephone conversations with René Vallejo, then a personal aide to Fidel Castro. Both sides spoke of the possibility of preparing a framework for discussion and the process was in full swing when Kennedy was assassinated. The contacts were suspended in January 1963, because Lyndon Johnson believed that they could pose a threat to his electoral campaign.[82]

On November 22, 1963, two events took place that are particularly illustrative of the nature of the "program of multiple ways." While in Paris, Nestor Sanchez, a CIA officer, handed to Rolando Cubelas the aforementioned hypodermic needle, and in Havana, journalist Jean Daniel and Fidel Castro himself discussed the possibility of an improvement in Cuba-U.S. relations. Daniel had previously met with Kennedy, who asked him to explore the attitude of the Cuban leader and meet with him again on his return. The president's assassination that same day left unanswered the question of the ultimate destiny of this course of events.

At first sight it seems contradictory that the myth of U.S. betrayal of the counterrevolution would be intensified by the experiences of the Bay of Pigs and Operation Mongoose, and that Kennedy, the president that went furthest in support of the counterrevolutionary cause, would become the most hated by the Cuban hard right. This contradiction reflects better than many examples the ideological essence of the counterrevolution. Whatever may have been their agenda or political discourse, they wagered from the start on U.S. military intervention. From the U.S. presidents they did not merely seek aid and recognition of belligerency rights—which they took for granted—but, rather, willingness to intervene. That is why they always supported politicians apparently willing to overstep that limit, and Kennedy, despite his support for covert activities, was unwilling to risk direct U.S. intervention. Besides, the Kennedy doctrine placed the counterrevolutionary phenomenon in different philosophical perspective and demanded that the oligarchy displaced from power renounce many of the privileges they had enjoyed in Cuba. The Kennedy counterrevolutionary formula, for Cuba and the rest of Latin America, proposed the rescue of the system of hegemony at the cost of the class that had inspired the counterrevolution. The conflict, therefore, was unavoidable. The role of Cuban counterrevolutionaries in the Dallas assassination may never be clarified. We will probably have to make do with the eclectic conclusion of the Select Committee of the U.S. House of Representatives, that a possible involvement of these groups could not be ruled out, whereby it included them among the principal suspects.

Chapter 5

The War over the Roads of the World

FOLLOWING THE DEATH of John F. Kennedy in November 1963, the secret war against Cuba was accorded a lower priority while the Vietnamese issue began to absorb the attention of the U.S. government. President Fidel Castro in his report to the first congress of the Partido Comunista de Cuba (PCC) in 1975 pointed out the importance of this factor in the change that took place in U.S. policy toward Cuba: "The subsequent conduct of the United States in Vietnam and the heroic resistance of their people resulted in a gradual decrease in military actions against Cuba, and our country was able to enjoy a period of relative peace."[1]

The civil reforms that Kennedy and Johnson undertook were consumed by the contradictions generated by this war. Its financial cost sparked the structural crisis of the U.S. economy. The society became polarized, and political and moral premises that until then had remained unquestioned were suddenly disputed. The Democratic Party's coalition broke down under the converging dissatisfaction of both the right and the left. It may very well be true that "the rebellion of the sixties constituted, overall, the great rehearsal of a postmodern revolutionary project of liberation."[2] But viewed from a contemporary perspective, the most transcendental result in the United States was the restructuring of the conservative sectors and the beginning of a counteroffensive that, scarcely twenty years later, allowed them to regain power.

Johnson was reelected in 1964 with the widest vote margin in the country's history. The African-American electorate, having received in Johnson's first term many rights that until then had been denied them, was a decisive factor in this victory. The president's platform was characterized by the pursuit of a deep process of domestic reforms. Under the Great Society program, taxes were lowered, education was reformed, the War against Poverty was launched, and civil rights were promoted more than ever before. But the natural allies of the War against Poverty were the enemies of the Vietnam War. Despite advances in these areas, results fell below expectations and the Democratic administration collapsed under the weight of its own contradictions. By 1968 it became evident that the war was unsustainable, that the domestic situation was becoming more explosive every day, and that the forces that previously had headed the reforms were now demoralized and dispersed. "The year 1968 was unusual. . . . It was a year in which everyone was protesting, it seemed: the South against blacks, the blacks against whites, the young against the war, the Northern working class against the young, and the 70 per cent of Democrats who remained faithful to their party against Richard Nixon."[3]

Johnson paid little attention to the Cuban issue, except as an example to remind him of what he would not tolerate again—as in the Dominican Republic in 1965, when he decided to send in 20,000 Marines. In January 1964 he suspended the conciliatory moves of William Attwood and in April he ordered all sabotage operations against Cuba halted.[4] The "program of multiple ways" ended up devoid of ways and the policy toward Cuba ran by pure inertia, which, for the Cuban Revolution, was nonetheless a relief after five years of intense confrontation. During his administration, from November 1963 through January 1969, the number of naval raids—until then the main from of counterrevolutionary attack—fell from 128 in 1964 to 12 in 1968, although other forms of terrorism rose.[5]

By the end of this period, the antiwar demonstrators took to the streets and riots in African-American neighborhoods became frequent. Johnson did not even try for reelection. The 1968 presidential campaign was notorious for the crisis of the Vietnam War, for the drama of the assassinations of Robert Kennedy and Martin Luther King, and for the skepticism of the liberal sectors over possible political options. The doors were open for Richard Nixon, heading the conservative alliance, to win the election. With that victory, one of the most controversial politicians in the history of the United States assumed the leadership of the nation. The Cuban counterrevolution received Nixon's victory with jubilation. He was an old friend, with ties to the Cuban oligarchy that went back years and the first of the U.S. political leaders to promote a hard line against the Revolution. But during his mandate Nixon demonstrated political talent and cold pragmatism, which allowed him to identify the limits of the system and act with a global vision that subordinated the Cuba issue to the search for new formulas of equilibrium with the USSR.

An uncontrolled nuclear race was economically unsustainable at the end of the sixties. Vietnam had demonstrated the limitations of the limited warfare doctrine for guaranteeing control of the Third World. Postwar inflation was progressively undermining the economy and social and economic problems demanded a greater priority for domestic affairs. These are the conditions under which Richard Nixon and Henry Kissinger proposed putting in practice a policy of "détente." Defined by Kissinger himself as a combination of "containment and cooperation," it was aimed at establishing a new international order that preserved the balance of power in favor of the United States and, at the same time, restrained the arms race. Into the framework of this strategy were inserted the policies of rapprochement with China, improvement of relations with the former European socialist camp, and a different approach to the Cuban problem.

Between 1973 and 1975, the U.S. government took steps that, without any fundamental change in its policy toward Cuba, indicated an interest in exploring the possibility for change. The Resolution on Foreign Policy of the first congress of the Cuban Communist Party analyzed the moment. "In the framework of a bankrupt anti-Cuban policy and the expansion of Cuba's diplomatic relations with the rest of the world, the U.S. vote before the OAS and the positive steps taken by Washington to eliminate some of the elements of the blockade that affected our relations with third countries, demonstrate that within the U.S. government there are influential sectors that begin to recognize this failure and postulate the need for a new policy toward Cuba that brings them nearer to the dominant current in Latin America."[6]

In February 1973 the two countries signed agreements to control air piracy and a year later—in April 1974—Congress approved a bill sponsored by senators Jacob Javits and Clairborne Pell that called for a revision of the policy toward Cuba. In June of that same year, Pat Holt, a staff member of the Senate Foreign Relations Committee, visited Cuba and met with Fidel Castro. This was the first official meeting of a U.S. government official with the Cuban president since relations were broken in 1961. Upon his return, Holt expressed his support for taking steps toward the normalization of relations and Secretary of State Dean Rusk expressed similar views. In July, also for the first time in many years, Castro granted journalist Frank Mankiewics an interview for U.S. television. Under the auspices of Mankiewics an exchange of letters took place between Kissinger and the Cuban leader.

In the 1972 elections Nixon practically demolished the Democratic candidate, George McGovern, a liberal politician and staunch adversary of the war in Vietnam who promoted changes in U.S. foreign policy, including the normalization of relations with Cuba. But Nixon's

Watergate nightmare began that same year. Much has been said about the considerable role played in this affair by a group of Cubans with a long counterrevolutionary history and historical ties to the CIA. The Watergate fiasco again attracted attention to the danger for the security of the nation that resulted from the indiscriminate training of hundreds of men in the techniques and mentality of subversive warfare. The scandal generalized the crisis of confidence in the system and brought about Nixon's resignation in 1974. In an unprecedented episode in U.S. history, the presidency went to Gerald Ford, a man who two years before had not even aspired to the vice presidency and who was considered a mediocre, albeit honest, politician. Ford inherited a country in the depths of the most serious economic recession of the postwar era, and was forced to order the humiliating retreat from Vietnam. Upon assuming the presidency he pronounced himself in favor of continuing to revise policy toward Cuba, taking into account the attitude adopted by the rest of the countries of the hemisphere.

In July 1975, culminating a process begun in November 1974, the OAS resolved to let each country decide, in accordance with its best interests, the question of relations with Cuba. The United States did not oppose this formula. In September Senators Javits and Pell visited Cuba to hold talks with Castro and make statements in favor of the normalization of relations. Various North American corporations also expressed interest in the possibility of reestablishing business dealings with Cuba. A few months before, in January 1975, Cuban and U.S. officials began to hold secret meetings in New York. In the first such meeting, the participants were Ramón Sánchez Parodi for Cuba and Lawrence Eagleburger, Kissinger's assistant, for the United States. For the second meeting, held July 29, these two were joined by, among others, William Rogers, assistant secretary of state for Latin America. Although the Cuban delegation at the meeting presented proposals of topics for discussion, the North American side avoided any concrete pronouncements. In general, a climate of conciliation prevailed, encouraged by visits to Cuba of important North American celebrities, such as Senator George McGovern in May 1975. Nevertheless, the Angolan question and Cuba's support for the independence of Puerto Rico became relevant obstacles for this process, which, together with the collapse of consensus around the policy of détente, determined that in August of that year the United States unilaterally suspended the talks. The pressures of the electoral campaign also influenced Ford to make an about-face in February 1976, when, in a political meeting in Florida, he spoke against normalization.[7]

The 1970s was a decade of strengthening for Cuba's international position. The economy improved significantly, the country joined the socialist economic system, ties were reestablished with many countries in Latin America, and Cuba's influence within the Movement of Nonaligned States was on the rise. This situation favorably influenced relations with the United States, as did the general North American strategy toward the USSR. This explains why Johnson distanced himself from Kennedy's policy toward Cuba and why Nixon, one of the proponents of the most intransigent position toward the Cuban Revolution, experimented with a number of conciliatory options. This was the atmosphere that prevailed from the mid-1960s on. However, the United States did not totally abandon subversive actions: they experimented with bacteriological and climatological aggressions,[8] they continued the attempts on Castro's life, and they maintained a precarious balance in their relations with the remaining counterrevolutionary groups.

Bankruptcy of the Original Counterrevolutionary Groups

The restrictions on U.S. support for the counterrevolutionary groups not only deprived them of their operational capacity but also of the resources that sustained a way of life, losses which encouraged the divisions that characterized them from the start. The pattern during this period was the constant rise and fall of small groups and circumstantial coalitions and the promotion of unrealistic projects intended to justify fund-raising efforts and maintain some relevance within the exile community. According to the estimates of Miami authorities, in 1969 there were 105 counterrevolutionary groups in the area.[9]

Although the funds earmarked for sustaining counterrevolutionary activity were significantly reduced, this shift in priorities in the secret war against Cuba was not followed up by substantial changes in diplomacy or public rhetoric. Counterrevolution continued to be the official line of the government of the United States with regard to Cuba; therefore, the climate of belligerence that sustained the organizations prevailed, and the counterrevolutionary groups continued to occupy a space in North American politics. The pressures of maintaining a basically hostile policy toward Cuba on the part of the U.S. government, combined with the interests of the counterrevolutionary groups, kept the Cuba issue at the center of exile politics, intensified political corruption, reduced the room for debate, and perpetuated very reactionary attitudes in the heart of the community. The maintenance of counterrevolutionary activity resulted in the perpetuation of a class of political parasites that profited from the "Cuban Cause" and fostered a climate of intolerance in the political behavior of the émigrés. A typical case in point was Alpha 66.

The capture of Menoyo, the separation of Veciana (who went on to carry out other missions on behalf of the CIA), and the gradual reduction of U.S. government support for the activities of the counterrevolutionary groups all affected the operational potential of Alpha 66. The leadership of the organization fell into the hands of the Sargén brothers, former Ortodoxo politicians connected with the Second National Front of the Escambray. The group's main task became raising funds for its own survival, for which they carried out sporadic naval attacks, organized military training camps on week-ends, prepared real or imaginary infiltrations, and encouraged from abroad terrorism within Cuba. Just like the other groups of this nature, they exerted pressure on the rest of the community that helped maintain the appearance of a great deal of cohesion in the community concerning the Cuba issue.

This apparent unity benefited not only the counterrevolutionary organizations but also the Cuban-American bourgeoisie that controlled the political life of the enclave, which explains why militarily ineffective and politically discredited groups have been able to remain active for so many years. Their role has been to keep alive what some people have labeled the counterrevolutionary industry—whether by contaminating the political climate with a rhetoric of intransigence that saturates the mass media, or by resorting to violent intimidation whenever necessary. Within certain limits, this constitutes the Cuban-American scenario generally convenient for North American policy toward Cuba—at least that which has been useful for those sectors promoting the continuation of hostility between the two countries. This, together with the historical conduct of the U.S. secret services with regard to the counterrevolution, explains the high degree of impunity with which these groups have functioned.

In mid-1964 the Representación Cubana en el Exilio (RECE) was formed.[10] It was sponsored by Pepín Bosch, general manager of Bacardí, who for many years headed an important sector of the national bourgeoisie and, some time later, a group of counterrevolutionary militants, native of Santiago de Cuba, who came to be called the *mafia santiaguera*. To head the organization they named individuals such as Vicente Rubiera, former leader of the telephone workers union in Cuba; Erneido Oliva, second-in-command of the Bay of Pigs Brigade, who went on to become a general in the U.S. Army; Ernesto Freyre, a lawyer who formed part of the team that negotiated the release of the Bay of Pigs invaders with the Cuban government; and Jorge Mas Canosa, who came from the Movimiento Demócrata

Cristiano and found in RECE the ideal vehicle for his launching as a political figure. Mas Canosa was assigned to the propaganda section and edited the RECE newsletter until November 1982.

RECE was one of the most important organizations of this period; it formed delegations in the centers of high concentrations of Cuban émigrés and collected funds for an invasion that never took place. It established alliances with other counterrevolutionary groups to carry out terrorist attacks against Cuban coastal objectives, in particular with Comandos L, an offshoot of Alpha 66 led by Tony Cuesta.[11] In July 1969 Cuesta collaborated with the landing of a group led by Amancio Mosquera that was to establish a guerrilla front in Baracoa, at the eastern end of the island, once again in the vicinity of Guantánamo Naval Base. But they were all captured and the operation ended in complete disaster. Published investigations reveal the existence of an FBI memorandum dated July 1965 stating that around this time, Jorge Mas Canosa received $5,000 from the CIA to finance an operation by the terrorist Luis Posada Carriles against Soviet and Cuban ships docked in the Mexican port of Veracruz. This proves that ties existed between RECE and the CIA and that the latter was involved in the terrorist actions carried out during this period.[12]

RECE took care of preparing and financing these operations, but its leadership did not participate directly in them. "Their dream is to name a president," claimed Felipe Rivero, leader of the Movimiento Nacionalista Cubano (MNC). "A huge bureaucratic apparatus. Famous for shooting the Havana Aquarium and killing a fish."[13] Given its conception and composition, RECE constituted to some degree the embryo of what later would become the Cuban-American National Foundation (CANF).[14] Marking the beginning of a new strategy, many of its activities in the 1970s were designed to influence both U.S. government policy and public opinion. This was the case with the creation in November 1975 of Americans for a Free Cuba, composed of seventeen congressmen opposed to Gerald Ford's policy of détente toward Cuba, although in reality, by this time that line had already been abandoned by the president. This group was promoted by conservative senators Jesse Helms and Richard Stone, and counted among its members some lawmakers still very active in U.S. politics, such as Robert Dole, Lawton Chiles, and Paul Laxalt.[15]

"The Operation in Defense of a Free Cuba has two objectives: (1) U.S. public opinion, and (2) the 435 members of the U.S. House of Representatives and the 100 members of the U.S. Senate. . . . In the Congress, the majority is apathetic with respect to Cuba and follows the lead of others. Unfortunately the leaders include senators like Kennedy and McGovern that are well informed about Cuba—from Castro's point of view. To counteract their influence and develop a leadership group in Congress that is well informed about what is really happening in Cuba, there should be a precise and careful educational campaign directed not only at Senators and Representatives but also at their staff." Based on this proposition RECE developed a sophisticated public relations and political influence plan that had at its disposal a budget of $230,000.[16] RECE announced its dissolution in mid-1988, but since the creation of the CANF in 1981, it existed only formally.

The last of the unifying efforts of the counterrevolution in the sixties was the Plan Torriente. Viewed as a whole, it turned out to be an improvised and fairly extravagant project. José Elías de la Torriente, an individual lacking in personality and political history, an unknown in Cuba as well as in the émigré community, was chosen to lead it. He had gone to school in the United States and subsequently worked as an accountant for North American companies and a horse breeder in Cuba. Some sources claim that Torriente had been recruited by the CIA before the victory of the Revolution.[17] In any case, there is no doubt that only with strong official backing could a man like this become overnight the leader of a movement that brought together most of the other groups. The Plan Torriente was "psychological warfare" aimed at provoking Cuba to take defensive measures that would hamper the 1970 sugar harvest, considered vital for the Revolution at the time. Despite estimates that that it raised over $4 million, the plan only carried out one operation of any significance: a sea raid on a small coastal village in Eastern Cuba. All indications are that a dispute over the organization's finances was the cause of the April 1974 assassination of Torriente in Miami.

By the early 1970s the prestige and influence of the counterrevolutionary groups established abroad showed definite signs of decay. Within Cuba there was a climate of nearly absolute peace: the principal counterrevolutionary organizations had been dismantled, no guerrilla foci had existed since 1965, and the majority of the opposition that had served as the social base for the counterrevolution had emigrated. From this moment on, the fundamental tendency of the migration was to establish themselves permanently in the United States, taking advantage, in the process, of the special benefits offered to them by that government. Possibly the migration would have taken place regardless of the evolution of the counterrevolutionary activity, but the decadence of that movement accelerated and expanded the process. These first generations of migrants[18] formed a relatively homogenous social group (the majority coming from the capitalists and upper middle class), had a high degree of family cohesion, and were predominantly white.

Together with the integration of the migrants into North American society came the first signs of participation of persons of Cuban origin in the political activity of that nation and the rise of new political tendencies—including the rise of an unexpected left movement. These new tendencies served to connect the Cuban immigrants more organically with the processes taking place in the society they lived in. But most significant in this period was the rise of fascist-oriented organizations that practiced a kind of terrorism novel in its objectives, if not in its methods. In this manner, right-wing terrorism and left-wing movements represented the extremes of the new Cuban émigré political spectrum. Both were minority movements not clearly incorporated into the North American political framework.

Fascist Terrorism

It is difficult to make conclusions about the concept of terrorism because its definition has been clouded by political manipulation.[19] The option of resorting to terrorism could be the result of a deviation that identifies vengeance and destruction as objectives in themselves —witness the irrational hatred present in some ethnic wars. Religious fanaticism has also engendered an indiscriminate terrorism apparently exempt of political goals. Nevertheless, in most cases, terrorism has been associated with the actions of minority political groups that try to force themselves on society in the midst of a socially and politically adverse climate.

Terrorism and armed struggle are not synonymous, although violence is common to both. One element that defines terrorism is the target of its actions. Terrorist activity is consciously oriented toward the civilian population, and its effectiveness is related to the brutality of its acts. Terrorism consists in domination through terror and its objective is to achieve a state of unreflecting panic that paralyzes the adversary's capacity to react and demoralizes his bases of support. By definition, terrorism is the opposite of persuasion. Terrorism is, typically, a form of political struggle. Thus, it is not defined by its methods but by the political philosophy that inspires its use. Yet, because strategy and tactics must correspond, in their condition as the opposite of persuasion terrorist methods require the same assistance and mobilization of the masses as every political movement that strives for popular support.

It was precisely because of the popular support enjoyed by the Cuban Revolution that, from the beginning, the counterrevolution had no other option but to resort to terrorism as a fundamental form of struggle. Terrorist activity requires limited material and human resources and exposes its participants to a minimum of danger. Therefore, excepting the bands of mountain guerrillas, the counterrevolutionary organizations concentrated on carrying out terrorist actions in the principal cities. Most of the bands themselves, despite assuming the model of guerrilla struggle, attempted to force themselves on the civilian rural population by means of terror.

The counterrevolutionary organizations of Cuban origin used essentially four kinds of terrorism: aggression against civilian objectives within the country; coastal raids and naval harassment from bases located abroad; attempts against Cuban installations and personnel abroad or against those abroad who had relations with Cuba; and terrorist activity meant to control the rest of the community of émigrés.

Urban terrorism—in the early years—and paramilitary activity in international waters and against Cuban shores had their heyday in the 1960s. This last form—the result of the alienation of the counterrevolution from Cuban territory—has been the most widely used form of attack against Cuba, and continues to be practiced even today. Some contributing factors have been the geographic location of the island, the length of its shoreline, the intense marine traffic in the area, and the country's dependence on international markets. Terrorism from the sea is relatively inexpensive, is guaranteed publicity, and benefits from the element of surprise. It can be accomplished by uneducated persons who are poorly qualified to compete in the North American labor market and are easy to manipulate politically. And, given these advantages, such terrorism can also be combined with drug trafficking and the contraband of illegal immigrants.

These activities could not be carried out without the support, or at least the consent, of the U.S. government. The vessels used have to be adapted and armed to carry out actions that have inevitable public repercussions, whereby the capabilities of its authors are enhanced. The operatives have been recruited and trained in the United States, and in most cases they have proceeded to broadcast their own actions in search of the maximum propaganda effect. Their ships are docked at ports and marinas located in the States. To operate they must leave and reenter U.S. territory, violating with complete immunity one of the world's most sophisticated surveillance systems.

Similarly, terrorist activity against Cuban installations and personnel located in third countries tended to increase in the late 1960s, as a reflection of the decreased official support for more extensive counterrevolutionary plans. This was with or without direct CIA participation, but certainly with the knowledge and without the opposition of the U.S. government. A new peak occurred during the mid-1970s due to a combination of factors, among them: U.S. efforts to improve relations with Cuba, conflicts between the Carter administration with the intelligence community, Cuba's support for the Angolan government, and the emergence of fascist dictatorships in Latin America. A new international terrorist offensive was launched from Miami, as was confirmed by the city's own police department.[20]

The first such group to adopt this form of terrorism as their principal tactic was the Movimiento Nacionalista Cubano (MNC), an openly fascist organization founded in 1964 by Felipe Rivero, a dramatically eccentric figure of the counterrevolution. A descendant of one of the most renowned families of the Cuban oligarchy, owners of the *Diario de la Marina,*[21] Rivero participated in the Bay of Pigs invasion and stood out as one of the few invaders to maintain a position consistent with his ideas during the public appearances and trial that followed. With this background, on his return to the United States he assembled a group of young Cubans, most of whom were living in the Northeast. He summoned them to a "War over the Roads of the World," a term that described a campaign of terror against Cuban officials, installations abroad, and anyone allegedly supporting the government of Cuba.

On December 1964, one of the founders of the MNC, Guillermo Novo Sampol, was arrested for firing a bazooka at the United Nations General Assembly at the moment that Che Guevara was speaking. Felipe Rivero was convicted for a similar crime committed at Expo 67 in Montreal. Both were later freed. Rivero moved to Miami, where he acquired the status of patrician and ideologue of Cuban fascism, a current favored by the Chilean military coup of September 1973.

Years later Rivero explained the impact this event had on the MNC: "I thought of what kind of help the Chileans could give us—maybe a statement calling the MNC the hope of Cuba. Chile was our pretty baby, our darling in the Cuban community. If we could get them to say we were the best, we'd be the new leaders of the Cuba exile movement. . . . [This meant] a slap in the face to our rivals in the Cuban community"[22]

Rivero's hopes were not unfounded. The Cuban community celebrated the Chilean coup d'état, and was so fascinated by it that in 1975 the Asociación de Veteranos de Bahía de Cochinos[23] awarded Augusto Pinochet its Medal of Liberty, a distinction no other foreigner has earned.[24] Fascism was spreading through the southern cone of Latin America. The Chileans organized a reign of terror that incorporated the police and armed forces of Argentina, Bolivia, Paraguay, and Uruguay, together with the paramilitary fascist groups of various countries. The Cuban terrorists also found a place in the endeavor, called Operation Condor. The FBI representative in Argentina in 1976 reported that Chile's military government maintained a "special relationship" with the Cuban anti-Castro groups, an alliance that included joint assassination missions. According to this report, Chile offered them the type of support once given by the CIA. FBI sources described a program whereby the Chilean junta vowed to recognize a Cuban government in exile based in Chile and supply them with arms, explosives, training, and asylum for fugitives.[25]

The MNC joined in this scheme and participated in various assassination attempts on behalf of the Chilean regime. Among them were the murder of General Carlos Prats and his wife in Argentina, the attempt on the lives of Christian Democratic leader Bernardo Leighton and his wife in Rome, and the killing of Chilean opposition leader Orlando Letelier and his secretary, Ronnie Moffitt, in Washington on September 21, 1976. This last assassination led to the capture and conviction of three of the principal leaders of the MNC. Another two participants fled and lived underground in the United States for nearly fifteen years. Guillermo Novo and Alvin Ross, initially sentenced to life imprisonment, later appealed and obtained their release. Guillermo Novo and his brother Ignacio, also sentenced to ten years in the same case, now work for the Cuban-American National Foundation.

Various other terrorists also made contact with the Chilean junta. Among them was Orlando Bosch, a pediatrician with a racketeering background who joined the counterrevolution early on in support of the Movimiento Insurreccional de Recuperación Revolucionaria (MIRR), a band of guerrillas that had operated in the Escambray Mountains since early 1960. Bosch quickly left the country to become their delegate abroad. He had received CIA training but for some reason was not included in the Bay of Pigs invasion, yet he devoted himself to carrying out raids against Cuban shores and shipping. In 1966 he was accused of extortion against Cuban émigrés in Miami and arrested by Collier County police when six bombs were found in the trunk of his car. In 1968 he was sentenced to ten years in jail for firing a bazooka at the Polish merchant ship *Polanica*, anchored in Miami. While in prison he founded Poder Cubano, an organization based in Miami, New York, and California, with the deliberate objective of attacking those who in the United States supported negotiations with Cuba or other so-called leftist causes—among them, opposition to the Vietnam War. That same year Poder Cubano placed dynamite at the New York consulates of Spain, Mexico, Canada, Japan, and Yugoslavia, at a Mexican tourism agency in Chicago, and the Cuban embassy in Tokyo. In Miami they carried out twenty-eight bomb attacks against objectives ranging from a Mexican airplane, the residence of the British consul, the Chilean consulate, the offices of Air Canada, and a number of agencies that sent family aid packages to Cuba.[26]

Despite all this, Bosch was granted parole in 1972. His release from prison coincided with the murder of José Elías de la Torriente—for which he was questioned—and the car bombing of Ricardo "Mono" Morales, a Cuban counterrevolutionary and CIA agent turned FBI informant, who testified against Bosch at the trial where he was convicted. Bosch fled the United States illegally and formed Acción Cubana. He immediately launched a campaign to raise $10 million, $3 million of which were to be a reward for anyone who murdered Fidel Castro. He was arrested for terrorist activity in 1974 in Venezuela. The Venezuelan government offered to extradite him to the United States, but this country refused to accept him. Bosch, therefore, was set free, whereupon he flew to Curaçao and from there to Chile, arriving on December 3, 1974.

One of his associates described this odyssey:

> Bosch contacted the Chileans through the Novo brothers, who accompany Bosch and Dionisio Suárez to Chile. When Bosch is released from jail in the United States he proposes to go immediately underground, to which I was initially opposed since no one was really pursuing him. However, Bosch argued that doing it like this had greater impact and I ended up helping with his passage to Puerto Rico and later by air to Santo Domingo. I think that afterward he went to Bahamas and from there to Venezuela and Chile. During all this time the organization supported him: we sent him $1,500 or $2,000 monthly and he raised other funds on his own. I visited him in Chile and the way he lived upset me. He had an expensive apartment and he even hired a maid that lived in his home, together with his wife and a girl who supposedly worked at the Chilean Ministry of Foreign Relations. We had gone to Chile to discuss the problem of Bosch's expenses and his tendency to act without consulting the rest of the organization.[27]

According to U.S. investigative reporters John Dinges and Saul Landau, Bosch reached an agreement with the Chilean junta and left for Costa Rica with false documents with the purpose of assassinating Pascal Allende, nephew of the ex-president and one of the leaders of the Chilean resistance. Bosch is also alleged to have planned to assassinate Henry Kissinger during a visit that the secretary of state was scheduled to make to Chile.[28] This account was confirmed before the

U.S. Senate by the Miami police, who declared they had obtained this information in February 1976 and passed it on to the FBI.[29] "The Pascal Allende thing was possible because Bosch acted on his own and moved in different circles, but the Kissinger thing I'm sure was a story that Mono Morales made up and told the FBI in order to gain prestige or money. I went to Costa Rica to receive Bosch. We rented a house for him that cost us $600 per month and I had to flee when the Costa Rican police themselves informed us of the attempt on Kissinger. Bosch stayed and was detained for a few days."[30]

The existence of an assassination attempt against Kissinger is not very probable. Although the counterrevolutionary group saw him as the "man of détente" and of conciliatory steps toward Cuba, an act of this kind would logically not be in the best interests of the Chilean junta. Kissinger had promoted the coup and was one of the most disposed to accommodate the military. On the other hand, it would have been truly difficult for Bosch to plan an action of this complexity on his own. The probability of a plan against Pascal Allende is much greater. Allende was one of the opposition leaders most hunted by the Chilean regime and it is known that another Cuban terrorist, Rolando Otero, coincided with Bosch in Costa Rica to carry out an identical mission for the Chileans.

Otero was a member of the terrorist group Frente de Liberación Nacional Cubano (FLNC), created in 1973 under the leadership of Frank Castro and made up of a combination of former members of various counterrevolutionary organizations. It stood out for mailing letter bombs to different Cuban embassies, for placing explosives at Cuban diplomatic missions in Mexico, Jamaica, Spain, and France, and for terrorist attacks against private entities in Miami and public places in Puerto Rico. Otero came from a family that formed part of the Cuban oligarchy. At sixteen he was the youngest recruit of the 2506th Brigade. He felt betrayed by the CIA and he included the U.S. government among his phobias. Between October and December 1975 he carried out a terrorist offensive in Miami that included placing explosive devices at the Miami International Airport, two post offices, the social security offices, the federal building, a bank, and even at FBI headquarters. He fled the United States and sought refuge in Chile, placing himself at the service of the junta, who assigned him the task of murdering Pascal Allende. After escaping arrest in Costa Rica, Otero returned to Chile but, unlike Bosch, the U.S. government insisted on his extradition and the Chilean regime was forced to turn him over.[31]

Bosch, on the other hand, was freed and left Costa Rica for the Dominican Republic, where he helped found the Comando de Organizaciones Revolucionarias Unidas (CORU).[32] This organization added a new dimension to the Cuban counterrevolution in that it then represented the integration of one of the largest and most aggressive terrorist networks in the world. CORU brought together the principal counterrevolutionary organizations in existence at the time. The Chilean fascist junta became a source of inspiration and support for that coalition, but creating something of that nature would have been impossible without the consent of the U.S. government. CORU was formed after Ford had abandoned the policy of seeking an understanding with Cuba and the Angola issue became the centerpiece of the conflict between the two countries. In fact, the excuse rendered for most of CORU's actions was Cuba's support for the Angolan revolution. In this regard, a veteran Miami antiterrorist police officer declared in 1979 to Dinges and Landau, "The Cubans held the CORU meeting at the request of the CIA. The Cuban groups . . . were running amok in the mid-70s, and the United States had lost control of them. So the United States backed the meeting to get them all going in the same direction again, under United States control. The basic signal was 'Go ahead and do what you want, but outside the United States.' "[33]

CORU was organized in Bonao, Dominican Republic, in June 1976. Among those attending the meeting were the Bay of Pigs Veterans

Association (Brigada 2506), Acción Cubana, Frente de Liberación Nacional Cubano, Movimiento Nacionalista Cubano, Alpha 66, and Agrupación Juvenil Abdala. The new organization was an undefined ideological grouping, joined only by their conviction of the need to extend international terrorism against Cuba. Although the meeting was organized by Frank Castro, the son-in-law of a high-ranking Dominican officer and head of the FLNC, it was Orlando Bosch who was chosen to head the alliance. The formation of CORU was not a marginal event in the counterrevolutionary movement, but rather an integral result of its evolution. Even politicians like Miró Cardona, generally associated with more moderate currents, expressed their support for this strategy. "We are alone, absolutely alone. . . . there is only one path to follow and we will follow it: violence, the internalization of the struggle for the liberty of Cuba at all levels."[34] The public participation of Abdala in this current also reaffirms this pattern. Up to that time they had presented themselves as a civic organization made up of young Cubans aimed at countering the progressive student movement opposed to the Vietnam War and in favor of a change in policy toward Cuba. Their incorporation into CORU confirmed the previous connections of Abdala with the terrorist groups, something the Miami police had already warned about, linking them to the FLNC although they may have had links with other organizations.[35]

Two months after CORU was created Orlando Bosch was expelled from Chile. The reasons are not clear, but this action, together with the delivery of Otero to U.S. authorities, raised serious doubts among the terrorist groups as to the loyalty of the Chilean regime. This did not prevent CORU, however, in barely one year from spreading terror throughout the American continent. In July 1976 they slipped a bomb into the luggage of a Cubana de Aviación flight out of Jamaica. It was set to explode on take-off but due to a departure delay it went off while the plane was still on the ground. That same month CORU carried out attacks with explosives at the offices of

British West Indies Airlines and on the car belonging to the manager of the Barbados office of Cubana de Aviación. In Colombia they machine-gunned the Cuban embassy and placed bombs at the Air Panama offices and in the car belonging to the Colombian official in charge of relations with Cuba. In Mexico CORU tried to kidnap the Cuban consul in Merida and in the process murdered an official who accompanied him. Finally, three members of the MNC were arrested in New York while placing a bomb at the Brooklyn Academy of Music, where a Cuban group was performing.

In August, CORU took credit for the kidnapping and murder of two Cuban diplomats in Argentina, an operation actually carried out by Argentinian fascist groups with the complicity of the country's repressive government forces. CORU placed a bomb at the Panama airport and another at the Cubana de Aviación office in that nation. In September they attacked the Guyanese embassy in Trinidad and Tobago with explosives, slipped a bomb aboard a Soviet merchant ship anchored in New Jersey, assassinated Orlando Letelier and Ronnie Moffit, and placed another bomb at the Palladium Theater in New York. In October a bomb placed on board a Cuban airliner in Barbados killed seventy-three people. The international revulsion provoked by this act of terror forced a number of governments to act. Two Venezuelans, arrested in Trinidad and Tobago, turned out to be the material authors of the crime. Both had connections with Bosch and Cuban terrorist Luis Posada Carriles.[36]

Posada Carriles, a sugar chemist linked to the Batista regime, was working for a North American company in Cuba when the Revolution came to power. In 1961 he moved to the United States, where he received specialized training from the CIA. Later he teamed up successively with JURE, RECE, and Comandos L. In 1967, to assist in the suppression of revolutionary movements, the agency sent him to Venezuela, where he occupied the post of inspector with the Venezuelan security police. He later formed a private detective agency and employed Hernán Ricardo and Freddy Lugo.

Ricardo and Lugo confessed to their involvement in the bombing and their relations with Posada and Bosch, and all four were arrested in Venezuela. Pressures of all kinds caused the judicial process in Venezuela to last over ten years. In the end Ricardo and Lugo were found guilty, Bosch was acquitted "because he was not physically present at the events," and Posada bribed his guards and easily escaped from jail. He settled in El Salvador, where, under the command of his good friend Félix Rodríguez, he served the CIA in supplying arms to the Nicaraguan contras. When the Iran-Contra scandal broke, the presence of Posada—an international terrorist and fugitive from Venezuelan justice—was one of the misdeeds reported by the press. (Despite this he was able to emigrate to Guatemala, where years later he was assassinated, once again gaining him international attention.) Posada declared to the U.S. press from a secret hideout in Central America that he was behind a series of terrorist bombings of tourist hotels and restaurants in Havana that took place in the 1990s. Posada further stated that CANF president Jorge Mas Canosa was informed of these actions and provided financial support. The CANF denied the charges.

Bosch, on the other hand, on being freed in Venezuela, entered the United States illegally in February 1988, turned himself in to the authorities, and was jailed for several months for violating his 1974 parole. Because of his terrorist background, the Department of Justice refused his request for political asylum and ordered him to be deported. No country in the world would accept him, although he was never offered to Cuba, who had claimed him since 1976. After a campaign headed by Cuban-American congresswoman Ileana Ros-Lethinen, which included personally lobbying President Bush, he was granted release and was allowed to remain in the United States. Again, the argument that he did not constitute a threat to public security turned out to be convincing. In fact, the arguments that truly convinced U.S. authorities were summarized by Jorge Mas Canosa—one of his mentors—in an interview published in 1988 by the *Washington*

Post. "The streets are quiet since he arrived. We want it that way. We first let the legal system take its course. I guarantee you that if he is sent to prision once again, or deported, there will be protests and demonstrations."[37] In 1991 Bosch was authorized to participate in a political rally, where he called for sending arms to Cuba, and in 1993, challenging the conditions placed on his legal status, he announced the formation of the Partido Protagonista del Pueblo, whose open objective is to collect funds to support armed attacks against Cuba. Asked if he did not fear reprisals by the U.S. government, he answered: "That is a problem for the authorities. I believe that the restrictions have expired." A spokesman for the district attorney declined to comment on this challenge.[38] Bosch now lives in Miami, has become a painter—a profession that apparently has become commonplace among retired terrorists—and "lives off his art."

A recurring theme throughout the investigation of the bombing of the Cuban airliner in Barbados has been the possible complicity of the Central Intelligence Agency. Ricardo and Lugo were found to have a diary containing the telephone numbers of CIA officers based in Venezuela,[39] and they themselves admitted they had maintained ties with the agency. Posada's relations with the CIA were public and notorious, and continued to be so when Félix Rodríguez's team was later formed in El Salvador.[40] The Posada-Bosch connection is itself full of gray areas. According to Duney Pérez Alamo they did not know each other until Bosch arrived in Venezuela. Posada had arranged everything and needlessly involved Bosch in the plan.[41] Posada was an agency man and Bosch was purportedly an enemy of the CIA. In addition, Bosch shared an apartment in Caracas with none other than Ricardo Morales, the agent that sent him to prison and that he apparently tried to kill. He had been sent there to carry out CIA missions similar to those of Posada. It is conceivable that Posada involved Bosch in order to dispel suspicion about the CIA role in the plan, and that the latter was aware that the U.S. government was apprised of the project and used this in his favor. The CIA involvement would explain the pressures exerted on the governments of Trinidad and Tobago, Barbados, and Venezuela to delay and distort the legal process and the treatment that both later received.

In bombing the Cuban airliner in Barbados, the Cuban counterrevolutionary groups transgressed all acceptable limits for international terrorism and as a result CORU fell into crisis. Nevertheless, no Cuban émigré individual or group—except for the left—had the nerve to publicly condemn this crime. On the contrary, the press and radio controlled by the Cuban right justified it in diverse ways, and some even celebrated the event. The results had been dramatic. In four months CORU's activities caused seventy-eight deaths. Independent of the CIA's direct participation in the Barbados bombing, the responsibility of the U.S. government lay in the policy of encouraging Cuban terrorism outside its shores. Even in the unlikely event that they had no previous knowledge of the plan, the United States was forced to exert pressure in favor of fixing the process. If they did not, other aspects of a policy openly in violation of international law and even dangerous to U.S. security could be made public. By encouraging Cuban terrorism, the U.S. government put itself in a position vulnerable to political blackmail, to the advantage of the Cuban counterrevolutionary groups.

The terrorist groups that operated during this stage were characterized by their openly fascist ideology and by the predominance among their ranks of individuals incapable of participating in the process of assimilation that was taking place within the immigration, thus occupying a relatively marginal place within the Cuban community. Their principal leaders came from the CIA-trained elite groups and were employed by the agency in counterinsurgency tasks in Latin America, Vietnam, and elsewhere. As a result they forged extensive connections among Latin American police forces, right-wing paramilitary groups, local U.S. authorities, and organized crime. Together with the support, complicity, or fear they inspired in certain segments of the émigré community, these terrorist groups were able to continue operating, this time with greater intensity, from within U.S. territory.

Between 1973 and 1976 the FBI investigated 103 bombings and six assassinations committed by these groups in the United States.[42] Studies in progress indicate that, in the 1970s, Cuban terrorist organizations carried out at least 279 actions throughout the world, more than half (144) on U.S. soil.[43] When the Carter administration announced its intention to improve relations with Cuba and an important sector of the Cuban community supported that policy, right-wing Cuban terrorism increased and came home to roost: 58 percent of all the terrorist actions of the decade were executed during those four years, and 68 percent of them were carried out in the United States.[44] According to FBI reports, the Cuban operation became the most dangerous terrorist network operating within the country, despite the fact that in all no more than 200 people were involved.[45]

The War over the Roads of the World constituted a new type of activity, different from that developed by the traditional counterrevolutionary groups. During the 1960s, 371 paramilitary actions were carried out against Cuban coasts and vessels and 156 terrorist acts were executed in the United States and other countries, whereas in the 1970s this proportion was reversed—to 16 and 279, respectively.[46] It is arguable that the new campaign turned out to be a desperate recourse to preserve a climate of belligerence that was quickly losing all pretexts. This situation is sharpened by the political impact of the process of assimilation of the Cuban émigrés into U.S. society and with the steps taken by the Carter administration toward improving relations with Cuba. The foundations on which the "counterrevolutionary industry" rested were shaken, affecting not only the most active terrorist groups but also a whole political infrastructure at the service of the interests of the majority of the Cuban-American bourgeoisie. Thus, from this moment on, terrorism —always playing a coercive role toward the rest of the émigré community—would make this objective its principal priority, reflecting the origin of a new political moment that would have as its distinctive element the competition for the control of the émigré community. Despite the absence of radical changes in its composition of the organizations, from now on terrorism would form part of the struggle for survival faced by the counterrevolutionary movement, and would become an element linked to the emergence of the Cuban-Americans in U.S. politics.

The Left and Coexistence

The left in the Cuban émigré community has its roots in the revolutionary groups that supported the struggle against the Batista dictatorship and later confronted the first counterrevolutionary organizations. This is the foundation of Casa de las Américas, a Cuban solidarity organization that continues to be a well-known meeting place for the Latin left in New York City. Casa can be considered a revolutionary remnant of the pre-1959 immigration and, although it subsequently associated with other émigré leftist groups, generational, cultural, and ideological reasons differentiate it from them and lend it an exceptional character.

In essence, the leftist movement originated in the early 1970s, mainly among Cuban young people influenced by the antiwar and civil rights movements in the United States. From the beginning it contemplated a search for a cultural identity expressed through the solidarity with the Cuban Revolution and the radicalization of its political positions in line with their own experiences in the United States. The majority of these youngsters did not escape the process of integration into North American society and evolved—often without intending to—toward a Cuban-American identity of a different political orientation from the majority of the immigrants. In fact, they often faced the dilemma brought about by their rejection of the mainstream immigrant society and the assimilation that inevitably ensued, as a result of the growing commitment of their political activity.

To a degree, this movement resulted from the alienation of these young people from the social milieu that the Cuban enclave offered them. This explains why the first groups were organized in areas distant from Miami, such as Gainesville—home of the University of Florida—Puerto Rico, and New York. These persons founded the Juventud Cubana Socialista (JCS), a fairly radical organization that became known by their slogan "Not all Cubans are *gusanos*"[47] and that included a relatively large group of young people.[48] Their objective lay in returning to Cuba and joining the revolutionary process, thereby not only fulfilling their political desires but also, from their point of view, solving the crisis of identity and belonging brought about by the uprooting of their migration. JCS was short lived, but formed the main bedrock for future leftist organizations and some of its principal leaders. The second feeder of the leftist movement were young people who reached the left after having taken the counterrevolutionary track, which they joined due mainly to their Catholic background. This latter was a politically more experienced group, in which Lourdes Casal became not only its most outstanding figure but also the most gifted of her generation of émigré intellectuals.

In 1974 these two groups, relatively informal organically, founded the magazine *Areíto*. The principal objective of this magazine was to serve as a vehicle for the left to identify itself and share opinions, but its impact transcended this purpose to the degree that it provided a dissonant note in an environment that pretended to be monolithic. In this manner *Areíto* enlarged the political spectrum of the Cuban community, which allowed other less radical positions to manifest themselves. In addition, it was a quality publication that won intellectual praise in the United States, Latin America, and Cuba, facilitating the contact of the leftist movement with its country of origin.

Almost simultaneous with the appearance of *Areíto* was the publication of *Joven Cuba*. Its publishers were a group of young Cubans that came from the radical movement in the United States. *Joven Cuba* provided an immature, but instinctively very realistic perspective of the situation of the Cuban émigré youth in the United States, and the future of its relations with Cuba. It proved ahead of its time in reflecting a tendency of integration into U.S. society which strove to express itself in its own voice. "*Joven Cuba* is the disenchantment we suffer when we think of ourselves as North Americans, and they [the Americans] remind us that we really are not. At the same time, our parents reject us for our sad efforts to avoid a Spanish accent, for dressing mod, and for trying to be more American than the Americans themselves. . . . *Joven Cuba* is the pride we feel when Martí or Maceo are mentioned, or when we listen to a *conga* or a *danzón*. It is also the anxiety we feel when we realize that we really know very little of our own roots. We touch but cannot feel the soul and rhythm of our fatherland."[49]

Areíto, which represented the predominant current within the left, assimilated the promoters of *Joven Cuba* and together they embarked on other political projects. The most important one turned out to be the Brigada Antonio Maceo (BAM), a decisive step in the consolidation of the émigré left movement. Although in theory BAM pretended to be a relatively wide movement, the requirements for membership, its political platform, and the open radicalism of its principal leaders marked it as a decidedly leftist organization—which, however, did not prevent hundreds of young people from joining its travel groups to Cuba. Their first trip to the island, in late 1977, had significant political repercussion, both in the United States and in Cuba, and opened a new stage in the relations between the émigrés and Cuban society, which received the group with sympathy and solidarity. The culmination of the visit was a meeting with Fidel Castro. This was the first organization of Cuban immigrants to visit the country after the victory of the Revolution, and the first to be received by the Cuban president.

Back in the United States, these persons faced the risk of physical aggression, the indiscriminate hostility of the counterrevolutionary media, the loss of certain job, study, and housing opportunities, and family conflicts brought about by their political positions. These challenges required an uncommon amount of commitment, valor, and personal integrity that have limited the group's numbers but certainly not its impact. The rise of an émigré left movement allowed two interdependent processes to manifest themselves. It revealed the heterogeneous political character of the émigrés and their polarization around the issue of relations with Cuba. Moreover, it accelerated the possibility of dialog between the Cuban government and that segment of the émigré community that supported reestablishing those contacts. The catalyst for this process was Jimmy Carter's victory in the 1976 presidential elections.

For Carter, the policy toward Cuba was part of the global view advocated by "trilateralism." David Rockefeller founded the Trilateral Commission in 1973 with the purpose of promoting those political conditions that would make the world better disposed to the products, technology, and capital flows of the great transnational corporations.[50] The intention, in brief, was to overcome the "crisis of democracy" and to accept the challenge of "peaceful coexistence," through the organization of a dominant block comprised of the leading developed capitalist countries[51] for the joint management of global issues and to take measures that would reduce the foci of regional tension.

With regard to Latin America, priorities were established according to the economic and political weight of each country or to its relation to potential conflict areas, as in the cases of Panama, Chile, and, later, Nicaragua. The management of the Cuba problem was also viewed on this basis, thus the Carter administration moved with relative celerity in search of solutions to the conflict between the United States and Cuba. Before the end of Carter's first year in office, the ban on travel to Cuba by U.S. citizens was lifted, agreements were signed on fishing rights, a hijacking agreement was renewed, and "interests sections" were opened in Washington and Havana following the success of normalization of relations with China. Diplomatic, academic, and cultural exchanges between the two countries increased dramatically, and even the U.S. secretary of state, Cyrus Vance, declared that the United States was willing to negotiate with Cuba without prior conditions. In fact, until 1979 there flourished a climate that pointed toward normalization, even though topics such as human rights, Cuba's relations with the USSR, and Cuban support for the governments of Angola and Ethiopia caused continued conflict.

In carrying out its foreign policy the Carter administration incorporated an ethical message of respect for human rights, which was in open contradiction to the indiscriminate support of counterrevolutionary activity against Cuba. This policy also had consequences for the intelligence services, which saw themselves severely limited in the area of special operations.[52] Therefore, the counterrevolutionary groups felt the effects not only on the political principles that served as bases of their support, but also on the structure of relations that up to that moment had served them to access the power structure of the United States. This marked a course of action that cut off the source of benefits to the exile community that resulted from performing their counterrevolutionary function. This proved to be a key element in understanding the political changes that would take place in important segments of this community and their consequences vis-à-vis the previously undisputed power of the extreme right.

The Carter administration tried to exert influence over the Cuban community following, on occasion, a pattern similar to that traditionally adopted by the Democratic Party toward other minorities. Thus they sponsored the National Coalition of Cuban-Americans (NCCA), an organization of professional Cuban-American politicians whose function was to take advantage of the funds assigned for public assistance programs to increase the influence of the party in the Cuban-American community. The NCCA was supposed to distance itself from the controversial issue of relations with Cuba, but this was not to be. In the end, the coalition was broken over this dispute. The

NCCA turned out to be the first organization of persons of Cuban origin that approached the problems of the community from a Cuban-American perspective. Its principal error lay precisely in attempting to apply to the Cuban community patterns that were not entirely its own, or at least that were not among its priorities. The question of the community's position regarding the Cuban Revolution not only constituted an emotional and historical issue, but also the principal source of benefits for that community and the basis of support of the Cuban-American bourgeoisie. Changing this required another language and other incentives.

The Carter administration, however, did not adequately capitalize on the rise of another movement, much more encompassing and transcendental. That was the coexistence current, which advocated a peaceful, negotiated solution to the problem of family reunification and contacts with Cuba. The main groups represented in this movement were the low-income, less socially integrated émigrés. Although it constituted a minority of the Cuban-American community and lacked a clear political projection, the most important characteristics of this movement were its popular character and its conflict with the paradigms imposed until then by the extreme right. In addition, its members never had adequate leadership, sufficient resources, or enough popular support to achieve their political potential. Their objectives and composition reflected a class conflict within the community that the exile rhetoric had kept hidden up to that time. Despite its limitations, the movement had a considerable impact on the political climate of the Cuban community, by subverting the bases of the counterrevolutionary discourse and questioning their as yet undisputed representation of that community. Paradoxically, the movement began to weaken as the process of normalization between the two countries moved forward and the demands that inspired and united them began to be met, without articulating others to replace them.

The best known coexistence group of this period was the one led by the Reverend Manuel Espinosa, who turned out to be a tragicomic character on the Miami political scene. With few scruples and a marvelous theatrical style—he fooled everyone—Espinosa played the same cards as the most sensationalist counterrevolutionary propaganda and used them to attract hundreds of people, more desperate than conscious, into a political movement that shook Miami. Following a pattern common to Cuban-exile politics, his objective was to gain publicity and make money exploiting those naive enough to believe that his message was sincere. Espinosa's ability lay in interpreting the sentiments of an important sector of the Cuban community and understanding that these people required a different agenda from the traditional counterrevolutionary line. After that gold mine had been discovered, others imitated him, corrupting the coexistence movement and undermining its goals.

The fear of a confrontation with the extreme right prevented the majority of the emerging Cuban-American democratic force—with some exceptions—from supporting the coexistence movement and strongly backing Carter's policy toward Cuba. In fact, the majority still had much in common with the ideological and political positions of the hard right. This had ominous consequences for the moderates, alienating them from their natural base of support. The resulting vacuum would later be filled by the extreme right, allied with the Republican Party. The left, at the time a relatively vigorous political force, was equally unable to distinguish essence from appearance and to capitalize on the rise of the coexistence movement.

From a more elaborate and elitist perspective, a variant of coexistence took hold among important segments of émigré intellectuals that called for a different approach to the analysis of Cuba and relations with Cuban society. As expected, this group was politically and ideologically heterogeneous, yet differed from the rest by the sophistication of its message, the impact of these persons on public opinion, their influence on U.S. policy toward Cuba, and by the fact that their support for a dialog weakened the theoretical and political tenets of the counterrevolution. The more cultivated elements of the left found a space, for the first time, in this sector thereby legitimizing and strengthening their positions. The most significant aspect of the intellectual movement was not its agreement with the Cuban Revolution—that was never a predominant tendency among them—but that it encouraged new patterns of analysis and behavior that undermined the credibility and control of the traditional counterrevolutionary groups. The importance of this group grew to the degree that some of its members began to participate in the design of the Cuba policy in their capacity as advisors of different U.S. administrations and specialized institutions, including the intelligence services.

Although this sector was never very organized, to some degree it centered on the Instituto de Estudios Cubanos (IEC), an association created in 1971 at the initiative of Prof. María Cristina Herrera. It had its origins in the Reuniones de Estudios Cubanos (Cuban Studies Meetings), a discussion forum on Cuba sponsored by former Christian-Democratic leaders and activists connected with the magazines *Exilio* and *Nueva Generación*. The IEC has made room for very diverse political tendencies. María Cristina Herrera, in an interview published in *Areíto* in 1974, defined this balance: "The members of the IEC are also active members of various other Cuban-exile civic, political, and cultural organizations and associations. Our institute is not a partisan political organization. In fact, one of our objectives has always been to promote the meeting and exchange of all [political] tendencies and opinions, including those of a political nature. The IEC will never be a party or a political movement, even though its members may be affiliated with them or carry out activities in this area."[53] The political tendencies that have predominated manifest a rather conservative, Christian-Democratic slant, and the relations of the IEC with Cuban society have not always been smooth. However, its positions in defense of pluralism and tolerance within the émigré community has brought it face to face with the extreme right, making it a frequent target of aggression, including the dynamite bombing of the home of María Cristina Herrera.

The Carter government attempted to promote and control the process of improvement of relations between the émigrés and Cuba, promoting figures acceptable to the Cuban government, as in the case of the banker Bernardo Benes. He was identified with a segment of Democratic, Cuban-American businessmen and politicians with whom he formed a group that traveled to Cuba and met with Fidel Castro on various occasions. According to Benes, these gestures received the personal approval of then-Secretary of State Cyrus Vance. The importance of this group was that it represented the interests and intentions of a relevant segment of the Cuban-American bourgeoisie that, with the consent of the U.S. government, supported improvement in relations between the two countries, in the belief that this could benefit them economically and politically.

This process was strengthened when the Cuban government sponsored in 1978 a Dialog with Representative Figures of the Community. President Castro himself advanced the possibility of celebrating this meeting at a press conference in Havana on September 6, 1978, with journalists linked to the Cuban community. The precedents for this meeting included the visit of the Brigada Antonio Maceo, the family trips of the followers of Rev. Espinosa, the interviews of Fidel Castro with Benes, and the liberation of a group of counterrevolutionary prisoners who waited to emigrate to the United States. At that press conference, President Castro defined, from the Cuban perspective, what made the Dialog possible: the consolidation of the Cuban Revolution, changes in U.S. policy toward Cuba, and diminished hostility on the part of the émigré community. The United States was excluded from the possible conversations for reasons of national sovereignty, he said, but at the same time he recognized the heterogeneity of the émigrés, the legitimacy of their interests in dealing with Cuba, and the will of the Cuban government to enter into dialog.[54]

The meetings were held in late 1978 and early 1979. On the part of the Cuban community the participants included a diverse but representative group that split from the traditional counterrevolution and adopted positions in defense of a negotiated solution of the problems. Among the 140 persons present in one or the other of the sessions of the meeting were 30 representatives of left groups, 34 intellectuals, 19 leaders of coexistence organizations, 5 clergyman, former members of the Batista government, former members of the 2506th Brigade, and former political prisoners. The agreements reached at the Dialog included the liberation of some 3,600 counterrevolutionary prisoners, a more flexible migration policy, and the possibility of visits to Cuba by Cuban émigrés. The participants founded Operación Reunificación Cubana, in charge of raising the necessary funds and organizing the travel of the ex-prisoners and their families to the United States. Altogether, some 12,000 Cubans migrated in this manner.[55]

As a result of the convergent policies of the Cuban and U.S. governments, the extreme right-wing sectors for the first time felt alienated from the rest of the community. Their capacity for action was reduced to the most irrational violence, which was practiced through whatever means at their disposal, including threats and propaganda. The Miami police themselves testified before a Senate committee that these activities had their origin in loss of support for the counterrevolution. "Failing support for funding in these areas, groups have resorted to bombings and extortion in an effort to gather support and individual funding for their cause. . . . Some Cuban groups purporting to be involved in terrorist type acts against the Cuban government are no more or no less than outright criminals, feeding upon the Cuban population and diverting the collected funding for their own purposes."[56]

In October 1973 the principal terrorist groups celebrated the Congreso contra la Coexistencia (Congress against Coexistence) in Puerto Rico, and two of the first proponents of this line, Luciano Nieves and Ramón Donéstevez, were assassinated in 1975 and 1976, respectively, as were Carlos Muñíz and Eulalio Negrín in 1979. The MNC, adopting the name Comandos 0,[57] published a communiqué that stated: "We consider any Cuban or Puerto Rican, in fact any American that travels to Cuba, independently of his motives, to be our enemy. We will be forced to judge any Cuban that goes to Cuba, in tour groups or individually, as we did with [Carlos] Muñíz Varela."[58]

Beginning then, the terrorist groups targeted the Cuban community as their prime objective. The principal terrorist group, Omega 7, became the most feared organization in the United States. Although they denied any organic ties with the MNC, the FBI considered Omega 7 the armed wing of this organization and their ties turned out in any case to be very tight. It likewise had its base in the small bedroom communities of New Jersey—also the origin of the MNC—with branches in Miami and Puerto Rico. The traditional home of the Italian Mafia, these northeastern U.S. cities also offered the Cuban terrorist groups the support of local authorities linked to organized crime. The mayor of Union City, later imprisoned for racketeering, maintained a team of Cuban assistants—among them the Cuban-American Bob Menendez, the current congressional representative from this district—that provided significant support to the terrorist groups that operated in this area. An analysis of the city budget in 1979 indicates that the mayor contributed $30,000 to financing the counterrevolutionary tabloids alone.[59] Something similar occurred in Puerto Rico where, with the support of the extreme right wing in the government and the complicity of the local security forces, Omega 7 acted under the cover of the tabloid *Crónica*. The most infamous of its actions was gunning down Carlos Muñíz Varela, a leader of the Brigada Antonio Maceo. The crime remains unsolved, despite the fact that many of those implicated—in some cases former chiefs of the Puerto Rico police—are in prison for other crimes and many of the facts are public knowledge.

Between 1975 and 1980, Omega 7 claimed responsibility for more than twenty terrorist acts, including placing explosive devices in the Soviet and Venezuelan missions to the UN, seven similar attacks on the Cuban mission in New York, the murders of Eulalio Negrín in 1979 and Cuban diplomat Félix Rodríguez in 1980, and a frustrated attempt on the life of Cuban UN ambassador Raúl Róa Kourí. Besides, Omega 7 terrorized the Cuban community, extorted contributions, compelled residents to participate in public rallies, threatened authorities and politicians, and silenced in one way or another anyone who dared criticize it. Some of its principal leaders were arrested in 1981 and the organization was disbanded after its chief, Eduardo Arocena, was sentenced to more than a hundred years in jail.

A Cuban-American sociologist, who would not give her name to a U.S. publication in 1980 for fear of reprisals, told of the results of her research on these groups: "Most of them," she explained, "came from the lower middle class in the old Cuba. Through the Revolution, they were victimized by peasants and the working class. In the United States, they feel victimized by the upper classes and a political culture which places a premium on being white. . . . Their world here is an alien and disconcerting place which confers on them little or no power and social status. . . . These men and women are easy prey for the movements and intelligence agencies in a society slowly, but systematically moving politically to the right and in the process of socioeconomic disintegration. . . . They are today's and tomorrow's bomb-throwers, Watergate plumbers, mercenaries, and most important today's and tomorrow's reactionary electorate."[60]

All this terror, however, was unable to slow the Dialog process. Despite the threats, over 100,000 Cuban immigrants visited Cuba in 1979. For this reason, if no other, the Dialog became one of the most effective measures of the Cuban government against the counterrevolutionary hard right. Nevertheless, the émigré group that participated did not have the cohesion, capacity for mobilization, or necessary resources to take advantage of the moment and gain sufficient influence in U.S. policy toward Cuba. Nor was Cuban society sufficiently prepared to assume the consequences of such an abrupt political change. Circumstances changed so quickly that the Cubans were unable to act in accordance with Fidel Castro's original foresight. Castro himself said, "Maybe the best thing would be to carry out these conversations with the greatest discretion, calm, and patience. This cannot be accomplished in twenty-four hours. We do not want anything spectacular. We do not believe that is the way."[61]

In fact, things happened differently. The decision to allow the émigré community to visit Cuba immediately and en masse polarized the Cuban émigrés to the detriment of the counterrevolutionary groups. On the other hand, it reduced the mobilization capacity of the left and coexistence sectors, it encouraged moneymaking attitudes both in Cuba and in the United States that devalued the political sense of the process, and it generated contradictions within Cuban society for which both the state and political institutions were unprepared. A national consensus around the Dialog and its agreements was not forged in Cuba. Immigrant families revisiting the island implied the collapse of the premises that until then had served to politically judge the act of migrating and constituted an emotional clash that had inevitable ideological and political consequences as well. If the process would have continued evolving in a normal manner it is possible that economic and political imperatives would have guided it to stability, but there was no time for that and the experience would be remembered by its worst manifestations.

The change in policy toward Cuba assumed by the Carter administration toward the end of his period weighed heavily on the Dialog process. Carter approached his reelection campaign burdened by a poor economy, the Iran hostage crisis in full swing, disunity within his own party due to some of his political projects, and the revitalization, with renewed force, of the neoconservative Republican sectors that organized an impressive political machine. This led him to make concessions to the right-wingers and assume ambivalent positions, which affected even more a capacity for leadership never truly consolidated. This situation deprived the Dialog of the political environment for which it was conceived and which constituted a precondition for its success, because it was precisely the attitude of the U.S. government that could tilt the balance against the counterrevolutionary far-right wing.

Thus came to an end a process of improvement in relations between the United States and Cuba that had advanced as never before during the revolutionary period and that had also witnessed significant progress in the relations of the Cuban immigration with the island, likewise consistent with the interests of the U.S. government. Carter's policy reversal toward Cuba left the pro-Dialog groups at the mercy of the extreme right, weakened the democratic segments of the community, and once again put the Cuban government in a defensive position that limited its capacity to maintain contact with the émigrés. It is this political background, intensified by the difficulties caused by the arrival to the labor force of the baby boomers born in the 1960s in the midst of a recession in the Cuban economy, that generated the conditions that gave rise to the events of Mariel in 1980.

The Mariel crisis was a dramatic, unexpected finale to a process that pointed toward reconciliation. It all began when groups of individuals interested in emigrating sought to gain entry to some Latin American embassies by force. The Cuban government negotiated the peaceful exit of these persons from these embassies, and even reached satisfactory agreements with the Peruvian ambassador, the most complicated case. As a result of pressures by Peruvian rightists, however, the government of Peru inexplicably disavowed its own ambassador and ordered him to return to embassy grounds those who had entered it illegally, and who calmly awaited their Peruvian visas in their homes. That decision unleashed a stream of illegal penetrations into the embassy until one of them caused the death of a Cuban embassy guard, and the revolutionary government decided to withdraw embassy protection. Some ten thousand people marched into the embassy grounds, an avalanche the Peruvian government was not interested or capable of receiving, more so since it was evident that the intention of nearly all was to emigrate to the United States. The OAS began to establish "Cuban refugee camps" in various Latin American countries, regionalizing the conflict. The Cuban government answered by opening the port of Mariel to any vessel that wanted to pick up Cuban emigrants. Thus in the following months some 120,000 persons abandoned the country to settle in the United States.

The Mariel crisis reversed all that had moved forward in the relations of Cuba with its immigrants. Once again the act of migrating took on a negative political connotation and the émigrés were branded as antisocial and treasonous. Although Carter spoke at first of receiving them with open arms and hearts, the U.S. government ended up treating the émigrés as criminals that required separate treatment.[62] The American press went so far as to label them "representative of the most contemptible migration in the nation's history."[63] For years the Mariel émigrés were limited to temporary residence in the United States, or parolee status, and they still may be imprisoned indefinitely for crimes committed in Cuba, or deported if they violate U.S. law. Based on their previous records, some 2,800 émigrés were arrested upon their arrival in the United States and twenty years later some are still in prison awaiting a court decision. Although the courts have ruled in their favor in 45 percent of the cases and nearly 400 have been deported to Cuba, approximately 2,400, considered "excludibles," continue in jail awaiting deportation.[64]

What followed was a period of dissatisfaction and uncertainty. In his address to the Second Congress of the Cuban Communist Party, Fidel Castro evaluated the results of this process: "In the current situation it is still not possible to make a definite evaluation of the policy toward the Cuban community living abroad. The visits were reduced to a minimum as a result of the great indignation that our people felt with the events that followed the repeated provocations at the Venezuelan and Peruvian embassies. Our policy in this regard will depend on the attitude taken by the new U.S. administration."[65]

In any case, after the Dialog and Mariel the Cuban community would never be the same. Key factors had changed, such as its social composition and the image of the community before North American society and before itself, and it became evident that the problem of relations with Cuba was an issue of interest for the majority, more so after the arrival of the new immigrants. The traditional counterrevolutionary groups exhausted their already limited capacity for mobilization and were left to play an eminently coercive role over the rest of the community and carry out minor paramilitary and propaganda activities against Cuba.

During the following twelve years of Republican government—from 1980 to 1992—only eighteen actions against Cuban coasts and fourteen other terrorist attempts were perpetrated.[66] The explanation lay in the fact that terrorism flourished to the degree that the counterrevolution found no other alternatives. But this situation changed with the victory of the neoconservative offensive, combined with greater maturity of the political, economic, and social integration of the Cuban immigrants. These developments gave rise to new counterrevolutionary groups, qualitatively different from the previous ones insofar as they were already a reflection of the emerging class interests and of links of a different nature with the U.S. power elite. The analysis of this process of migration-integration, its economic, political, and psychological conditions, and their corresponding consequences are therefore necessary for understanding the complexity of the Cuban counterrevolutionary phenomenon.

Chapter 6

Immigration and Counterrevolution

STUDY OF THE Cuban migration to the United States suggests establishing two periods, differentiated both by the nature of the migration and the social composition of the migrants. The victory of the Revolution in 1959 is the watershed between the two periods.

Prerevolutionary migration was essentially an economic phenomenon. Although political migration from Cuba to the United States had been relatively common since the nineteenth century, most of the immigrants were workers in search of better jobs, and were accepted into the United States in accordance with the need for labor that the North American economy had at any given time. Material incentive has also inspired immigrants after 1959. In fact, it is accurate to say that behind the veil of political dissidence, it has been the fundamental motivation of individuals. But in contrast with the previous period, postrevolutionary migration was carried out in accordance with the political interests of the United States, giving it a political connotation and determining its social composition.

The political or economic nature of migratory processes has become a frequent topic of debate among specialists. U.S. sociologist

Robert Bach has concluded: "the defining characteristics of migration flows are found at the level of social and economic organization and international politics, not among individual perceptions and motivations. . . . The difference lies in how similar problems of both an economic and political nature get interpreted by the two principal actors in any migration flow, the sending and receiving states."[1]

Migrating constitutes an individual option whose achievement requires above all the willingness of the receiving state. The political, economic, and humanitarian foundation that defines that posture determines the specific migratory phenomenon at a social level, even though the motivations of individuals are always very complex and diverse:

> The act of migrating is typically a very complex decision, traumatic and multicausal, that reflects a certain degree of dissatisfaction of the individuals with their situation, with their expectations of life and with a given sociopolitical environment. In this context it is nearly impossible to determine where the economic factors end and the political or even psychological begin. . . . Political nonconformity is not, in and of itself, a determining factor for deserving the status of political refugee. There needs to be present a certain degree of persecution which makes it impossible for the person to continue living in his or her country, which has not been the case for the majority of the Cuban émigrés. . . . Nevertheless, the Cuban migratory phenomenon after the victory of the Revolution is essentially political because it was made possible by political causes and they determined its characteristics.[2]

The differences between pre- and postrevolutionary migrants can also be found in their class characteristics, social status, race, and dominant ideology, as well as in the role—symbolic or real—played by these persons in influencing U.S. policy toward Cuba and the weight of that circumstance on their social positioning, culture, and relations with their country of origin. Cuban politics also influenced the generalized political standard of postrevolutionary migration.

Fidel Castro, in a speech given in New York, commented: "We ourselves did not sufficiently understand that many of those immigrants were economic, and we saw them as adversaries of the Revolution due to the statements they made on arrival here in order to receive aid. . . . Perhaps with our experience, with what we know today, we should have made a clear differentiation between those who were immigrants—because they were not exiles, nobody expelled them—for political reasons and those who were immigrants for economic reasons."[3] For these reasons, it would not be correct to establish an organic continuity in the Cuban migratory process; on the contrary, the significance from a historical point of view is the break that occurs between one period and the next.

Prerevolutionary Migration

The most significant migration flow in contemporary history was that which gave rise to the United States. In the nineteenth century, immigration was responsible for 30 percent of the population growth of that nation, and even in the first half of the twentieth it represented 10 percent of that increase. Until 1950 the immigrants were primarily of European origin, but from then on close to 50 percent of immigrants have been Latin Americans.

Since the nineteenth century, the United States has become the natural destination for Cuban migrants for various reasons, among them geographic proximity, economic ties between the two countries, and the extraordinary privileges that, at times, the United States granted to that migration. Since the 1820s there have been significant Cuban settlements in the United States. At that time Cuban immigrants numbered around one thousand and were primarily intellectuals or political figures that emigrated from the colony, fleeing persecution by the regime or seeking greater freedom in North America.[4] Among this group are some of the most important exponents of Creole liberal bourgeois thinking, such as José A. Saco; the pioneers of independence, headed by Félix Varela; and the first proponents of annexation, represented by Narciso López.

In the 1870s the number of Cuban immigrants increased significantly, reaching 12,000 persons. It is estimated that 4,500 settled in New York, 3,000 in New Orleans, 2,000 in Key West, and another 2,500 in the rest of the country. The bulk of the Creole elite was concentrated in New York. But here, as in the rest of the cities, the majority were workers of different races that migrated in response to the end of the Civil War, the beginning of the first Cuban war of independence, and the move to the United States of an important part of the Cuban cigar-rolling industry.[5]

The end of the war in Cuba, in 1878, permitted the return of many of these people as well as the concentration of the remaining immigrants—and others that joined them—in very defined communities of tobacco workers in Key West and Tampa, where some 20,000 Cubans had settled by 1890.[6] The proletarian character and racial diversity of these communities generated a different political environment from that of the Spanish colony they left behind. Their cohesion and political radicalism favored the development of a labor movement very advanced for its times. Nevertheless, the center of political attention was always the question of Cuban independence. The biggest associations and principal leaders rose around this issue. The role of immigration in the independence struggle of José Martí and in the formation of the Partido Revolucionario Cubano is well known.

Nevertheless, these communities were not homogeneous. Beginning in the 1870s, changes in the social composition took place that gave rise to class, racial, and ideological conflicts among the immigrants. Martí's success is precisely that he was able to subordinate these contradictions to the question of independence and to convince the immigrants that their role consisted in supporting the revolutionary movement on the island, not leading it, as some wealthy Cuban immigrants pretended to do. There is evidence that, contrary to the radical revolutionary attitude taken by the immigrant workers, there also existed within the immigration a significant sector of the bourgeoisie that flirted with annexation to the United States, favored the penetration of the oligarchy into the revolutionary ranks, and promoted the adulteration of the political aims of the Cuban Revolutionary Party after the death of José Martí on the battlefield on May 19, 1895. Some of these men lent legitimacy to the North American intervention in Cuba's war against Spain and to the consummation of a neocolonial state in Cuba. The most relevant figure among them was Tomás Estrada Palma, José Martí's substitute as party delegate and the first president of Cuba in 1902.[7]

The end of the War of Independence in 1898 transformed the political priorities of the Cuban émigré communities and accentuated their integration into U.S. society. A good many of the immigrants returned then to fight for independence, or immediately after Spanish colonialism was defeated. By the century's end the Cuban immigrant population had fallen to some 11,000 persons.[8] Nevertheless, the survival of social enclaves, organized around cigar production, allowed for an environment to endure until the 1930s that was favorable to the preservation of traditions and a conscience of national identity. Beginning in the thirties the cigar-rolling industry entered a crisis and the enclaves tended to disperse. The creation of these enclaves constituted a significant historical and cultural experience insofar as they gave rise to communities with ethnic and cultural characteristics that differentiated them from the rest of U.S. society as well as from the Cuban society from which they had come. The experience is repeated—for other reasons and with other sociopolitical peculiarities—with the formation of the Cuban-American enclave in Miami beginning in 1959.[9]

Domestic political conflicts encouraged migratory outflows from Cuba during the republican period (1902–59), but the exile constituted a minority that possessed the means to leave the country and settle abroad. The United States also became the preferred country of residence for a good part of the Cuban bourgeoisie, and it was quite common for that class, as well as for the upper middle class, to send their children to study there and to travel there frequently on business or pleasure. However, the distinctive characteristic of pre-revolutionary Cuban immigration was that it flourished at a time when the economic conditions in the United States required a supply of immigrant laborers.

During the first decade of the twentieth century 40,149 Cubans migrated to the United States, encouraged by an immigration policy that allowed over 8.5 million people to enter the country in ten years. Another 27,837 Cubans moved north in the 1910s, and 15,608 in the 1920s. The Depression, which severely affected cigar production and the general economy of Florida, together with the anti-immigrant sentiments that such conditions generate, resulted in a sensible decrease in immigrants during the 1930s; only 4,122 Cubans arrived in that decade. The employment opportunities generated by World War II once again spurred an increase in immigration in the 1940s, to 15,415, and it is estimated that 40,000 Cubans immigrated to the United States from 1950 through 1959. Official figures for persons of Cuban origin living in the United States in 1958 are contradictory, insofar as the traffic was very dynamic and not all who were in the country at any one time necessarily sought permanent residence. The most realistic estimate, according to the first report of the Cuban Refugee Program, is that in 1958—after the wave of repatriations following the revolutionary victory—125,000 Cuban-born persons and their descendants resided in the United States, of which 50,000 were settled in Miami.[10]

The most disadvantaged sectors of a society are not generally those who immigrate. To migrate one needs a minimum of resources and training that insures certain capacity for insertion into the new society. Therefore, the migration has never been representative of the average Cuban population. Nevertheless, in the prerevolutionary period it was primarily working class persons who immigrated, and they settled under conditions similar to those of other Latin American immigrant groups, which prevented them from rising significantly up the social ladder, as would be the case years later. On the contrary, life was not easy for most of those who settled in southern Florida. The racism, anti-unionism, McCarthyism, and anti-Catholicism that dominated the region during the 1950s particularly affected Cuban workers and revolutionaries—more so if they were black, as the "Cuban niggers" were especially scorned and persecuted by the Ku Klux Klan.[11]

Miami became the political center of exile opposition during the years of struggle against the Batista dictatorship. The Auténticos, with more resources and contacts than the rest of the groups, capitalized on the support of the wealthier émigré opposition sectors. In 1955 Fidel Castro traveled to the United States and for six weeks devoted his efforts to organizing patriotic clubs of the 26 of July Movement. The basis of these organizations were immigrant workers, who donated a day's pay if they were employed or one dollar per month if they were not.[12] Meeting with Cuban immigrants in Miami, Fidel Castro established the differences between exiles and immigrants: "You are more than exiles, you are immigrants from hunger. . . . the exiles are few and some of them are millionaire thieves."[13]

Unlike the workers, the Cuban bourgeoisie living in the United States was almost totally white, conservative, and often Protestant, which made for notable social differences between the two groups. This is not surprising. As noted by Professors James and Judith Olson, given the strong ties between the Cuban elite and the United States, it was normal for wealthy immigrants to be "as American as they were Cuban."[14] This no doubt influenced the fact that the most conservative sectors of the anti-Batista movement found in the émigrés their natural environment. The first groups that migrated beginning in 1959 resembled these well-to-do sectors already in the Unites States. However, in the 1950s the majority of immigrants were working class, and although it did not play a significant role in the insurrection process, this community was characterized by its massive rejection of the dictatorship and its support for the revolutionary cause. This explains the massive repatriation that occurred immediately after the revolutionary triumph.

Counterrevolutionary Emigration

U.S. belligerence toward the Cuban Revolution required the creation of powerful stimuli to emigrate from the island.[15] Therefore, only hours after deciding to put into effect the plans that culminated with the Bay of Pigs invasion, Eisenhower sought congressional support for a policy of promotion and assistance for Cuban immigration.[16] Emigration played an important function within the counterrevolutionary strategy. It drained Cuba of the human capital that the country's economy demanded, discredited the revolutionary political model, and established the social base that would lend support to the counterrevolutionary movement. Some specialists have calculated that, out of a population of 6 million, the migration potential resulting from the conflicts of the Revolution with those sectors most interested in maintaining the status quo—bourgeoisie, small bourgeoisie, professionals, business leaders, merchants, and others—numbered some 600,000 persons. This is in fact the number of those who abandoned the country during the first two postrevolutionary migratory waves.[17] It indicates that the U.S. policy of encouraging migration from Cuba was extraordinarily aggressive and encompassing, and fulfilled the aims for which it was designed.

Although it would be a mistake to equate political disagreement with a militant counterrevolutionary attitude, in fact the immigrants voted with their feet and became a fundamental component of the political opposition to the revolutionary government. By satisfying this political function, a role-benefit relation was established that explains the persistent priority of the Cuban issue in the political agenda of the émigrés and the extraordinary privileges granted by the U.S. government to this immigrant group. Moreover, this relation has not been expressed in a linear or unwavering manner throughout the years. Rather, it has been conditioned by the contingencies of U.S. policy toward Cuba, the characteristics of the various generations of immigrants of the postrevolutionary period, and the attitude that this nation has taken at any given time toward the migratory question.

The indiscriminate application of the category of "political refugee" to the majority of the immigrants coming from Cuba reflected an intention of political manipulation. This corresponds with the intention of framing the Cuban question within the context of the Cold War and giving these immigrants a similar treatment as that received by the immigrants from the socialist bloc. In fact, originally the Cubans entered the country under the aegis of the Walter-McCarran Act, passed in 1952 to encourage immigration from the European socialist countries.

Among the first immigrants were those who could truthfully be considered political exiles, since in many cases they were elements of the Batista dictatorship that fled to the United States. They were later joined by nearly all the national oligarchy, followed by the rest of the privileged sectors of the country, including a significant portion of the most qualified professionals and technical personnel. From a quantitative perspective, 31 percent of this emigration were businessmen, professionals, and technicians, and another 33 percent were officials and merchants. The equivalent proportions in the Cuban population, according to the 1953 census, were 9.2 percent and 13.7 percent, respectively. Even more illustrative are the indicators comparing the level of education of these immigrants with that of the general Cuban population at the time: 36 percent of the migrants were high school graduates, versus 4 percent of the population as a whole. Conversely, only 4 percent of the migrants had less than four years of schooling, while 52 percent of the Cuban population were in that situation.[18] In 1960 less than 7 percent of the Cubans in the

United States were black, and ten years later the figure had fallen to 2.6 percent.[19]

The 200,000 persons who left Cuba between the victory of the Revolution in January 1959 and the missile crisis of October 1962 constituted the first generation of immigrants to the United States.[20] In correspondence with the above-mentioned strategy, these persons received from U.S. officials the maximum assistance for entry. Private persons and entities such as the Catholic Church were even granted visa waivers—conceived for cases of extreme emergency—when the United States broke diplomatic relations with Cuba in January 1961. Proportionately, these immigrants participated to a greater degree than later immigrants in counterrevolutionary activities. They formed part of the first counterrevolutionary groups, joined the Bay of Pigs invasion brigade, participated massively in the secret war organized by the CIA, and contributed the principal leaders of the counterrevolutionary movement. This conduct was justified on class grounds: this first wave of immigrants constituted the group truly displaced from power in Cuba and those most affected economically by the Revolution. The leadership assumed by these early immigrants within the counterrevolutionary movement, and the economic and political benefits this brought them, made the integration of this group into U.S. society all the more advantageous. This incorporation would later have important consequences for the class structure and the ideological and political orientation of the Cuban émigré community in the United States. The result is that, in the class recomposition that would follow in the émigré community, the Cuban-American bourgeoisie would be composed predominantly of persons who occupied that same position in Cuba.

The results of the October missile crisis undoubtedly transformed the North American vision of the endurance of the Cuban Revolution and, correspondingly, how the question of immigration should be treated. At the end of 1962, President Kennedy suspended direct flights to Cuba, and tens of thousands of persons hoping to emigrate were left stranded in the country. This, combined with the policy of indiscriminately harboring illegal Cuban immigrants, created a tremendous incentive to illegal immigration, which in this period reached one of its highest levels of the revolutionary years. The expectation of emigrating, with the utmost guarantees of receiving preferential treatment in a highly developed country like the United States, constituted in and of itself a destabilizing element in Cuban society. In addition, migration through illegal means proved a dramatic angle that could be lavishly exploited by U.S. propaganda. It also implied risks, not only for the security of the immigrants but also for the potential victims of airplane and boat hijackings and of those charged with protecting these resources. Between 1962 and 1965 some 30,000 Cuban immigrants entered the United States illegally.[21]

To reverse this situation, the Cuban government authorized those émigrés who wished to pick up their relatives in Cuba to do so freely and safely. The port of Camarioca, on the northern coast of Matanzas, was outfitted for that purpose, from which some 2,700 persons migrated between October and November of 1965.[22] This provoked a situation which resulted in the signing of the so-called Memorandum of Understanding, the first bilateral agreement to regulate the migratory flow. Approximately 250,000 persons immigrated to the United States during the eight years this agreement was in effect,[23] of which 90 percent had relatives in the United States,[24] and therefore the process of family reunification was nearly complete. This would have a significant impact on the demographic makeup of the Cuban émigré community and its subsequent relation with Cuba. However, the agreement neither suggested nor produced an improvement of relations between the two countries. Despite the fact that those who emigrated did so of their own free will, by mutual agreement of the two governments, employing normal migratory procedures and adequate means of transportation, they continued to be considered political refugees. The airlift became known as the Freedom Flights, and no distinctions were established between legal and illegal immigration.

During this period another 10,500 Cubans reached U.S. territory by illegal means.[25]

In 1973, President Richard Nixon decided to end the airlift and suspend the migratory agreements that gave rise to it, thereby returning the migratory problem to the state it had been in 1965. The political and economic situation in the United States, the spread of strong anti-immigrant feelings, and the rejection of the prerogatives enjoyed by the Cubans contributed to that decision. Moreover, this corresponded with the interest of the Cuban government in reducing the drain that this indiscriminate emigration constituted, and which they had tried to curtail by a series of restrictions since 1969. By this date what can be considered as the second generation of immigrants of the revolutionary era had finally settled in their new country. Some 600,000 Cubans had emigrated to the United States since 1962, contributing to a total population of 803,226 persons of Cuban origin, according to the 1980 census.[26] From a sociological perspective, this population continued to represent a segment of the privileged white classes of Cuban society that settled in the United States under particularly favorable conditions, thereby reinforcing the pattern of the first generation. They were older than the U.S. national average, it was common for three generations to share the same household, and a greater number of women joined the labor force compared to the other minority groups. The average annual family income was $18,245, below the national average of $19,917, but above that of Mexican-Americans ($14,765) and Puerto Ricans ($10,734). Only 11.7 percent lived below the poverty line, close to the national average of 9.6 percent. In 1970 only 1,000 Cubans owned businesses in Miami, but ten years later the figure climbed to 10,000.[27]

The deep transformations introduced by the Cuban Revolution in the Cuban social structure altered the points of reference—political, ideological, and cultural—of the first generations of immigrants vis-à-vis Cuba. Their conflict with the Revolution encompassed not only interests related to the recuperation of their lost status, property, and privileges, but also included values deep seated in a way of life and individual goals that contrasted with the new patterns of Cuban society. A significant degree of class heterogeneity could already be found among these immigrants, and was intensified in the course of their settlement in the United States. Yet their predominant social composition, their political references, and their links to the former Cuban elite maintained the pattern of significant sociological differences with respect to Cuban society and, consequently, the alienation of the émigré political groups from life in Cuba. Therefore, those who emigrated later, regardless of their motives, responded to another reality and their conflict with the Revolution has not had the class consistency present in the first generations of émigrés.

The numeric and functional predominance of the first generations over the totality of the Cuban émigré community in the United States emphasized the class conflict. Combined with the counterrevolutionary interest of U.S. policy, this predominance encouraged a process of political polarization that reasserted the convergence of the migratory phenomenon with opposition to the Cuban system. Although the changes introduced by the Carter administration in U.S. policy toward Cuba and the rise of the coexistence movement demonstrated the fragility of the consensus, the objective of overthrowing the Cuban regime prevailed, in general, over issues such as family reunification or maintaining ties with Cuban society. Nor has this agenda been representative of the common needs and interests of the average immigrant. This helps to explain important differences historically observed between the political priorities of the Cuban immigrants and those of the rest of the country's minority groups.

In contrast with the tendency manifested in the first generations, only 40 percent of those who emigrated in 1980 had relatives in the United States;[28] in addition, 40 percent were black. Their social composition reflected the changes that had taken place in Cuban society throughout the revolutionary period. As a result, the post-1980 migration added a new element of heterogeneity to the social segmentation and class polarization already present in the Cuban-American community. This group, an essential component of the 1980–1989 migratory flow, which can be accurately classified as the third generation, maintained closer ties to Cuban society and their political priorities have been related to the issue of divided families. Also, their political and social references are different and the bases of cultural contact more current, thus their participation in counterrevolutionary activities has been much more limited, despite having arrived in the United States at a time of a new counterrevolutionary boom.

As a result of the economic recession in the United States in the 1970s, the events of Mariel occurred at a time of rising anti-immigrant feelings there. This climate is reflected in the character of the 1980 Refugee Act, which had been under discussion before these events. In any case, Mariel increased the fear of a massive and uncontrolled influx of Cubans and altered the patterns whereby U.S. public opinion has accepted the supposed exceptional nature of these immigrants. Beginning in 1980, the United States enacted more selective policies for legal immigration, which was reflected in the spirit and implementation of the migratory agreements signed in 1984. In contrast to 1965, the 1984 agreements reflected a high degree of incompatibility between the U.S. requirements and the characteristics of the migratory potential. Since the priorities established by U.S. law were basically the same, the difference lay in the composition of those who sought to migrate and their degree of family relations in that country. The inflexible application of these parameters determined that between 1985 and 1990, only 7,428 Cubans were able to emigrate legally, compared with the ceiling of 100,000 established by the agreements.[29] Nevertheless, there was no increase in illegal exits; on the contrary, they declined to the lowest level in all of the revolutionary years, to only 1,000 in five years.[30] This figure demonstrates a relatively high degree of social stability in Cuba until the 1991 economic crisis gripped the country and the illegal exodus once again exploded.

It is, therefore, the economic crisis that set the pattern that differentiates the fourth generation of Cuban immigrants. It can be affirmed that the new migrants were persons who felt prepared to face the challenge of migration and, thus, sought to increase their options in a more developed society. A study carried out at the University of Havana with a sample of these potential immigrants suggests that most were relatively young white males, well educated and motivated essentially by aspirations of personal realization that they believed could not be fulfilled given the economic crisis in their country. Nonetheless, most did not consider the American way of life to be their ideal model of society, but rather expressed their preference for Cuban society before the crisis.[31] The novelty of this situation lies in how it reflects a different historical period and, therefore, the motivations and composition of the immigrant groups are essentially different.

Another distinctive characteristic of this generation of immigrants is that the majority left Cuba illegally. Between 1991 and July 1994, the United States received 12,808 illegal Cuban immigrants, but granted only 3,794 requests for legal entry.[32] Although the Mariel Syndrome has been a permanent preoccupation of U.S. authorities throughout the 1990s, their policy flirted with stimulating this migration, confident that the restrictions Cuba imposed on illegal exits would maintain the volume within levels economically and politically manageable for the United States. In fact, the retaining wall was truly the Cuban government, since they prevented the illegal exit of 37,801 persons between January 1990 and July 1994.[33]

The pressure for legal migration generated by the Cuban economic crisis led to social turmoil in the summer of 1994. The continuous hijackings of vessels, with loss of lives in a number of cases, as well as riots in Havana, resulted in the Cuban government's decision on August 12 to lift restrictions on exits by sea. The Clinton administration responded to the situation thus created, fearful of negative consequences for the reelection campaign of Florida's Democratic governor and of the president himself in 1996. On August 19, Washington did a complete turnabout in its policy of immigration from Cuba and announced that it would block the entry of "rafters"[34] to its territory. Reversing the exceptional treatment received for thirty-five years, those captured offshore would be interned in camps outside U.S. territory, thus becoming ineligible to enjoy the benefits of the Cuban Adjustment Act of 1966, and would likewise be ineligible for refugee status. In a few days, more than 30,000 Cuban immigrants ended up interned in U.S. military bases in Guantánamo and Panama.

Logically, the majority of the Cuban-American population rejected these measures, not only on account of the emotional issues that surrounded the situation, but also because they significantly affected the historic preferential treatment they had received that influenced other aspects of life in that community. The Clinton administration maneuvered between rival pressures. On the one hand, the Cuban-American right demanded a toughening of the policy toward Cuba. On the other, an important part of U.S. public opinion preferred finding a solution to the problem and adopting a strategy aimed at the normalization of relations between the two countries. In the end, the Democratic administration opted for negotiations that led to new migratory agreements. The first, signed on September 9, 1994, became the first bilateral agreement specifically aimed at curbing illegal immigration, representing a radical change in the policy that the United States had historically taken toward Cuba. In a second agreement intended to normalize the flow of legal immigration, the U.S. government committed to granting a minimum of 20,000 visas annually and other concessions to potential Cuban immigrants. The Cuban government, for its part, assumed responsibility for controlling the illegal migratory flow from its coasts to the United States.[35]

However, the problem of the 30,000 rafters interned in virtual concentration camps outside U.S. territory remained to be solved. Therefore, new talks were held in April; on May 2, 1995, both governments made public an extension of the agreement that called for the gradual admission into the United States of those confined in

Guantánamo and the return to Cuba of those illegal immigrants captured on the high seas from that moment on. In addition, the United States agreed to suspend the practice of granting automatic asylum to those who arrived illegally on its shores, and Cuba to receive these persons back and not take judicial action against them, which required a change in the law that penalized any attempt to exit the country illegally.[36] U.S. Attorney General Janet Reno announced her government's decision and emphasized that these measures represented a new step toward standardizing migratory procedures with respect to Cuba, a humanitarian solution to the situation in Guantánamo and the deterrence of another dangerous and uncontrolled current of immigrants from the island.[37]

Sending the illegal Cuban immigrants to Guantánamo and Panama satisfied the general U.S. consensus on how to handle the issue and corresponded to the electoral interests of the Democrats, but risked alienating the Cuban-American right, a sector that both Governor Lawton Chiles and President Clinton had been cultivating since 1992. Therefore, Clinton received a delegation of the Cuban-American right-wingers at the White House and accepted their demands to counterbalance this measure by outlawing family remittances to Cuba, suspending travel by Cuban-Americans to the island, and increasing radio and TV transmissions aimed at Cuba. Jorge Mas Canosa, the most prominent figure of this group, was highly pleased with the treatment received and supported the action of confining the rafters outside U.S. territory. He called Clinton "a man who stood for democracy and freedom, and argued that what the U.S. president did had nothing to do with politics but rather came from his own convictions."[38] The dynamics of the migratory conflict required, however, that new steps be taken and this led to expanding the May accords. The Cuban-American right was totally excluded from this negotiating process for two reasons. First, because their positions were in contradiction with U.S. strategic interests, backed by a wide consensus within North American society. Second, because the emergence of different voices within the Cuban-American community and the electoral results themselves proved that the right wing's control over this community was much more limited than what had been believed. This explains why Mas Canosa now reacted violently against the agreement and equated it with the "Bay of Pigs treason."[39]

Not surprising, if we consider that by outlawing illegal immigration, the agreements had strategic impact on the bilateral relations that transcended the migratory issue and eliminated the preferential treatment received by the Cuban immigrants since the Revolution came to power, thereby annulling the political connotation traditionally given to the act of migrating to the United States. Stimulating emigration from Cuba—or the expectations of migrating—and exploiting this politically constituted a pivotal element of U.S. policy toward Cuba. The accords materially changed the entire policy insofar as they transformed one of its principal ingredients. Moreover, they modified the ideological basis of that policy. From now on, Cuban immigrants would be considered the same, at least before the law, as all other immigrants entering the United States. No longer did Cuban-Americans have guaranteed entrée right to the top levels of U.S. national politics.

Counterrevolution and Social Integration

The naturalization of the Cuban immigrants has been presented as a model of success of the American Way of Life. However, this so-called golden exile is the only such example, at least from Latin America. The nature of this exception can be found, on the one hand, in its class composition. No other Latin American immigrant group has been better prepared to adjust to North American society than the Cuban immigrants. But, above all, it is the result of the preferential treatment rendered by the U.S. government and the connections resulting from their counterrevolutionary role in Cuba and the rest of

Latin America. In the end the "golden exile" is also fruit of the Cuban Revolution.

The process of integration of the Cuban immigrants into North American society has in fact been comparatively successful. This is true despite the presence of distinct class differences and the dramatic psychological and social consequences that the process of uprooting and settling has had for many of those immigrants. Compared to Cuban society it is evident that the immigrants' standard of living is higher, but this is true for all Latin American immigrants in the United States, even those at the lower income levels. If this were not the case the problem of massive illegal immigration that so worries North American society would not exist.

The Cubans have been successful even when compared to all other North American minority groups, although their income does not match the national average and it is well below that of the white middle class. In 1986, 13 percent of Cuban-Americans lived below the poverty level, compared to the national average of 11 percent. The figure for Mexican-Americans was 25 percent and for Puerto Rican–Americans, 38 percent. From an occupational perspective, 54 percent of Cuban-Americans had what were considered well-paying jobs, close to the national average of 56 percent, versus 33 percent of Mexican-Americans and 47 percent of Puerto Ricans. [40]

Various factors have contributed to and conditioned the process of integration[41] of the Cuban immigrants into North American society, which in turn has influenced its counterrevolutionary behavior. So great has been its impact that the Cuban counterrevolution evolved to become a domestic issue for the United States. On the one side are the events that directly influenced the formation of the Cuban-American enclave in Miami, the milieu where most of the immigrants settled, with its particular social and cultural characteristics. On the other are those that influenced the totality of the émigrés, in particular the preferential aid policy whose pillar was the establishment, in February 1961, of the Cuban Refugee Program.

This program was developed on the basis of the experience of handling the Hungarian refugees in 1956 and had the double purpose of encouraging migration from Cuba and, at the same time, neutralizing the increasing opposition that the massive arrival of immigrants generated in Florida. Thinking that these persons would quickly return to Cuba, the program's developers initially estimated its cost at only $4 million, and set as one of its principal objectives the temporary relocation of the Cuban immigrants in other states. The Cuban-American demographer Félix Masud-Piloto has documented that of the 447,795 immigrants registered in the program between 1961 and 1972, 66.3 percent were at some time relocated to other areas.[42] The relocation plan, however, confronted realities that in the long run made it impractical. First, these persons ended up staying in the United States for life, contrary to anyone's expectations. This reinforced the attraction of the Miami enclave and, consequently, most of those who had been relocated to other places returned there. Second, the dispersion was contrary to the counterrevolutionary function the U.S. government had assigned to the émigrés, which required a certain degree of demographic concentration. In the end, the Cuban Refugee Program ran until 1975 and spent over $100 million per year,[43] becoming the biggest and costliest program of its kind ever carried out in the United States.

To reduce these costs as well as to ease the process of obtaining permanent residence and citizenship in the United States, the Johnson administration sponsored in 1966 the Cuban Adjustment Act. The law reaffirmed the special character of this group as compared to all other immigrants. Cubans were automatically granted political asylum, they were exempt from the quota restrictions established by the Immigration Act of 1965, and after one year they could opt for permanent residency without having to exit the country, as required for all the rest. This meant that practically all Cubans living in the United States were immediately eligible to become residents or citizens. Nevertheless, while the Cuban Refugee Program was in effect it had limited impact on their status, since by remaining refugees they enjoyed privileges not enjoyed even by U.S. nationals. But once the program ended, it motivated an increase in naturalizations, promoted their participation in U.S. political affairs, and encouraged the subsequent illegal immigration.

The political objective of converting the Cuban-American community into a model of success vis-à-vis the Cuban Revolution made it possible for them to be assimilated more quickly and become more prosperous than other immigrant groups. As early as 1970, Lourdes Casal stated:

> the studies of assimilation and adjustment appear to indicate that the Cubans have adjusted significantly well in the United States, that after their initial influx took Miami by surprise they have not become a social problem. All indicators of social disorganization and maladjustment are low (dependency, crime, juvenile delinquency, mental illness, etc.). A very singular program of social assistance for refugees is in fact partially responsible for this success, but the characteristics of the refugees themselves have certainly been a factor. The adoption of the new culture has been adequate, varying with the degree of social and economic compensation derived from their current life in the United States as compared to their pre-exile experience and with the presence or absence of a strong Cuban community.[44]

For Casal, as for most sociologists of the time, the presence of strong ethnic communities delayed the process of social integration. However, by 1980 it was possible to speak of the category "Cuban-American" within the North American social structure.

It is difficult to establish absolute patterns to characterize the process of social integration in a nation such as the United States, comprised of successive waves of immigrants of various national and class origins, who arrived in the country at diverse historical periods. Integration is synonymous with acceptance, but insertion into a new society does not occur at the same pace for all individuals. Objective and subjective conditions establish so many differences that when speaking of social integration one should only think in terms of tendencies that characterize a social process rich in individual manifestations. Things are not the same for the first generation of immigrants as for their descendants, nor can we disregard the economic and social status of the group in question compared to the rest of society. It is not even an issue exclusive to immigrants: it must be remembered that most of the Hispanic population of the United States did not have to migrate, rather it was those already living in the territories of Mexico and Puerto Rico who were victims of U.S. colonization. It is more probable that a recently arrived European felt more integrated into U.S. society than an African-American whose grandparents arrived 150 years before. At least integration means different things to each. The issue of integration does not have the same importance for all persons. It is of particular interest to subordinate groups, because it implies a certain abatement of the discrimination to which they have been victims. It is no coincidence that the condition of minority is emphasized—with an underlying discriminatory intention—precisely in the surnames of the less advantaged groups: *African-American* and *Hispanic-American* are terms used much more frequently than those that refer to groups of European origin.

For those scholars who embrace the extreme version of the melting pot,[45] *assimilation* means that the individual breaks with his culture of origin to insert himself within the dominant culture, and that he distances himself from his ethnic group or even that those groups disappear—a sociological theory termed *acculturation.*

> Despite appearances, however, the processes of modernization, acculturation, and assimilation have been inexorable, constantly working to transform minority values and loyalties and bring them in line with those of larger society. Each immigrant group has had to adjust Old World values and associate itself with larger groups. . . . Cuban immigrants, no less than any of their immigrant predecessors, have faced the forces of acculturation and assimilation, and although they are still in an early stage, those social, political, and economic forces are

> working their "melting pot" magic. . . . For many Cuban-Americans, the acculturation process—the tendency of immigrants to adopt the material culture and language of their new society—had already started before they arrived in the United States.[46]

Without denying that the process of social integration objectively implies the mixture and adaptation of minority groups, the melting pot theory reflects a rather simplistic vision of the cultural and ethnic homogeneity achieved by North American society and demonstrates a certain xenophobic reaction toward the new immigrants. On the contrary, other scholars emphasize that the multiethnic character of that society tends to reaffirm the identity of origin of the individuals and to preserve the structures that give life to their communities, without this being an obstacle to their integration into the whole insofar as they simultaneously assume the values common to the general society.[47] Analyzing the migratory issue in the United States, historian Hugh Brogan explains that the immigrants generally tend to remain attached to their ethnic communities due to the need for the solidarity of their reference group.[48] I might add that in the case of U.S. society, this is a process that transcends the context of the immigrants and is reproduced in their descendants, which constitutes a specific form of organization of society. This does not always imply, however, the survival of the enclaves.

Without pretending to say the final word on a matter so debated, I believe that the Cubans, like most immigrants to the United States, have integrated to the degree that their ethnic group has perceived itself as North American and has been accepted as such by society as a whole. This is a process that implies the formation of a new identity, which assumes the values, norms, and aspirations of the receptive society, modifying—but not eliminating—the ethnic and national-origin features that give the immigrant group a unique character and convert it into what some anthropological currents denote as an ethnic-national minority. This concept entails a class connotation, insofar as it refers not only to the cultural and national-origin characteristics of these groups, but also to their subordinate position within a given scheme of national dominance. Social integration constitutes, therefore, a phenomenon with origins in the economic relations established by subordinate groups with the dominant group, which consequently expresses itself at the cultural and political superstructure at both levels. Important indicators to gauge the degree of integration are economic adjustment, consolidation of a unique social structure, and degree of participation in national politics. At the limit, the political and social rights granted to an ethnic group and that they can exercise in the receptive society are a result and reflection of their integration.

Although integration is not an outcome that depends exclusively on individuals' determination, and at times occurs in spite of it, no doubt the desire to assimilate, and to be accepted, constitute powerful incentives in the integration process. In 1966, 83 percent of the Cuban immigrants living in Miami declared their intention to return to Cuba if the revolutionary government was overthrown.[49] Barely a decade later, in 1979, surveys carried out by Cuban-American sociologist Alejandro Portes indicate that 95.9 percent would settle permanently in the United States, only 22.6 percent considered the possibility of returning in the event of political change in Cuba, and 62.5 percent did not feel discriminated against in the United States.[50] In another survey, taken by Sergio Bendixen in 1992, only 20 percent considered the possibility of returning to Cuba if there was a political change on the island.[51] And a poll carried out in Miami and Union City by researchers at Florida International University in 1995 shows an increase in this figure to 31 percent, a result possibly influenced by the new arrivals.[52]

In analyzing the process of integration of the Cuban immigrants, we observe that these persons came from a society that belongs to the scant 10 percent of nations that are ethnically homogeneous, only to become uprooted and integrate into North American society as a minority group. This was unique to Cuban society, whose culture and ethnic characteristics had, until then, maintained a singular expression within the context of its national territory. The Cuban-American constitutes a unique social being, connected to Cuban society through strong emotional ties and common historical and cultural roots, yet different from a member of that society as to many acquired values—so different are their goals, motivations, and priorities resulting from the conditions of their existence and, especially, their patriotic point of reference.

Nevertheless, integration through the acceptance of an ethnic group reinforces the need to preserve the unique ethnicity that fuels the integration process. Thus, the ties with their country of origin become essential for reinforcing this identity, particularly in the young. This explains the importance for the Cuban-American community of a solution to the political dispute with Cuba. It is crucial to their cultural survival, with all the economic, political, and social implications this has. Only by maintaining these contacts can the Cuban-American community keep alive the cultural traditions that tend to vanish because of existential imperatives. Recent studies indicate that, although Spanish continues to predominate in 90 percent of Cuban-American homes, 65 percent of those who make up the second generation of immigrants (U.S. born of Cuban parents) prefer English and this preference extends to 100 percent of the third generation. Increasingly we observe tendencies toward dispersion in specific zones of residence and toward interethnic marriage.[53]

Social integration is followed by the development of a unique ideology that incorporates both old and new values and adapts them to the current reality. This ideology constitutes a relevant element for the immigrants' relations with the rest of the society and significantly influences the possibilities for communication with the country origin. The core of the Cuban-American ideology has been a counterrevolutionary purpose that has decisively influenced the rest of its components. This interest has modified political standards and heightened a conservative fanaticism uncommon in Cuban political tradition, extending it to areas of political interest beyond the Cuban issue. The conceptual core of the counterrevolutionary ideology has been Plattism (see chapter 1).

Abel Prieto defines Plattism as the tendency of "castrated Cubanness"—born prior to the revolutionary victory and even independence, present in the émigrés as well as in the country—that accepts the most superficial and external aspects of Cuban culture to become "accomplices of Cuba's denationalization." He argues that annexationism "sleeps in all manifestations of this culture, regardless of how noisily 'Cuban' they are presented,"[54] and adds some interesting hypotheses about its manner of expression among the émigrés. "The first exiles are the bearers, on the one hand, of a very vigorous national culture; but on the other, they brought with them a cultural legacy of Plattism that, once grafted onto the North American society, is enriched in various ways. . . . The political and class profile of the first exiles, and the governmental programs of aid and manipulation, in favor of U.S. interests, together with the pressure and political maneuvers of the annexationist sectors of the immigration, have contributed to the consolidation of this variant of the culture of dependency. . . . Certain paradoxes can be observed in the conservation of this superficial 'Cubanness': it is not a question of resisting integration into North American society, but rather a particular alternative of integration."[55]

While in effect as a supplement to the Cuban constitution, the Platt Amendment was a crude expression of the limits imposed on the sovereignty of the nation—certainly an imperfect formula of neocolonial domination, given its transparency. At the extreme of the Plattist spectrum are those who, before and after 1959, advocated U.S. military intervention whenever they felt their interests were threatened and believed the nation's problems were impossible for the Cubans themselves to solve. This option, endorsed by almost all counterrevolutionary groups, has enjoyed the backing of the majority of the postrevolutionary émigrés on many occasions, constituting an ideological barrier against the essence of nationalist thinking in Cuba. In the words of José Martí, this nationalism implies "a competent Cuban, master of himself, jealous of his humblest rights, accustomed to the intercourse of the rights of others, irate only when less proven Cubans consider him incompetent, strong of body and soul to conquer liberty and preserve it."[56] The conflict between Cuba and the United States has established political conditions for the émigrés that have nurtured this culture of dependency. One variant of this attitude advocates economic strangulation through blockade and other measures. But even some who reject the most aggressive measures propose peaceful solutions and recognize the need to respect certain national rights, in many cases encourage other forms of intervention, and grant the United States unjustified authority over the Cuban nation.

Other issues related to the welfare and political interests of the émigrés have similarly influenced the ideology that accompanies integration. Economic neoliberalism, capital flight, and trade inequality between the United States and Latin America have been particularly fruitful for the economy of Miami and influential on the positions of the Cuban-American community toward the problems of the region. The coincidence in points of view between the Cuban-American community and North American conservatives, together with the preferential treatment received by the former from the U.S. government, have determined the role played by the Cuban-Americans within the Hispanic movement and their electoral preferences to date. As a result Cuban-Americans have become one of the most conservative groups in U.S. society, and have adopted a political posture that nourishes, for new reasons and in new ways, their counterrevolutionary vocation. The Cuban-American enclave in Miami has been the base of support for these positions. From there they have strengthened the political power of Cuban-Americans in southern Florida and allowed them a disproportionate representation at the national level.

The Capital of the Counterrevolution

The Cuban-American enclave in Miami constitutes the epicenter of the Cuban community in the United States and serves as the cultural standard even for those who live outside the area. At Florida's southeastern tip, Miami-Dade County[57] has a population in excess of 2 million people. Over half are of Latin origin—in fact, Miami is the only major U.S. city whose population is mainly Hispanic—and some 500,000 are Cuban-Americans. This region constitutes the third richest Hispanic market in the country and its members consume 37.1 percent of the goods and services produced in the area.[58] It is also one of the principal centers of Catholicism in the United States, although as of 1995, only 25 of its 600 priests are of Cuban origin.[59]

Miami's economic structure depends to a great degree on foreign trade, with tourism from and services to Latin America. Approximately 200 multinational corporations have their Latin American offices in the area. Fifty percent of Florida's foreign trade is generated in Miami, and its ports and airports handle 90 percent of U.S. shipments to Latin America. In 1993 the foreign trade of the Miami region was valued at $25.6 billion, and its 4.7 million foreign visitors generated an additional $7.2 billion in business. Foreign deposits in southern Florida banks—mostly capital fleeing from Latin America—totaled $25 billion in that year, which generated additional financial, legal, and technical services.[60] In the last three decades Miami has been one of the fastest growing U.S. cities. The economic, political, and social context of that growth must be understood in order to correctly analyze the role played by the Cuban-Americans at different levels of U.S. politics. Miami has become the center of U.S. trade with Latin America, an important financial market, and the port of entry of a good share of the illegal drugs consumed in the United States.

The arrival of the Cuban immigrants beginning in 1959 initially caused an increase in unemployment, a reduction in wages, and a deterioration of social assistance to the area. However, the Cuban

Refugee Program and the government funds related to the secret war against Cuba significantly stimulated the region's economy. Not only did the CIA spend vast resources there, but those investments also generated an economic infrastructure that developed its own dynamics, provided other incomes, and provided contacts that allowed many immigrants, originally linked to counterrevolutionary activities, to establish businesses permanently. Therefore, it is precisely the CIA's intervention in the area, organizing a network of interests based on a policy of hostility toward Cuba, that was a key factor in the process that would transform the counterrevolution into a domestic political issue in the United States.

This infrastructure also served as cover for drug running, turning Miami into one of the principal centers of international drug traffic. Seventy percent of the cocaine and marijuana distributed in the United States enters the country through southern Florida, a business estimated nationally at $80 billion annually.[61] Illegal drug traffic has influenced the entire Miami economy as well as the legal and political functioning of its society. In particular, the banking system and the real estate market have been connected in various ways to the drug market. It is estimated that half the $15 billion that on average are invested annually in real estate in the region comes from illegal sources, as well as half the annual cash surplus of banks, calculated at between $6 and $8 billion. This illegal share is double the national average.[62]

In Miami the presence of organized crime goes back to the 1930s and since its origin it has included links with elements of Cuban origin, a connection that has had political connotations for Cuba, both in the republican period as well as in the subsequent counterrevolutionary activity. Nevertheless, it was in the 1970s that the Miami Cubans–organized crime connection assumed its current proportion and profile. The role of the Cubans in drug trafficking has evolved, from one of dealing and distribution to tasks more related to money laundering and legal and financial support. Moreover, perfectly legitimate businesses today had their origin in drug trafficking. Due to this evolution, the drug business has ceased being a marginal activity and become a prime source of employment and inserted itself into the political structure of the region. In 1993 Miami ranked first in drug-related crime among the largest metropolitan areas in the United States. It was also first in violent crimes and crimes against property.[63] Add to this the high level of racial tensions that at various times have exploded into rioting.

The massive arrival of Cuban immigrants beginning in 1959 coincided with the increase in U.S. investments in the most productive sectors of the Latin American economies and with a renewed political interest in the region, not unrelated to the Cuban Revolution. This meant an increase in job opportunities for many of the first Cuban immigrants, who besides having the necessary qualifications had the advantage of prior ties with North American corporations and the trust that their political background inspired. The first wave of immigrants was thus able to take advantage of a favorable situation and, at the same time, provide part of the human capital essential to the development of southern Florida. These immigrants served also as a base for the development of an ethnic Hispanic market that easily linked up with the Latin American market. Many Cuban-Americans took management, technical, and professional positions in large U.S. corporations oriented toward Latin America. This intermediary role in the service of North American multinationals established a community of interest that reflected their political attitudes. In part, the Cuban-American community took advantage quickly, from a privileged position, of the emergence of a process of economic globalization that required a technocracy capable of interacting with dependent Latin American markets.

This role was strengthened to the degree that Miami also became the political center of the Latin American right. More than a refuge for its capital and a traditional haven for the groups displaced from power, the Latin American oligarchy found here a center for its political activity. With the support of the Cuban-American community, the city provided the links and professional services that allowed these groups to receive counsel and broaden their influence in the United States. Miami has also served as a focal point for conspiracies and operations of the counterrevolution in the continent and one of the key hubs of international arms traffic.

The influence of Cuban-Americans in southern Florida has multiplied their impact over the rest of the Hispanic-American movement. Even though Cuban-Americans represent only 4.8 percent of the Hispanic population of the United States, Miami is home to nearly a third of the fifty largest Hispanic companies in the nation, two of the country's three Hispanic television networks, two of the five top Spanish-language newspapers, nine Spanish-language radio stations, and most of the Latin-music record labels.[64] Among the seventy wealthiest Hispanic millionaires in the United States—those with assets in excess of $25 million—twenty-five are Cuban-American and eighteen of those live in southern Florida.[65]

As has been pointed out by Cuban-American sociologists Marifeli Pérez-Stable and Miren Uriarte, much of the Cuban-American labor force has managed to improve its status at each juncture of the development of Miami's economy. In 1960 one-third of the labor force was employed in the manufacturing sector, but the occupational distribution evolved rather quickly to specialized services such as banking, trade, and tourism, which by 1988 employed 23.6 percent of the economically active Cuban-American population.[66] This hypothesis is also supported by the Cuban-American demographers Portes and Rumbaut, who argue that, although Cuban-American workers have generally benefited from the selective employment established within the enclave, such practices offer limited opportunities,[67] and, one might add, restrain the possibilities for climbing the social ladder.

The occupational distribution of the Miami Cubans within the economy also changed significantly in the process that accompanies their social integration. While in 1970 only 14 percent occupied positions as managers, professionals, and technicians, by 1988 this ratio increased to 31.2 percent. Similarly, the proportion employed in less skilled jobs such as office clerks, salespersons, and manual and service workers decreased from 71 percent to 59 percent.[68] At the same time that a segment of this community had risen on the employment ladder, another was stranded in some of the lowest-paying jobs in the area, resulting in a highly polarized employment structure.[69] On the basis of these elements, Pérez-Stable and Uriarte conclude that, despite the preferential treatment they received, only 20 percent of the labor force matches the image of economic success that some have generalized for the whole community.

These differences are particularly evident when the first wave of immigrants is compared with those that arrived later, beginning with the third generation of émigrés. Even though they came from another sociological context, the newer immigrants possessed levels of education and training that should have allowed them to adapt just as well to the requirements of the receptive society. However, studies carried out at the University of Florida demonstrate that after 1980 the adaptation of Cuban immigrants was much less successful. These groups exhibit economic indices similar to those of African-Americans, who are at the bottom of the economic scale in the region.[70]

Taken as a whole the social and economic indicators of Cuban-Americans in southern Florida lie somewhere between those of non-Latin whites and the blacks, although, viewed historically, the trend is toward improvement over time, evidence of their integration into the overall economy. A significant indicator is that over time Cuban-Americans have received, on average, less discriminatory pay for the same jobs, indicating that they are approaching the more privileged sectors of the society at a faster pace than other minorities.[71] This process has occurred amid deep and sometimes dramatic racial tensions. Discriminated against by whites, Cuban-Americans appear, in turn, to discriminate against all other Latin American groups and especially against blacks, who accuse them of having taken their jobs and having received preferential treatment from the government, and who refuse to do business with them in the enclave. The Mariel crisis and the difference in treatment received by the illegal Haitian immigrants reinforced this animosity and, even though it was not the only or even the most important cause, it became a contributing factor to the social explosions that led to rioting by Miami blacks in 1968, 1980, and 1982.

In reference to the Cuban-American bourgeoisie and petite bourgeoisie, studies by Cuban economists Roxana Brizuela and Luis Fernández-Tabío indicate that they are proprietors of 61,470 businesses, with earnings of $54 billion annually. Ninety percent of these, however, are small businesses within the enclave that together generate only 34 percent of the enclave's income. The principal economic power is concentrated in 600 corporations that account for over 60 percent of the earnings.[72] According to the *Miami Herald,* in 1986 there were 700 millionaires in the Cuban community in the United States.[73]

On the basis of these data, we can conclude that the assets of the Cuban-American bourgeoisie, within the enclave and beyond, come from four main sources. First are investments in multinational corporations, resulting mostly from capital of the Cuban national bourgeoisie that at the time of the revolutionary victory was already connected with large U.S. corporations. Second are the businesses of the enclave, which do not possess the biggest assets but are certainly the most numerous. The other two sources are assets linked to U.S. corporations with investments in Florida and capital accumulated from drug trafficking, which has ramifications in other sectors of the economy. The composition of this capital helps to explain certain political behavior of its owners. Until now the stratum of the bourgeoisie that dominates the political life of the community has been precisely that which depends on enclave businesses. This is logical, since it is crucial for this group to strengthen the influence of the Cuban-Americans in local politics. It can be argued that these assets have their origin in counterrevolutionary activity and that this is the key to maintaining the political status that assures Cuban-Americans their access to the principal centers of power in the United States. Thus the predominance of this group has been accompanied necessarily by very conservative positions, interested in maintaining the focus of attention on Cuba on the basis of attitudes that encourage maximum hostility.

It is difficult to assess the impact of the sector connected to drug trafficking, although the experience of some judicial proceedings suggests that their participation in the community's political affairs is widespread, for reasons similar to the Miami bourgeoisie, from which many of the individuals involved in drug trafficking came. The Cuban-American sector connected to North American corporations based in Florida is notably lacking in political representation in the enclave, although they are duly inserted into the region's economic and political elite. The Cuban-American executives of large corporations show little interest in local politics. However, in the last few years there has been an increase in contacts between this sector and the Cuban-American political groups in the enclave, possibly in order to take advantage of the political contacts that the latter have developed in the various U.S. centers of power.

Available data does not permit an exact quantification of the class distribution of the Cuban-American community established in the enclave. As an approximation of reality I will attempt to define a social pyramid within the economically active population. At the top is the bourgeoisie, representing no more than one percent of the total. Next comes the middle class, from which about 8 percent are small business owners and 30 percent executives and professionals. The working class comprises the remaining 60 percent, of which the bottom 40 percent of the pyramid hold the lowest-paid jobs. Unemployment has historically fluctuated between 5 and 10 percent of the active labor force. Retirees, and the aged in general, constitute one of the lowest and most disadvantaged groups in the enclave's social scale, and an undetermined but significant number of persons live off marginal and unlawful activities. These indicators reproduce rather accurately the occupational composition (which is not the same as social status) and class structure that this population exhibited in Cuba before the Revolution.[74]

According to reports by Americas Watch, the political climate of Miami is among the most repressive in the country and includes everything from physical force to the extensive use of the mass media and pressures on businesses, employment, and social life of those who stray from counterrevolutionary positions. But it would be erroneous to suppose that the political and ideological patterns of the counterrevolutionary bourgeoisie have been imposed purely by coercive means. The counterrevolutionary bourgeoisie is a product of a policy that has benefited, to a greater or lesser degree, the entire Cuban immigration, and this preferential relationship with the U.S. system, independently of its contradictions, has imposed a counterrevolutionary ideology on the majority of the émigré community. The basis for the counterrevolutionary attitude, reproduced time and time again under different conditions, lies in U.S. policy toward Cuba and the interests generated therefrom. The Cuban-American bourgeoisie opposes a rapprochement between the United States and Cuba not only for historical reasons, but also because through the counterrevolution it found a source of benefits and political space that is a determining factor in maintaining its dominance within the enclave and its ascendancy in national politics. This, above all, explains the renewed vigor of its intransigence.

Cuban-Americans in U.S. Politics

In the 1960s a Cuban immigrant that adopted U.S. citizenship was considered a traitor to his country by the counterrevolutionary movement. José Miró Cardona, testifying before the U.S. Senate in late 1961, summarized the counterrevolutionary position regarding integration: "[Cuban] men, women, and children [in the U.S.] have just one purpose: to go back [to Cuba] and fight . They would rather fight and die than try to remake their lives in a friendly but foreign country. Every day they await the order to take up arms, to fight communism, and, especially, to fight it in Cuba. They want to keep their dignity intact. They do not fear adversity; they want to go back. Therein lies the fundamental reason for the Cuban exiles' determination to stay in Miami, one hour's flight from Cuba."[75]

The historical reality was that those who had to give the "order" never gave it, and things changed rapidly thereafter. A new rationale was found for naturalization: it increased the influence of Cuban-Americans in the United States and thus helped the Cuban cause. Almost immediately after Cuban Refugee Program was halted, some 178,000 residents of Cuban origin became naturalized citizens. This figure represented almost 30 percent of all Cuban immigrants and 12 percent of all naturalizations that took place in the 1970s.[76] According to the U.S. Immigration and Naturalization Service, in the 1980s another 109,077 Cubans took that step.[77]

According to the 1990 census, the number of persons of Cuban origin living in the United States was 1,053,197. Of those, 71.7 percent were Cuban-born (of whom 50.3 percent had been naturalized), and the remaining 28.3 percent were born in the United States to Cuban parents. Of the entire Cuban-American community in the United States, 678,345 persons (64.4 percent) were U.S. citizens. Studies by Ernesto Rodríguez indicate that in 1990 the number of Cuban-American voters was approximately 400,000. According to the 1990 census, 561,868 Cuban-Americans lived specifically in Miami-Dade County, of whom 65 percent were U.S. citizens, which works out to approximately 180,000 eligible Cuban-American voters.[78]

It is much more difficult to ascertain the number of these citizens that registered to vote and actually went to the polls, since voting statistics do not include voters' national origin, but refer only to general ethnic group (e.g., Hispanic). Studies carried out in the Miami area by Portes indicate that Cuban-Americans exhibit a higher degree of voter participation than other minority groups, and thus are closer to the national average.[79] Nevertheless, in absolute terms their electoral impact is very limited: Cuban-Americans represent less than 5 percent of the electorate in Florida and less than 1 percent of the nation's. Nor is their financial contribution relevant to the national political campaigns, whose costs total hundreds of millions of dollars. These indicators demonstrate that the impact of the Cuban-American electorate on U.S. political processes cannot be evaluated by their specific national weight, but by the way in which Cuban-Americans empower their local capacities and interact in the political system. It is not only a question of political culture. The Cuban-American bourgeoisie has created political machinery capable of mobilizing this vote, collecting funds and interrelating with other interests, negotiating support for causes that increase their real force, and allowing them to insert themselves into the operation of the U.S. political system.

The search for consensus in U.S. politics constitutes a complex process of alliances and compromises in which the specific weight of each ingredient expresses itself through multiple factors. Among these are: the relative importance of different regions, the organization and control of political forces, the desire to participate, the interest for the issue at hand, and the influence and personality of the politicians involved. Viewed from this perspective, the weight of Cuban-Americans in issues as controversial as abortion or welfare is insignificant, but that group does affect issues such as relations with Cuba, a long-standing and often debated topic that nevertheless lacks the force to mobilize or polarize most of the nation's electorate.

The weight of the Cuba question in the political behavior of the Cuban-American community has tilted their preference toward conservative politicians who pronounce themselves in favor of maintaining an intransigent policy toward Cuba and encourage the hope of intervention. In 1983, although 47 percent were registered Democrats, Cuban-Americans were the U.S. population group that most supported Ronald Reagan, and even in the 1996 election 75 percent voted for George Bush over Bill Clinton. At present, according to surveys carried out at Florida International University, 37 percent are registered Republicans and only 11 percent Democrats,[80] a pattern very different from other Hispanics. However, the majority favored social welfare programs, in open contradiction to basic conservative tenets, according to studies carried out in the 1980s.[81] Recently Cuban-American voters have continued to oppose budget cuts and the immigration policies proposed by the Republican majority in Congress. Nevertheless, these concerns have not significantly affected their electoral conduct. This conservative, pro-Republican attitude has limited the capacity of Cuban-Americans to penetrate the Hispanic movement, despite both the efforts of the Republican Party since 1980 to attract their votes and the role played by Cuban-American politicians in this endeavor.

In terms of domestic politics, the success of the Cuban-Americans has been centered in the influence they have acquired in southern Florida. The only place where the Cuban-American vote can be decisive is in Miami, where it represents over 40 percent of the electorate. According to studies by Guillermo Grenier of Florida International University, in contrast with most cities with a large Hispanic electorate, whose political alienation allows them to be practically ignored, no politician can hope to win an election in Miami-Dade County by ignoring the Cuban-American vote.[82]

The first associations with certain domestic political objectives were the "municipalities in exile," social organizations that organized and mobilized relatively wide sectors of the émigré community. In the mid-1970s, Manolo Reboso, an associate of Manuel Artime, was the first Cuban-American elected to public office in the United States.[83] His election was related to the victory of Puerto Rican Maurice Ferre for mayor of Miami that broke a historic electoral pattern in that city's politics and emphasized the growing importance of the Cuban-American vote. The process continued and after a few unsuccessful attempts, in 1982 the Cuban-American candidate Raúl Martínez was elected mayor of Hialeah, the second most important city in Miami-Dade County, and Xavier Suárez became the first Cuban-American mayor of Miami in 1985. Today Cuban-Americans control the management of all the municipalities where they are concentrated, enjoy a five-member majority on the County Commission, and in the state legislature their representation has increased from three representatives in 1982 to ten representatives and three senators.

Two Cuban-Americans from Florida and one from New Jersey hold seats in the U.S. House of Representatives. The presence of three Cuban-Americans in the U.S. Congress represents a significant representation in the debate over those issues affecting the Cuban-American community—including the relations with Cuba—and a greater conservative influence over the "Hispanic Caucus," comprised of seventeen legislators. Cuban-Americans are thus the best represented, proportionately, of any minority group in the country. Florida Congresspersons Ileana Ros and Lincoln Díaz-Balart, both Republicans, represent the forces of the extreme right of the Cuban-American bourgeoisie that control the politics of the enclave. New Jersey Democrat Bob Menéndez, for his part, has allegedly maintained historical ties with the terrorist groups based in Union City, his home district, and with the Italian-American political machine linked to organized crime in the region.

It is interesting to note that the first attempts at political participation by the Cuban-American community took place within the structures of the Democratic Party. Reboso, Martínez, and rest of the first wave of Cuban-American politicians elected in Florida belonged to that party, and a Cuban-American—Alfredo Durán—was even named chairman of the Democratic Party in the state in 1976. This trend was influenced by the historical dominance of the Democrats in the South and the policy of the party in favor of capturing the minority vote. The participation of the Cubans in U.S. politics, channeled through the Democratic machine, showed a certain tendency—still largely undefined—to break with the counterrevolutionary pattern of placing the Cuba issue before the existential problems of the community. This situation changed radically in 1980 as a result of the rise to power of the neoconservative Republicans and their policy of alliance with the counterrevolutionary extreme right, which in this manner breaks into the domestic political scene, becoming the principal force of the Republican Party in the state.

During the 1980s the Cuban-American groups in Miami organized political machines capable of capitalizing to the maximum the political potential arising from their electoral and financial capacity and their contacts with the North American centers of power. They were able to make themselves felt in U.S. policy toward Cuba to a degree that was obviously above their real weight in the economic and political life of the country. Various factors contributed to these inroads of Cuban-Americans into U.S. domestic politics. First was the high concentration of this population in an area of economic boom. Second was the consolidation within this enclave of an elite with sufficient economic power and political experience to organize and control this electoral base and interact with the rest of the system. Third was the convenience for the North American power elite of counting on these émigrés in their policy toward Cuba and in the overall policy toward Latin America. Finally, there was the ideological coincidence with those sectors that have dominated national politics since the 1980s, which assigned the Cuban-American community new political functions, this time related to the growth of Republican influence in Florida and the rise of conservative sectors within the Hispanic movement.

The key element in this process was precisely the coincidence between the emergence of a neoconservative offensive in U.S. politics, and the maturity of the process of social integration of the Cuban-American community. This correspondence permitted the extreme-right political sectors to introduce themselves into this process, contributing their control over a small but militant and well-placed electorate that likewise provided a certain degree of legitimacy to the policy that the Reagan administration pretended to put in place toward Cuba. The counterrevolutionary function of the Cuban émigrés was thereby revitalized and once again it proved a source of important benefits for their economic welfare and their participation in the political affairs of the nation. This process was accompanied by a crucial change in the nature of the counterrevolution: as of this moment it became essentially a domestic issue. The new counterrevolutionary organizations would define themselves as North American entities whose function was to influence the system as a whole in order that the United States pursue a policy toward Cuba in accordance with their opinions and interests. Plattism thus assumed its crudest form. Independent of its nationalist rhetoric, we are in the presence of an annexationist current because their Cuban-American actors have already been formally and spiritually annexed.

Chapter 7

The Counterrevolution Renewed

JUST AS THE Keynesian Welfare State turned out to be the solution to the crisis of governability faced by the U.S. political system in the 1930s, the New Right movement pretended to become the unqualified answer to the crisis of hegemony that challenged the United States fifty years later. The victory of the Cuban Revolution, the U.S. defeat in Vietnam, racial rioting, Watergate, the Iranian Revolution, the growth of national liberation movements in Africa and Latin America, the energy crisis, and the recurrent cycles of inflation and recession shattered the consensus that had sustained U.S. postwar politics and caused the voters to lose faith in the system.

The 1980 political platform of the Republican Party described the crisis in the most somber terms:

> The U.S. is aimless. Our nation drifts in agony, without course, almost without design, in one of the most dangerous and disorderly periods in history. . . . Domestically our economy totters: early this year inflation reached the highest level in over a century; weeks later the economy plummeted, registering the steepest downturn ever recorded. Prices are increasing at over 10 percent annually. Over 8 million people

> are looking for work. Factories are closing all over the country. The hopes and ambitions of our people are being drowned. Internationally, the already dangerous conditions are deteriorating. For the first time the Soviet Union is acquiring the means to destroy or dismantle our system of land-based missiles and threaten us into submission. Marxist tyrannies are expanding ever more rapidly in the Third World and Latin America. Our alliances in Europe and the rest of the world are wearing down. Our energy sources are dependent more and more each day on unreliable foreign suppliers. . . . In the last humiliation suffered in Iran, militant terrorists continue to play with the lives of Americans.[1]

The neoconservative movement demanded a profound renewal of values and methods capable of restoring their legitimacy and popular support. Until that time the conservatives had distanced themselves from the premises that had inspired the expansion of U.S. capitalism, defying a liberal tradition deeply rooted in the nation's history. But the crisis revitalized conservative principles related to family, religion, and individual liberty versus the growing power of government bureaucracy, turning them into powerful ideological resources for the mobilization of important sectors of the population, especially the middle class, that were dissatisfied with their situation and concerned for the future of the nation. Neoconservatives magnified these fears, encouraged rigid and primitive religious and ethical principles, and incorporated them into a new right-wing vision of capitalism. This view accepted the logic of monopolies and rejected the traditional isolationism of the conservative message, openly defending the alleged right of the United States to claim supreme power over the rest of humanity. Just as trilateralism had done before, neoconservatism fulfilled the function of legitimizing and reordering the U.S. system of hegemony. But this time it was from another angle of the global perspective—emphasizing military and geopolitical aspects—in line with the specific conditions of contemporary transnational capitalism.

Groups representing diverse and occasionally contradictory schools of thought joined forces in the neoconservative movement, united by the desire to remodel the political system and empower U.S. hegemony throughout the world. The were joined by neoconservative philosophers, designers of the ideological support base of the movement; economists of the neoliberal schools; religious fundamentalists; the New Right, bent on modernizing conservative political practices; and political circles urging a "confrontation of civilizations" in the context of the return to the more aggressive postures of the Cold War.[2] Conservative criticism was not only directed at the Democrats. The neoconservatives questioned practically everything: the legitimacy of the welfare function of the state, the New Deal strategy, environmental protection laws, the entire U.S. foreign policy, and the gains for minorities obtained by the civil rights movement since the 1960s. The core of the neoconservative challenge was their rejection of the doctrine of Soviet contention, and specifically the policy of détente, proposing instead that those political processes that were not compatible with U.S. interests could be reversed.

But despite its outward projection and international consequences, the neoconservative offensive was fundamentally directed at North American society. The conservative message inspired a domestic ideological movement that was to recover legitimacy and forge a consensus. Therefore, neoconservatism became in the first place a movement of political influence directed at U.S. public opinion. Its participants included a respectable corps of scholars, research centers, modern propaganda devices, and political action committees. Ronald Reagan, an exponent of traditional conservatism, was adopted by the new conservatives to serve as advanced guard in this crusade. His shallow political culture and simple arguments did not prevent his communications skills and undisputed personal charisma from contributing significantly to popularizing the neoconservative message.

The New Right considered that U.S. policy toward Latin America in particular required deep changes. The Santa Fe Committee was a conservative think tank that put forward many of the ideas that would undergird for the Reagan administration's policy toward Latin America. In 1980 it declared, "Latin America is vital for the U.S.: the projection of the U.S. as a world power has always rested on a cooperative Caribbean and a supportive Latin America. For the U.S. isolationism is impossible. Containing the Soviet Union is not enough. Détente is dead."[3] The committee expressly assumed the premises of the Monroe Doctrine, proposing that in defining its hemispheric relations the United States should seek to further its interests over any other consideration. Consequently, it argued in favor of: strengthening the role of the Latin American military and accepting those right-wing dictatorships that were necessary for maintaining order in the region; reorganizing the Inter-American Defense Board and placing the Panama Canal under its custody; abandoning the policy of support for human rights when it was to the detriment of governments allied with the United States; equating domestic revolution with external aggression and acting decisively against any manifestation of social rebellion, including "liberation theology"; and implementing reforms in economic relations with Latin America based on stimulating private capital, free trade, and direct investment.

Cuba, Brazil, and Mexico were the three countries in the region that the United States should prioritize. Cuba was considered the most important adversary in the hemisphere and a challenge to the credibility of U.S. hegemony in Latin America. "The United States can only restore its credibility by taking immediate action," stated the Santa Fe Committee in reference to Cuba.[4] It proposed taking "openly punitive" actions that would reverse the steps taken by the Carter administration to improve bilateral relations; launching a political and ideological offensive that would include radio transmissions "openly sponsored by the United States"; and promoting counterrevolution without ruling out armed intervention. At the same time, it recommended letting the Cuban government know that the United States could abandon this policy and be "very generous" if Cuba broke its alliance with the USSR.[5]

In line with the neoconservative strategy of "raising the consciousness" of North American society with a view toward embarking on a new political course, the policy toward the island also required instruments that would facilitate achieving the required consensus. It was necessary, in the first place, to paint such a devilish picture of the Cuban system as to justify any offensive option. "We reclaim the fundamental principle of treating a friend as such and self-proclaimed enemies as such, without excuses," stated the Republican platform.[6] And Cuba was defined by neoconservative rhetoric as a Soviet "vassal," as an "extra-continental aggressor" state, and as the "organizer" of subversion in Latin American and the Caribbean.[7] Ronald Reagan summarized the message: "Cuba is for all practical purposes a Soviet colony."[8]

The policy to follow toward Cuba was detailed in early 1981 by *National Security Directive no. 17 of the President of the United States,* according to which the objective was to develop public pressure against Cuba, bringing to light human and political rights issues and using the Cuban exile community to transmit this message.[9] This plan included creating Cuban-American political instruments that would lend legitimacy and win allies for the government's policy. New right-wing Cuban-American organizations were thus created and the policy toward Cuba was consolidated as part of the domestic ideological debate.

The Cuban-American Ultraright

At the beginning of Cuba's neocolonial period, the ideological denominations of the political parties had little practical significance and were subordinate to specific political alliances. Nevertheless, the

Conservatives were defined more clearly than other tendencies, as the successors of the anti-independence, pro-autonomy movement and open supporters of the Plattist tendency that took shape after the U.S. intervention of 1898. Raimundo Cabrera, one of its principal theorists, stated in 1907, "Undoubtedly the most important thing in the political state of the country is its relations with the United States. What essentially separates the Liberals from the Conservatives in Cuba is the opinion as to whether to establish a greater or lesser dependence between the two peoples. . . . Being a Conservative means allowing our own republican government to be reborn, with the participation and responsibility of the government of the United States in its orderly maintenance. . . . All those who have faith and hope in the future of the country, for the patriotic effort of its children and the guiding and saving action of the United States, should join the ranks of the Conservative Party and lend it their moral and practical support."[10] Beginning in the 1930s the Conservatives drifted toward fascism with the creation of the ABC, one of the anti-Machado groups that joined in the U.S.-sponsored mediation. Later it evolved into the Falangist movement and into organizations of the Catholic right, such as the Agrupación Católica Universitaria, which became some of the principal components of the post-1959 counterrevolution.

The Cuban ultraright, therefore, had organic roots in the counterrevolution and an ideological definition based on some of the most dependent tendencies of neocolonial power in Cuba. In contrast with recent Cuban history, where conservative thinking represented a minority of the population, in the Cuban-American community it had established itself as the predominant ideological trend. This strengthened their union with the U.S. conservative movement.

The Cuban-American ultraright joined the neoconservative movement because of ideological agreement and in order to obtain the political and economic benefits that accompanied this alliance. The union was the logical political expression of a process of social integration marked by the counterrevolutionary function of the émigrés and by the recomposition of a bourgeoisie that had its origins in the Cuban oligarchy, imposing its ideological standards on the rest of society. The Cuban-American counterrevolution subordinated its objectives to U.S. policy, just as previous counterrevolutionary groups had done. The uniqueness of this new counterrevolutionary proposal lies in the way in which they related to the country's power elite. By capitalizing on its contradictions, they took on a role that went beyond the exclusively operational function that they had played in the past.

Beginning in 1980 the counterrevolution joined the most conservative sectors of North American society to influence U.S. public opinion in order to lend legitimacy to a policy of maximum hostility toward Cuba. They contributed their vision, interests, and experience to the analysis and design of the actions that put this policy in practice and collaborated on other domestic and foreign policy projects of the neoconservative movement. In particular, they offered the New Right access to the Hispanic movement, additional strength for their alliance in Florida, and support for Reagan's policy toward Latin America. In exchange for these services they received the recognition necessary to break into the national political system, support for their political machines, and the economic and symbolic benefits that resulted from the increase in their relative political power.

The Cuban-American National Foundation

The Cuban-American National Foundation was formed in 1981 on the initiative of the U.S. government as part of Project Democracy. The CANF was an idea pushed by William Casey, then director of the Central Intelligence Agency, with the objective of obtaining support, inside and outside the United States, for the foreign policy that the Reagan administration sought to carry out. Project Democracy sought to promote new means of intervention through the development of "political assistance" to friendly groups in the Third World.

This assistance would complement the diplomatic efforts, economic aid, and military cooperation that constituted the support mechanisms of the postwar North American system of hegemony. Project Democracy spawned, in December 1983, the National Endowment for Democracy (NED), a public instrument created to channel this political intervention, as well as plans for covert operations—among them the illegal aid to the Nicaraguan counterrevolution, which led to the Iran-Contra scandal.

Until then, political intervention projects had been handled by the CIA and, due to their possible international repercussions, had been done so covertly. The NED—more specialized in its methods and with a long-term focus that the CIA's plans generally lacked—was created with the aim of perfecting this instrument, legitimizing and strengthening its role within the arsenal of resources employed by U.S. policymakers. The legislation approving the NED established that it was a bipartisan project designed

> to encourage free and democratic institutions throughout the world through private sector initiatives; to facilitate exchanges between U.S. private sector groups and democratic groups abroad; to promote U.S. non-governmental participation in democratic training programs and democratic institution-building abroad; to strengthen democratic electoral processes abroad through timely measures in cooperation with indigenous democratic forces; to support the participation of the two major American political parties, labor, business, and other U.S. private sector groups in fostering cooperation with those abroad dedicated to the cultural values, institutions, and organizations of democratic pluralism; and to encourage the establishment and growth of democratic development in a manner consistent both with the broad concerns of the United States' national interests and with the specific requirements of the democratic groups in other countries which are aided by programs funded by the Endowment.[11]

The NED was charged with financing political parties, labor unions, business groups, news media, and civic organizations. The

Democratic and Republican Parties and the unions affiliated with the AFL-CIO procured the majority of the funds and executed or served as a smoke screen for many of the projects. The NED's early projects were associated with the conservative "anticommunist crusade" of the 1980s, but it later adapted to post–Cold War conditions and today constitutes a sophisticated instrument for penetrating political systems and civil societies in those countries that constitute foreign policy objectives.[12]

The implementation of the plans to form a "conservative Cuban-American lobby" was entrusted to Richard Allen, the national security advisor. Allen delegated the task of selecting the leadership of this organization to his assistant, the Cuban-American Mario Elgarresta.[13] The CANF constituted, therefore, an effort similar to that employed by the neoconservative movement in other sectors of North American society, but distinctive in its interrelation with covert operations programs and with plans for foreign political intervention carried out by the Reagan administration. Thus the CANF was an active participant in supplying the Nicaraguan Contras, supporting the UNITA bands in Angola and other operations of this nature.

Cuban-Americans Raúl Masvidal and Carlos Salmán were called to Washington to form the CANF. Some time later they were joined by Jorge Mas Canosa, a business associate of Elgarresta. All three were men with a counterrevolutionary history and acknowledged CIA connections, representatives of those Cuban-American sectors that aroused the greatest interest for the U.S. conservative movement. Masvidal came from family of Cuban oligarchs historically active in national politics. He participated in the Bay of Pigs invasion and, as he himself declared, later carried out missions for the CIA, culminating his career as a prominent Miami banker.[14] Salmán was one of the first Cuban émigrés active in the Republican Party in Florida. Jorge Mas Canosa, a professional counterrevolutionary turned businessman, had no defined party affiliation. They later called upon Frank Calzón, a familiar Cuban-American Washington lobbyist well connected with U.S. neoconservative organizations, to serve as the CANF's executive director and to develop its original design. Initially they conceived a relatively modest project, with a budget of $59,000,[15] that entailed, in practice, uniting the three groups most representative of the Cuban-American ultraright: conservative intellectuals, politicians linked to the Republican Party, and the Miami counterrevolutionary bourgeoisie.

The neoconservative Cuban-American intellectuals were a relatively informal group of scholars, most of whom were connected with the Center for International and Strategic Studies at Georgetown University in Washington, D.C., one of the ideological centers of the U.S. neoconservative movement. The most prominent figures of this group were José Sorzano, Otto Reich, Ernesto Betancourt, and Luis Aguilar León.[16] Some of them later occupied relatively important posts in the Reagan administration, making them the Cuban-American ultraright sector best integrated into the neoconservative movement. They tried to establish themselves as the CANF ideologists, monopolize relations with Washington, and take over the foundation's propaganda. However, their almost exclusive interest in foreign policy issues and their detachment from the rest of the Cuban-American community limited their capacity for influence. Eventually the majority broke with the CANF because of leadership disputes and contradictions as to the foundation's role in Miami politics.

The Cuban-American politicians connected with the Republican Party constituted a small group. The principal figure was Tirso del Junco, a California politician that went on to become the Republican Party's president in that state during the Bush administration. Personally connected with Ronald Reagan, during this period del Junco headed the president's political campaign within the Hispanic Republican movement and thus never associated in an official manner with the CANF. The influence of the Hispanic Republicans in Florida was slight and they were eventually displaced by new politicians with ties to other sectors of the Cuban-American bourgeoisie. Thus

Carlos Salmán and his followers also split from the foundation in the end.

The Miami counterrevolutionary bourgeoisie was barely organized politically in the early 1980s. Situated in the enclave's center of economic power, it had distanced itself from the traditional counterrevolutionary groups and had yet to find a space within the limited domestic political efforts carried out by a few Cuban-American Democratic politicians. The creation of the CANF filled the void and rapidly strengthened this group. Their connections with the neoconservative sectors were weaker than those of the conservative intellectuals and Cuban-American Republican politicians. However, they were better suited to control the rest of the community and mobilize the necessary resources to carry out the plan of the U.S. conservative movement. This won them the leadership of the Cuban-American neoconservative movement and eventually absolute supremacy over the foundation in the person of Jorge Mas Canosa.

The promotion of Mas Canosa to the first level of the counterrevolutionary leadership shows his ability to play by the rules of U.S. domestic politics and capitalize on the economic advantages of these contacts. At no time did he participate in military actions. After a brief period of membership in the Christian Democratic Movement in Cuba, he migrated early on and joined the Bay of Pigs project, forming part of the Nino Díaz group that failed to land. He received training at Fort Benning in 1963 yet he did not participate in paramilitary actions, before or after. His activity within RECE was limited to propaganda: he stood out among the first to foresee the benefits of combining counterrevolutionary activity with U.S. domestic policy. In 1974 Mas Canosa participated in the electoral campaign of the future Democratic senator from Florida, Richard Stone, but in 1980 he switched sides and backed Stone's opponent, Republican Paula Hawkins, becoming one of her chief advisors. His leadership of the CANF assured him a swift rise to political prominence. Before his death in 1997 he came to have access to the three last U.S. presidents and more than twenty foreign leaders.

Even more astounding was Mas Canosa's rise in the business world. In 1968 he was employed by Church and Tower, Inc., in 1971 he bought the company for $50,000, and barely a year later it generated a profit of one million dollars, multiplying ninefold by 1979.[17] Between 1976 and 1980 he faced six lawsuits for nonpayment and for negligence in occupational safety and health. In 1983 his bodyguards, following his orders, shot one of the plaintiffs. In a business-related conflict he beat his brother Ricardo in 1985 and one year later he challenged Miami Commissioner Joe Carollo to a duel when the latter ruined a business operation worth over $100 million.[18] The conflicts with Ricardo continued until 1990, when Jorge was found guilty of defamation and forced to pay over $1 million in indemnity. In the 1980s he faced five more lawsuits. In 1993, Dade[19] County inspectors discover that MBL Paving, listed as a company owned by African-Americans and thus a beneficiary of contracts assigned by law to firms owned by this minority group, had in fact been the property of Mas Canosa since 1984. He thereby illegally obtained contracts worth $61 million.[20] He also had public conflicts with Armando Codina, one of the directors of the CANF, who accused him of manipulating the County Commission for his own benefit.[21]

Church and Tower's contracts were limited to two clients: installing telephone poles for Southern Bell and constructing public works for Dade County. While many companies of its kind failed in that period, Church and Tower recorded profits of 27.5 percent. Of this, 68 percent came from its telephone company contracts and most of the rest from a contract with the county to build a prison whose initial budget was $9.2 million but ended up costing $33 million. The telephone business generated profits of 73 percent in 1991, 88 percent in 1992, and 43 percent in 1993, extraordinary figures when compared to the national average of 12 percent and the fact that in Florida the other two companies that did this work suffered losses. The results were incredible for many specialists, even taking into account the benefits derived from Mas Canosa's political influence in the county and his (suspiciously) special relationship with Southern Bell.

In March 1994, Church and Tower merged with the contracting firm Burnup and Sims to create Mas Tec, in which the Mas family owned 65 percent of the shares and controlled the company. Once again, Mas Canosa had landed in clover. Immediately after the takeover, the share price of the new company shot up from $2 to $8, converting an initial joint capital investment of $10.2 million into $80 million. Despite operating at a sizable loss, Burnup and Sims was a company with clients nationwide, which gave Mas Tec the base to expand into Latin America and other parts of the world. According to some analysts, this reflected Mas Canosa's interest in creating a base for capitalizing on the eventual collapse of the Cuban regime.[22] Mas Tec invested $1.5 million in El Salvador and $7.5 million in Argentina. They even tried doing business in China—demonstrating their lack of political scruples—but the ensuing scandal paralyzed the operation. In this manner, Mas Canosa's capital since assuming the presidency of the CANF catapulted from $9 to $105 million, making him the third richest Hispanic capitalist in the United States, according to the magazine *Hispanic Business.*[23]

Some one hundred Cuban-American businessmen from Miami originally joined the foundation. This group was comprised primarily of first generation immigrants, with a class background that linked them to the old Cuban oligarchy and the Batista regime. Many had been active participants in the first counterrevolutionary organizations and boasted CIA connections. They represented the group that benefited most from government spending in the area, without excluding profiteers from drug trafficking and money laundering. It can be argued that, being relatively young in the 1960s, this group of counterrevolutionaries had a greater opportunity to adapt to the system and capitalize on the benefits derived from their contacts with the power elite. They reflected, to some degree, the midpoint in the mutation process that the Cuban bourgeoisie went through in integrating into U.S. society.

On the advice of Richard Allen, the CANF was modeled after the "Jewish lobby" in the U.S. The design was fashioned by the celebrated attorney of the America-Israel Public Affairs Committee, Barney Barnet.[24] He crafted a complex structure that included the CANF as a nonprofit organization dedicated to education and research, the Cuban-American Foundation charged with lobbying at the various levels of government, and a supposedly independent political action committee whose function was to channel financial contributions without committing the rest of the organization, as established by U.S. laws. On this basis the CANF charted its project of national influence, utilizing more and more professional North American institutions for that aim, such as the lobbying firm Hill and Knowlton, the public relations firms MWW/Strategic Communications and Gray and Co. II, and various law firms in Miami and Washington.

A decisive factor in this organization achieving so much influence has been its capacity to mobilize financial resources for political aims, multiplied by its government connections. In 1992 the CANF reported political contributions to senatorial and congressional campaigns of nearly $400,000. This is only the tip of the iceberg; the foundation contributed a much greater quantity from organizing fund-raising activities, soliciting donations from individuals connected to the foundation, and making unregistered donations, a common practice in U.S. politics. A good part of this money is not even expended by the donors: studies by Prof. John Nichols in 1988 demonstrate a nearly total correlation between the funds that the CANF received from the NED[25] and its contributions to friendly politicians.[26] But it is not only a question of the volume of contributions but also their convenient timing and direction. With relatively small sums of money the CANF has been able to exert influence over important national politicians by choosing the right moment. This was the case with President William Clinton, for whom the foundation raised over $400,000 at a difficult time in his campaign, thus influencing, according to various public sources in the United States, his decision to support the 1992 Torricelli Act.[27]

With regard to control of the enclave, the CANF has left little margin for the opposition. Beyond their influence, given their contacts at different levels of the U.S. power structure, the organization redeemed the most aggressive canons of the counterrevolutionary tradition and took advantage of the remaining organizations to form an alliance that would guarantee, also by means of coercion, the control of enclave politics. Most of the mass media in the area succumbed to the CANF, either out of fear or self-interest, and those that did not—such as the *Miami Herald*—became victims of its hostility.[28] To carry out this policy of intimidation, in 1990 the foundation created in Miami the Commission of Information. The Novo Sampol brothers—notorious terrorists implicated in the murder of Orlando Letelier—joined the commission, establishing an office in the city from where they kept records on their enemies and maintained systematic contacts with police and intelligence services. They even held weekly meetings with the FBI, according to Ramón Cernuda.[29] This commission was announced to be the result of the unification of "the two historic tendencies" of the counterrevolution: one that proposed working within the U.S. system and the other through terrorism. The *Washington Post* and the *New York Times*, among other media, criticized these practices.[30]

The candidates backed by the foundation began to occupy all sorts of posts in public office and administration throughout the region. "It is incredible," proudly declared one of his associates, referring to Mas Canosa, "to watch him deal with the commissioners and treat them like chauffeurs."[31] Even the "law" took sides in favor of the CANF. District Attorney Dexter Lehtinen,[32] husband of Rep. Ileana Ros-Lehtinen, selectively assailed the enemies of the CANF, and numerous Cuban-American liberal politicians found themselves accused of everything from fraud to drug running.[33] The most notorious case was that of Ramón Cernuda. In May 1989 fourteen U.S. Treasury agents raided his office and residence, and confiscated 200 works of art, accusing Cernuda of violating the U.S. embargo against Cuba. Mas Canosa—lacking any legal authority—publicly assumed responsibility for the act, declaring, "I'm going to continue trying to get an investigation of Cernuda and of twenty—or two hundred or two thousand—other 'Cernudas' in Miami."[34] Thus began six months of harassment that led Cernuda to claim, "Under the surface of Miami society, a police state was being structured."[35] The Miami Cuban Museum was bombed; an institution headed by Cernuda, it had been the object of a systematic campaign by the Cuban right "for treason against the principles of 'Cubanness' and for assuming a political agenda not shared by the majority of the community."[36] FBI investigators confirmed this: "The individuals believed responsible for these actions have targeted businesses, museums, and individuals whom the subjects believe have advocated a better relationship with Castro's Cuba."[37] Two years later a judge ruled in favor of Cernuda, declaring that "the city appears to have fallen victim to the local community's intolerance for those who chose to provide a forum for controversial artists."[38]

In August 1992 the organization Americas Watch published for the first time a report on human rights violations in the United States. Entitled *Dangerous Dialog,* it spoke of the "violence and intimidation of dissident political voices in the Cuban-American community of Miami." The CANF was singled out for suppressing the opposition through repeated attempts to close museums and verbal attacks against newspapers, radio stations, and individuals. At the same time, the report blamed the government for the political support it provided and the funds it channeled to the CANF through the NED and Radio Martí.[39]

These charges did not provoke any change in the situation, however. Under pressure from the CANF, Governor Lawton Chiles signed into law an act prohibiting any company in Florida from doing business with Cuba, which was interpreted as invalidating federal licenses allowing for travel, family aid packages and remittances, and other activities excluded from the embargo. The foundation's aim was to eliminate opposition politicians, such as Francisco González Aruca, who were proprietors of businesses of this nature. A group of these companies sued the state government for unconstitutional attempts to regulate the nation's foreign trade. Although the attorneys for the state of Florida argued that these companies were not covered by the law (since they were protected by a federal license), Mas Canosa insisted on using it to finish off Marazul Travel, Aruca's company.[40]

Abel Holtz, president of Capital Bank of Miami, also told the press about his concerns for the political practices of the CANF and its consequences for the region. "The Foundation has gone beyond an international policy toward Cuba. They have used their ability to raise money to participate in local politics, in terms of appointments of judges and so on; and, in terms of radio and television, to be censor of public opinion. The Latin Builders' Association is actually controlled by the Foundation, and it's very strong. If you have a local election, [the foundation] would go to the Builders' Association and say you have to support this one for mayor and this one for councilman. So they are involved in every aspect of the community."[41]

In exchange for their collaboration the foundation has provided its directors and associates a degree of political power that translates into significant economic benefits. Among the advantages accompanying this association with the CANF are: business opportunities through Ronald Reagan's Caribbean Basin Program,[42] access to bank loans without the customary collateral, changes in zoning benefiting certain real estate deals, preferences in obtaining government contracts, and relations with business groups in other parts of the country.

The creation of the CANF meant, therefore, a qualitative change in the nature of the counterrevolution. In this case, the counterrevolutionary organization ceased to be a marginal instrument of the system and became one of its integral parts, once again associating relations with Cuba with domestic interests that complicate a solution to the Cuba issue. In fact, this is not unique to the Cuban case. Something similar occurs with Israel, despite differences in national impact and political reasoning. However, contrary to what occurs with the Jewish-American community, the root of the matter lies not in the absolute power of the Cuban-American ultraright but in the way they have been used by the U.S. neoconservatives and the process generated by these connections.

This combination of domestic factors and foreign policy, combined with the lack of maturity and the intolerance of the systems of participation in the Cuban-American community, explain the disproportionate influence achieved by the CANF in U.S. policy toward Cuba over the last few years. The CANF constitutes not only the strategy of a particular class. It is practically the only organization capable of reconciling the specific interests of the dominant group within the Miami Cuban-American bourgeoisie with those of the U.S. power elite and projecting them as part of an ideology that serves to attract most of the Cuban émigrés living in the United States. The alteration of any of these variables would significantly modify the foundation's influence in U.S. politics and that of the enclave itself. Once again the Cuban issue, more specifically the counterrevolutionary role assigned by the U.S. system to Cuban immigration, catapulted the influence of the Cuban-American right to national and international levels and reported extraordinary benefits for its bourgeoisie. The neoconservative offensive found in the CANF a resource of practically undisputed legitimacy for its policy toward Cuba and a political machine that augmented its possibilities in southern Florida.

The decisive factor in the success of this operation has been the absence, both in and out of the enclave, of any true opposition to the premises behind the policy against Cuba. According to a study on U.S. policy options toward Cuba performed by Donald Shultz for the U.S. Army War College,

> The U.S. dilemma, of course, is complicated substantially by the fact that there is a large, politically influential and viscerally anti-Castro Cuban-American community in [primarily] southern Florida. It would be going too far to say that our Cuban policy has been "made in Miami." Nevertheless, Cuban-American influence—primarily through the Cuban American National Foundation—has been palpable and has strengthened the hard-line inclinations already dominant in U.S. foreign policy circles. This influence has been all the more potent because there is no political constituency for a "softer" or more flexible line towards Cuba. There are no domestic political gains to be made by changing current policy, while the political costs are obvious. The upshot is that the Cuban-American community has been able to exercise a virtual veto over U.S. policy.[43]

Only the existence of this correlation has permitted the CANF to play such an crucial role in U.S. policy toward Cuba.

Against the opposition of the North American broadcasters, in 1985 the CANF succeeded in getting approval for Radio Martí, an official U.S. government radio station aimed at Cuba with the purpose of destabilizing that nation's government, which costs the U.S. taxpayers close to $20 million annually. This project, in clear violation of established international agreements and with the open opposition of various sectors of the society, was expanded in 1990 with Television Martí, which matched the costs of the radio operation. TV Martí continues despite the proven fact that the interference created by the Cuban government blocks its signal from being received on the island. The CANF possesses its own radio station aimed at Cuban territory as well, La Voz de la Fundación, and helps finance transmissions by other organizations. In total, nearly 1,000 hours of counterrevolutionary broadcasts are transmitted toward Cuba each week.

In 1985, thanks to its influence over Florida legislators, the CANF succeeded in getting Congress to repeal the Clark Amendment, which prohibited federal aid to the Angolan counterrevolution, opening the way to the intensification of the war. Mas Canosa visited the rebel zone in 1988 and received a hero's welcome from UNITA chief Jonas Savimbi. It is during this period that the foundation became involved in covert aid to the Nicaraguan Contras, on the premise that "the road to Havana passes through Managua." This participation included financing terrorist Luis Posada Carriles's escape from his Venezuelan jail and moving him to El Salvador to join the project of supplying the contras.[44] In 1988 the U.S. Senate investigated—with little success—the participation of the CANF in the Iran-Contra scandal. In his diary Oliver North mentions payments of more than $80,000 to Jorge Mas Canosa. According to testimony of a State Department official, Mas Canosa introduced Félix Rodríguez[45] into the operation and later placed Posada Carriles under his command.[46]

The CANF encouraged a campaign against alleged human rights violations in Cuba, despite the reticence of the neoconservatives toward this issue. The campaign included getting former Cuban counterrevolutionary prisoner Armando Valladares named as U.S. ambassador to the UN Commission on Human Rights. Valladares had been the object of a media campaign that promoted him as a crippled poet suffering political imprisonment in Cuba, but his credibility was seriously compromised when the Cuban government's claims that he was neither a cripple nor a poet were proven true. But what is most incredible about the decision, and its importance for understanding the ideological nature of the CANF, was his sudden "appointment" as a U.S. citizen and diplomat, convinced that with this status he could legitimately represent the Cuban people.[47] The international political environment of the 1980s was not conducive to significant advances in this policy. Thus, the accusations against Cuba did not thrive until the collapse of the Eastern European bloc. U.S. pressures were then successful in getting the UN commission to place Cuba under investigation and name a "special envoy," which the Cuban government never accepted.

In 1988 the foundation became the only private organization in the United States with immigration faculties. That year the government of that country approved putting into action the Exodus Program, while at the same time tightening as much as possible the program of legal immigration from Cuba. Thanks to this program some 8,500 Cubans residing in third countries were allowed to enter the U.S. sponsored by the CANF. Lest they become a public liability the families of the intended immigrants were required to purchase an insurance policy that covered their health and social assistance. The company chosen for this was Winterthur International of Bermuda, which did not have a license to operate in Florida and did not comply with the required coverage specified by the State Department in the agreements. This gave rise to problems with hospital payments, and many immigrants ended up resorting to state-funded health services, in violation of the agreement. Nancy Wittenberg, director of the Florida Refugee Assistance Program, rated the services offered by the CANF as "atrocious" and questioned the legality and honesty of the operation. After Mas Canosa personally appealed to Gov. Lawton Chiles, the official was forced to publicly recant her statements. Nevertheless, the project—a recipient of nearly $2 million in federal funds—was under question and was finally suspended in 1993.[48]

During the Reagan and Bush administrations, the CANF acted as an extension of the U.S. government's foreign policy and as a tool of domestic pressure to impose that policy. According to investigator Gaeton Fonzi, during this period the foundation received more than $200 million in public funds to carry out this task.[49] The CANF became an integral part of the system, in effect joining the select group of organizations of North American civil society that participated in structuring this system of hegemony. This participation made the CANF unique among counterrevolutionary organizations. Thus its influence has been bipartisan, encompassing not only electoral politics but also the government bureaucracy at the different levels.

In summary, a number of factors that probably can never be duplicated coalesced around the CANF to establish its effectiveness. These included its coincidence with official U.S. policy and with the conservative positions that dominated the political debate in that country during the last few years; as a result, the foundation enjoyed a degree of access to the power elite previously unknown to other counterrevolutionary groups. On the other hand, the Cuban-American bourgeoisie had given rise to a sector now capable of articulating a political movement within the boundaries of the U.S. system and influencing certain aspects of that nation's local and national politics. In addition, this bourgeoisie shared a similar ideology with the rest of the Cuban-American community and was capable of controlling, practically without opposition, the mechanisms of political participation within the enclave. Finally, the CANF put together a political machine that in each case accurately chose its targets and methods, projecting an image of power, exaggerated at times, under a fanatically tenacious leadership, unscrupulous at using any means to achieve its ends.

Paradoxically, it was the crisis in Eastern Europe beginning in 1989 that revitalized the belief in the imminent collapse of the Cuban Revolution, which gave rise to new competitors for the CANF. This collapse generated a climate of counterrevolutionary euphoria, reactivated all the existing variants of counterrevolution, and widened the spectrum with new entrants, more in tune with the international climate and the new adjustments in U.S. foreign policy.

Crisis and Counterrevolution

The first reaction of the U.S. government to the growing impact on Cuban society of the decline of the socialist bloc was to bet on the immediate collapse of the Revolution. They expected a process of social and political chaos to unfold similar to what was occurring in Eastern Europe, without anticipating the consequences that would have for the United States. Therefore, U.S. actions were directed at abetting the crisis, reinforcing measures that could hamper Cuba's traditional trade relations with the former socialist countries and the still-existing USSR and prevent Cuba's entrance into other economic spheres, particularly Latin America and Europe. Within this scheme, any means of destabilization was welcome, leading the way to the encouragement of all forms of counterrevolution, including terrorism.

This situation had a distinct impact on the political attitudes of the Cuban-American community toward Cuba. In 1988 a survey by the prestigious Gallup reported that 41 percent favored negotiations with Cuba and 39 percent supported lifting the embargo. Another study that same year by the Institute for Public Research at Florida International University confirmed these figures: 43 percent of those surveyed were inclined toward improving relations. By 1991, these attitudes changed radically. New studies at the same university revealed a significant increase in hostility and intransigence toward the Cuban Revolution: 88 percent believed that the Revolution would not survive more than five years, 91 percent wanted U.S. support for counterrevolutionary groups within the country, 90 percent backed the internalization of economic pressures, 88 percent voted for strengthening the embargo, 80 percent opposed any new diplomatic or commercial relations, 73 percent backed armed military actions from abroad, and 54 percent supported open U.S. military intervention. Although support for a dialog with the Cuban government continued to be evenly divided, this reflected more a tactical question, since many expected this to yield similar results to those achieved by means of armed pressure.[50]

The Cuban-American community perceived the disappearance of the USSR as the confirmation of the apocalyptic predictions of the counterrevolution with respect to the future of the Cuban Revolution. In 1991 the counterrevolutionary groups openly debated how to dispose of the properties that they would eventually recover when the Revolutionary government fell. Proposed reconstruction programs included sending thousands of Cuban-American technicians to organize the country's return to capitalism. New constitutions were drafted and steps were even taken to form a "provisional government" where "seniority in exile" was to be the main selection criterion. Meanwhile, as the "war fever" intensified, the number of terrorist plans increased. Some of these materialized in attempts to infiltrate small armed groups and in attacks against the Cuban coastline.[51]

The CANF identified with U.S. policy objectives and tried to project its influence outward, in particular toward the former socialist camp, receiving tokens of support from the new governments of Czechoslovakia, Hungary, and Poland. In May 1990, in an unprecedented event, thirteen Soviet officials and scholars visited Miami at the invitation of the CANF. Interviews with Mas Canosa were published in the Soviet press, and even Yuri Pavlov, then head of Latin American affairs at the Soviet Ministry of Foreign Relations, traveled to Miami and met with counterrevolutionary leaders.[52] The foundation's principal directors visited Moscow late that year hoping that Mikhail Gorbachev would receive them to discuss "the future of Cuba." Although they were not granted the interview they were received by other Soviet government officials.

The collapse of the USSR in 1991 heightened even more the expectations of high-level contacts with Russian authorities. The CANF opened an office in Moscow and used the Exodus Program to benefit some Cuban students who had decided to emigrate to the United States. Dazzled by the "discovery" of the seeming economic and political power of the Cuban-Americans, some Russian leaders took seriously the promise that this organization had sufficient clout in Washington to secure economic benefits for Russia. They even claimed to be capable of assuring the supply of sugar if Russia suspended trade with Cuba. This served the interests of the Fanjul family, former sugar tycoons in Cuba and current owners of the sugar corporations La Romana in the Dominican Republic and Gulf and Western in the United States. Beginning then, the Fanjuls affiliated with the CANF and became the principal Cuban-American contributors to the Clinton campaign. Interested mainly in economic benefits that the foundation could not truly deliver, the Russians became disillusioned with the Cuban counterrevolutionaries, and they in turn with the Russian leaders, who did not take a decisive anti-Cuban position.

The CANF also directed its lobbying efforts toward Latin America: their directors were received by several presidents and established contacts with most of the governments in the region. But with the exception of Argentina these gestures did not result in any lasting influence; moreover, the Latin Americans rejected CANF as a favored option. Nevertheless, the propaganda gains from these meetings benefited the foundation by exaggerating their importance.

Like the foundation, many counterrevolutionary organizations from earlier periods, now practically extinct, reinitiated their activities in the hopes of gaining merits for the post-Castro Cuba. These groups were politically depleted and had an extremely limited following and range of action. Yet a number of training camps were reactivated and some minor armed attacks were launched for obvious propaganda purposes. Attempts were also made to encourage the reorganization of former counterrevolutionary organizations in Cuba to carry out violent actions within the country, using the counterrevolutionary radio stations beamed at the island and reactivating old contacts. In 1990 the CANF promoted the creation of Unidad Cubana, a coalition of these organizations that served, above all, to increase the climate of political intolerance within the Cuban-American community.

The CANF has been, therefore, a proponent of the most intransigent positions and most of the counterrevolutionary groups have allied with it. This attitude responds not only to a rigid ideological code but also to objective political interests. Maintaining a counterrevolutionary climate constitutes the basis of power of the far right in the enclave, its national impact in the United States, and the guarantee of a predominant role in the future of Cuba if the Revolution is defeated. To reinforce this image the CANF set about creating institutions charged with designing the "reordering" of postrevolutionary

Cuban society and establishing their roles in the new contingency. In 1989 the state of Florida and the CANF jointly financed a research program on Cuba at the University of Miami, its budget estimated at $2 million. The initial offer was made to Florida International University, but the conditions imposed implied such limitations on academic freedom—one requirement was that two-thirds of the board of directors would be chosen by the foundation—that the faculty and the State Board of Regents refused to accept the grant and publicly condemned it. Despite this the state legislature assigned the money so that the CANF could carry out the program in the institution it deemed appropriate.[53]

Also with this aim, 1993 saw the creation of the Blue Ribbon Commission on the Economic Development of Cuba, which presented a project for the "reconstruction" of the Cuban economy at the Mid-America Committee of International Business and Government Corporations. The project proposed to compensate former property owners in Cuba through a program that would privatize all Cuban state enterprises. This commission had as its honorary presidents the patricians of neoliberalism, Marcus Forbes Jr. and Arthur Laffer. The twenty-seven other members included Senators Bob Graham (D-Fla.) and Connie Mack (R-Fla.), Rep. Ileana Ros (R-Fla.) and former representative Larry Smith (D-Fla.), former ambassador Jeanne Kirkpatrick, and a dozen representatives of large U.S. corporations, among them Hyatt Hotels, Royal Caribbean Cruise Lines, and BellSouth. These companies were promised economic benefits once the foundation rose to power in Cuba. The investment firm Lazard Frerez was hired to develop a project "for the adequate industrial development of post-Castro Cuba," whose central proposition consisted of a privatization plan of such magnitude that *U.S. News and World Report* defined it as a scheme "designed to sell Cuba to Wall Street."[54] Mas Canosa did not hide this purpose: "You cannot go little by little. We should have a very aggressive privatization program. It has to be radical and it has to be immediate. Privatize everything in the hands of the Cuban government. . . . I believe in absolutely open capitalism."[55]

These actions were not meant to sway the Cuban people. The logic behind these projects lies in assuring the greatest degree of control possible over what were considered to be the mechanisms that the U.S. government would establish in dealing with the Cuban case once the Revolution was defeated. According to Domingo Moreira, one of the directors of the foundation, "whoever takes power once the change occurs will have a place to go to solve the immediate problems, and that place is the United States."[56] The Strategy for Leadership, developed for the foundation by MWW/Strategic Communications, also revealed the premises behind this conception: "Although various exile groups have ideas on how to organize the Cuban government after Castro, the group with the most visibility in the United States . . . will wield the greatest influence over U.S. policy and investments in the post-Castro era."[57]

The CANF has made an effort to be known inside Cuba. The Voice of the Foundation and the pressure by Mas Canosa to have himself promoted on Radio Martí are proof of this.[58] But at the same time, the foundation has discredited and discouraged the development of any internal alternative that could become a rival in the future. Unconcerned with being represented inside the country, the CANF has publicly declared its low esteem for the prospects and integrity of the small counterrevolutionary groups that appeared on the island. The CANF's projects and conduct betray such disdain for Cuban society that its Plattism assumes insulting proportions, even for other currents of the counterrevolutionary movement. The foundation, however, had no choice but to join the counterrevolutionary efforts that sought to gain a space within Cuban society, since that constituted an essential element for gaining legitimacy in the face of international public opinion. In 1991 the CANF embarked on the task of organizing and publicizing the existence of the Coalición Democrática Cubana, a very small group of persons that gave the appearance of representing the foundation within Cuba. The CANF conceived of this group as expendable and encouraged it to carry out clearly provocative actions designed to provoke a repressive reaction by the Cuban government, in the hopes of unchaining a series of domestic conflicts that would justify a "humanitarian intervention" by the United States. The project backfired, however, when Héctor Castañeda, the organization's chief in Cuba, turned out to be an agent of Cuban State Security and publicly denounced the plans in 1992.[59]

The limited results of its international dealings and the failure of its subversive efforts within Cuba led the foundation to concentrate once again on lobbying activities within the United States, aimed at preventing a change in U.S. policy toward Cuba. The most significant step in this direction was the sponsorship of the Cuban Democracy Act—the Torricelli Act—passed in 1992 by the U.S. Congress by a wide margin and supported by the presidential candidates of both parties in the elections of that year.

The text of the law encompassed three parts: strengthening the sanctions, opening up communications, and expressing a willingness toward calibrated responses to stipulated changes carried out by the Cuban side. In this sense the law established an exception with regard to telephone communications with Cuba—notably, the principal business of Jorge Mas Canosa—and opened up the possibilities of increasing the volume of mail. It also eased the restrictions on activities related to the press, academic research, and transmission of information in both directions, but assigning to these a subversive role that compromised those involved and raised suspicions that complicated the law's implementation. In essence, the law was one more step in the direction of increasing pressure for the economic and diplomatic isolation of Cuba, seeking to bring back relations between the two countries to the worst they had ever been. To satisfy an old dream of the Cuban-American far right, it also proposed restrictions on the contacts émigrés had with the island, insofar as it established limits on expenditures while in Cuba and on the amount of goods and cash they could send their relatives still in Cuba.

However, the law was unique in codifying a qualitative change in the arguments that justified the policy toward Cuba. And, in the words of journalist Peter Slevin, "by setting the terms of North American aid toward Cuba after Castro, the law also established a possible role of mediator for Mas Canosa himself"[60]—that is, a role for the CANF in the new machinery of domination that the United States pretended to restore in Cuba. The law had no choice but to establish the inadmissibility of the Cuban political regime as the core of the dispute. Notwithstanding the inevitable influence of the Cold War on the dissension between the United States and Cuba, the heart of the conflict always was that the Revolution broke with a state of dependency that formed an integral part of the North American system of hegemony. U.S. rhetoric avoided labeling the contradiction in these terms and instead gave as an excuse the position that Cuba occupied within the East-West conflict, thus U.S. demands revolved until then around the international role of the island and its links with the USSR. The end of the Cold War radically transformed these points of reference. Therefore, the new policy required a new message: the Cuban political system was allegedly incompatible with the post–Cold War international order. The Torricelli Act cannot hide the interventionist nature of its objectives, which are "to seek a peaceful transition to democracy and a resumption of economic growth in Cuba through the careful applications of sanctions . . . to seek the cooperation of other democratic countries in this policy [and] to make clear to other countries that, in determining its relations with them, the United States will take into account their willingness to cooperate in such a policy."[61]

The core of the law, striving to disrupt Cuba's foreign relations, is directed toward international trade, credits, and assistance. These ideas form part of the components logically accompanying a policy of economic strangulation, but the law's strategic aim is much more encompassing. It constitutes a crude application of the Monroe Doctrine in the contemporary world, a warning to Europe, and an imposition of standards of conduct on the Latin American countries. It is not fortuitous that there is an international consensus, expressed though continuous resolutions of the UN General Assembly, condemning this policy, particularly its extraterritorial character and the precedents it establishes in international relations.[62]

Conscious of these costs, the Bush administration initially opposed the enactment of the Torricelli Act. Mas Canosa then utilized Rep. Stephen Solarz (D-N.Y.) to obtain Clinton's support. At first Clinton likewise hesitated in supporting the initiative, but the need for campaign funds, his commitments to Sen. Robert Torricelli (D-N.J.), and the political convenience of taking the initiative away from the administration in an issue with few other electoral consequences, persuaded him to support the law.[63] In the end Bush had no choice but to accept it—after negotiating amendments with regard to the obligation of the president to comply with all of its sections—and he signed it into law at a rally organized by the CANF in Miami on October 23, 1992.

The Torricelli Act synthesizes the foundation's strategy. It is a process that begins with the control of the Cuban-American community and extends to the creation of a network of interests with North American political sectors that will assure the continuation of a policy of maximum hostility toward Cuba. This policy includes pressures on third countries, aimed at aggravating the economic crisis to the point of stirring up social disorder, which will in turn justify a U.S. intervention. The fundamental difference between the CANF and other U.S. political groups—and the danger that its approach entails for U.S. national security—is that the promotion of social chaos in Cuba is crucial to CANF interests since it is what assures the foundation a role as protagonist in the conflict. From this perspective the CANF would fill the power vacuum that would result from this situation—a role upheld by the U.S. law itself. The foundation's project leaves absolutely no room for conciliation, nor even for a tactic of "peaceful subversion." This would require compromises and set in motion a process that would reduce the foundation's role and dampen its expectations for the future that it, and the sectors it represents, contemplates for Cuba.

The CANF's actions have been set in a race against time. They are destined to avoid at all cost any change not only in the objectives but also in the form that U.S. policy toward Cuba takes, and in the perception of the foundation's role in an eventual postrevolutionary Cuba. On this basis, its activities, aimed at presenting a bloated image of its power, seek an insertion into the U.S. system that assures it will continue to be taken into account in tracing U.S. policy toward Cuba and in the future outcome of this situation. To do this the CANF has had no qualms in affirming that it has the capacity to raise $4 billion in the Cuban-American community and another $1 billion from Wall Street to aid in the "reconstruction" of Cuba. "Many people think the Foundation is so powerful that they want to be on good terms with it," argues James Suchlicki, professor at the University of Miami and sometime contributor to the CANF.[64]

The passage of the Torricelli Act and the election of three Cuban-Americans to the U.S. Congress became points in the foundation's favor, because they served to establish the limits of the agenda and maintain a dominant presence in the debate over Cuba policy. Nevertheless, in the 1992 elections the CANF suffered significant political erosion because of inconsistencies in its support for Republican candidates and the fact that Clinton's election damaged twelve years of contacts and alliances, despite Mas Canosa's efforts to win over the Democrats.

The end of the Cold War also entangled the ideological environment for counterrevolutionary politics. The much-proclaimed End of Socialism turned into an anachronism the argument that Cuba was a satellite of the USSR, a justification that served as basis for the traditional hostility of U.S. policy. Fear for the consequences of an eruption of social chaos on the island was felt internationally, even within the United States. Finally, the probable establishment of a far-right regime in Cuba, absolutely allied with U.S. interests, was perceived as a destabilizing influence on the political balance in Latin America and an obstacle for the expansion of Europe's relations with the region. The "internalization of the counterrevolution" required, therefore, a new image for Cuba's counterrevolutionary groups, an element that tended to weaken the supremacy of the far right within the counterrevolutionary options. This loss gives rise to the logical resistance of the far right toward this "new image" and a sense of urgency for their political project that explains many of their later actions. "It's hard," said a director of the foundation, "when one has been sacrificing for ten years and now when it's time to reap the fruits, all these other groups spring up."[65]

In this way three tendencies, reflecting contradictions present in the context of U.S. policy toward Cuba, began to emerge within the Cuban counterrevolution. One trend assumed that the defeat of the Cuban Revolution was imminent and sought to hasten it through open U.S. intervention, whether by applying economic pressure, seeking to isolate Cuba from the international community, or even by direct military intervention. This group conferred a subordinate role on the domestic counterrevolutionary front, which would subordinate itself to the leadership of the groups established abroad. A second trend, although stemming from the same premises, sought an international arrangement and called for a moderation of the anti-Castro rhetoric, an apparent distancing from the United States, and greater legitimacy based on greater links with domestic counterrevolutionary groups. The third current analyzed the Cuban situation more from a long-term perspective and based its strategy on the gradual development of the internal counterrevolution.

For some sectors of the counterrevolution the established objective was an absolute return to the past, completely ignoring the logic implicit in the political evolution of almost three generations of Cubans. Others, conscious of the practical impossibility of this proposal and more adapted to the strategic premises of the new international global order, proposed formulas based on the reconstruction of a system of dependency from which they would obtain significant advantages, but that required the support of the new sectors of the Cuban population. In reality these are different versions of a project that, inspired by the trend of globalization of contemporary transnational capitalism, proposes the reinsertion of Cuba in the international community on the basis of an absolute return to capitalism under conditions especially favorable for the Cuban-American bourgeoisie.

In line with the conciliatory language that emerged after the Cold War, none of the groups have openly rejected—at least in theory—the possibility of a dialog, whether with the government or other sectors of Cuban society. But for them, dialog is assumed to be a way for the Cuban government to back down from its position, rather than a means for the resolution of conflict. The CANF—who in fact opposes any form of negotiation—proposes a dialog conditioned on the exclusion of Fidel and Raúl Castro, which makes their proposal more an inducement to conspiracy than a formula for negotiation. Other groups condition a dialog on the debate over the "democratic transition," establishing as a precondition the illegitimacy of the current political system in Cuba and their intention to change it. In practice these positions lead to the same contradiction as in the past: they constitute challenges to the power structure that, given their antagonistic character, can hardly result in consensus.

With respect to Cuba both the Bush and Clinton administrations faced contradictions similar to those that have appeared in other issues of post-Cold War U.S. policy. The cohesiveness engendered by the confrontation with the USSR has disappeared. The political debate has wavered between powerful domestic support for extremely conservative positions—such as those of the CANF—and international demands for new strategies based on forging a consensus that would assure the stability of the hegemonic system with minimum use of unilateral force. Conscious of this dilemma, important power sectors in the United States, including a branch of the conservatives, promoted the development of other counterrevolutionary currents more amenable to this environment. This other face of the counterrevolutionary was signified by the creation of the Plataforma Democrática Cubana (PDC) and the proliferation inside and outside the island of the so-called human rights groups, who have now begun to assume positions more clearly defined as political opposition.

The Other Face of the Counterrevolution

The PDC, whose formation was publicly announced in 1990 in Madrid, is a coalition of the Unión Liberal Cubana, headed by Carlos Alberto Montaner; the Coordinadora Socialdemócrata, whose main figure was Enrique Baloyra; and the Partido Demócrata Cristiano Cubano, then led by José Ignacio Rasco. The PDC assumed the immediate and inevitable collapse of the Cuban Revolution, therefore its thesis was to prevent this from leading to social chaos that would serve to "justify" a North American intervention. Its plan therefore consisted of "organizing the democratic transition" of Cuba, through negotiations between the Cuban government and representatives of the counterrevolutionary groups inside and outside the island. In order to get the Cuban government to accept this formula they called for increased international pressure on Cuba, making their proposal consistent with the interests of U.S. policy.

The PDC presented itself as an alliance representing the Cuban currents of liberalism, Christian democracy, and social democracy. In a confidential letter to the domestic counterrevolutionary groups, Montaner explained the reasons that led them to assume these positions: "We did not embark on the creation of the Platform solely for love of ideological convictions . . . but because in this strategic concept there is an enormous wealth of potential aid . . . the weight of hundreds of political parties from all over the world, and it even opens the way to assistance that European foundations grant to political causes."[66]

The PDC's plans were aimed at joining the international coalition of each ideological tendency, winning the support of European and Latin American intellectual circles, and incorporating the domestic counterrevolutionary groups into this scheme. In furtherance of these objectives they carried out an active international campaign that included interviewing dozens of governments, organizing international conferences, and establishing contacts with existing opposition groups in Cuba. It has been alleged that the Platform also sought to establish a conservative wing represented by the foundation, but the latter did not accept the proposition and instead was critical of the PDC, insofar as it perceived it as a political rival. Nonetheless, the PDC has abstained from acting within North American territory, for reasons that probably have to do with the origin of its funds and the restrictions of U.S. law.[67]

Without a doubt the Platform was an undertaking that intended to be more in tune with the politics of the post–Cold War period. Its objective was to moderate the counterrevolutionary platform in order to incorporate new forces into the pressures against the Cuban Revolution and in this manner counter the increasing international isolation faced by U.S. policy toward Cuba. Its expectations were based on the existence of a political environment that justified the belief that the Cuban Revolution was in no condition to survive the collapse of the socialist bloc. Based on this, it stimulated the interest of various governments and Western political movements to establish a presence in an eventual postrevolutionary Cuba. At the same time, it attempted to exploit the concern for the effect that a state of social chaos, a possible U.S. intervention, and the establishment of a far right regime in Cuba would have on the stability and future of the region. The PDC even appealed to the sentiments of sectors traditionally allied with the Cuban Revolution in the hope that, given the right moment, they would back what was presented as the "least worst" alternative for the Cuban people.

To satisfy these concerns the PDC sold an image of pluralism, moderation, humanitarian concern, pacifism, independence from the United States, and capacity to control Cuba's internal situation. The Platform has received economic and political assistance from the German foundations Neuman and Adenauer, from the Spanish government, from the liberal and Christian Democrat Internationals, and from the U.S. government by way of the NED and, allegedly, the CIA. In reality the PDC is a superstructure of leaders without a political membership base to stand on. The three organizations that comprise it were created expressly to integrate the coalition and, with the exception of the Christian Democratic Party, which boasts a long-standing membership, the other groups have no known liberal or social democrat credentials. By all appearances this is an effort designed to find areas of contact with the ideological currents that have dominated the European political scene since World War II, but whose transplant to Latin America, and particularly Cuba, has been traditionally limited by economic restrictions. These limitations have reduced the capacity of these political tendencies from becoming classic parties. More often they become circumstantial political alliances within the power struggle of the Latin American national elites.

These positions have even less appeal in the Cuban-American community, which was never organized along international ideological patterns. Proof that the Platform has no base of support within the émigrés is that neither the Unión Liberal Cubana nor the Coordinadora Socialdemócrata can boast of having more than twenty members. Nor does the organization have the weight it claims to have in Cuba. It would not enjoy such influence even if it had achieved the alliance of the domestic counterrevolutionary groups, as it proposed to do; its support within the United States is very limited. Even though the PDC line underscores the activity of these groups, in practice it views them as subordinates, just as it does the foundation, fulfilling the role of legitimizing the counterrevolutionary activity that is carried out from abroad. This perspective is not only a reflection of the struggle for leadership that is traditional in the counterrevolution. It is also based objectively on true capacity of the domestic groups, who, for a long time, have expressed themselves as an ingredient of a movement launched from abroad and toward world public opinion, and who thus complement the fundamental line of U.S. policy toward Cuba over the last few years.

After nearly two decades during which the counterrevolution was practically nonexistent on the Cuban domestic political scene, the so-called human rights groups began to appear in 1976, precisely when Carter made this issue one of the premises of his foreign policy. Moreover, they achieved relative political relevance beginning in 1980, when they joined the network of counterrevolutionary groups and projects encouraged by the Reagan administration and received official NED financing and covert economic aid from other sources. From that moment, the Western press turned them into a topic of constant attention and any action on their part typically won them disproportionate international importance. They also maintain systematic contact with European and Latin American embassies on the island and are visited by whatever foreigner wants to present an image of impartiality on the Cuban issue. Finally, the "human rights" groups are a permanent source of information for the counterrevolutionary groups established abroad and for the U.S. press, with whom they maintain fluid personal and telephone links.

At first these groups came forth under the pretext of the defense of human rights, but later evolved and adopted definitely political platforms, within the scheme of a "transition to democracy," which corresponds with the priorities and methods adopted at each occasion by U.S. policy. The PDC was very active in trying to provide these groups a concrete political sense and organize them on the basis of the ideological categories on which the coalition was built. "Of course the denunciations that your groups have made have been instrumental in unmasking Castroism, but—in our judgment—you have to take a qualitative leap and plunge into the realm of political opposition. . . . Naturally, this change in strategy puts those who follow it in a certain state of illegality, making them more vulnerable to repression. . . . Moreover, it would be necessary to take precautions in case the signatories are imprisoned. . . . In the final analysis, if this would happen, let us not forget that shortly before occupying their places in history, Havel, as well as Wałesa and Sakharov, were also imprisoned."[68] Montaner concluded this exhortation to the domestic dissidents by establishing the ideological denomination that each should assume in order to join the PDC. Although the majority refused to accept this apostolic invitation, the government of the United States, through the NED, distributed close to one million dollars between 1990 and 1992 to finance these activities.[69]

The alleged lack of connection between the PDC and the U.S. government is hard to fathom. Its three principal leaders boasted a long counterrevolutionary history and well-known links with the U.S. intelligence services. José Ignacio Rasco founded the Christian Democratic Movement and formed part of the Frente Revolucionario Democrático and the Consejo Revolucionario Cubano, civilian facades for the Bay of Pigs invasion. Enrique Baloyra's origins are also in the Catholic right. He was a member of the Movimiento de Recuperación Revolucionaria and the Directorio Revolucionario Estudiantil, received specialized intelligence training at Fort Benning, and collaborated with the Pentagon in the analysis of the Latin American situation —particularly that of El Salvador. Montaner comes from a family linked to pro-Batista groups. He joined the counterrevolution in his early years, also formed part of the select group that the CIA trained at Fort Benning in 1963, and later participated in various counterrevolutionary projects.

In addition, U.S. support for the PDC has been publicly reported on many occasions. Typically it has been channeled through the NED and coincidentally the first group benefited has been the Coordinadora Socialdemócrata, the member of the coalition that has received the least international support. The NED has also financed events of the PDC in various parts of the world. U.S. meddling in the organization became so obvious that in 1992 a sector of the Social Democratic wing denounced this situation and split from the organization.

The erroneous premise on which the PDC was founded—the inevitable and imminent fall of the revolutionary government—its lack of political and ideological legitimacy, and its limited capacity to mobilize people within the island and in the Cuban-American community are all factors that tended to gradually weaken the credibility of the organization and its internal unity. The PDC was disabled from playing a positive role in a process of real improvement in relations between Cuba and the United States. The PDC was thus a project that reminds us of subversive efforts similar to those applied toward the ex-socialist bloc, conceived for a strategy that corresponded to the Bush administration's plans against the Cuban Revolution. Yet the project is capable of adapting to the requirements of a more long-term policy, as long as it continues to enjoy the backing of the United States. The question currently on the table is, In its attempt to dismantle the Cuban revolutionary system will the counterrevolution continue to cling to glaring forms of confrontation or will they opt for other more subtle forms of penetration?

Chapter 8

The Counterrevolution after the Cold War

THE COLLAPSE OF the Eastern European socialist camp and the disappearance of the USSR led to a qualitative change in the evaluation of the Cuban Revolution's capacity for survival and the corresponding revitalization of the various trends of the counterrevolution. Counterrevolutionary euphoria marked U.S. policy toward Cuba in the period immediately after the end of the Cold War and established standards that, although questioned at times, remain in force today. In any case, the debate is about the methods, not about the objectives. Different views of U.S. policy toward Cuba share the objective—and the alleged feasibility—of dismantling the socialist system and the possible integration of the country into the schemes of domination and hegemony conceived for the post–Cold War era. A key element in this strategy is to question the compatibility of the Cuban political system with the new international order that the United States seeks to impose. This order has found its rationale, and its excuse, in the doctrine that relates the strategic objectives of U.S. foreign policy with the "promotion of democracy" throughout the world.

Although it was always been applied selectively, this concept began to gain strength in the mid-1970s, becoming one of the focal points of the trilateralist strategy that guided Carter's foreign policy. Reagan and Bush, for their part, utilized the argument, although they began from more restricted premises, as the basis for their policies against socialist and Third World nationalist governments, but avoiding conflicts with right-wing regimes allied with the United States. "Although the term 'democracy' appeared regularly in the language of foreign policymakers for reasons of convenience, or under specific circumstances, it has not been the predominant way in which the United States has historically exercised its hegemony, especially in the years of the Global Empire following the Second World War. In fact, the predominant form was the development of strategic alliances with authoritarian and dictatorial right-wing regimes."[1]

The dictatorships served to slow the pace of revolution in Latin America. But the chronic breakdowns originated by popular rejection of these systems, the tremendous political cost for the United States of this commitment, and the paralysis and bewilderment that the dismantling of the socialist camp brought about in the revolutionary ranks led to a modification in this policy. "Promotion of democracy became the base of support of the new international order that the United States wanted to impose. Confident that the resources of neoliberalism would contain the revolutionary forces and probably euphoric with the postmodern utopia that decreed the end of ideologies, the North American system has defined the promotion of democracy as one of the three basic objectives of its foreign policy, in conjunction with developing free trade and maintaining military supremacy.[2]

For the proponents of this policy, democracy is not defined as the will of the people or the common good, but rather as a system of distribution of power based on elections that permit the political interplay between the government and the opposition.[3] This opposition—when speaking of "established democratic regimes"—should fulfill the condition of being "loyal," in which loyalty is defined as playing by the rules of the game and not propounding a qualitative transformation of the system. In effect, it is a local tactical exercise that in no way compromises the strategic global thrust nor the supranational relations of dependency that serve as its foundation. As expressed by Cuban philosopher Juan Antonio Blanco, "to date, democracy has been but *one* of the systems—among others—of administering those areas of power that the dominant class of a society entrusts to its government." This poses a contradiction that has its origin in the rise of capitalism itself. "Liberal politics is directed at facilitating the accumulation of capital and free trade, cementing both in an ideology of individualism and selfishness as the engine for the general welfare. Democracy, on the other hand, was in its origins an anti-capitalist ideology insofar as it proposed two things: participation and equality of opportunities. . . . The secret [for reconciling this conflict] lies in the skillful combination of liberalism and democracy: within a system of equal *liberties*—but brutal asymmetry of *opportunities*—it was possible to compete advantageously and win, almost invariably, the majority vote. *Symmetric* liberties exercised from *asymmetric* opportunities is the central axiom of liberal democracy."[4]

Blanco himself defines the features of the democratic system that is to be generalized: "reduce the expectations of having a government of the people, by the people, and for the people, to choosing the best possible option from the electoral menu at each visit to the ballot box. The fetishism of multiparty elections thereby replaces, conceptually, the previous democratic definition; lowering expectations as to what a system of democratic government—even under electoral fetishism—can contribute as a *result* of its operation. The emphasis here is again placed on the procedural, not the substantive element: what is supposedly important is the 'democratic' capacity to administer conflicts within the status quo, not providing favorable final results in the interest of the majority. The participative expectations are reduced, not just to being simply represented by elected officials, but to [the hope] that a technostructure of specialized political operatives in executive positions and with more actual, daily decision-making power than the former, do not distance themselves too much—in their *uncontrolled* hegemony—from the desires of most of the electorate."[5]

The strategy of promoting democracy is related to the retreat of the world revolutionary movement and the needs of economic globalization. Economic globalization facilitates putting these mechanisms into effect, on the one hand, because neoliberalism tends to fragment the society and absolutely alienate a segment that supposedly will carry little weight in the political life of the country, and on the other, because transnational capital, organically inserted into the national economies, does not have as much need as previously for the traditional national oligarchies in order to maintain the instruments of hegemony. A novel element in this new order is precisely that it tends to replace—or transform—the old oligarchies with a technocratic bourgeoisie integrated with transnational capital, which finds its allies in a privileged social stratum, inserted into the mechanisms of global production that are characteristic of the global system of domination. Therefore, societies can carry out internal reforms at the cost of the traditional oligarchies and promote a democratic game in which transnational hegemonic power never looses, insofar as it is applied through multiple resources.

Representative democracy is conceived for the manipulation of the middle class, a social segment particularly benefited by economic globalization. In summary, "promotion of democracy" constitutes an effort to achieve the most convenient national political organization for the new international order that is presumed to follow the Cold War. Its objective is to achieve the stability needed by the globalized system of production, the basis for a supranational power that is also expressed in the manipulation of multinational political institutions, in the transnational control of mass media, in the open and subliminal imposition of a cultural model, and in many other aspects of contemporary life. It is a new design for domination, encompassing all of dependent society, through the use of the most advanced techniques of social communication and the instruments of representative democracy. It is a qualitative leap, truly globalizing, for neocolonialism.

"Peaceful subversion" forms part of the arsenal of weapons with which to impose this new model of hegemony. Carl Gershman, president of the National Endowment for Democracy, argued that "in a world of advanced communications and expansion of knowledge, it is no longer possible to depend exclusively on force to promote stability and defend national security. Persuasion is more important every day, and the United States must improve its capacity to persuade developing techniques to reach people at many different levels."[6] But peaceful subversion is an option that does not exclude other alternatives. Establishing this pattern of international conduct does not preclude the use of force. On the contrary, an interventionist philosophy, based on the concept of limited sovereignty and the establishment of supranational powers, accompanies this proposal to "democratize" the world.

> This point is not concealed. Describing the new Pentagon budget in January 1990, the press reports that "In [Defense Secretary Dick] Cheney's view, which is shared by President Bush, the United States will continue to need a large Navy (and intervention forces generally) to deal with brushfire conflicts and threats to American interest in places like Latin America and Asia." . . . The same questions are addressed by Marine Corps Commandant General A. M. Gray. The end of the Cold War will only reorient our security policies, he advises, but not change them significantly. . . . "The underdeveloped world's growing dissatisfaction over the gap between rich and poor nations will create a fertile breeding ground for insurgencies. These insurgencies have the potential to jeopardize regional stability and our access to vital economic and military resources." The National Security Strategy Report sent to Congress two months later described the

> Third World as a probable locus of conflict: "In a new era, we foresee that our military power will remain an essential underpinning of the global balance, but less prominent and in different ways. We see that the more likely demands for the use of our military forces may not involve the Soviet Union and may be in the Third World, where new capabilities and approaches may be required." . . . In reality, the "threat to our interests had always been indigenous nationalism."[7]

"Promotion of democracy" does not constitute, in reality, a new formula. Historically, a threatened power resorts to violence to impose itself, and to persuasion to perpetuate itself once the danger has been overcome. This is the first impression of the U.S. system, once it feels it has won the Cold War. Nationalism establishes the resistance to this policy and brings to light its conceptual and organic limitations. The national state reinforces its role as protective barrier against foreign domination, serving not only the segments of the bourgeoisie that fear being displaced—the historical reason that originated that state—but wide sectors of the population, who assume it as a defense against a process of economic rationalization that tends to alienate them from their own social context.

On the local scale, democratic manipulation is not always sustained within the desired limits. The inclusion of the marginal sectors becomes a goal for the revolutionary circles, and therefore a source of destabilization for the model. "The game of 'democratizing' bourgeois hegemony to widen the consensus, that old game of advantage that capitalism is obliged to play because of its nature, always has the disadvantage that it expands political activities and representations to more and more dispossessed masses, whose development makes them increasingly more capable of demanding what the system cannot deliver without undermining the bases of domination themselves. Reformism is essential for averting revolution, but at the risk that the revolution will emerge in the same medium that reformism creates, through its active, radical, and effective repudiation."[8]

For promotion of democracy the United States has defined two types of programs of political intervention: those directed at long-term "democratic political development," and those directed at a "democratic transition," that is, a change of regime. The programs of political development are aimed at stabilizing and consolidating the political systems in societies already considered democratic and are applied particularly in Latin America and the former socialist countries. In the second case, two types of transitions are identified: from right-wing or authoritarian dictatorships to civil elitist regimes, and from socialist, nationalist, or popular regimes conceived as adversaries of the United States, wherein lies the case of Cuba.[9] Here the precondition that the opposition behave "loyally" is waived. On the contrary, U.S. policy is directed at creating what the Marxists call the necessary "objective and subjective conditions" for revolutionary—or counterrevolutionary, as the case may be—change to occur.

With respect to Cuba, the objective conditions are associated with maintaining the economic crisis as a destabilizing element, and the subjective conditions with stimulating the rise of "new power alternatives" capable of serving as catalysts for a political crisis. In other words, intensifying the economic blockade and encouraging political dissidents to continue to be the core of U.S. policy toward the island. Both tactics do not always combine harmonically. The difficulty in the Cuban case lies in the lack of domestic elements capable of putting this project in practice. In the absence of a strong and credible counterrevolutionary movement within Cuba, various North American political circles propose the need for an opening in their relations with Cuban society, through which they can increase their influence. This objective contradicts the essence of the blockade, the interests of the Cuban-American right wing, and the sense of immediacy assumed by U.S. policy for the defeat of the Cuban Revolution. The dichotomy has permitted the coexistence of various currents of thought within U.S. policy and explains why the counterrevolution has expressed itself in alternatives that seem contradictory and hard to conjugate.

Counterrevolutionary Restoration

In February 1995, the draft of the Cuban Liberty and Democratic Solidarity Act, sponsored in the U.S. Congress by Sen. Jesse Helms (R-N.C.) and Rep. Dan Burton (R-Ind.), was made public. It had been promoted by the Cuban-American National Foundation and drafted with the participation of attorneys from Bacardí, the Asociación de Industriales Azucareros y Colonos Cubanos en el Exilio, and other institutions of the prerevolutionary Cuban oligarchy. One year later it was passed by a wide margin in both chambers, and President Clinton signed it into law.

This bill clearly reflects, as no other document does, the essence of Cuban-American right-wing thinking, their proposals for the future of Cuba, and the interests that lie behind these politicians. In a way the bill breaks with the logic of the evolution of the counterrevolution with respect to the role that they are destined to assume in the future of Cuba under an eventual reversal of the revolutionary process. It reintroduces the claims for restoration of the old Cuban national oligarchy. The law stresses, above any other consideration, the interests of this class in recuperating its wealth and its political and social status on the island. The oligarchy's natural ally, for reasons of philosophy and opportunistic political benefits, is the most reactionary segment of the North American right wing, thus complicating the application of other policies, more adapted to contemporary reality and even to the thinking of the more advanced neoconservative circles.

The law constitutes a reflection of the preponderance of the right wing in the current Cuban-American bourgeoisie, but also the anachronism of its positions and the divorce between its goals and the most basic interests of the Cuban people. Until then, the CANF had avoided defining itself around these interests. The contradictions between this sector—ex-proprietors of large fortunes in Cuba—and a stratum of the less wealthy prerevolutionary bourgeoisie and middle class that today also form part of the Cuban-American bourgeoisie, were manifest within the Cuban-American ultraright. Given the language of the bill, the latter would be at a disadvantage in competing for Cuba's principal resources. The law also contradicts the image that this organization had tried to transmit to the Cuban people. Jorge Mas Canosa, in a video sent clandestinely to Cuba in 1992, stated: "I have said and I reiterate that the Cuban exiles will not go to Cuba in search of something, to reclaim anything. The foundation is responsible for having totally changed the mentality of the Cuban exiles."[10] This mutation is only conceivable given its loss of influence over the totality of the Cuban-American bourgeoisie and the U.S. government, as well as by its desperation to avert possible changes in U.S. policy toward Cuba.

The provisions of the law are aimed at strengthening the economic blockade and applying more rigorously the extraterritorial articles of the Torricelli Act, oriented not only toward trade but also foreign investment in Cuba. They go so far as to prohibit entry into the United States of persons who invest in Cuba, and their families, penalizing the countries that do business with the island and banning access to the U.S. market of products containing Cuban sugar. But the most telling aspect of the Helms-Burton Act is its provisions regarding properties nationalized by Cuba and the conditions established for the relations of the United States with the government that they hope to install there.[11]

The right of nationalization of private property constitutes a sovereign right that most nations have applied at one time or another, and both the U.S. government and its courts have recognized the authority of the Cuban government in this regard.[12] Nevertheless, the Helms-Burton Act conditions any future settlement with Cuba on the return of the properties or the compensation of the claimants. This refers not only to nationalized U.S. properties—pending negotiation since 1960 at the request of Cuba[13]—but also those of former Cuban citizens. This is one of the most extraordinary novelties of the law. When referring to properties of U.S. citizens seized by the government of Cuba on January 1, 1959, or thereafter, it includes in this notion those Cubans who at a later date became naturalized U.S. citizens. Here the law not only ignores the rights of the Cuban state over its own citizens, but also violates the U.S. legal doctrine itself and creates a dangerous legal precedent for Cuba's future relations with other countries. The January 1st date is not without significance, either. Before the Agrarian Reform of May 1959, in Cuba there were no expropriations except those of acknowledged embezzlers of the Batista regime, some of whom today have significant influence within the foundation.

Theoretically, this law burdens the Cuban people—even if the revolutionary government were overthrown—with the obligation to pay a sum that, according to U.S. government estimates, exceeds $100 billion,[14] many times the country's gross national product. It also questions the rights acquired not only over productive installations that for thirty-five years were the object of capital investments by the Cuban state and more recently by foreign investors, but also over housing, health centers, schools, preschool centers, and many other services that today operate from locations that could be considered properties subject to claims by anyone who left the country. The passage of this law has put the question of payment of compensation of legitimate North American properties on a dead end track, insofar as the revolutionary government could never accept a claim of this nature, for reasons of economics as well as sovereignty. This concern has been voiced by some large U.S. corporations that for thirty years have awaited a solution to the dispute, allowing them to make effective their claims.[15]

But the proponents of the law were not only thinking of a solution to the political future of Cuba that would favor them. Its provisions would also permit immediate claims to foreign companies with investments in Cuba. "The Cuban-American proprietors of sugar mills, tobacco farms, cattle ranches, and other businesses confiscated after the Cuban Revolution are closely following the proposed Helms-

Burton bill. For the first time in over three decades the law could give them the opportunity to go to court, allowing them—even though they were not U.S. citizens at the moment their properties were seized—to bring suit in the United States against foreign companies that 'traffic' in confiscated Cuban properties."[16]

The Helms-Burton Act also requires that the "future democratic government of Cuba," in order to be legitimate, be approved by the U.S. government, fulfill these and other conditions set by the United States, and in effect subordinate itself to a U.S.-Cuba Council that would coordinate the relations between the U.S. government and private sector, and its Cuban counterparts; a role made to order for the CANF. In this manner, the foundation satisfied, at least temporarily, the objective of averting the process toward a revision of the Cuba policy, as had been suggested by the majority of the main news organizations and key political figures, including noted spokespersons of neoconservative currents.

The promotion of this project was not alien to the domestic situation in the United States. The victory of the conservative Republicans in the mid-term elections of 1994 significantly weakened the Clinton administration and projected the neoconservative sector to the race for the presidency in 1996. The cohesion that this effort required prompted the neoconservatives to temporize with elements such as Senator Helms. An old ally of the CANF, the greatest exponent in Congress of extreme reactionary thinking, and a hard-liner incapable of adapting to the requirements of the new order, Helms nevertheless enjoyed substantial support from ultraconservative elements in the United States. This situation turned out to be particularly favorable for the foundation, because it coincided with its fallout with the administration as a result of the expansion of migratory accords with Cuba signed in May 1995.[17]

The Clinton administration initially opposed the Helms-Burton bill because of the international problems that its extraterritorial nature would evoke. However, the Clinton strategists in the campaign against Bob Dole recommended its approval when Cuban Air Force fighters shot down two airplanes belonging to the organization Hermanos al Rescate (Brothers to the Rescue) on February 24, 1996. In the beginning this organization searched the waters of the Straits of Florida for illegal Cuban immigrants, with the consent and cooperation of U.S. authorities. After the signing of the migratory accords they began to fly over Cuban air space for propaganda purposes. These overflights received wide coverage in the U.S. media and the U.S. government even sent messages to its Cuban counterpart warning of these occurrences and promising to put a stop to them. They did not, giving rise to the incident that cost the lives of four Rescate pilots. The U.S. government then adopted a different position: it backed the enactment of Helms-Burton, imposed other sanctions on Cuba, and took the case to the UN Security Council. After a controversial process that included investigations by international experts and contradictory rulings by the International Civil Aviation Organization, the Security Council approved a mild resolution condemning Cuba and called attention to the responsibility of the States to control the adequate use of civil aviation, an implied reference to the United States. The passage of the Helms-Burton Act has sharpened the contradictions between the United States and its allies—the European Union, Mexico, and Canada—within the context of the North American Free Trade Agreement (NAFTA) and the World Trade Organization (WTO). Even the Organization of American States has declared the law to be an unacceptable violation of the principles of territoriality and sovereignty, free trade, the unity of the international market, and respect for human rights. It became, in fact, a dangerous precedent that was rapidly extended to other countries, such as Libya and Iran, through the enactment of the D'Amato-Kennedy Act only months after Helms-Burton was passed.

Its role in the approval of this law placed the CANF squarely in favor of coercion as a component of the strategy of "promoting democracy" in Cuba. This position contradicts the more general projections of U.S. strategy after the Cold War because it leads to social chaos and the restoration of a historically displaced social class, compromising the stability of the regime they aim to impose. By reflecting the aspirations of the oligarchy and the pro-Batista circles that migrated in the initial stage, the law reduces the capacity for maneuvering of U.S. policy and compromises other interests. Therefore, in the post–Cold War situation, the counterrevolution debates whether to continue encouraging this option or using other resources that some consider more effective for dismantling the Cuban revolutionary system.

Pluralism and Counterrevolution

In the corner opposite of the post–Cold War counterrevolutionary options are the currents of thought that focus on strengthening the internal opposition. This line will tend to evolve—in fact, such an evolution is already evident—according to the patterns of what Robinson predicts will be the new forms of North American intervention in Cuba:

> Washington has already begun to foment a national opposition network inside and outside of Cuba, backed by a wide international support network that includes human rights groups, political parties, labor unions, media, youth and women's groups, civic associations, etc., following the same pattern as the *Nicaraguan model*. These programs of *political aid* would attempt to give the opposition network the capacity for political action and public visibility within the Cuban population. Such a democratic network would have an interconnected leadership that would share a common program. It will not be a covert or violent opposition. Its political platform will be moderate, even nationalist, and will not call for the overthrow of the Cuban government, rather for a dialog leading to a political opening and peaceful change. It will raise delicate questions for the Cuban population

> with emphasis on the economic wants and aspirations of the younger generation born after 1959. North American strategists will try to build a social base for the political opposition among the groups linked to the emerging foreign sector of the dual economy, exploiting the incipient social stratification, the resentments, and the legitimate gripes.[18]

The efforts of the external counterrevolutionary groups that defend this line of action have, until now, been directed at building, organizing, and legitimizing the internal opposition, which they believe possible only after a change in U.S. policy toward Cuba. This explains why their platform consisted in recognizing certain achievements of the Revolution and giving assurances to the Cuban people, validating the internal opposition by emphasizing its moderation, criticizing the anachronisms of U.S. policy, and facing up to the intransigent positions of the Cuban-American extreme right wing. The positions of these counterrevolutionaries correspond with those of the Plataforma Democrática Cubana, differing only in a longer-term vision that does not take for granted the supposed immediacy of the fall of the Cuban government.

Apparently these groups' demands toward Cuba are limited to favoring the development of "political pluralism," understood as the reinsertion of the émigré political groups in national life and the expansion of opportunities for the internal counterrevolutionary groups—with the corresponding assistance from abroad—to participate in the domestic political debate. Seemingly, this boils down to appealing to the Cuban government for greater "tolerance" for the opposition. Only in this case they propose a level of tolerance that capitalism has never allowed for itself. Tolerance and power are interconnected by a relation of dependency that establishes the limits of each. The limit to democratic toleration in capitalist countries has always been the capacity of the system to survive. The class issue determines the sense of tolerance and, therefore, of repression. The market constitutes the means of repression par excellence of the neoliberal representative democracies, insofar as it establishes the limits between real opportunities and tolerable expectations. "In this cleansing of the society the market is once again a fundamental factor, because it plays the role of showing each individual, every day, like a mirror, who he really is, what he has and does not have access to. And this ends up establishing what this school calls the new social rationality that leads to an ordered society, a rational society."[19]

In Cuba the degree of tolerance is limited by the antagonism of the positions—the aim is to transform the model of political organization of the society, not the government—and the aggressiveness of the United States. This constitutes a real threat, present in all aspects of national life by way of the economic blockade and the promotion of counterrevolution through multiple means. On the other hand, tolerance is enhanced by the level of support enjoyed by the Revolution, which makes unnecessary—and not functional under the specific Cuban conditions—the use of forms of repression common in most parts of the world. This proposal suggests, in fact, opening once again a domestic space to all manifestations of counterrevolution and, for its part, to North American domination, which corresponds precisely to the "programs for transition to democracy" designed by the U.S. government.

Therefore, this is not a new twist in the North American theory of subversion. It was, in fact, applied intensively against the former socialist camp and became an essential part of the doctrines applied in the so-called low-intensity conflicts in the Third World. This explains the resistance offered by the Cuban revolutionary forces to granting any space to this trend. But the implementation of this line of action has been hampered not only by the opposition of the Cuban government and revolutionary circles, but also by the inflexibility of U.S. policy, by the incapacity of the foreign counterrevolution to renovate and adjust to the new Cuban reality, and by the lack of organization and popularity of the counterrevolutionary groups within Cuba.

This counterrevolutionary current responds to a less structured organizational body whose operation is based on more diffuse, and therefore more deceptive, ideological premises. Thus on many occasions this current is confused with other efforts truly aimed at normalizing relations between the United States and Cuba and with a legitimate internal debate directed at overcoming the imperfections of the system, which complicates the Cuban response and leads to mistakes in identifying its enemies. This constitutes, by the way, one of the objectives. This group can be distinguished from other natural positions in the contemporary ideological debate—conferring on it a specific counterrevolutionary character—by the fact that its radius of action is not limited to the ideological sphere, rather it is structured to act on the Cuban reality with clearly political ends. These are to organize the internal opposition from positions more acceptable to certain European and Latin American circles, and more adjusted to the requirements of the new international order.

The theoretical challenge is to find the formulas that permit the divorce between the society and the state and apply them to Cuba as was done in other socialist countries; in essence, to fracture the popular cohesion around the Cuban revolutionary project, undoubtedly the principal determinant of its survival. These groups have found a receptive ear among North American liberal sectors, circles of the international social democracy, and various human rights groups particularly in the United States. Similarly they have been challenged by the more aggressive counterrevolutionary circles who consider that they have backed down, and their message has found little echo in the mainstream of the Cuban-American community, more inclined toward conservative attitudes.

The best-known figure of this current of thought is Ramón Cernuda, an art collector from Miami who presents himself as the foreign representative of the dissident groups of social democratic persuasion that exist on the island. Both Cernuda and the Platform made the linchpin of their political program a call for a "national dialog," which the principal internal counterrevolutionary groups convened in June 1990. It constituted an effort at a counterrevolutionary arrangement around the theme of a democratic transition, with the singularity that it originated from within Cuba and it enjoyed the personal support of then president George Bush.[20] However, the CANF and other traditional counterrevolutionary groups labeled it treason, and the projected attempt at a union was aborted in the midst of a bitter dispute.

Despite the limited effectiveness demonstrated to date, this political line fills a space within the U.S. strategy and responds to a model that is particularly effective as a tactic for creating a climate of political opening. Its shortcoming lies in its dependence on three assumptions that are unlikely to happen: a significant moderation of U.S. policy toward Cuba; renewed strength, unity, and political capacity of the internal counterrevolution; and the growing support of the Cuban-American community to a thesis that breaks with the traditional patterns of the counterrevolution and affects sensitive interests.

The hierarchy of the Catholic Church, after a period of confrontation with the Revolution that endured until 1962, admitted having assumed a "quiet posture" until 1986, when it adopted a truly conciliatory position in the Encuentro Nacional Eclesial Cubano (Cuban national ecclesiastic encounter), an event in which both clergy and laity participated. The conclusions of this event went so far as to affirm that "our society has made serious efforts to promote social rights, such as life, nutrition, medical assistance, education, adequately paid employment. We consider that this occupies a primary place; and we know that the full exercise of these constitutes not only the condition for authentic liberty, but also an already manifest way of being free. . . . Socialist society has helped Christians to value the human person more. . . . It has taught us to give for the sake of justice what before we gave as charity; appreciate human labor more, not only as a factor of production but also as an element of personal development; and comprehend the need for structural changes for a better distribution of goods and services."[21]

These positions—interpreted as attempts at accommodation nonexclusive of other contradictions with the revolutionary process—significantly improved relations between the Cuban Catholic hierarchy and the state and eased the way for harmonizing with the various religious expressions that existed in the country.[22] This attitude, however, changed drastically from the moment the crisis occurred, the Church once again adopting very critical postures toward the Revolution. The Catholic hierarchy then launched a call for a "national reconciliation"—supported by the Vatican—which some scholars considered to be

> a redefinition of an alternative challenge, centered on the unconditional acceptance of the exiles and of the expressions [real and potential] of an internal opposition, in an ambiguous combination of family reunification and politics. Basically, we are not witnessing here a gesture of toughening on the part of the hierarchy. Rather it is the exteriorization of the Church's own project, that despite seeing its sphere of influence decrease, never ceased being the only legalized opposition environment within a unitary, homogenous, doctrinaire, and even ideologically exclusive political spectrum, as has been the case with Cuba. . . . Now it is not essentially a question of dialog between Church and state [although it is present] nor of Marxists and Christians. What is essential for the bishops is now the dialog between the island and its émigrés, which, interspersed with the dialog between the Revolution and the opposition, is the theme that marks the text.[23]

In this manner the Cuban Catholic hierarchy—while trying to distance itself from extremist counterrevolutionary groups and facing their accusations of vacillation—is clearly included within the strategy of "promotion of democracy," strengthening its role as a possible "agent of change" that Samuel Huntington attributes to it in the Cuban case. It is the same role that, according to that scholar, it played with great success during the 1970s and 1980s in various parts of the world. The collaboration between the Vatican and the Reagan government in carrying out a policy of subversion in Poland has been well documented.[24]

Alternative Political Currents

In the context of the aggravated climate of intransigence of Cuban immigrants toward the revolutionary process that existed after 1989, it was nevertheless significant that over 50 percent of those polled favored improvement in family contacts, 39 percent approved excluding food and medicines from the embargo, and 25 percent supported its complete lifting. Younger immigrants with more education and higher incomes comprised the least hostile group in the sample. Women exhibited more opposition to the embargo, and those who had left their country more recently expressed a greater interest in maintaining contact.[25]

These attitudes are basically driven by the desire to maintain ties with family living in Cuba but, due to the connection established between the positions of the extreme right and rejection of those ties, they also express a certain distancing from that reactionary posture. The figures can be analyzed in the context of studies by sociologist Alejandro Portes, who in 1993 attempted to classify the political attitudes of the Cuban-American community—despite the imprecision of political definitions within the North American system. Portes found that 3.6 percent were in the extreme left (very liberal), 19.3 percent in the moderate left (liberals), 22.5 percent in the center (moderate), 48.5 percent in the moderate right (conservative), and 6 percent in the extreme right (very conservative).[26]

These results demonstrate the conservative ideological pattern that predominates in the Cuban-American community. However, they also indicate that at least 20 percent of that community maintains a different position, in many cases favorable to the normalization of relations between the two countries. That 20 percent is composed, first of all, of individuals considered liberals in the U.S. context, the majority of them voting Democrats, without implying that all the liberal Democrats are included. Also included are persons who prioritize contacts with Cuban society and see in the improvement of relations the way to achieve that goal. Finally, there are the progressive sectors that manifest support—more or less critical—for the Cuban revolutionary process. These segments of the population, very heterogeneous in socioeconomic composition and attitudes, constitute the basis for alternative currents to the counterrevolution in the heart of the Cuban-American community. Within this line one finds both the more progressive thinkers as well as those who disagree with the premises of the Cuban system and therefore favor a change, yet are not militant and tend toward formulas that will lead to a compromise.

The left continues to be in the minority, particularly affected by the reversal that has taken place in the international revolutionary movement and the empowerment of the right wing in U.S. politics. Despite this, organizations such as the Brigada Antonio Maceo, Casa de las Américas, Alianza de Trabajadores de la Comunidad (Community workers' alliance), and the Cuban-American Committee have survived and maintain a presence in the political debate on Cuba. One element that stands out in the work of these groups is the way in which they have recently mobilized a small but growing segment of the Cuban-American community and incorporated it into the movement for humanitarian aid to Cuba. In this manner they exploit the contradictions in the counterrevolutionary movement by challenging them with attitudes promoting social and humanitarian values.

The intellectuals constitute, relatively speaking, the most liberal segment of the community. This definition has to be understood in the rather imprecise terms used in the United States to differentiate between liberal and conservative positions, particularly in relation to the role of the state, care for the underprivileged, and a less aggressive foreign policy. In the case of the Cuban-American community, liberalism translates into a distancing from the counterrevolutionary extreme right, a different ethics, and a greater degree of tolerance in the political debate. Even though the far right has attempted to gain a foothold in this sector—and the foundation in particular has tried to control it—their efforts have not met with success due, primarily, to the resistance of the intellectuals themselves. The influence of the right wing in this sector is circumscribed to a group of academics of limited professional prestige controlled by the CANF and the group of neoconservative intellectuals connected with the U.S. New Right, who have succeeded in making a significant impact on the system as a whole.

The predominance of liberalism within the fundamental body of the Cuban-American intellectual movement links it to the corresponding currents of North American political thought. These contemporary liberals adhere to the belief that the concept of national sovereignty is not an inalienable part of international relations, assume neoliberalism as the standard of global economic organization, and consider illegitimate any other form of government apart from representative democracy. These conceptions as applied to Cuba lead at the minimum to the conviction that the Cuban system is not viable and that the Revolution is incapable of surviving under current conditions. Therefore, they share the views that call for reforms according to U.S. demands. Thus, even without committing to the counterrevolutionary groups, most Cuban-American intellectuals have adopted positions that legitimize U.S. meddling in Cuban affairs and, in fact, have participated prominently in the elaboration of the various policy positions toward Cuba that are currently debated in that nation's circles of power. These papers have stressed the criteria of "promotion of democracy" from a perspective adjusted to the concept of "calibrated response" to eventual concessions that the intellectuals expect the Cuban government will make to U.S. demands.

The Moderates

One of the most interesting processes of the last few years leading to alternatives to classic counterrevolution has been the political infighting in the heart of the Cuban-American community itself, especially after the Democratic electoral victory of 1992, which brought about the development of the so-called moderate political current. The moderates cannot be defined on the basis of what they want for Cuba, because a wide range of interests and proposals find room within this tendency. They can be defined by what they do *not* want for the island. They clearly do not want social chaos, which leads them to oppose the economic blockade and the growing pressures to isolate Cuba. Nor do they want, for Cuba or Miami, the Cuban-American extreme right.

The moderates are ideologically and politically opposed to the revolutionary system in Cuba, the majority of its leaders have an active counterrevolutionary pedigree—including public links to the CIA—and often their proposals dovetail with the more advanced projections of the neocolonial domination scheme developed for the post–Cold War era. Nevertheless, their opposition to maintaining the economic blockade puts them outside the currently prevailing standard of counterrevolutionary strategy toward Cuba, not only because the blockade has been at the center of that policy but because its preservation responds to a philosophy that is not satisfied with influencing the Cuban political process. They want to lead it into a crisis and discredit it as a political alternative, achieving in this manner one of the objectives of the strategy for dealing with low-intensity conflicts: destroying or at least incapacitating the enemy. The opposition of the moderates to promoting chaos in Cuba, their rejection of the blockade, and their confrontation with the ultraright establish a different tone in the debate with respect to Cuba and constitute points of contact with Cuban society. This explains some of the steps taken by the revolutionary government to widen the possibilities for dialog with certain segments of this trend, even though they also constitute a form of external political opposition.

The moderates do not enjoy solid bases of support in the Cuban society, nor sufficient organization among the émigrés, to consider them at this time an alternative equivalent to the extreme right. However, the importance of this movement lies precisely in its disposition to compete with the hard right for political control of the Cuban-American community. Nevertheless, their positions with respect to Cuba are often laced with a counterrevolutionary rhetoric that they consider necessary in order to gain access to their electors and adjust to the North American political codes. The moderates reflect a strategic tendency that in perspective could favorably influence the contacts between Cuba and its immigration, as well as the direction of future U.S. policy toward the island and, in the course of local politics within the enclave, toward increased tolerance. This constitutes the desire of 64 percent of the community, according to the latest polls taken by Florida International University.[27]

The most representative groups in this line have been Cambio Cubano and the Comité Cubano para la Democracia (CCD). The declared objective of both organizations is to promote the "transition to democracy" in Cuba through negotiations with its government. Although their positions are definitely critical of U.S. policy, their proposals for the future of Cuba do not differ much from those promoted by the PDC and other groups of that nature. The novelty of these organizations lies in their composition and their tactic of presenting a message of conciliation free of the threats and preconditions characteristic of counterrevolutionary language.

Cambio Cubano, created in 1993 under the leadership of Eloy Gutiérrez Menoyo, is made up of individuals most of whom come from the most aggressive counterrevolutionary groups, which puts them in a favorable position for accessing a wider social base, more representative of the center of the Cuban-American population. The group's counterrevolutionary past, combined with the liberal and conciliatory image it now projects, makes it an attractive option for European and Latin American circles that favor changes in U.S. policy toward Cuba. It also allows them to confront the opposition—the Cuban-American ultraright—from a position of credibility and project themselves within the North American system as an alternative attractive to important power groups, some of them within the Clinton administration.

Cambio Cubano has labeled the Torricelli Act a new Platt Amendment, considering "unacceptable that a foreign Congress determine the future of Cuban democracy." In clear contraposition to the CANF, Cambio Cubano proposes to be a "trustworthy bridge with the island, not a group that coerces or conquers the people there." It claims to represent a "silent majority of the exiles" that favors tolerance and "peaceful transition" of the current Cuban political system along lines similar to those proposed by the Inter-American Dialog. Their approximation to the positions of that organization is not fortuitous, given that the principal foreign policymakers of the current U.S. administration have participated in this analysis and political action group. The Inter-American Dialog's proposal for the island consists of reforms to U.S. policy that relax some aspects of the blockade in order to "humanize" it, as a sign of good will, whereupon it will be easier to obtain continental support for the demand for changes in the Cuban political system. Essentially, the blockade will continue to be applied as a factor of additional pressure on the country until these changes take place. The Inter-American Dialog also favors increasing selective contacts between the two countries, aimed at influencing Cuban society.[28] Coinciding with these recommendations, Cambio Cubano considered at first that the lifting of the embargo could be used as a pawn in the negotiations, but later their position evolved toward support for its immediate and unconditional end. Its current position is that "the war is over," an attitude that led Cuba to authorize Gutiérrez Menoyo to visit the island on more than one occasion, beginning in June 1995, where he held various meetings with Fidel Castro.[29]

The specific weight of Cambio Cubano in the U.S. political debate on Cuba is still to be defined and will depend, above all, on the course that North American political interests take. At this moment, this group enjoys scant influence over the power elite in the United States, lacks a professional political machine, and lacks the resources and experience necessary to function within the system and make effective its potential capacity to mobilize the Cuban-American community. Therefore, the degree of impact on the United States depends still on the "use" that the establishment wants to make of this organization and the relative influence of its allies in the debate on Cuba. Nevertheless, it constitutes an interesting political alternative because it responds to a natural process of evolution originating in the heart of the émigrés, within traditionally counterrevolutionary sectors that came in conflict with the predominant political forces. This allows them the possibility to communicate with what until now has been the political base of the ultraright, a capacity that no other group opposed to this line has.

The Comité Cubano para la Democracia, also formed in mid-1993, groups a number of persons united—in their own words—by their criticism of the current U.S. policy toward Cuba and their opposition to the predominance of the extreme right in the political life of the Cuban-American community. It has been headed by Marcelino Miyares and Alfredo Durán, two participants in the Bay of Pigs invasion who later gained prominence in business and political circles in the United States. The rest of the group is composed primarily of prestigious liberal intellectuals scarcely integrated into the rest of the community and, consequently, with limited capacity for mobilization.

The CCD defines itself as an exponent of the positions of the moderate groups within the Cuban-American community, which, according to them, have until now been inadequately represented. It is opposed to "punitive measures" by the U.S. government against the island. The CCD proposes negotiations with the Cuban side to "put an end to authoritarian rule" and to pledge respect for those "civil and political rights" that it proclaims as the basis of its platform, extending this tolerance to the Cuban-American community, where it favors the "expansion of the political space." In contrast to other moderate groups, the CCD defines its counterpart in Cuba as the domestic dissident groups and pretends to act in favor of their development, denoting a degree of convergence with some tendencies of the counterrevolutionary movement.[30] Better prepared to deal within the North American system than Cambio Cubano, the CCD, however, does not share the latter's authority within potentially wide segments of the Cuban-American community. It is an elitist effort that intends to compete with the CANF in the struggle for political influence in Washington, for which it has the experience, capacity, and necessary contacts, but still lacks the financial backing that this enterprise demands. Nor has the CCD demonstrated the will needed to assume the consequences of a debate with the extreme right, which makes the organization seem inconsistent and vulnerable.

Somewhere between the traditional left and the more conservative moderate groups, Miami has witnessed two efforts at mass communications with particular impact in the United States and Cuba. These were the radio station Radio Progreso Alternativa and the magazine *Contrapunto,* headed by Francisco González Aruca and Nicolás Ríos, respectively. Both constitute unusual examples of persons that have found a space both in Cuba and in Cuban-American society. They have established communication bridges that, despite their limitations and conditionings, are of strategic value to the degree that they have become a standard of what is possible—on both sides of the Straits of Florida—and the adequate means to achieve it.

Radio Progreso Alternativa has the merit of launching a different voice among Miami radio stations and legitimizing a different approach to the Cuba issue in the day-to-day political debate within the Cuban-American community. Structured on the basis of a dynamic form of listener participation that includes live discussions and call-ins, its programs have achieved ratings that compete with the rest of the radio stations. The power of mass communications has given Radio Progreso Alternativa a capacity for mobilizing public opinion that the progressive groups had been unable to achieve to date and that covers a wide segment of the Cuban-American community. It reaches in particular those for whom relations with Cuban society are a priority and have yet to find an effective vehicle of representation. On the other hand, the station has faced a climate of intransigence whose breakdown is a question of interest to the various political forces in the area. This makes the project, and specifically the person of Aruca, converge with wider efforts—inside and outside the Cuban-American community—aimed at counteracting the dominance of the ultraright in the enclave and its influence over policy toward the island. In Cuba, Radio Progreso Alternativa is a well-known station and its programs and newscasts are sometimes heard through retransmission. Aruca is a recognized political figure with access to the most varied information sources and contacts with the country's leadership, including Fidel Castro.

Contrapunto magazine was an editorial effort directed by Nicolás Ríos. A journalist, former college professor, and prominent Christian Democratic leader in Cuba, Ríos has stood out for his criticisms of the extreme right and his defense of Cuban national values. Although the magazine had a limited circulation in the United States as a result of the systematic boycott by the right wing, it was a product of professional quality. Its appeal was its notable access to authoritative sources at the highest levels in Cuba and its penchant for open debate—giving access to the most varied positions—something not common to the forms of communication directed at the Cuban-American community. In Cuba, *Contrapunto* circulated regularly in academic and cultural circles, where it enjoyed an assiduous readership that frequently collaborated with the publication.[31]

In addition, Ríos, together with Armando Fiallo—also a well-known Christian Democratic figure—was involved in organizing seminars on "participative democracy," a forum of education and debate promoted by the Fundación pro Hombre headed by Fiallo in Venezuela with the financial sponsorship of the Hans Seidel Foundation, a German, Christian democrat organization. The seminars on participative democracy were held in Miami and on various occasions in Cuba. The assistants included persons from various segments of the population and constituted an unusual forum for discussion that won the respect of very diverse currents of thought. The activity of Ríos and Fiallo was reported relatively widely on the island and both have met with Fidel Castro and other members of the leadership.

The Absentees

Having made an inventory of the most important political tendencies among the émigrés and the segments where they are located, two absences are particularly worth noting. The immigrant youth is not represented in a significant manner in any of the political currents. It is the segment of the population that least travels to Cuba and there is no evidence that its members manifest special concern for any other topic. Rather, their behavior is characterized by apathy. There are no studies that provide an adequate explanation for this attitude but, whatever the causes, it is analogous to a very generalized attitude among North American youth and undoubtedly forebodes important changes in the medium run in the political orientation of the Cuban-American community toward the Cuba issue. This is even more true to the degree that the great majority of these persons no longer comprise a community of immigrants—as Mercedes Arce has accurately noted—and, therefore, they approach the subject from different premises than those that have conditioned the attitudes of their elders.

Another group whose absence from the political arena has become relevant and is in some manner related, for generational reasons, to the former is composed of corporate executives. This group has transcended the limits of the Cuban-American enclave and has inserted itself into the economic mainstream of the country, whether forming part of large U.S. corporations or of the principal sectors of the Florida economy. Without a doubt, this is an economically powerful group linked to some of the more important power blocs in the United States. Most are trained within the system and thus this segment brings together the most qualified elements of the Cuban-American community. We can assume that this group participates in many ways in the U.S. political system, yet it is not possible to identify where and how. Their influence in the debate on the Cuba issue has likewise been irrelevant.

The explanation can be found, perhaps, in the fact that their interests do not depend directly on the life of the enclave and that their relations with the island are not a priority for them. Nevertheless, the logical generational change that is taking place within the immigration, the consequences of the process of social integration, and the growing interest of North American business in gaining access to the Cuban market foreshadow a new role for this group. It should increase its level of political participation and assume greater leadership over the rest of the Cuban-American community. As in the case of Cuban-American youth, it is difficult to define their ideological leanings and the impact they could conceivably have on attitudes toward Cuba. But whatever these may be, these executives will respond to new premises and inevitably reflect another political environment.

The Future of the Counterrevolution

The so-called postmodern era in the history of humanity has begun. It is characterized by the contradictions resulting from having achieved tremendous technological advances that globalize production, information, and, therefore, culture, as well as the predominance of a political system that pretends to perpetuate ancestral inequalities and the indiscriminate exploitation of natural resources in favor of transnationalized capital. This international capital must act within the conditions imposed by an international order in which nations deal with their own internal conflicts and offer greater or lesser resistance to the control of the industrialized powers.

The United States is the center—rather than the pole—of this international arena, which is in the process of adjustment and remodeling. The end of the Cold War did away with the basis that sustained the consensus for the politics of force that characterized U.S. conduct after WWII and the corresponding ideological standards that facilitated internal cohesion, introducing both domestic and international complications in both spheres. Nuclear power, once the basis for the strategic balance with the USSR, has lost that function under the current conditions, and the indiscriminate use of military force—although events of the last few years suggest the opposite—faces increased domestic and international opposition that makes its application more difficult. Added to this is the impact of its costs on the budget deficit and other aspects of the U.S. economy, and the contradiction between these investments and the significant reduction in expenditures for the social sector advocated by the conservatives, precisely as an excuse to reduce the economic imbalance. Zbigniew Brzezinski writes that while the United States has no rival capable of contesting its vast power, domestic problems inhibit the length of its reach and prevent converting that power into a recognized global authority. In consequence, the United States cannot be the world's policeman, he continues, nor the global banker nor even the global moralist. The first requires legitimacy, the second must be based on liquidity, and the third depends on setting an immaculate example.[32]

The undisputed element of U.S. supremacy lies in its military power, which logically translates into the basis of its political hegemony. The prosperity of the U.S. economy also depends on this political might. Thus, the psychology of intimidation is an intrinsic part of the ideology that constitutes the basis for the North American power system. It can be asserted that the characteristic trait of the current political situation in the United States is strategic confusion and widespread mistrust of the mechanisms of government. For many North American scholars, the principal problem of national security that the country faces today lies precisely in these domestic contradictions.[33]

Most U.S. policymakers and analysts agree that, in the absence of a bipolar world, North American hegemony must be exercised in a casuistic manner, depending on the regional, subregional, and national conditions and requirements of the case in question. Thus, no option is barred: the policy may be economic, political, ideological, or military, and executed unilaterally or multilaterally. In reality, the aim is to be prepared to use a combination of all, varying the emphasis depending on the situation—an objective that requires, first of all, being well informed about the local reality and anticipating its evolution. This has modified to a certain degree the significance of espionage—one of the reasons for the reforms that have taken place in the intelligence services—and assigns a greater role to academic studies and interpersonal contacts in foreign policy design.

In consequence, the strategic orientation of U.S. foreign policy does not slant it inexorably toward a specific policy with respect to Cuba. Within reason, this could be either maintaining the blockade, military invasion, or a political opening that would favor peaceful penetration. The strategy is still to destroy the Revolution, but no global projection determines, for the moment, the tactics to be employed, as opposed to what often happened in the context of the Cold War. On one hand, the current situation does not favor maintaining a policy of maximum hostility toward Cuba. The absence of adequate justification, international opposition, and concern for the consequences for the United States of social chaos in Cuba are powerful arguments against this strategy. Nevertheless, a weakened central government, an ultraconservative ideology in vogue that is particularly intransigent with respect to Cuba, and the dealings of political campaigns characterized by the lack of credibility of the candidates open too much space for inertia and political opportunism.

The counterrevolution is currently polarized between those that propose the gradual and peaceful dismantling of the system—a line of thought better adjusted to the currents that predominate in the U.S. media and academic centers but still lacking in concrete political expression—and the extreme right. The latter prefers the apocalyptic alternative, and nevertheless enjoys the support that results from the political influence and advantage accumulated in thirty-five years of campaigns aimed at demonizing the Cuban regime. Because of this, the counterrevolution is today capable of expressing itself in many ways and influencing Cuban society through various channels. Cuba has been inevitably exposed to more capitalism and has made necessary adjustments as required by the new international order, which constitute, in and of themselves, challenges of unavoidable consequences for the Revolution. This generates an ideological climate favorable to counterrevolutionary activity, which additionally enjoys powerful external political advocates.

The counterrevolution will possibly tend to employ more subtle and long-term methods than those it has historically applied. But that has not happened yet. On the contrary, what presently characterizes the Cuban counterrevolution is the aggressiveness, intransigence, and blunt plan of restoration and dependency outlined in the political platform of the Cuban-American extreme right. Thanks to the support of the most reactionary segments of U.S. society, this continues to be the official policy of this country toward Cuba after the Cold War. The most widely disseminated alternative to the current policy has been to ease the economic embargo but keep it as an instrument of pressure and combine it with measures that would facilitate the ideological and political penetration of the United States into Cuban society. This formula of "peaceful subversion," not a totally new element in U.S. strategy, tends nevertheless to be designed with greater care and gains popularity as an option for the United States.

This is due to the singularity of the Cuban case with respect to North American policy toward other countries and the apparent validation of these tactics when viewed as contributing elements to the collapse of the European socialist camp.

However, the extreme right is correct in affirming that reducing the blockade to a bilateral action—an embargo—is not a sustainable option for U.S. policy. Either the United States applies the blockade in full strength, emphasizing its extraterritorial aspects—discouraging investment and trade by other countries in Cuba—regardless of the feasibility or political cost, or it unshackles the chains that accompany this policy and seeks equal opportunities to compete for the Cuban market and influence its society. The latter is hampered by the Monroe Doctrine logic that lies beneath U.S. policy toward Latin America. On the other hand, it is ever clearer that crisis leads to social chaos and, therefore, crisis and the "peaceful transition" advocated by certain sectors of the U.S. political spectrum are incompatible. It is this contradiction, together with the weight of growing international pressure and the capacity for resistance that the Cuban people demonstrate, that could motivate a change in policy toward Cuba.

Despite the presence of a strong current in favor of this change, the Clinton administration has not decided to advance beyond a solution to the migratory issue, which enjoys a solid national consensus. It has not taken advantage of the spaces that the Torricelli Act opened for promoting communications, increasing nongovernmental relations and manifesting a willingness for "calibrated response" to changes they expect will take place in Cuba, assuming this line of action from the openly subversive perspective outlined above.

The internal factor is a decisive element for the feasibility of U.S. plans and, consequently, for the future of the counterrevolution. The economic crisis constitutes, without a doubt, a source of personal dissatisfaction that tends to complicate the domestic political scene. The collapse of the socialist camp caused widespread confusion within the revolutionary ranks, from which Cuba could not escape unhurt. Economic reforms bring with them new contradictions and the emergence of social sectors that alter the homogeneity achieved during the revolutionary process. "The duality of the internal market; the reappearance of inequalities; the massive influx of tourism; the current constraints for the state in furthering social integration through full employment; the subjective impact of the crisis of the Soviet paradigm; the emergence of new socioeconomic actors and with them the de facto restructuring of the country's political economy; these and many other elements have particular material, psychological, and social repercussion for the various sectors (workers, farmers, students, intellectuals), the perspectives and expectations of their respective organizations, as well as the view of reality that each takes in light of the new and rapidly changing circumstances."[34] As Fidel Castro has stated, the most serious consequence of this situation is a certain degree of social disorder and corruption. They become, in fact, destabilizing factors for a revolutionary power that, since the mid-1980s, had recognized its bureaucratic imperfections and launched a process that came to be known as the "rectification of errors and negative tendencies."

U.S. policy pretends to exploit these new circumstances precisely in order to stimulate internal counterrevolution, conceived as the "social actor" chosen to convert the economic breakdown into a political alternative. Given the current conditions in Cuba, a rather common error among contemporary Cubanologists is to confuse counterrevolution with the logical internal debate, often encouraged by the Cuban leadership itself and situated within the space offered by the nation's own institutions. Others such as Huntington—whom Zbigniew Brzezinski called, possibly in praise, the Machiavelli of democracy—hope that from the legitimate debate will rise the forces capable of reversing the revolutionary process.[35] Nevertheless, substantial qualitative differences separate the need for reforms of a particular political system and the structured opposition to its projections and premises. In the Cuban case, this design collides with other factors that constitute powerful stimuli for maintaining national cohesion in support of this process:

- A rich nationalist and anti-imperialist tradition has forged an ideology that, in concrete political terms, transcends occasional conflicts and serves as a compass for the general aspirations of the nation. Combined with the educational level it has attained, the Cuban people have developed a political culture that allows them to realistically gauge their alternatives and pursue their interests.
- Cuba's socialism has turned out to be a genuine process with wide popular support and active participation. It is morally gratifying to generations of Cubans who, having been educated in this system of beliefs, make it the factor that gives meaning to their lives. It also has produced concrete material and social benefits for the population that, even under current circumstances, are of great value when compared to other underdeveloped countries.
- Social stratification is minimal compared with other countries and —possibly more important—it takes on particular characteristics within the socialist structure, benefiting sectors that would otherwise not be in a capacity to compete.[36]
- The manner in which the Cuban state has managed the crisis has allowed it to maintain an adequate level of egalitarian social assistance, instead of abandoning the less fortunate, and to uphold relatively well a collective approach to problem solving. This has served as a palliative to the selfishness that every situation of this nature generates.
- This function of the state as a guarantor of social welfare—deeply rooted in Cuban political tradition—is reinforced as the first signs of recuperation of the crisis appear. It becomes evident that public mediation in the control of the commercial mechanisms introduced by the reforms is beneficial to the general public. This perception is strengthened by the power of cohesion and mobilization that the personality of Fidel Castro contributes to Cuban political life.

In light of these realities, the counterrevolution sees its perspectives limited by objective historical factors, which makes the Cuban case different from other experiences. The counterrevolution does not have a class base in the country, it does not represent the specific interests of certain segments of society, and it offers no viable alternatives for the nation as a whole. Although studies on the evolution of social classes in Cuba are still in progress, it is evident that the Revolution totally alienated the bourgeoisie from the national scene and significantly amalgamated all other social classes. The massive migration of the groups better situated in the prerevolutionary social pyramid favored this process and limited their impact within society.

For the sake of an internal political analysis, it would be more appropriate to speak of the segments that make up Cuban society. Workers, farmers, professionals, intellectuals, government officials, military personnel, and political operatives comprise a social structure that is a mixture of social origins, educational levels, philosophical tendencies, and personal aspirations. Although the emergence of sectors linked to the reforms of agricultural property, the dollar economy, and the private market adds new elements to the traditional social structure, it would be a mistake to attribute to one or another sector qualities specific to the concept of social class. Beyond the many theoretical questions posed by this approach to the problem, in practical terms, sectorization does not have as wide an expression in the context of the family as generally occurs with class differences.

It is not correct, therefore, to speak of soft sectors when attempting to diagnose Cuban society. Paradoxically, this mistake has been made both by certain tendencies of Cuban political theory and in the design of North American subversive activity. Without a doubt, the dialectics of the historical process determines periods of greater or reduced stability and the crisis of recent years has been a cause of the weakening of positions that, at other times, appeared very firm. This, however, is valid for individuals of any sector and age group, which does not prevent these problems from being expressed with greater emphasis among certain groups—as evidenced by the predominance of young people among illegal immigrants—or that their repercussions are greater depending on the particular sector in question.

After being practically displaced from the national scene, the internal counterrevolution experienced a resurgence in the latter half of the 1970s through the variant of the human rights defense groups. This form, characteristic of the policy assumed by the Carter administration, reflects the beginning of a strategy aimed at remodeling the methods of influence of the North American system of hegemony. The Reagan administration gave a decisive thrust to this option, without excluding other more aggressive weapons in its arsenal against Cuba. Project Democracy and the subsequent creation of the National Endowment for Democracy integrate these groups within a subversive concept that includes financing them and promoting their activities abroad. The excessive sense of triumph after the Cold War presages—probably before its time—their conversion into open political opposition.

The internal counterrevolutionary groups, however, do not reflect emerging alternatives in the domestic political debate, nor do they represent any specific sector of Cuban society. Just like the groups that have settled abroad, an analysis of their evolution reveals a direct relationship between their positions and current U.S. policy toward Cuba and similar strategic aims. On the other hand, this relationship gains them an international repercussion that transcends their real capacities but limits their legitimacy in the Cuban environment. Comprised of individuals alienated from the mainstream of society, with scant authority and capacity of assembly, and inspired mainly by the desire to emigrate from the country, there is little indication that these groups will ever play a significant role in Cuban political life. They will likely continue to play a legitimizing function for a political opposition that has its base outside the country and depends on North American sponsorship. The counterrevolution will continue to be, in the foreseeable future, a phenomenon determined by exogenous forces and organized primarily from abroad, emphasizing the dependency of its domestic expressions.

Each day the Cuban émigrés will be less capable of fulfilling the counterrevolutionary function traditionally assigned to them by the North American system. The extreme right has been able to articulate this policy because it has counted on a social base that acts in correspondence with these codes. But the process of integration accompanied by the inevitable transfer among generations adds a new vision of the relations with Cuba and other political priorities. The enclave tends to be more a cultural reference than a socioeconomic reality. The individualist and consumerist culture itself—possibly the characteristic and unifying element par excellence in U.S. culture—will decrease the degree of politicization of the Cuban-American community and reorient its interests in a way similar to what has occurred with other ethnic groups in that society, prioritizing the issues that directly affect their daily lives. The new immigrants—even maintaining the relatively high figures established by the current accords—reflect another social composition and different political inclinations from the first generations. More than the possibility of becoming a source of revitalization of counterrevolutionary activity, their concerns are geared, initially, to surviving in a setting that is no longer so welcoming and, later, to maintaining the most normal and fluid relations possible with the family they left behind in Cuba. The Cuban policy toward new immigrants will undoubtedly contribute to this tendency.

The counterrevolutionary attitude of the Cuban émigrés prevalent since 1989 and the correlation to its domestic political projections has remained nearly unaltered. This is confirmed by the survey carried out by Florida International University in 1995—the fourth since 1991—this time in Miami and Union City, the areas of greatest concentration of Cuban-Americans in the United States. Over 70 percent declared that the position of the candidates toward Cuba has strong bearing in determining their electoral preferences. Nevertheless, the study registered changes in the way these attitudes are expressed, the most significant being the relative frustration regarding eventual political change in Cuba. The expectation that the Revolution would not survive more than five years fell from 88 percent in 1991 to 41 percent in 1995. Once again those who migrated after 1970 are more favorable than those who left before 1970 toward the search for negotiated solutions, and there exists a marked division between generations; the young tend to support this position without combining it with pressure tactics. Only 7.4 percent belong to organizations oriented specifically toward the Cuban issue and of these only 4.2 percent consider themselves active militants, which gives an idea of the limited real potential of the counterrevolutionary organizations.[37]

In U.S. relations with Latin America, the role of Miami tends to keep alive an interest in Cuba that does not depend on historical or generational factors but rather on the situation of the region, the interests of the United States, and the specific policy it follows with regard to Cuba. Thus it can lean in the traditional direction—maintaining to a certain degree the counterrevolutionary inclinations in the new generations—or accommodate to new interests related to the benefits resulting from possible business with Cuba. For small and medium-size companies—which characterize the economic structure of the enclave—the relations of the émigrés with Cuban society already signify a lucrative business. Even though a portion of the money spent as a result of these contacts benefits Cuba, the majority ends up in the hands of North Americans, in particular Cuban-Americans with businesses in the enclave. This tendency would be reinforced with an eventual opening of trade between the two countries. Despite the existence of industries in which the economies of Cuba and Florida compete, those related to the ethnic market would be complementary. Geographical proximity, the quality of the Cuban-American workforce, and the infrastructure already existing in Miami associated with tourism and trade with Latin America put the region in a privileged position should that opportunity occur. Thus, the growing interest of U.S. firms in doing business with Cuba should have repercussions in the attitude adopted by the Cuban-American community toward the issue in the future.

In a similar manner, the eventual course of U.S. domestic policy and the evolution of its ideological tendencies will influence the enclaves, in one way or another. Whatever this process may be, the most relevant effect will be that, as a result of their integration, the émigrés will be increasingly perceived as part of North American society, and their claim to eventual political rights in Cuba—an objective that has been at the center of the counterrevolutionary strategy—will lose legitimacy. The Cuban-American community constitutes an element of Cuban foreign policy and a factor of domestic influence because of its links with Cuban society and its cultural implications, but it cannot be considered a constituent element of its domestic policy. Notwithstanding the conflicts that determined their migration, the great majority did so freely, not as political exiles, and with the intention of settling and procreating in their new destination. It was a migration plagued with anomalies and many problems will have to be solved for relations with their country of origin to be truly normalized, including the right of return of those who desire to do so.[38] But the solution to this problem cannot be expected through the granting of political rights—decisive for the future of the "Cubans in Cuba"—to persons who, in legal and practical terms, are citizens of another country. More so when that country is the United States, with whom Cuba has had so many disagreements in which this migration has played such an active role.

The sustained advance of New Right forces within the U.S. political system poses new questions as to the future of U.S. policy toward Cuba, but the future of the Cubans cannot depend on decisions made in Washington. An aspect in which Fidel Castro and Monsignor Carlos Manuel de Céspedes—vicar general of the Archdiocese of Havana—agree is the exceptional historical character of the moment and the consequences that a frustration of the possibilities for independent development could have for the destiny of the Cuban nation.[39] This is precisely the nationalist challenge faced by the Revolution in Cuba. Given the historical dependence of the country on the North American system of hegemony and its consequences for the development of an independent bourgeoisie—a condition accentuated by Cuban migration and the formation of the Cuban-American community—the triumph of the counterrevolution would mean absolute dependence on the United States. I am not talking about actual annexation of the country since, as in the case of Puerto Rico, this would be too costly for the United States. Rather, it would be an organic subordination that would not require actual legalization, with implications even for the national psychology, insofar as the Plattist ideology would become historically validated. The Cuban-American community—whether or not its individual components are fully conscious of it—would be called on to play a significantly useful role in this process.

The challenge for Cuba continues to be perfecting the socialist system—defined as the realization of "Martí's postulate of national liberation with social justice,"[40] guarantor of the essential national consensus—and adapting it to the new international conditions without in the process losing self-esteem for the values of our race and our traditions of independence. The future will have to be decided in Cuba, by the Cubans, taking into account the international environment and particularly the turns taken by U.S. policy, but based on original and independent decisions adapted to the nation's reality. This is far from the proposals of those who, as expressed by José Martí, "admire without sufficient examination the institutions of the North American people, without seeing that they have not prevented the conversion of the democratic and worldly Yankee into the authoritarian, greedy, aggressive Yankee, and that those institutions are nothing more than the regulation of the rights that must be molded to the people where they are in force, and that they hurt them more than they help them when they do not conform, from the beginning, to their nature."[41]

This is not a utopia. At the same time that globalization presents new challenges to the sovereignty of nations—a sovereignty, by the way, that capitalism never guaranteed to the dependent countries—the logic of transnationalization also comes into conflict with the narrow geopolitical criteria that have guided the expansion of U.S. imperialism. Under these conditions it is difficult to prevent Cuba from broadening the scope of its international economic relations and becoming inserted into a system of global interdependence. Even with the injustices and disadvantages associated with underdevelopment, being part of a global system, this will always be better than the unipolar subordination that the United States has historically tried to impose and that has been at the core of the strategic objectives of the counterrevolution. The capacity demonstrated by the Cuban system for surviving under the most difficult conditions, with a high degree of domestic tranquillity—a very scarce commodity in the contemporary world—high cultural level of the population, and the presence of a very advanced economic and social infrastructure for a Third World country, assures the stability desired by international capital for its investments. These are the reasons why foreign investment has increased steadily in recent years, despite the intensification of the U.S. blockade.

Popular support for the Revolution continues to be the key to the country's political equation. The Revolution, by its nature and the powers it confronts, cannot survive without this support. Beyond the dissatisfactions and contradictions present in all societies and magnified by the crisis, all indicators point to a continuing high level of support for the Cuban political system. The results of the last two elections reflect this tendency and correspond with independent studies carried out by foreign specialists. In November 1994, a Gallup poll, sponsored by the *Miami Herald,* of more than a thousand Cubans determined that a majority believes that the Revolution has had more successes than failures. A significant number of those polled mentioned the U.S. embargo rather than the political system as the reason for their "economic misery"; a solid majority expected 1995 to be a better year, continuing with a set of highly popular economic reforms; most are still willing to support their Revolution. The picture of the Cubans that emerges from the survey is one of a sociable people, highly satisfied with their personal lives.[42] The counterrevolutionary has been unable to offer an alternative for improving—objectively and subjectively—this social reality. Herein lie its insufficiency and its estrangement from the general aspirations of the Cuban people. Its relevance is only commensurate to the persistence of the bilateral conflict between the United States and Cuba, emphasizing its dependent and antinationalist nature.

The flow of migrants toward the United States will continue, because it is the reflection of the economic differences between the two countries and the result of the pressures exerted by the separation of families. But we can expect that in the future it will respond less to the logic imposed by its confrontation with the Revolution, insofar as its social composition and its priorities are different. Above all, the flow will continue because it is untenable for the United States to continue paying the political and material price required for immigration to play its traditional counterrevolutionary role indefinitely. To the degree that this happens, a full normalization of the relations between the Cuban society and its émigrés will be possible. It would be a connection representative of the contemporary manner in which our ethnic and national roots are manifested, enriching respectively the Cuban culture and the welfare of both communities. At least, that is the hope.

Abbreviations in Notes and Bibliography

ANSA	(Italian news agency)
CEA	Centro de Estudios de América
CEAP	Centro de Estudios de Alternativos Políticas
CEASEN	Centro de Estudios sobre Asuntos de Seguridad Nacional
CESEU	Centro de Estudios sobre Estados Unidos
CIDE	Centro de Investigación y Docencia Económicas
EU	Estados Unidos (United States)
MES	Ministerio de Educación Superior
MININT	Ministerio del Interior (Ministry of the Interior)
MINREX	Ministerio de Relaciones Exteriores
UH	Universidad de La Habana

Notes

Introduction

1. "By bourgeoisie we mean the class of modern capitalists, which are the owners of the social means of production and employ salaried labor." Note by F. Engels to the English edition (1888) of Karl Marx, *The Communist Manifesto.*

2. Karl Marx, "Las luchas de clases en Francia de 1848 a 1850," in *Obras escogidas en dos tomos* (Moscow: Editorial Progreso, 1955), 1:124.

3. Jean Paul Sartre, "Huracán sobre el azúcar," in *Sartre visita a Cuba* (Havana: Edicion Revolucionaria, 1960), 160.

Chapter 1

1. Ramiro Guerra, *Manual de historia de Cuba (económica, social, y política): Desde su descubrimiento hasta 1868 y un apéndice con la historia contemporánea* (Havana: Consejo Nacional de Cultura, 1962), 490.

2. Ramiro Guerra, *La Guerra de los Diez Años,* 2 vols. (Havana: Editorial Ciencias Sociales, 1972), 1:28–29.

3. On the ethnoracial characteristics in the formation of the Cuban nationality, see Jesús Guanche Pérez, *Aspectos etnodemográficos de la nación cubana: Problemas y fuentes de estudio,* paper presented at the 18th Congress of ALAS, Havana, 1991.

4. Sergio Aguirre, *Eco de caminos* (Havana: Editorial de Ciencias Sociales, 1974), 86.

5. Ibid., 94.

6. Emilio Roig de Leuchsenring, *Tres estudios martianos* (Havana: Editorial de Ciencias Sociales, 1984), 26.

7. André Gunder Frank, *Lumpenburguesía: Lumpendesarrollo* (Mexico City: Ediciones Era, 1971), 13.

8. Carlos Rafael Rodríguez, *Cuba en el tránsito al socialismo* (Havana: Editorial de Ciencias Sociales, 1985), 34.

9. Michael J. Mazarr, *Semper Fidel: America and Cuba, 1776–1988* (Baltimore: Nautical and Aviation Publishing Company of America, 1988), 91.

10. Juan Luis Martín, interview by author, November 1995.

11. James S. Olson and Judith E. Olson, *Cuban-Americans: From Trauma to Triumph* (New York: Twayne Publishers, 1995), 34.

12. The Platt Amendment was a resolution of the U.S. Congress that established the right of that country to intervene in the internal affairs of Cuba.

13. Ramiro Guerra, *La expansión territorial de los Estados Unidos a expensas de España y los demás países latinoamericanos* (Havana: Editorial Ciencias Sociales, 1975), 425.

14. Ibid., 390.

15. Olson and Olson, *Cuban-Americans,* 34.

16. Carlos Rafael Rodríguez, *Cuba en el tránsito,* 308.

17. Ramón de Armas, Francisco López Segrera, y Germán Sánchez, *Los partidos políticos burgueses en Cuba neocolonial 1899–1952* (Havana: Editorial de Ciencias Sociales, 1985), 183.

18. Ibid., 175.

19. Ibid., 348–51.

20. Olson and Olson, *Cuban-Americans,* 48.

21. Armas, López Segrera, and Sánchez, *Partidos políticos,* 191.

22. Carlos Rafael Rodríguez, *Cuba en el tránsito,* 318.

23. Nevertheless, it is unlikely that it made up a third of the population, as suggested by Marifeli Pérez-Stable in *The Cuban Revolution* (New York: Oxford University Press, 1993), 27. For this calculation, Pérez-Stable includes within this class everyone that earned a monthly salary above 75 pesos, but in the Cuban economy of the time, this income was much closer to the poverty level than to the middle class, what I here call the petite bourgeoisie.

24. Carlos Rafael Rodríguez, *Cuba en el tránsito,* 318.

25. Ibid., 312.

26. Marifeli Pérez-Stable, *Cuban Revolution,* 87.

27. Carlos Rafael Rodríguez, *Cuba en el tránsito,* 313.

28. Ibid., 314.

29. Robert Scheer and Maurice Zeitlin, *Cuba: An American Tragedy* (Harmondsworth: Penguin, 1964), 26.

30. Ibid., 24.

31. Armas, López Segrera, and Sánchez, *Partidos políticos,* 164.

32. Thomas G. Paterson, *Contesting Castro: The United States and the Triumph of the Cuban Revolution* (New York: Oxford University Press, 1994), 48.

33. Refers to Ramón Grau's regime. "Mongo" is a nickname for Ramón.

34. Raúl Roa, *Retorno a la alborada,* 2 vols. (Santa Clara: Universidad Central de Las Villas, 1964), 1:63.

35. Hortensia Pichardo, *Documentos para la historia de Cuba,* 3 vols. (Havana: Editorial Ciencias Sociales, 1963), 3:546–47.

36. Armas, López Segrera, and Sánchez, *Partidos políticos,* 216.

37. Ibid., 217–18.

38. Eduardo Chibás, "En Cuba" section, *Bohemia* (Havana), May 25, 1947.

39. Unless otherwise noted, the data is taken from Scheer and Zeitlin, *Cuba,* 17–30.

40. Paterson, *Contesting Castro,* 39.

41. Ibid., 147.

42. Ibid., 26, 38.

43. Ibid., 35–54.

44. Noam Chomsky, *Deterring Democracy* (New York: Hill and Wang, 1992), 49.

45. Comité Central del Partido Comunista de Cuba [PCC], *Informe al Primer Congreso del Partido Comunista de Cuba* (Havana: Departamento de Orientación Revolucionaria del CC-PCC, 1975), 26–27.

46. Carlos Rafael Rodríguez, *Cuba en el tránsito,* 364.

47. In March 1958 the U.S. government suspended military aid, in response to attacks that these arms, conceived ostensibly for hemispheric defense, were being used for domestic repression. Nevertheless, through the use of various subterfuges—such as the supply of spare parts—they were able to maintain the combat capacity of Batista's troops. Other forms of cooperation remained unaltered.

48. Carlos Forment, *Caribbean Geopolitics and Foreign State-Sponsored Social Movements: The Case of Cuban Exile Militancy, 1959–1979* (Boston: Center for the Study of the Cuban Community, 1984), 76.

49. Testimony of Luis María Buch, testimony to author, February 14, 1995. Includes copies of the report sent to Comandante Fidel Castro, August 18, 1958, on the interview with Lyman Kirkpatrick, and another report dated September 12 of that year in which he includes the questions posed to

the U.S. embassy in Venezuela and their answers. The originals of both documents are kept in the Office of Historical Affairs of the Cuban Council of State.

50. Ibid.

51. Ibid.

52. Ibid.

53. Paterson, *Contesting Castro,* 209–25.

Chapter 2

1. Chomsky, *Deterring Democracy,* 16, 27.

2. Ernesto Guevara, "Cuba: An Exceptional Case?" *Monthly Review,* July–August 1961, 58.

3. Tad Szulc, *Fidel: A Critical Portrait* (New York: Morrow, 1986), 480, 488.

4. The Bay of Pigs describes an area that includes Larga and Girón Beaches. Since the invasion encompassed both beaches, I prefer the former term. The last redoubt of the invaders was Girón Beach; thus it is correct to speak of the Victory at Playa Girón, the term commonly employed in Cuba to refer to this event.

5. Fabián Escalante Font, *La guerra secreta de la CIA* (Havana: Editorial Capitán San Luis, 1993), 25.

6. Rafael is also the father of Lincoln Díaz-Balart (R-Fla.), one of the three Cuban-American Congressmen and a strong proponent of a hard line toward Cuba. It is rumored that the father engineered the son's political career and views his protégé as a future president of a "free Cuba."

7. Comandante William Morgan, foster son of the North American Mafioso Dominic Bartoni. He served prison terms in the United States for assault and robbery and was wanted as a deserter from the Korean War. In Cuba he had been linked to figures of organized crime like Meyer Lansky and Santos Traficante. Under orders of the U.S. intelligence services he joined the Second National Front of the Escambray and went on to become a trusted associate of Gutiérrez Menoyo. He was later convicted of espionage and subversion and condemned to death by the revolutionary courts. José Duarte Oropesa, *Historiología cubana,* 4 vols. (Miami: Ediciones Universal, 1974), 4:123–25.

8. Julio Crespo Francisco, *Bandidismo en el Escambray: 1960–1965* (Havana: Editorial Ciencias Sociales, 1986), 18.

9. Ibid., 18–19.

10. Masferrer was an ex-senator of the Batista bloc whose political career ranged from communism to the extreme right. During the dictatorship he headed a paramilitary band that committed countless crimes and abuses. After fleeing the island he was linked to various plans against Cuba and other countries—among them, an invasion of Haiti said to have been encouraged by drug traffickers. He was shot to death in Miami.

11. Márquez-Sterling had a long political career that included the presidency of the Constitutional Assembly in 1940; having been one of the opposition candidates to the Batista bloc in the 1958 elections, he was rebuffed by the majority of the Cuban political groups.

12. Ministerio del Interior, Dirección de Inteligencia, G-2, Estado Mayor del Ejército Rebelde, *File of Operation Opera,* MININT Records, Havana, March 17, 1960, 228–31.

13. Raúl Gutiérrez Serrano, "Survey Nacional: El pueblo opina sobre el Gobierno de la Revolución," *Bohemia* (Havana), February 22, 1959, 75–81.

14. Raul Gutiérrez Serrano, "El pueblo opina sobre el Gobierno Revolucionario y la Reforma Agraria," *Bohemia* (Havana), June 21, 1959, suppl., 8–13.

15. Fidel Castro in "En Cuba" section, *Bohemia,* March 8, 1959, 87.

16. Antonio Núñez Jiménez, *En marcha con Fidel* (Havana: Editorial Letras Cubanas, 1982), 458.

17. Carlos Prío, "En Cuba" section, *Bohemia,* November 29, 1959, 80.

18. The Constitution of 1940, one of the most advanced of its time in Latin America, established the need to carry out agrarian reform in the country, but the complementary laws needed to implement it were never enacted. The 1959 Agrarian Reform Law established a property limit of 400 hectares (960 acres), which affected only the owners of the largest landholdings, the majority of them U.S. corporations. Some 100,000 peasants became owners of their land as a result of this law, although the majority of the large landholdings were organized as cooperatives and state farms.

19. "¡Diez mil novillas cargadas! Un aporte más de todos los ganaderos de Cuba a la Revolución," *Bohemia* (Havana), March 8, 1959, suppl., 16.

20. Núñez Jiménez, *En marcha con Fidel.*

21. Raúl Gómez Serrano, "En Cuba" section, *Bohemia,* June 21, 1959, suppl., 16.

22. Specifically, the Punta Alegre Sugar Company, Cuban Land, Atlántica del Golfo, Vertientes-Camagüey, and the United Fruit Company.

23. Serrano, "En Cuba" Section, *Bohemia,* June 21, 1959, suppl., 16.

24. "El pensamiento vivo de Fidel: Frases de un discurso para los trabajadores azucareros," *Bohemia* (Havana), February 21, 1959, 69.

25. Pérez-Stable, *Cuban Revolution,* 83.

26. "En Cuba," April 7, 1959, 83.

27. Pérez-Stable, *Cuban Revolution,* 65–68.

28. Comité Central del PCC, *Primer congreso del Partido Comunista,* 34.

29. Fidel Castro, "Bajo la bandera del 26 de Julio: El nuevo ejecutivo de la CTC," *Bohemia* (Havana), November 29, 1959.

30. Fidel Castro, "En Cuba," March 8, 1959, 87.

31. Núñez Jiménez, *En marcha con Fidel,* 214.

32. Ibid., 212.

33. Pérez Alamo had been a prominent guerrilla fighter under the command of Fidel Castro. He joined Column 9 and was one of the officers who later accompanied Matos to Camagüey. He became involved in the events surrounding the Matos mutiny but was acquitted at the trial. Nevertheless, he left the country and joined the counterrevolution. Testimony to author, February 3, 1995.

34. Núñez Jiménez, *En marcha con Fidel,* 441.

35. Arsenio García, testimony to author, January 17, 1995.

36. Ministers of Public Works and Labor, respectively.

37. Duney Pérez Alamo, testimony to author, February 3, 1995.

38. Ibid.

39. Núñez Jiménez, *En marcha con Fidel,* 442–48.

40. Testimony of Duney Pérez Alamo to the author, February 3, 1995.

41. Escalante Font, *Guerra secreta,* 49.

42. Dirección de Inteligencia, "Informe sobre Manuel Artime," MININT Archives, Havana, January 25, 1960.

43. Dirección de Inteligencia, *Circulación por las unidades de ese Mando del ex-Cmdte. ER Higinio Díaz Ante, complicado en la frustrada conspiración de Húber Matos, que trata de salir del país por la vía de asilo político, Dir. Int. G—2, Emer.* MININT Archives, March 24, 1960.

44. Dirección de Inteligencia, *Informe sobre la organización contrarrevolucionaria MRR, Operación América.* MININT Archives, November 28, 1961.

45. Justo Carrillo, *A Cuba le tocó perder* (Miami: Ediciones Universal, 1993), 169.

46. Ernesto Guevara, "Un pecado de la Revolución," *Verde olivo* (Havana), February 12, 1961.

47. U.S. Senate, Select Committee to Study Governmental Operations with Respect to Intelligence Activities, *Alleged Assassination Plots Involving Foreign Leaders,* Senate Report 94–465, November 20, 1975, 93.

48. As a major landholder itself, the Catholic Church was, in fact, a part of the native oligarchy.

49. Duarte Oropesa, *Historiología cubana,* 4:357. This source mentions 815 churches, but that figure is impossible when compared to the number of priests. The figure of 200 churches was taken from Olson and Olson, *Cuban-Americans,* 45. The rest of the figures in the two sources match approximately.

50. Olson and Olson, *Cuban-Americans,* 45.

51. Aurelio Alonso, "Iglesia católica y política cubana en los noventa," *Cuadernos de nuestra América* (CEA, Havana) 11.22 (July–December 1994): 64.

52. Dirección de Inteligencia, "Declaraciones del detenido Reynold González," MININT Archives, Havana, October 18, 1961.

53. MRR, "Informe del Movimiento de Recuperación Revolucionaria (MRR) a la opinión pública de América y del Mundo," Costa Rica, June 8, 1960.

54. Dirección de Inteligencia, "Declaraciones del detenido Manuel Reyes García," MININT Archives, Havana, August 1, 1962, 1.

55. Dirección de Inteligencia, *Resolución del Tribunal Superior Electoral del 14 de octubre de 1957 reconociendo vigencia como Partido Político y existencia legal al Partido de Liberación Radical con el carácter de Partido Nacional,* MININT Archives, Havana, 1957.

56. Sorí Marín was an attorney who came from Organización Auténtica before joining the Rebel Army and attaining the rank of comandante and the position of auditor general of the guerrilla troop in the Sierra Maestra. After the victory he was named minister of agriculture, but he came into early conflict with the revolutionary program and he played a key role in the first conspiracies. The moment and way in which he became associated with the Catholic hard right awaits further study, but evidently Sorí Marín became a close collaborator of theirs, possibly since before the victory of the Revolution, perhaps as a result of his contacts with the CIA since that time.

57. Howard Hunt was one of the CIA officers who oversaw the political front for the Bay of Pigs invasion. He was subsequently convicted for his role in the Watergate break-in.

58. E. Howard Hunt, *Give Us This Day* (New York: Paperback Library, 1973), 215; Carrillo, *A Cuba,* 105.

59. Rubén Castillo Ramos, "Cruzada redentora en la Sierra," *Bohemia* (Havana), April 26, 1959.

60. Dirección de Inteligencia, "Expediente de Manuel Artime Buesa, Informe de Rodrigo Rivas Vega, Delegado del Buró Agrario de Manzanillo," MININT Archives, Manzanillo, June 15, 1959, 6.

61. Dirección de Inteligencia, "Expediente de Manuel Artime Buesa, Informe relacionado con la actuación del Teniente Manuel Artime Buesa en la región de Manzanillo." MININT Archives, Manzanillo, November 19, 1959.

62. Manuel Artime in *Historia de una agresión* (Havana: Editorial de Ciencias Sociales, 1974), 63.

63. I have the tape-recordings of the statements of this source.

64. Angel Fernández Varela, "Entrevista a Angel Fernández Varela," *Contrapunto* (Miami) 4.10 (18 October–14 November 1993).

65. Dirección de Inteligencia, *Informe del MRR.*

66. José Ignacio Rasco, "El Quinto Congreso Internacional de la Democracia Cristiana," *Bohemia* (Havana), December 6, 1959, 38.

67. Enrique Ros, *Playa Girón: La verdadera historia* (Miami: Ediciones Universal, 1994), 21–22.

68. This term takes its name from Eusebio Mujal, the Auténtico labor leader who assumed power of the central union when the Communists were swept out by the government of Carlos Prío. Mujal later negotiated a pact with the dictatorship and became their practical ally.

69. Artime in *Historia de una agresión,* 71.

70. U.S. House of Representatives, Select Committee for the Investigation of Assassinations, *Appendix on Anti-Castro Activities and Organizations,* Washington, D.C., March 1970, par. 44.

71. Ros, *Playa Girón,* 161–63.

72. Centro de Estudios Operativos del MININT, "Operación 700, no hubo casualidad," *Cuadernos de estudios* (Havana), April 1994, 15.

73. Izaguirre de la Riva, handwritten statement, MININT Archives, n.d., 14.

74. Justo Carrillo was an economist who had been president of the Banco de Fomento Agrícola e Industrial during the administration of the Auténticos and who was returned to that post after the victory of the Revolution. During the struggle against the dictatorship he formed part of the "conspiracy of the pure ones" (see chap. 1).

75. Other reports give the date as October 1960; the confusion probably arose because the organization made its manifesto public in October.

76. Dirección de Inteligencia, *Informe sobre la creación del MRP por el traidor Manuel Ray Rivero,* MININT Archives, September 20, 1961.

77. Roberto Padrón Larrazábal, *Manifiestos de Cuba* (Seville: Universidad de Sevilla, 1975), 254–73.

78. Duarte Oropesa, *Historiología cubana,* 4:268.

79. Ministerio del Interior, Departamento de Seguridad del Estado, *Declaraciones de Reynold González,* MININT Archives, Havana, January 5, 1977.

80. Roberto Orihuela, *Nunca fui un traidor: Retrato de un farsante* (Havana: Editorial Capitán San Luis, 1991), 282.

81. Hunt, *Give Us This Day,* 105.

Chapter 3

1. "Informe elaborado por la Comisión Taylor sobre el fracaso del Plan Zapata," in *Playa Girón: La gran conjura* (Havana: Editorial Capitán San Luis, 1981), 38. This report of the commission headed by Gen. Maxwell Taylor created to investigate the Bay of Pigs fiasco recounts the handling of the Cuban case before the victory of the Revolution (see also chap. 1 of this book).

2. Ibid.

3. Ibid., 39. See also the following declassified CIA documents: U.S. Central Intelligence Agency, "A Program of Covert Action against the Castro Regime," Washington, D.C., March 15, 1960; "Memorandum of Conference with the President," Washington, D.C., March 18, 1960.

4. Artime in *Historia de una agresión,* 68.

5. Carrillo, *A Cuba,* 106.

6. Testimony of a source with direct access to this information who refused to be identified; recorded interview in the possession of the author. Various persons have affirmed this CIA connection with potential members of the coalition. As a result of my investigations, I tend to believe that it was Angel Fernández Varela who made these contacts.

7. Ros, *Playa Girón,* 18–19.

8. Carrillo, *A Cuba,* 107.

9. Hunt, *Give Us This Day,* 45.

10. Ibid., 81.

11. Arthur Schlesinger Jr., *Los mil días de Kennedy* (Havana: Editorial de Ciencias Sociales, 1970), 188.

12. Ros, *Playa Girón,* 35–41.

13. Artime in *Historia de una agresión,* 71–72.

14. Testimony of a source who asked to remain anonymous; tape-recorded interview in possession of the author.

15. Thomas Powers, *The Man Who Kept the Secrets: Richard Helms and the CIA* (New York: Knopf, 1979), 112.

16. "Informe elaborado por la Comisión Taylor," 40.

17. Ibid., 48.

18. Ibid., 44.

19. Allen Dulles, "My Answer to the Bay of Pigs," declassified CIA document, 2d draft, master copy, n.d., 12.

20. John F. Kennedy, "The President's News Conference of April 12, 1961," in *Public Papers of the Presidents of the United States: Kennedy, 1961–63* (Washington D.C.: GPO, January 1962), 259.

21. Hunt, *Give Us This Day,* 77.

22. Ibid., 188.

23. Richard Bissell, assistant director of the CIA, assumed direct command of the operation. Quoted in Powers, *Man Who Kept the Secrets,* 116–17.

24. Hunt, *Give Us This Day,* 81.

25. At the beginning of the 1968 War of Independence, a sector of the bourgeoisie headed the struggle, but this group did not represent the majority of the entire class nor did it constitute the bulk of the troops.

26. Defense attorney Antonio Cejas Sánchez in *Historia de una agresión,* 312.

27. Ibid.

28. Centro de Estudios Operativos del MININT, "Team de infiltración, la avanzada terrorista," *Cuadernos de estudios* (Havana), April 1994.

29. Felix Rodríguez and John Weisman, *Shadow Warrior* (New York: Simon and Schuster, 1989), 61.

30. Ibid., 60. Rodríguez worked for the CIA for many years. According to his own testimony, he participated in covert operations in various countries and in the training of repressive forces in Latin America. He was involved in the assassination of Che Guevara in Bolivia and the Iran-Contra scandal during the Reagan administration.

31. Hunt, *Give Us This Day,* 76, 164.

32. Dirección de Inteligencia, "Expediente de Higinio Díaz Ane," MININT Archives, Havana, n.d.

33. Ros, *Playa Girón,* 206.

34. "Informe elaborado por la Comisión Taylor," 55.

35. Quintín Pino Machado, *La batalla de Girón: Razones de una victoria* (Havana: Editorial Ciencias Sociales, 1984), 278.

36. Ros, *Playa Girón,* 196.

37. Hunt, *Give Us This Day,* 143.

38. Ibid., 49.

39. Ros, *Playa Girón,* 117.

40. Hunt, *Give Us This Day,* 151.

41. Testimony of a source that prefers to remain anonymous.

42. Carrillo, *A Cuba,* 105.

43. Schlesinger, *Mil días de Kennedy,* 212.

44. Carrillo, *A Cuba,* 112–19.

45. *Playa Girón: La gran conjura,* 56.

46. Ros, *Playa Girón,* 163.

47. Dirección de Inteligencia, "Declaraciones del detenido Humberto Sorí Marín," MININT Archives, Havana, n.d., 2.

48. Hunt was later implicated in the Watergate scandal.

49. Escalante Font, *Guerra secreta,* 92.

50. Dirección de Inteligencia, *Historia en prisión de las organizaciones contrarrevolicionarias*, MININT Archives, n.d., 2.

51. The socialist character of the Cuban Revolution was enunciated by Fidel Castro at a mass rally that was held as a memorial to the victims of the April 15 air strike that preceded the invasion.

52. U.S. House, Select Committee, *Anti-Castro Activities,* par. 26.

53. Dirección de Inteligencia, "Declaraciones del detenido Alfredo Izaguirre de la Riva," MININT Archives, Havana, October 1961, 25–27.

54. Dirección de Inteligencia, *Informe de la Operación Candela,* MININT Archives, June 8, 1961.

55. Escalante Font, *Guerra secreta,* 155.

56. Ibid., 116–18.

57. Warren Hinckle and William Turner, *The Fish Is Red* (London: Harper and Row, 1981), 120–21.

58. On the recruitment of Venciana by CIA officer David Phillips, see U.S. House, Select Committee, *Anti-Castro Activities,* par. 119; Hinckle and Turner, *Fish Is Red,* 169; and Escalante Font, *Guerra secreta,* 120.

59. Ministerio del Interior, Dirección de Inteligencia, "Informe al Jefe de la Sección Q sobre planes de sabotages," MININT Archives, Havana, August 15, 1961.

60. Ministerio del Interior, Dirección de Inteligencia, *Declaraciones del detenido González.*

61. Powers, *Man Who Kept the Secrets,* 136.

Chapter 4

1. John F. Kennedy, "Special Message to the Congress on the Defense Budget, March 28, 1961," in *Public Papers of the Presidents* (1962), 229–40.

2. John F. Kennedy, "Radio and Television Report to the American People on Returning from Europe, June 6, 1961," in *Public Papers of the Presidents* (1962), 445.

3. John F. Kennedy, "Address at the White House Reception for Members of Congress and for the Diplomatic Corps of Latin American Republics, March 13, 1961," in *Public Papers of the Presidents* (1962), 174.

4. John F. Kennedy, "Address in Berkeley at the University of California, March 23, 1962," in *Public Papers of the Presidents* (1963), 266.

5. John F. Kennedy, "Address before the American Society of Newspaper Editors, April 20, 1961," in *Public Papers of the Presidents* (1962), 304.

6. Ample information on Operation Mongoose, including a chronology and declassified documents, can be found in Laurence Chang and Peter Kornbluh, *The Cuban Missile Crisis, 1962: A National Security Archive Documents Reader* (New York: New Press, 1992); and in Escalante Font, *Guerra secreta.* For additional information, see U.S. Senate, Select Committee, *Alleged Assassination Plots.* The information I have used comes primarily from these sources.

7. General Lansdale, an expert on covert operations, was put in charge of coordinating Project Cuba. The SGA, where the principal agencies of the U.S. foreign-policy establishment and the intelligence community were represented, was the group charged with overseeing the operation. In practice, Robert Kennedy, assisted by Gen. Maxwell Taylor, directed this operation.

8. Chang and Kornbluh, *Cuban Missile Crisis,* 5.

9. Ibid., 350.

10. In fact, as a result of the measures adopted by the Eisenhower administration and the climate surrounding the bilateral relations, trade between the two countries by that time had fallen to a mere $23 million and was limited to Cuban imports of U.S. food and medicines.

11. "Guidelines for Operation Mongoose," in Chang and Kornbluh, *Cuban Missile Crisis,* 38.

12. Escalante Font, *Guerra secreta,* 160–66.

13. "Memorandum for the Special Group (Augmented), July 25, 1962," in Chang and Kornbluh, *Cuban Missile Crisis,* 40.

14. For an analysis of this situation that agrees with many of these statements, see Powers, *Man Who Kept the Secrets,* 138.

15. Escalante Font, *Guerra secreta,* 223.

16. Chang and Kornbluh, *Cuban Missile Crisis,* 353.

17. More details about this plan can be found in Escalante Font, *Guerra secreta,* 152–55.

18. U. S. Central Intelligence Agency, "Spontaneous Revolts in Cuba: Contingency Planning," declassified document, Washington, D.C., January 5, 1989.

19. There is practically little to add to the events leading to the 1962 missile crisis. Politicians and academics of the three countries have met on various occasions to clarify this historic episode. In these events it was demonstrated that the Cuban government insisted to their Soviet counterpart that the agreements should be made public, in accord with the sovereign right of each country to install within its territory those weapons it considered necessary for its defense. In fact, this was standard practice for the United States and its allies, but the Soviet government was not persuaded by this good judgment and acted in secret. The validity of Soviet intentions thus lost legitimacy in the court of international public opinion.

20. Chang and Kornbluh, *Cuban Missile Crisis,* 357.

21. Ibid., 360.

22. Ibid., 368.

23. Escalante Font, *Guerra secreta,* 172–73.

24. Dirección de Inteligencia, "Resumen sobre el caso Operación 'Santa Clara.'" MININT Archives, Havana, February 18, 1965. Also, Escalante Font, *Guerra secreta,* 174.

25. Dirección de Inteligencia, "Declaraciones del detenido Juan Falcón Zammar," MININT Archives, Havana, August 1962, 34, 36.

26. Escalante Font, *Guerra secreta,* 148.

27. Ibid., 149.

28. Ibid.

29. Dirección de Inteligencia, "Declaraciones del detenido Falcón," 47.

30. Escalante Font, *Guerra secreta,* 156.

31. John F. Kennedy, "The President's News Conference of September 13, 1962," in *Public Papers of the Presidents* (1963), 674.

32. Germán Borrell Plasencias, "La labor político-ideológica durante la lucha contra bandidos en el Escambray," Instituto Superior Pedagógico "Capitán Silveiro Blanco Núñez," Sancti Spíritus, 1987, 48–49.

33. Ibid., 49.

34. Ibid., 54.

35. Crespo, *Bandidismo,* 137.

36. Escalante Font, *Guerra secreta,* 150.

37. "Ley 988," *Gaceta oficial de la República de Cuba* (Havana), November 29, 1961, 1.

38. Escalante Font, *Guerra secreta,* 151.

39. "Segunda Ley de Reforma Agraria," *Gaceta oficial de la República de Cuba* (Havana), October 3, 1963.

40. Fidel Castro, "Discurso en el duodécimo aniversario del asalto al Cuartel Moncada," in Borrell, "Labor político-ideológica," 67.

41. Dirección de Inteligencia, "Declaración del detenido Izaguirre," 25–27.

42. Miró Cardona, José. "U.S. Senate, Subcommittee on Refugees and Escapees of the Committee on the Judiciary," Washington, D.C., December 6, 1961, in Carlos E. Cortés, ed., *Cuban Refugee Programs* (New York: Arno Press, 1980), 6.

43. Most of these figures correspond with those supplied by Ray Cline, the most authoritative of sources, having been assistant director of the CIA, quoted in Powers, *Man Who Kept the Secrets,* 338. Other authors tend to accept lower figures, but in no case do they claim fewer than 200 officers and 2,000 agents, and all agree that Mongoose was the largest CIA operation ever conducted. In fact, Joan Didion calculates that as many as 120,000 persons were involved in these activities. Didion, *Miami* (New York: Simon and Schuster, 1987), 90.

44. Hinckle and Turner, *Fish Is Red,* 152.

45. José Luis Méndez, "Terrorismo de origen cubano," Ph.D. dissertation in process, MES, Havana, 1995.

46. Ibid., 231–32.

47. Ibid., 180.

48. Hinckle and Turner, *Fish Is Red,* 131.

49. John F. Kennedy, foreword to *Public Papers of the Presidents of the United States: Kennedy, 1961–63* (Washington, D.C.: GPO, 1963), v–vi.

50. The Special Group was an agency of the National Security Council.

The Special Group (Augmented), comprised of the Special Group plus other officials, was created solely to follow the development of Operation Mongoose and was disbanded after the latter's demise.

51. Chang and Kornbluh, *Cuban Missile Crisis,* 395.

52. Ibid., 394.

53. Hinckle and Turner, *Fish Is Red,* 158.

54. Duarte Oropesa, *Historiología cubana,* 4:398–99.

55. Chang and Kornbluh, *Cuban Missile Crisis,* 396.

56. David Corn, *Blond Ghost* (New York: Simon and Schuster, 1994), 87.

57. U.S. House, Select Committee, *Anti-Castro Activities,* par. 2.

58. John F. Kennedy, "Remarks in Miami at the Presentation of the Flag of the Cuban Invasion Brigade, December 29, 1962," in *Public Papers of the Presidents of the United States* (1963), 911. Apparently Kennedy was told that the brigade members had kept the flag hidden from Cuban authorities, a virtual impossibility, given the way they were captured and imprisoned for over a year in Cuba. Artime confessed to Howard Hunt that the flag was in fact a replica. (See Hunt, *Give Us This Day,* 221.) Subsequently, in retaliation for Kennedy's pledge not to invade Cuba, the brigade requested that the flag be returned, and later there was talk of delivering it to Gen. Augusto Pinochet for safekeeping.

59. Rodríguez and Weisman, *Shadow Warrior,* 119.

60. Hinckle and Turner, *Fish Is Red,* 62; Corn, *Blond Ghost,* 98.

61. Corn, *Blond Ghost,* 115.

62. Ibid., 118.

63. *Declaración de Río Cañas: Manifiesto de la constitución de la Junta Revolucionaria del Pueblo,* Puerto Rico, September 16, 1963, author's archives.

64. Corn, *Blond Ghost,* 115.

65. JURE's contact with *Time* constitutes a mystery in the organization's history, because at the time, that magazine's interest in the Cuban issue was related to the role played in the conflict by the most conservative sectors of North American society. Nor is the connection with Eloy Gutiérrez Menoyo clear: JURE promoted Gutiérrez Menoyo in Puerto Rico and for some reason, at the same time they announced Ray's alleged landing in Cuba, they announced Menoyo's as well.

66. "Cuba: Can't Anyone Here Play This Game?" *Time,* June 12, 1964.

67. Lorelei Albanese, "Manolo Ray: Protest in Exile," *San Juan Star Magazine,* August 1, 1971, 2.

68. Corn, *Blond Ghost,* 115.

69. Duney Pérez Alamo, testimony to author, June 7, 1995.

70. Hinckle and Turner, *Fish Is Red,* 171.

71. For more information on the Veciana-Phillips connection, including the possible implication of both in Kennedy's assassination see Gaeton Fonzi, *The Last Investigation* (New York: Thunder's Mouth Press, 1993).

72. Hinckle and Turner, *Fish Is Red,* 167–69.

73. Ibid., 103; Orihuela, *Traidor,* 305.

74. Hinckle and Turner, *Fish Is Red,* 153–62.

75. Bradley Earl Ayers, *The War That Never Was* (Canoga Park, Calif.: Major Books, 1976), 197.

76. Hinckle and Turner, *Fish Is Red,* 191–93.

77. Ibid., 199–203.

78. Robert Blakey and Richard Billings, *The Fatal Hour* (New York: Berkeley Books, 1992), 195–99.

79. Ibid.

80. Méndez, "Terrorismo de origen cubano," app.

81. The action prepared in cooperation with Cubelas, assigned the code name AMLASH, was one of those uncovered by the Church Commission and was possibly the best known of the attempts to assassinate Fidel Castro —perhaps due to its sensationalism and to the fact that it coincided with Kennedy's slaying.

82. Three of the principal protagonists of this event have written about it: William Attwood, *The Twilight Struggle* (New York: Harper and Row, 1987), 258–59; Jean Daniel, "Unofficial Envoy: A Historical Report from Two Capitals," *New Republic,* 1992; and Carlos Lechuga, *In the Eye of the Storm* (Melbourne: Ocean Press, 1995), 197–211.

Chapter 5

1. Comité Central del PCC, *Primer congreso del Partido Comunista de Cuba,* 235.

2. Juan Antonio Blanco, *Tercer milenio: Una visión alternativa de la posmodernidad* (Havana: Centro Félix Varela, 1995), 102.

3. Hugh Brogan, *The Longman History of the United States of America* (New York: Morrow, 1986), 682.

4. Corn, *Blond Ghost,* 112.

5. Méndez, "Terrorismo de origen cubano," app.

6. Comité Central del Partido Comunista de Cuba [PCC], *Tesis y resoluciones del Primer Congreso del Partido Comunista de Cuba* (Havana: Departamento de Orientación Revolucionaria del CC-PCC, 1987), 524.

7. National Security Cuba Documentation Project, *United States and Cuba Détente: 1974–75 Initiative and the Angolan Intervention,* National Security Archive, (Washington, D.C.: 1993), 1–21.

8. Hinckle and Turner, *Fish Is Red,* 322–24.

9. U.S. Senate, Judiciary Committee, *Terroristic Activity: Terrorism in the Miami Area,* 94th Cong., 2d sess. (Washington, D.C.: GPO, 1976), 616.

10. Although its members celebrate January 5 as the anniversary of their founding, RECE went public in April with a call for a plebiscite among the exiles, ostensibly to choose their representatives.

11. On May 30, 1966, Cuesta was discovered in one of these operations. In the ensuing battle he was wounded and as a consequence lost his eyesight and was crippled. Imprisoned until 1978, he publicly thanked the Cuban government for the attentions he had received, criticized his former comrades for abandoning him, and adopted a position of peaceful coexistence. However, upon his return to Miami he reactivated Comandos L and promoted new terrorist actions. He died in 1993.

12. Gaetón Fonzi, "Who Is Jorge Mas Canosa?" *Esquire,* January 1993, 20.

13. He is referring to a November 15, 1965, attack sponsored by RECE in which a boat off the Havana coast shot at the aquarium, the Hotel Riviera, and an apartment building. Cited in *Miami Herald,* March 16, 1966.

14. The last chapter of this book is dedicated to the CANF.

15. *Diario de las Américas* (Miami), November 15, 1975. Quoted in Saul Landau, "Chronology of Activities of the Cuban-American National Foundation," unpublished.

16. *Diario de las Américas* (Miami), December 4, 1975.

17. Didion, *Miami,* 62.

18. Most authors have preferred to classify the postrevolutionary migration flows in stages, determined primarily by the immigration policies adopted by both governments, but especially by the United States. Even though this classification has practical value, in my opinion, it does not accurately express the class differences present in this process, nor the relation between the decision to migrate and the migrants' conflicts with Cuban society. I therefore classify them as "generations of migrants." The first generation covers the period between 1959 and 1962 and the second, from 1962 to 1973. The reader should not confuse the concept of "generation of

migrants" with that of "generation of immigrants": the latter is used to differentiate between immigrants and their descendants. This topic is covered in greater detail in the next chapter; for more information, see Jesús Arboleya, *Havana-Miami: The U.S.-Cuba Migration Conflict* (Melbourne: Ocean Press, 1995).

19. See Jesús Arboleya, "Terrorismo y contrarrevolución," *Cuadernos de estudios* (CEASEN, Havana), 1995.

20. U.S. Senate, Judiciary Committee, *Terrorist Activity,* 608.

21. The *Diario de la Marina* distinguished itself by its support of Spanish colonialism and by representing the most conservative sectors of prerevolutionary Cuban society.

22. John Dinges and Saul Landau, *Assassination on Embassy Row* (New York: Pantheon Books, 1980), 149.

23. After the members of the 2506th Brigade returned from Cuban prisons they formed the Asociación de Veteranos de Bahía de Cochinos. Besides the invaders, the organization was joined by many others that supposedly were to participate in the invasion but could not, for reasons beyond their control. The 2506th, as it has continued to be known, has been involved in terrorist activities as well as in the social life and local politics of Miami.

24. Dinges and Landau, *Assassination on Embassy Row,* 147.

25. Ibid., 265.

26. Duarte Oropesa, *Historiografía cubana,* 4:467–69. According to Oropesa, he was the head of Poder Cubano in California.

27. Duney Pérez Alamo, testimony to author, June 7, 1995. Pérez Alamo was one of the principal leaders of Acción Cubana.

28. Dinges and Landau, *Assassination on Embassy Row,* 250.

29. U.S. Senate, Judiciary Committee, *Terrorist Activity,* 639.

30. Duney Pérez Alamo, testimony to author, June 7, 1995.

31. Dinges and Landau, *Assassination on Embassy Row,* 294.

32. Information on the history of Orlando Bosch appears in various Cuban and foreign publications, among them: Carlos Rivero Collado, *Los sobrinos del Tío Sam* (Havana: Editorial de Ciencias Sociales, 1976); Dinges and Landau, *Assassination on Embassy Row;* Hinckle and Turner, *Fish Is Red;* Julio Lara Alonso, *La verdad irrebatible sobre el crimen de Barbados* (Havana: Editora Política, 1986); Alicia Herrera, *Pusimos la bomba—¿y qué?* (Havana: Editorial de Ciencias Sociales, 198); and Duarte Oropesa, *Historiografía cubana,* vol. 4.

33. Dinges and Landau, *Assassination on Embassy Row,* 251.

34. Hilda Inclán, "Cardona Inspires Acción Cubana: Anti-Castro Leader Seeks Unity," *Miami News,* March 22, 1974. Quoted in Landau, "Cronología."

35. U.S. Senate, Judiciary Committee, *Terrorist Activity,* 636.

36. Dinges and Landau, *Assassination on Embassy Row,* 251–52.

37. "Of Burning Ambition and Orlando Bosch," *Washington Post,* May 12, 1988. Quoted in Landau, "Cronología."

38. *Miami Herald,* October 16, 1993. Quoted in Landau, "Cronología."

39. Lara, *Verdad irrebatible,* 69.

40. Félix Rodríguez had formed part of the gray teams during the Bay of Pigs project. He subsequently joined Artime's group and later served the CIA in missions in Vietnam, Bolivia, and other places. He has confessed to participating in the capture and murder of Che Guevara. Lastly, he was implicated in the Iran-Contra scandal, while in charge of operations to supply the Nicaraguan contras from Salvadorian territory.

41. Duney Pérez Alamo, testimony to author, June 7, 1995.

42. Félix R. Masud-Piloto, *With Open Arms: Cuban Migration to the United States* (Totowa, N.J.: Rowman and Littlefield, 1988), 77.

43. Méndez, "Terrorismo de origen cubano."

44. Ibid.

45. Forment, *Caribbean Geopolitics,* 86.

46. Ibid.

47. The term *gusano* (worm) was used in the early days of the Revolution to describe the counterrevolutionaries and others who opposed the process. This usage has its origins in the writings of José Martí.

48. Unless otherwise specified, the sources that served to reconstruct the story of the émigré left movement are testimonies of the principal protagonists that I have gathered over the years, private collections of *Areíto, Joven Cuba,* and other publications, and my personal experience in my relations with these groups while I worked as a Cuban diplomat in the United States.

49. Grupo Areíto, *Contra viento y marea* (Havana: Casa de las Américas, 1979), 255.

50. Luis Maira, *América Latina y la crisis de la hegemonía norteamericana* (Lima: DESCO, 1982), 206.

51. Although the more developed socialist countries, in particular the USSR, were not excluded.

52. Hedrick Smith et al., *Reagan: The Man, the President* (New York: Macmillan, 1980), 7.

53. María Cristina Herrera, "¿Qué es el Instituto de Estudios Cubanos?" *Areíto,* October 1974, 36.

54. Fidel Castro, *Entrevista con periodistas que escriben para la comunidad cubana en el exterior, 6 de septiembre de 1978* (Havana: Editorial de Ciencias Sociales, 1978).

55. Olson and Olson, *Cuban-Americans,* 76.

56. U.S. Senate, Judiciary Committee, *Terrorist Activity,* 608.

57. The terrorist groups operated under various names, and sometimes different groups used the same name to claim responsibility for their actions. The MNC used the name Comandos 0 on various occasions, although there is a possibility that other groups used it too.

58. Masud-Piloto, *With Open Arms,* 77.

59. Jeff Stein, "Face to Face with Omega 7," *Cuba Times* (New York), Spring 1980, 7.

60. Ibid., 12.

61. Castro, *Entrevista con periodistas,* 16.

62. Both judgments turned out to be exaggerated. Only 16 percent had criminal records; 74 percent were working in Cuba before they left, and 9 percent were professionals. In truth, in the fifteen years that they have lived in the United States, of the 125,000 persons who settled in that country as a result of the events of Mariel, only 600 have committed serious criminal acts and fewer than 100 are confined in psychiatric institutions. Political factors had little effect on the individual motivation of the majority and in fact the Mariel émigrés have become the segment most favorable to improvement of relations with Cuba. For an analysis of the migration flow, see Jesús Arboleya, *Havana-Miami.*

63. Masud-Piloto, *With Open Arms,* 94.

64. Olson and Olson, *Cuban-Americans,* 89–91.

65. Comité Central del PCC, *Informe Central al II Congreso del Partido Comunista de Cuba,* Editora Política, Havana, 1980.

66. Méndez, "Terrorismo de origen cubano."

Chapter 6

1. Robert Bach, "The Cuban Exodus: Political and Economic Motivations," in *The Caribbean Exodus* (New York: Praeger, 1987), 10.

2. Jesús Arboleya, *Havana-Miami,* 12–13.

3. Fidel Castro, "Discurso en el distrito del Bronx," *Granma* (Havana), October 26, 1995, 4–5.

4. The most detailed studies on nineteenth-century Cuban immigration have been undertaken by Professors Gerald E. Poyo at the University of Texas and Louis A. Pérez at the University of South Florida. Some of their publications are cited in this book.

5. Gerald E. Poyo, "The Cuban Experience in the United States, 1865–1940: Migration, Community, and Identity," *Cuba Indies 21* (Center for Latin American Studies, University of Pittsburgh Press, 1991): 24. Other studies suggest lower figures for 1870s immigration: some 5,000 on the basis of the Census of 1870, and nearly 7,000 a decade later. See Olson and Olson, *Cuban-Americans,* 20.

6. Poyo, "Cuban Experience," 25.

7. Further reading on this topic can be found in Armas, Segrera, and Sánchez, *Partidos políticos,* 24–26.

8. Olson and Olson, *Cuban-Americans,* 28.

9. I define *enclave* as a differentiated economic, social, and cultural structure that responds to an ethnic concentration, with its corresponding preferential market located in a particular area. The term *Cuban-American community* refers to all the immigrants of Cuban origin living in the United States, not only those residing in the enclave.

10. It is difficult to find precise figures for this period. The majority of the data come from Olson and Olson, *Cuban-Americans,* table 1 and pp. 39, 49, 93. Other sources consulted were *Atlas of U.S. History* (1979); *U.S. Hispanic Market 1980; Spanish-Americans in the U.S.: Changing Demographic Characteristics;* Comité Estatal de Estadísticas de Cuba, *Estadísticas de las migraciones externas y el turismo* (Havana: Comité Estatal de Estadísticas, 1982); Lisandro Pérez, "Cubans," in *Harvard Encyclopedia of American Ethnic Groups* (Cambridge, Mass.: Belknap Press, 1980); and Cortés, *Cuban Refugee Programs.*

11. Olson and Olson, *Cuban-Americans,* 43.

12. Fidel Castro sought out Carlos Prío for financing the Granma expedition in 1956, but this was an isolated case in his organizational work among the immigrants.

13. Fidel Castro, *Revolutionary Struggle, 1947–1958,* ed. Rolando Bonachea and Nelson Valdeés (Cambridge, Mass.: MIT Press, 1972), 285.

14. Olson and Olson, *Cuban-Americans,* 47.

15. For an analysis of the effect of the migratory question in relations between Cuba and the United States, see Jesús Arboleya, *Havana-Miami.*

16. Masud-Piloto, *With Open Arms,* 34.

17. Olson and Olson, *Cuban-Americans,* 49.

18. Bach, "Cuban Exodus," 112.

19. Olson and Olson, *Cuban-Americans,* 84.

20. In previous writings I have placed in this first generation all those who migrated until 1973. Further studies suggest separating this group into two parts, due primarily to differences in social composition.

21. Mercedes Arce et al., "La emigración en Cuba, 1959–1990," manuscript, CEAP, Universidad de La Habana, 1991, 5.

22. Ibid.

23. Masud-Piloto, *With Open Arms,* 68.

24. Bach, "Cuban Exodus," 11.

25. Arce et al., "Emigración en Cuba," 6.

26. Between 1973 and 1979, 37,973 Cubans entered the United States, the majority from third countries. Masud-Piloto, *With Open Arms,* 3. The census data were taken from Olson and Olson, *Cuban-Americans,* 77.

27. Olson and Olson, *Cuban-Americans,* 77.

28. Masud-Piloto, *With Open Arms,* 97.

29. Fidel Castro, "Comparecencia ante la televisión cubana el 24 de agosto de 1994," *Granma* (Havana), August 28, 1994, 3.

30. Antonio Aja Díaz, "La emigración ilegal hacia los EU," *Areíto* (Miami), March 1994, 8.

31. Centro de Estudios de Alternativas Políticas, *Estudio de los intentos de salidas ilegales por la vía marítima hacia Estados Unidos*, CEAP, Universidad de La Habana, January 1994, 87–91.

32. Fidel Castro, "Comparecencia ante la televisión," 1.

33. Ibid.

34. Thus named because of the crude vessels that were generally used for the voyage.

35. Conversaciones Cuba–Estados Unidos, "Comunicado conjunto," *Granma* (Havana), September 10, 1994, 6.

36. "Declaración conjunta Cuba–Estados Unidos," *Granma* (Havana), May 3, 1995, 4.

37. Alejandro Rodrigo, ANSA, Washington, D.C., May 2, 1995.

38. *New York Times,* August 26, 1994.

39. The belief that Kennedy betrayed them by refusing to intervene directly in the 1961 invasion is an opinion widely held among the Cuban counterrevolutionary groups. Some analysts have tied this attitude to the alleged participation of Cuban counterrevolutionary elements in the assassination of the president.

40. Olson and Olson, *Cuban-Americans,* 94.

41. The terminology relating to this topic is not unanimous. I have chosen the term *integration* to define the process of insertion of the immigrants and their descendants into the new society and its cultural consequences. In this respect, see María Isabel Domínguez, "Inserción social y tolerancia," *Acuario* (Centro Félix Varela, Havana) 7 (1995): 8. Following the example of Fernando Ortíz, the Cuban psychologist Mercedes Arce uses the term *transculturation* to characterize the process of integration of Cuban immigrants in South Florida. See Fernando Ortíz, *Contrapunteo cubano del tabaco y el azúcar* (Havana: Editorial de Ciencias Sociales, 1983); and Mercedes Arce, "El proceso de transculturación de la comunidad cubana en Miami: Características sociopsicológicas predominantes," Ph.D. dissertation, MES, Havana, 1994.

42. Masud-Piloto, *With Open Arms,* 53.

43. Ibid.

44. Lourdes Casal, "Cubans in the U.S.," *Nueva generación* (New York), December 1972, 14.

45. The melting pot characterizes North American society as a mixture of many ingredients that are united to form a single new product.

46. Olson and Olson, *Cuban-Americans,* 102.

47. For an analysis of the various theories on the topic, see Alejandro Portes and Rubén Rumbaut, *Immigrant America* (Berkeley: University of California Press, 1990); and Mercedes Arce, "Transculturación de la comunidad cubana."

48. Brogan, *History of the United States,* 416.

49. Olson and Olson, *Cuban-Americans,* 74.

50. Grupo Areíto, *Contra viento y marea.*

51. Reginald Meyers, "Exilados esperan pronto fin del régimen castrista," *Nuevo herald* (Miami), February 20, 1992, 1.

52. Guillermo Grenier et al., *The 1995 FIU Cuba Poll: Views on Policy Options toward Cuba Held by Cuban-American Residents of Dade County, Florida, and Union City, New Jersey* (Miami: Florida International University, April 11, 1995), 9.

53. Olson and Olson, *Cuban-Americans,* 103.

54. Abel Prieto, "Cultura, cubanidad, cubanía," paper presented at the conference "La nación y la emigración," Havana, April 1992, 2.

55. Ibid., 10.

56. José Martí, Periódico *Patria* (New York), July 30, 1892, in *Obras completas*. Havana: Editorial Tierra Nueva, 1961, XXII:360.

57. Miami-Dade (formerly Dade), one of sixty-seven counties in Florida, is made up of twenty-eight municipalities, the most important being the City of Miami. We use the name Miami to refer to the county as a whole, except when I specify the city.

58. Mimi Whitfield, "Publicidad en español tienta a anunciantes," *Nuevo herald* (Miami), October 30, 1995, B-3.

59. Olson and Olson, *Cuban-Americans,* 100.

60. Cathy Booth, "Miami, the Capital of Latin America," *Time,* Fall 1993 (special issue), 82.

61. It is almost impossible to get exact figures. I chose $80 billion because it is close to the average and is the estimate quoted most often.

62. Penny Lernoux, "The Golden Door for Drugs: The Miami Connection," *Nation,* February 18, 1984.

63. Dan Keating and Charles Strousse, "Miami Area Again Leads U.S. in Crime," *Miami Herald,* December 5, 1994, A-6.

64. Booth, "Miami," 84.

65. "The 1995 Hispanic Business Rich List," *Hispanic Business,* March 1995, 24.

66. Marifeli Pérez-Stable and Miren Uriarte, *Cubans in the Changing Economy of Miami* (Boston: Inter-University Program of Latino Research, University of Massachusetts, 1991), 13

67. Portes and Rumbaut, *Immigrant America,* 35.

68. Pérez-Stable and Uriarte, *Cubans in the Changing Economy,* table 2.

69. Antonio Jorge and Raúl Moncarz, *General Overview of the Cuban Influx since 1959* (The Hague: Research Group for European Migration Problems, 1981), 18.

70. Gregg Fields, "Ponen en duda 'éxito cubano,'" *Nuevo herald* (Miami), June 27, 1988, A-1.

71. Pérez-Stable and Uriarte, *Cubans in the Changing Economy,* table 5.

72. Roxana Brizuela and Luis Fernández-Tabío, "El potencial económico de las empresas pertenecientes a cubanoamericanos en Estados Unidos," manuscript, Universidad de La Habana, 1992, 2.

73. *Nuevo herald,* March 3, 1986, A-1.

74. U.S. Department of Commerce, Bureau of the Census, *Persons of Hispanic Origin in the United States, March 1979–October 1980,* Population Characteristics Series P–20, no. 354 (Washington, D.C.: GPO, 1981).

75. Cortés, *Cuban Refugee Programs,* 7.

76. Alejandro Portes and Rafael Mozo, *Patterns of Naturalization and Voting in the Cuban Community* (Boston, 1984), 2.

77. U.S. Department of Justice, Immigration and Naturalization Service, *1990 Statistical Yearbook of the Immigration and Naturalization Service* (Washington, D.C.: GPO, 1991).

78. Ernesto Rodríguez, *Sobre la ciudadanía norteamericana: Análisis estadístico preliminar* (Havana: CEA, 1995). This study argues that 42.2 percent of the Cuban-American population are U.S. citizens under twenty-five years of age; 49.9 percent are over twenty-five. My estimates are based on these figures. Figures for the Cuban-American population in Miami-Dade County were obtained from Maria A. Morales, "Comienza campaña, para naturalizar a inmigrantes," *Nuevo herald* (Miami), April 12, 1995, A-1.

79. Portes and Mozo, *Naturalization and Voting*, 5.

80. Grenier et al., *1995 FIU Cuba Poll*, 10.

81. Portes and Mozo, *Naturalization and Voting*, 165.

82. Jannice Reyes and Alfonso Chardy, "Estudio: Dade no se gana sin el voto cubano," *Nuevo herald* (Miami), February 6, 1993, B-1.

83. After 1959, that is. In the nineteenth century various Cubans occupied public office in the émigré communities.

Chapter 7

1. Partido Republicano de Estados Unidos, "Selección de la plataforma del Partido Republicano," *Cuadernos semestrales* (CIDE, Mexico City), 1981, 273.

2. The neoconservative movement has been studied by numerous specialists from various countries. The Centro de Investigación y Docencia Económica (CIDE) of Mexico has specialized in researching its impact on U.S. policy toward Latin America.

3. Comité de Santa Fe, "Las relaciones interamericanas: Escudo de la seguridad del Nuevo Mundo y espada de la proyección del poder de Estados Unidos," *Cuadernos semestrales* (CIDE, Mexico City) 9 (May 1981): 214.

4. Ibid., 208.

5. Ibid., 209.

6. Partido Republicano de Estados Unidos, "Selección de la plataforma," 295.

7. Luis Maira, "América Latina, pieza clave en la política de contención de la administración Reagan," *Cuadernos semestrales* (CIDE, Mexico City) 9 (May 1981): 238–39.

8. Ibid., 238.

9. María Teresa Miyar, "La comunidad cubana y el tema de las relaciones Cuba–Estados Unidos," in *Temas de estudio* (Havana: CESEU, 1989), 2.

10. Raimundo Cabrera, "Sobre los partidos políticos," *Cuba y América* (Havana), March 16, 1907. Quoted in *Selecciones de lecturas del pensamiento político cubano* (Havana: Facultad de Filosofía e Historia, Universidad de La Habana, 1985), 506.

11. Joel M. Woldman, *The National Endowment for Democracy,* Foreign Affairs and National Defense Division, Congressional Research Service, Washington, June 21, 1985, 9.

12. See William Robinson, "El rol de la democracia en la política exterior norteamericana en el caso de Cuba," In *La democracia en Cuba y el diferendo con los Estados Unidos* (Havana: CEA, 1995), 32.

13. Fonzi, *Last Investigation,* 121.

14. Masvidal split from the CANF in 1985, as did Salmán and Calzón two years later. In all cases it was the result of political differences with Mas Canosa, the only one of the founders who remained in the organization.

15. *Miami Herald,* November 26, 1993. Quoted in Landau, "Cronología."

16. These are the Cuban-American intellectuals directly linked with the CANF. Others, such as Edward González and Pedro Sanjuan, who also formed part of the ideological current, remained active in academia.

17. The most widely accepted story is that he concealed new contracts from the stockholders and delayed collection of debts in order to acquire the company at the lowest possible price. It is alleged that the disloyalty of Mas Canosa provoked the suicide of Mario Torres, one of the owners of the company, who accused him in a public letter to RECE. See *Miami Herald,* April 10, 1988; *Orlando Sentinel Tribune,* January 17, 1993; and Reinaldo Taladrid and Lázaro Barredo, *El Chairman soy yo: La "verdadera" historia de Jorge Mas Canosa* (Havana: Ediciones Trébol, 1994), 310–12.

18. This operation centered around a juicy contract for the development of Watson Island. A number of CANF directors and important officials of the Reagan administration, including Ambassador Jane Kirkpatrick, were implicated in the operation. Probably due to his exclusion, Carollo, noted for his political opportunism, denounced the deal. Afterward, Mas Canosa tried to destroy Carollo's political career.

19. Dade County was later renamed Miami-Dade County.

20. District of Miami cases 76–31470, 76–31376, 76–33427, 77–7049,

78–188627, 80–11376, 85–22503, 86–55395, 87–52896. Quoted in Saul Landau, "Cronología."

21. Codina, one of the foundation's most influential directors due to his personal and business association with Jeb Bush, son of the ex-president, left the CANF over this dispute and over what he considered Mas Canosa's betrayal of the Republican Party, his support of Bill Clinton in the 1992 elections.

22. David Poppe, "Mas," *Florida Trend,* November 1994, 41–42.

23. "1995 Hispanic Business Rich List," 24.

24. John Newhouse, "A Reporter at Large: A Second Havana," *New Yorker,* May 19, 1987, 76.

25. In the case of Cuba, the NED has been used to channel funds to the domestic counterrevolution and to sustain some offshore counterrevolutionary organizations. The CANF has been one of the principal recipients of these funds. In its first four years, the NED contributed over half a million dollars to the CANF for anti-Cuba campaigns in Europe and Latin America. Part of this money also served as indirect financing for domestic counterrevolutionary groups.

26. Fonzi, *Last Investigation,* 119.

27. Just the banquet held by the CANF in April 1992 in Miami, where Clinton announced his support for the Torricelli Act, netted Clinton $125,000 in contributions. Carla Anne Robbins, "Dateline Washington. Cuban-American Clout," *Foreign Policy* 4 (Fall 1992). Quoted in Landau, "Cronología." The Torricelli Act, named for its sponsor, Rep. Robert Torricelli (D-N.J.), is also known as the Cuban Democracy Act.

28. The campaigns against the *Miami Herald* were denounced by the Inter-American Press Society and reported by the rest of the U.S. press as unusual and intimidating episodes. The CANF's actions included boycotts of the newspaper, destruction and vandalism of newsstands, and terrorist threats.

29. Ramón Cernuda, interview by Saul Landau, September 14, 1994. Quoted in Landau, "Cronología."

30. Jack Anderson and Dale Van Atta, *Washington Post,* July 18, 1990; *New York Times,* November 27, 1990.

31. Peter Slevin, "Mas Canosa traza el futuro de Cuba," *Nuevo herald* (Miami), October 11, 1992, A-14.

32. Wounded in the Vietnam War, Lehtinen is publicly described by many sources, including some former professional associates, as emotionally

unstable and prone to violence, including wife beating. Faced with certain opposition from Congress, the Bush administration never sought ratification for his candidacy; Lehtinen thus served for years as U.S. district attorney in Dade County without being ratified in that post.

33. Among those accused were Pedro Ramón López and his wife, Teresa Saldice, for tax evasion, and Alfredo Durán, accused of participation in drug trafficking in the Dominican Republic. Cernuda and Durán were found innocent but López and his wife fled the United States and are still under investigation.

34. Transcript of a radio declaration. Quoted in Landau, "Cronología."

35. Ramón Cernuda, interview by Saul Landau, September 14, 1994. Quoted in Landau, "Cronología."

36. *Diario de las Américas* (Miami), December 15, 1989.

37. *Washington Post,* June 15, 1990. Quoted in Landau, "Cronología."

38. February 1992. Quoted in Landau, "Cronología."

39. Americas Watch, *Dangerous Dialog* (Washington, D.C.: Americas Watch, August 1992). Quoted in Landau, "Cronología."

40. *Miami Herald,* May 21, 1993, and June 15, 1993. Quoted in Landau, "Cronología."

41. *Town and Country,* July 1993. Quoted in Landau, "Cronología."

42. Since 1982, with the help of this program, the directors of the CANF—Jorge Mas Canosa, Francisco Hernández, Domingo Moreira, and José Luis Rodríguez—started businesses in the Dominican Republic, Guatemala, and other countries. Rodríguez later accused the others of dishonest management and broke with the CANF, sparking a scandal that spilled into the nation's press. District of Miami, case no. 90–12926. Quoted in Landau, "Cronología."

43. Donald E. Shultz, *The United States and Cuba: From a Strategy of Conflict to Constructive Engagement,* Strategy Studies Institute, U.S. Army War College, Carlisle Barracks, Pa., May 12, 1993, 119.

44. In September 1988, Félix Rodríguez testified before the U.S. Senate that he collaborated in Posada's breakout and his transfer to El Salvador "on the request of a wealthy benefactor from Miami who financed the escape." Although Rodríguez refused to name him, three exile leaders and two close associates of Posada identified the man as Jorge Mas Canosa (UPI, April 4, 1988). The chief of the Venezuelan prison, Andrés José Arana Méndez, also admitted having been offered a $28,000 bribe, but claimed that he never received the cash (FBI, April 23, 1985). Quoted in Landau, "Cronología."

45. Rodríguez took part in the gray teams (see chap. 3) during the Bay of

Pigs invasion, in Manuel Artimes's Central American project, and in CIA activities in Vietnam and Bolivia, including the capture and murder of Ernesto Che Guevara.

46. Alfonso Chardy, "Vinculan a Jorge Mas Canosa con activista cubano," *Nuevo herald* (Miami), July 19, 1988, A-1.

47. Valladares split from the CANF in 1993 and created his own foundation. The CANF saw it as a competitor and set about discrediting him, to the point that Kristina Arriga, executive director of the Valladares Foundation, declared to the *Miami Herald* that "these people remind me of the Mafia." *Miami Herald,* May 24, 1993. Quoted in Landau, "Cronología."

48. *Miami Herald,* April 12 and 14, 1991; Fonzi, *Last Investigation,* 119.

49. Fonzi, *Last Investigation,* 86.

50. Guillermo Grenier et al., *Views on Policy Options toward Cuba Held by Cuban-American Residents of Dade County, Florida: The Results of the Second 1991 Cuba Poll* (Miami: Florida International University, October 1991), 2–9; Mercedes Arce et al., *Análisis de las encuestas llevadas a cabo por el Institute of Public Opinion Research de FIU en octubre de 1991,* manuscript, CEAP, Universidad de La Habana, 1991.

51. For a description of the prevailing climate see Donald Shultz, *The United States and Cuba: From a Strategy of Conflict to Constructive Engagement,* ed. cit., May 12, 1993, p. 21.

52. Alfonso Chardy, "Grupo de exiliados planea diálogo con Moscú sobre el futuro de Cuba," *Nuevo herald* (Miami), October 15, 1990, A-1.

53. It was unprecedented for the state legislature to approve public funds for a private institution such as the University of Miami that met the conditions set by the CANF after these conditions were rejected by the board of regents that supervises public higher education in the state.

54. *Report of the Blue Ribbon Commission* and *U.S. News and World Report,* May 4, 1992. Quoted in Landau, "Cronología."

55. *Orlando (Fla.) Sentinel,* November 25, 1994. Quoted in Landau, "Cronología."

56. Slevin, "Mas Canosa," A-15.

57. Ibid.

58. Mas Canosa's interference in the editorial and news policy of Radio Martí, aimed at promoting himself and the activities of the CANF, constituted one of the reasons for the resignation of Ernesto Betancourt as director of this station. This interference was also the object of investigation by agencies of the executive and legislative branches of the U.S. government.

59. Taladrid and Barredo, *Chairman soy yo,* 187.

60. Slevin, "Mas Canosa," A-14.

61. "Cuban Democracy Act," *Congressional Record,* title 17, 1992, 271.

62. Every year since 1993, the UN General Assembly has voted against the U.S. blockade of Cuba, with a growing majority, especially in 1994 and 1996, when more than a hundred countries voted in favor of the resolution. The United States's position, on the other hand, has never been supported by more than four votes (1993).

63. This maneuver significantly affected relations between the CANF and the Bush administration and campaign staff. *Miami Herald,* April 26, 1992. Quoted in Landau, "Cronología."

64. Slevin, "Mas Canosa."

65. Ibid., A-18.

66. Carlos Alberto Montaner, *Carta de Carlos Alberto Montaner a Gustavo, María Elena, Luque, Payá, y Elizardo,* Madrid, July 29, 1991. Made public in a press conference held by Cuban authorities.

67. For more information on the political projection of the PDC, see Jesús Arboleya, "Nuevas vertientes de la contrarrevolución cubana: Una imagen fabricada para Europa," *Revista de estudios europeos* (Havana), January–June 1993.

68. Montaner, *Carta.*

69. *Miami Herald,* February 9, 1992. The NED handed out $190,000 in 1990, $462,132 in 1991, and planned to distribute over half a million dollars in 1993.

Chapter 8

1. William Robinson, "Rol de la democracia," 15.

2. Ibid., 10.

3. Samuel P. Huntington, *The Third Wave* (Norman: University of Oklahoma Press, 1993), 9–10.

4. Blanco, *Tercer milenio,* 52, 57; emphasis mine.

5. Ibid., 66; emphasis mine.

6. Carl Gershman, "Fostering Democracy Abroad: The Role of the National Endowment for Democracy," speech before the American Political Science Foundation, August 29, 1986. Quoted in Robinson, "Rol de la democracia," 12.

7. Chomsky, *Deterring Democracy,* 28–31.

8. Fernando Martínez Heredia, "'Nuestra América': El presente y el proyecto de América Latina," *Anuario del Centro de Estudios Martianos* (Havana), 1991.

9. Robinson, "Rol de la democracia," 32–33.

10. *Nuevo herald* (Miami), July 23, 1992. Quoted in Landau, "Cronología."

11. *Proyecto de ley Helms-Burton,* 104th Cong., 1st sess. (Havana: Editora Política, May 1995).

12. A U.S. State Department diplomatic note dated June 29, 1959, referring to the Cuban agrarian reform, and a March 23, 1964, ruling of the U.S. Supreme Court in the "Sabbatino" case, recognize the right of the Cuban state to carry out these nationalizations invoking the doctrine of the Act of a Sovereign Power. See Olga Miranda, "Nacionalizaciones cubanas acorde a las leyes internacionales . . . ," in *Aquí no queremos amos,* Editora Política, Havana, May 3, 1995, 23, 28.

13. The Cuban government recognized and resolved the problem of compensation with all claimant countries *except* the United States, who has refused to negotiate this matter, despite Cuban requests that date back to 1960. See Miranda, "Nacionalizaciones cubanas," 27.

14. Wendy R. Sherman, Assistant Secretary of the Department of State to the President of the Committee on International Relations of the House of Representatives of the United States, Washington, D.C., April 28, 1995.

15. Mimi Whitefield, "Reclamantes de Estados Unidos opuestos al plan Helms-Burton," *Nuevo herald* (Miami), October 2, 1995, B3.

16. Ibid.

17. Regarding this process of negotiation, see chapter 4.

18. Robinson, "Rol de la democracia," 36; emphasis mine.

19. Julio Carranza, "Economía y tolerancia." *Acuario* (Centro Félix Varela, Havana) 7 (1995): 14.

20. "Carta del Presidente George Bush," *Nuevo herald* (Miami), February 27, 1992, A7.

21. Quoted in Alonso, "Iglesia católica," 59–60.

22. Although the right of worship was always respected, as a result of the confrontations of the early years and dogmatic interpretations of Marxism, religious believers were stigmatized for a long time. Nevertheless, political contradictions were limited almost exclusively to the Catholic Church. In the 1980s this situation began to change, culminating in 1993 with a total

revision of these positions, and the acceptance of believers within the ranks of the Communist Party as well as modifications to the Constitution, and in 1998 with the pope's visit to Cuba. See Alonso, "Iglesia católica."

23. The text referred to is the document "El amor todo lo espera" (Love awaits all), circulated by the Cuban bishops to all Catholics in September, 1993. Quoted in Alonso, "Iglesia católica," 55, 66.

24. Huntington, *Third Wave,* 282.

25. Grenier et al., *Results of the Second 1991 Cuba Poll,* 2–9.

26. Alejandro Portes, "The Cuban-American Community Today: A Brief Portrait," quoted in Alonso, "Iglesia católica," 58.

27. Grenier et al., *1995 FIU Cuba Poll,* 10.

28. Diálogo Interamericano, "Cuba en las Américas: Desafíos recíprocos," manuscript, 1992.

29. There is a wide range of public information referring to these positions and events. However, because of its relevance from a programmatic and doctrinal view, I recommend reading the declarations of Cambio Cubano, "Por Cuba. Por el Cambio," *Nuevo herald* (Miami), March 19, 1993; and "Declaración de Cambio Cubano," *Nuevo herald* (Miami), August 23, 1993.

30. "Para todos los cubanos una propuesta real del Comité Cubano para la Democracia," *Nuevo herald* (Miami), August 22, 1993, B5.

31. The magazine folded in 1997 for lack of circulation and advertising.

32. Zbigniew Brzezinski, *Out of Control: Global Turmoil on the Eve of the Twenty-First Century* (New York: Collier, 1993), 149.

33. Amos A. Jordan, William J. Taylor Jr., and Lawrence J. Korb, *American National Security* (Baltimore: Johns Hopkins University Press, 1993).

34. MINREX and Centro Félix Varela, *El conflicto de baja intensidad y el carril II de Torricelli,* document sponsored by MINREX and Centro Félix Varela, Havana, August 1995.

35. Huntington, *Third Wave,* 141.

36. An analysis of the magnitude and impact of this phenomenon in Cuban society can be found in Domínguez, "Integración social y tolerancia," 10.

37. Grenier et al., *1995 FIU Cuba Poll,* 2–4.

38. A strategic step in the direction of this normalization was taken when the Cuban government decided that Cuban-Americans could invest in the country, even though the state of relations between the United States and Cuba, and specifically the prohibitions of the blockade, prevent this possibility from materializing in most cases.

39. Carlos Manuel de Céspedes García-Menocal, "Promoción humana, realidad cubana y perspectivas," paper presented at the Second Catholic Social Week, Havana, November 17–20, 1994, 34.

40. Martínez Heredia, "Nuestra América," 188.

41. Martí, *Patria.*

42. Mimi Whitefield and Mary Beth Sheridan, "Cuba Poll: The Findings," *Miami Herald*, December 18, 1994, A1, A39.

Bibliography

Aguirre, Sergio. *Eco de caminos.* Havana: Editorial de Ciencias Sociales, 1974.

Aja Diaz, Antonio. "La emigración ilegal hacia los EU." *Areíto* (Miami), March 1994.

Akzin, Benjamin. *Estado y nación.* Mexico City: Fondo de Cultura Económica, 1968.

Albanese, Lorelei. "Manolo Ray: Protest in Exile." *San Juan Star Magazine,* August 1, 1971.

Alfonso, Pablo. "Clinton pasa a la ofensiva." *Nuevo herald,* Miami. August 20, 1994.

Alonso, Aurelio. "Iglesia católica y política cubana en los noventa." *Cuadernos de nuestra América* (CEA, Havana) 11.22 (July–December 1994).

Americas Watch. *Dangerous Dialog.* Washington, D.C.: Americas Watch, August 1992.

Arboleya, Carlos. "Miami's Cubans." *Diario las Américas* (Miami), May 17, 1985.

Arboleya, Jesús. "Las corrientes políticas en la comunidad de origen cubano en EU." Ph.D. dissertation, MES, Havana, 1994.

——. *Havana-Miami: The U.S.-Cuba Migration Conflict.* Melbourne: Ocean Press, 1995.

——. "Nuevas vertientes de la contrarrevolución cubana: Una imagen fabricada para Europa." *Revista de estudios europeos* (Havana), January–June 1993.

——. "El 'poder' de la extrema derecha cubanoamericana." *Correo de Cuba* (Havana) 1.1 (October–December 1995).

——. "Terrorismo y contrarrevolución." *Cuadernos de estudio* (CEASEN, Havana), 1995.

Arce, Mercedes. "El proceso de transculturación de la comunidad cubana en Miami: Características socio-psicológicas predominantes." Ph.D. dissertation, MES, Havana, 1994.

Arce, Mercedes, et al. "Análisis de las encuestas llevadas a cabo por el Institute of Public Opinion Research de FIU, en octubre de 1991." Document, CEAP, Universidad de La Habana, 1991.

Arce, Mercedes. "La emigración en Cuba: 1959–1990." Document, CEAP, Universidad de La Habana, 1991.

Arguelles, Loudes, et al. "Cubanos emigrados en Puerto Rico: Coloniaje y terrorismo." *Areíto* (Miami) 31 (1982).

Armas, Ramón de, Francisco López Segrera, and Germán Sánchez. *Los partidos políticos burgueses en Cuba neocolonial, 1899–1952.* Havana: Editorial de Ciencias Sociales, 1985.

Atlas of United States History. Maplewood, N.J.: Hammond, Inc., 1979.

Attwood, William. *The Twilight Struggle: Tales of the Cold War.* New York: Harper and Row, 1987.

Ayers, Bradley Earl. *The War That Never Was.* Canoga Park, Calif.: Major Books, 1976.

Bach, Robert. "The Cuban Exodus: Political and Economic Motivations." In *The Caribbean Exodus.* New York: Praeger, 1987.

Bernal, Guillermo. *Cuban Families.* Boston: Center for the Study of the Cuban Community, 1984.

Blakey, G. Robert, and Richard Billings. *Fatal Hour: The Assassination of President Kennedy by Organized Crime.* New York: Berkeley Books, 1992.

Blanco, Juan Antonio. "La administración Reagan: Tiempo de transición." *Cuadernos de nuestra América* (CEA, Havana) 6 (July–December 1986).

———. *Tercer milenio: Una visión alternativa de la posmodernidad.* Havana: Centro Félix Varela, 1995.

Booth, Cathy. "Miami, the Capital of Latin America." *Time*, Fall 1993 (special issue).

Borm, Atilio. "La crisis norteamericana y la racionalidad neoconservadora." *Cuadernos semestrales* (CIDE, Mexico) 9, first semester (1981).

Borrel Placensias, Germán E. "La labor político-ideológica durante la lucha contra bandidos en el Escambray." Thesis, Instituto Superior Pedagógico "Capitán Silveiro Blanco Núñez," Sancti-Spíritus, Cuba, 1987.

Brizuela, Roxana, and Luis Fernández-Tabio. "El potencial económico de las empresas pertenecientes a cubano-americanos en Estados Unidos." Document, Universidad de La Habana, 1992.

Brogan, Hugh. *The Longman History of the United States of America.* New York: Morrow, 1986.

Brzezinski, Zbigniew. *Out of Control: Global Turmoil on the Eve of the Twenty-first Century.* New York: Collier, 1993.

———. "U.S. Foreign Policy." *Foreign Affairs,* 1973.

Buckley, William F. "It's a Matter of Pride." *Miami Herald,* September 4, 1994.

Buezas, Roberto. "La política económica del gobierno republicano: Contenido, obstáculos, y perspectivas." *Cuadernos semestrales* (CIDE, Mexico) 9 (1981).

Carranza, Julio. "Economía y tolerancia." *Acuario* (Centro Félix Varela, Havana) 7 (1995).

Carrillo, Justo. *A Cuba le tocó perder.* Miami: Ediciones Universal, 1993.

Carter, Jimmy. *Keeping Faith: Memoirs of a President.* New York: Bantam Books, 1982.

Casal, Lourdes. "Cubans in the U.S." *Nueva generación* (New York), December 1972.

Castells, Manuel. *La Crisis económica mundial y capitalismo americano.* Barcelona: LAIA, 1978.

Castillo Ramos, Rubén. "Cruzada redentora en la Sierra." *Bohemia* (Havana), April 26, 1959.

Castro, Fidel. "Bajo la bandera del 26 de Julio: El nuevo ejecutivo de la CTC." *Bohemia* (Havana), November 29, 1959.

———. "Comparecencia ante la televisión cubana el 24 de agosto de 1994." *Granma* (Havana), August 28, 1994.

———. "Conversación con Fidel." Interview by Luis Rumbaut. *Areíto* (New York) 3–4 (1978).

———. "Discurso en el Distrito del Bronx." *Granma* (Havana), October 26, 1995.

———. *Discurso en la velada conmemorativa por los Cien Años de Lucha.* Havana: Editorial de Ciencias Sociales, 1976.

———. "En Cuba" section. *Bohemia* (Havana), March 8, 1959.

———. *Un encuentro con Fidel.* Interview by Gianni Miná. Havana: Oficina de Publicaciones del Consejo de Estado, 1987.

———. *Entrevista con periodistas que escriben para la comunidad cubana en el exterior, 6 de septiembre de 1978.* Havana: Editorial de Ciencias Sociales, 1978.

———. *Un grano de maíz: Conversación con Tomás Borge.* Havana: Oficina de Publicaciones del Consejo de Estado, 1992.

———. *Nada podrá detener la marcha de la historia: Entrevista concedida a Jeffrey Elliot y Mervyn Dymally sobre multiples temas económicos, políticos, e históricos.* Havana: Editora Política, 1985.

———. *Revolutionary Struggle, 1947–1958.* Ed. Rolando Bonachea and Nelson P. Valdés. Cambridge, Mass.: MIT Press, 1972.

Castro, Soraya, and María Teresa Miyar. *U.S. Immigration Policy towards Cuba, 1959–1987.* Havana: Editorial José Martí, 1989.

Centro de Estudios de Alternativas Políticas. *Estudios de los intentos de salidas ilegales por la vía marítima hacia Estados Unidos.* CEAP, Universidad de La Habana, January 1994.

Centro de Estudios Operativos del Ministerio del Interior. "Operación 700, no hubo casualidad." *Cuadernos de estudio* (Havana), April 1994.

———. "Team de infiltración, la avanzada terrorista." *Cuadernos de estudios* (Havana), April 1994.

Céspedes García-Menocal, Carlos Manuel de. "Promoción humana, realidad cubana y perspectivas." Paper presented at the Second Catholic Social Week, Havana, November 17–20, 1994.

Chang, Laurence, and Peter Kornbluh, eds. *The Cuban Missile Crisis, 1962: A National Security Archive Documents Reader.* New York: New Press, 1992.

Chardy, Alfonso. "Vinculan a Jorge Mas Canosa con activista cubano." *Nuevo Herald* (Miami), October 15, 1990.

Chibás, Eduardo. "En Cuba" section. *Bohemia* (Havana), May 25, 1947.

Chomsky, Noam. *Deterring Democracy*. New York: Hill and Wang, 1992.

Christopher, Warren. *Declaraciones ante la Comisión de Relaciones Exteriores de la Cámara de Representantes de Estados Unidos*. ANSA, Washington, D.C., August 8, 1994.

Comisión Nacional Bipartidista Centroamérica (Kissinger Commission). Mexico City: Editorial Diana, 1984.

Comité Central del Partido Comunista de Cuba [PCC]. *Informe del Primer Congreso del Partido Comunista de Cuba*. Havana: Departamento de Orientación Revolucionaria del CC-PCC, 1975.

———. *Tesis y resoluciones del Primer Congreso del Partido Comunista de Cuba*. Havana: Departamento de Orientación Revolucionaria del CC-PCC, 1987.

Comité de Santa Fe. "Las relaciones interamericanas: Escudo de la seguridad del Nuevo Mundo y espada de la proyección del poder global de Estados Unidos." *Cuadernos semestrales* (CIDE, Mexico) 9 (May 1981).

Comité Especial para Investigación de Asesinatos de la Cámara de Representantes de Estados Unidos. *Anexo sobre actividades y organizaciones anticastristas*. Washington, D.C.: GPO, March 1979.

Comité Estatal de Estadísticas. *Estadísticas de migraciones externas y turismo*. Havana: Comité Estatal de Estadísticas, 1982.

"Conversaciones Cuba–Estados Unidos. Comunicado conjunto." *Granma* (Havana), September 10, 1994.

Corn, David. *Blond Ghost: Ted Shackley and the CIA's Crusades*. New York: Simon and Schuster, 1994.

Cortés, Carlos E., ed. *Cuban Refugee Programs*. New York: Arno Press, 1980.

Corzo, Cinthia. "Cambio en la política deja en un limbo la Ley de Ajuste." *Nuevo Herald* (Miami), August 20, 1994.

Crespo Francisco, Julio. *Bandidismo en el Escambray: 1960–1965*. Havana: Editorial de Ciencias Sociales, 1986.

"Cuba: Can't Anyone Here Play This Game?" *Time*, June 12, 1964.

"Cuba: Regulaciones sobre el embargo." *Cuadernos de nuestra América* (CEA, Havana), January–June 1983.

"Daniel, Jean. "Unofficial Envoy: A Historical Report from Two Capitals." *New Republic,* 1992.

"Declaración conjunta Cuba–Estados Unidos." *Granma* (Havana), May 3, 1995.

Declaración de Río Cañas: Manifiesto de la constitución de la Junta Revolucionaria del Pueblo. Rio Cañas, Puerto Rico, September 16, 1963.

Diálogo Interamericano. "Cuba en las Américas: Desafíos recíprocos." Document, 1992.

Díaz-Briquets, Sergio. "Cuban-Owned Businesses in the U.S." *Cuban Studies* (Center for Latin American Studies, University of Pittsburgh Press), Summer 1984.

Didion, Joan. *Miami.* New York: Simon and Schuster, 1987.

"¡Diez mil novillas cargadas! Un aporte más de todos los ganaderos de Cuba a la Revolución." *Bohemia* (Havana), March 8, 1959.

Dinges, John, and Saul Landau. *Assassination on Embassy Row.* New York: Pantheon Books, 1980.

Dirección de Inmigración y Extranjería de Cuba y Centro de Estudios de Alternativas Políticas de la Universidad de La Habana. *La emigración en Cuba, 1959–1990.* Havana, 1991.

Domínguez, Jorge I. *To Make a World Safe for Revolution: Cuba's Foreign Policy.* Cambridge, Mass.: Harvard University Press, 1989.

Domínguez, María Isabel. "Integración social y tolerancia." *Acuario* (Centro Félix Varela, Havana) 7 (1995).

Duarte Oropesa, José. *Historiología cubana.* 4 vols. Miami: Ediciones Universal, 1974.

Dulles, Allan. "My Answer on the Bay of Pigs." 2d draft, master copy. Declassified CIA document, n.d.

Dumpierre, Erasmo. *Biografía de Julio Antonio Mella.* Havana: Editorial Orbe, 1975.

Ediciones Entorno. *El gobierno de Estados Unidos contra Cuba.* Havana: Ediciones Entorno, 1992.

Editorial Capitán San Luis. *Playa Girón: La gran conjura.* Havana: Editorial Capitán San Luis, 1981.

Editorial de Ciencias Sociales. Equipo de Ediciones Especiales. *La juventud acusa al imperialismo.* Havana: Editorial de Ciencias Sociales, 1980.

Escalante Font, Fabián. *Cuba, la guerra secreta de la CIA.* Havana: Editorial Capitán San Luis, 1993.

"Exiliados en Estados Unidos están vendiendo Cuba." *Economía hoy* (Mexico City), 1992.

Fernández Retamar, Roberto. *Introducción a José Martí.* Havana: Casa de las Américas, 1978.

Fernández Varela, Ángel. "Entrevista a Ángel Fernández Varela." *Contrapunto* (Miami) 4.10 (1993).

Fields, Gregg. "Ponen en duda 'éxito cubano.'" *Nuevo herald* (Miami), June 27, 1988.

Foner, Philip. *Historia de Cuba y sus relaciones con Estados Unidos.* 2d ed. Havana: Editorial de Ciencias Sociales, 1973.

Fonzi, Gaeton. *The Last Investigation.* New York: Thunder's Mouth Press, 1993.

———. "Who Is Jorge Mas Canosa?" *Esquire,* January 1993.

Forment, Carlos. *Caribbean Geopolitics and Foreign State-Sponsored Social Movements: The Case of Cuban Exile Militancy, 1959–1979.* Boston: Center for the Study of the Cuban Community, 1984.

Frank, André Gunder. *Lumpenburguesía: Lumpendesarrollo.* Mexico City: Ediciones Era, 1971.

García Azuero, Francisco. "Sector privado teme consecuencias del éxodo." *Nuevo herald* (Miami), September 2, 1994.

Garthoff, Raymond L. *Détente and Confrontation: American-Soviet Relations from Nixon to Reagan.* Washington, D.C.: Brookings Institution, 1985.

González, Edward. *El futuro de Cuba en un mundo posterior al comunismo.* Instituto Nacional de Investigaciones, Rand Corporation, June 1992.

Gramsci, Antonio. *Antología.* Havana: Editorial de Ciencias Sociales, 1973.

Grenier, Guillermo et al. *Views on Policy Options toward Cuba Held by Cuban-American Residents of Dade County, Florida: The Results of the*

First 1991 Cuba Poll. Miami: Florida International University, March 1991.

———. The 1993 FIU Cuba Poll: *Views on Policy Options toward Cuba Held by Cuban-American Residents of Dade County, Florida.* Miami: Florida International University, October 1991.

———. *Views on Policy Options toward Cuba Held by Cuban-American Residents of Dade County, Florida: The Results of the 1993 Cuba Poll.* Miami: Florida International University, July 1993.

———. *The 1995 FIU Cuba Poll: Views on Policy Options toward Cuba Held by Cuban-American Residents of Dade County, Florida, and Union City, New Jersey.* Miami: Florida International University, April 11, 1995.

Grupo Areíto. *Contra viento y marea.* Havana: Casa de las Américas, 1979.

Guanche Pérez, Jesús. "Aspectos etnodemográficos de la nación cubana: Problemas y fuentes de estudio." Havana, 1991.

Guerra, Ramiro. *Azúcar y población en las Antillas.* Havana: Editorial de Ciencias Sociales, 1970.

———. *La expansión territorial de los Estados Unidos a expensas de España y de los países hispanoamericanos.* 4th ed. Havana: Editorial de Ciencias Sociales, 1975.

———. *La Guerra de los Diez Años.* 2 vols. Havana: Editorial de Ciencias Sociales, 1972.

———. *Manual de historia de Cuba (económica, social, y política): Desde su descubrimiento hasta 1868 y un apéndice con la historia contemporánea.* 2d ed. Havana: Consejo Nacional de Cultura, 1962.

Guevara, Ernesto. *Che periodista.* (Articles previously published in *Verde olivo.*) Havana: Editorial Pablo de la Torriente Brau, 1988.

———. "Cuba: Exceptional Case?" *Monthly Review,* July–August 1961.

———. *Escritos y discursos.* 9 vols. Havana: Editorial de Ciencias Sociales, 1985.

———. "Un pecado de la Revolución." *Verde olivo* (Havana), February 12, 1961.

Gugliotta, Guy, and Jeff Leen. *Kings of Cocaine: Inside the Medellín Cartel.* New York: Simon and Schuster, 1989.

Gutiérrez Serrano, Raúl. "El pueblo opina sobre el Gobierno Revolucionario y la Reforma Agraria." *Bohemia* (Havana), June 21, 1959, suppl.

———. "Survey Nacional: El pueblo opina sobre el Gobierno de la Revolución." *Bohemia* (Havana), February 22, 1959.

Hepburn, James. *Arde América.* Madrid: Ibérico Europea de Ediciones, 1968.

Hernández, Rafael. "La lógica de las fronteras en las relaciones Estados Unidos–Cuba." *Cuadernos de nuestra América* (CEA, Havana) 7 (January–June 1987).

Herrera, Alicia. *Pusimos la bomba—¿y qué?* Havana: Editorial de Ciencias Sociales, 1981.

Herrera, María Cristina. "¿Qué es el Instituto de Estudios Cubanos?" *Areíto,* New York, October 1974.

Hinckle, Warren, and William Turner. *The Fish Is Red: The Story of the Secret War against Castro.* New York: Harper and Row, 1981.

Historia de una agresión. Havana: Editorial de Ciencias Sociales, 1977.

Hunt, E. Howard. *Give Us This Day.* New York: Paperback Library, 1973.

Huntington, Samuel P. *The Third Wave: Democratization in the Late Twentieth Century.* Norman: University of Oklahoma Press, 1993.

Ianni, Francis. *Black Mafia: Ethnic Succession in Organized Crime.* New York: Simon and Schuster, 1974.

"Informe elaborado por la Comisión Taylor sobre el fracaso del Plan Zapata." In *Playa Girón: La gran conjura.* Havana: Editorial Capitán San Luis, 1981.

Jaramillo, Isabel. "El conflicto de baja intensidad en el Caribe: La fase preventiva." *Cuadernos de nuestra América* (CEA, Havana) 6 (July–December 1986).

———. "Estados Unidos y la readecuación de su estrategia global: El conflicto de baja intensidad." Ph.D. dissertation, MES, Havana, 1995.

Johnson, Tim. "Some Pollsters Harassed; Most Eager to Talk." *Miami Herald,* December 18, 1994.

Jordan, Amos A., William J. Taylor Jr., and Lawrence J. Korb. *American Na-*

tional Security: Policy and Process. 4th ed. Baltimore: Johns Hopkins University Press, 1993.

Jorge, Antonio, and Raúl Moncarz. *The Cuban Entrepeneur and the Economic Development of Miami S.M.S.A.* The Hague: Research Group for European Migration Problems, 1981.

———. *General Overview of the Cuban Influx since 1959.* The Hague: Research Group for European Migration Problems, 1981.

———. *International Factor Movement and Complementary: Growth and Entrepreneurship under Conditions of Cultural Variation.* The Hague: Research Group for European Migration Problems, 1981.

Keating, Dan, and Charles Strousse. "Miami Area Again Leads U.S. in Crime." *Miami Herald,* December 5, 1994.

Kennedy, John F. *Public Papers of the Presidents of the United States: Kennedy, 1961–63.* Washington, D.C.: GPO, 1962.

———. *Public Papers of the Presidents of the United States: Kennedy, 1961–63.* Washington, D.C.: GPO, 1963.

Kissinger, Henry. *Diplomacy.* New York: Simon and Schuster, 1994.

———. *Years of Upheaval.* Boston: Little, Brown, 1982.

Lage, Carlos. *Intervención en la conferencia "La nación y la emigración."* Havana, April 1994.

Landau, David. *Kissinger.* Barcelona: Ediciones Grijalbo, 1973.

Landau, Saul. "Chronology of the Activities of the Cuban-American National Foundation." Unpublished.

Lara Alonso, Julio. *La verdad irrebatible sobre el crimen de Barbados.* Havana: Editora Política, 1986.

Lechuga, Carlos. *In the Eye of the Storm: Castro, Khrushchev, Kennedy, and the Missile Crisis.* Melbourne: Ocean Press, 1995.

Lenin, V. I. *Acerca del programa nacional del POSDR.* Moscow: Editorial Progreso, 1978.

———. *Balance de la discusión sobre la autodeterminación.* Moscow: Editorial Progreso, 1978.

———. *La lucha de los pueblos y las colonias y paises dependientes contra el imperialismo.* Moscow: Editorial Progreso, 1978.

——. *Obras escogidas.* 3 vols. Moscow: Ediciones Lenguas Extranjeras, 1960.

——. *El orgullo nacional de los grandes rusos.* Moscow: Editorial Progreso, 1978.

——. *La revolución socialista y el derecho de las naciones a la autodeterminación.* Moscow: Editorial Progreso, 1978.

León Cotayo, Nicanor. *El bloqueo a Cuba.* Havana: Editorial de Ciencias Sociales, 1983.

——. *Sitiada la esperanza: Bloqueo económico de EE.UU. a Cuba.* Havana: Editora Política, 1992.

Le Riverend, Julio. *La república: Dependencia y revolución.* Havana: Editorial Universitaria, 1966.

Lernoux, Penny. "The Golden Door for Drugs: The Miami Connection." *Nation,* February 18, 1984.

"Ley 988." *Gaceta oficial de la República de Cuba* (Havana), November 29, 1961.

López y Rivas, Gilberto, and Alicia Castellanos Guerrero. *El debate de la nación: Cuestión nacional, racismo y autonomía.* Mexico City: Claves Latinoamericanas, 1992.

López Segrera, Francisco. *Cuba: Capitalismo dependiente y subdesarrollo (1510–1959).* Havana: Casa de las Américas, 1976.

Maira, Luis. "América Latina, pieza clave en la política de contención de la Administración Reagan." *Cuadernos semestrales* (CIDE, Mexico City) 9 (May 1981).

——. *América Latina y la crisis de la hegemonía norteamericana.* Lima: DESCO, 1982.

Mandel, Ernest. *Ensayos sobre el neocapitalismo.* Mexico City: Ediciones Era, 1971.

Mankiewicz, Frank, and Kirby Jones. *With Fidel: A Portrait of Castro and Cuba.* Chicago: Playboy Press, 1975.

Martí, José. *Obras completas.* Havana:Editorial Tierra Nueva, 1961.

Martínez Heredia, Fernando. "'Nuestra América': El presente y el proyecto de la América Latina." *Anuario del Centro de Estudios Martianos* (Havana), 1991.

Marx, Karl. "Futuros resultados de la dominación británica en la India." In *Obras escogidas en dos tomos.* Moscow: Editorial Progreso, 1955.

———. "Las luchas de clases en Francia de 1848 a 1850." In *Obras escogidas en dos tomos.* Moscow: Editorial Progreso, 1955.

Marx, Karl, and Friedrich Engels. *La guerra civil en Francia.* Havana: Editorial de Ciencias Sociales, 1973.

———. "El Manifiesto Comunista." In *Obras escogidas en dos tomos.* Moscow: Editorial Progreso, 1955.

Masud-Piloto, Félix Roberto. *With Open Arms: Cuban Migration to the United States.* Totowa, N.J.: Rowman and Littlefield, 1988.

Mazarr, J. Michael. *Semper Fidel: America and Cuba, 1776–1988.* Baltimore: Nautical and Aviation Publishing Company of America, 1988.

Medina Castro, Manuel. *Estados Unidos y América Latina, siglo diecinueve.* Havana: Casa de las Américas, 1968.

Méndez, José Luis. "Terrorismo de origen cubano." Ph.D. dissertation, MES, Havana, 1995.

Mesa-Lago, Carmelo. "Will Cuba's Economic Reforms Work?" *Miami Herald,* January 2, 1994.

Meyers, Reginald. "Exiliados esperan pronto fin del régimen castrista." *Nuevo herald* (Miami), February 20, 1992.

Ministerio del Interior. Dirección de Inteligencia, G-2, Estado Mayor del Ejército Rebelde. *Circulación por las unidades de ese Mando del ex-Cmdte. ER Higinio Díaz Ante, complicado en la frustrada conspiración de HÚBER MATOS, que trata de salir del país por la vía del asilo político.* MININT Archives, Havana, March 24, 1960.

———. *Declaraciones del detenido Alfredo Izaguirre de la Riva.* MININT Archives, Havana, October 1961.

———. *Declaraciones del detenido Humber Sorí Marín.* MININT Archives, Havana, n.d.

———. *Declaraciones del detenido Juan Falcón Zammar.* MININT Archives, Havana, August 1962.

———. *Declaraciones del detenido Manuel Reyes García.* MININT Archives, Havana, August 1, 1962.

———. *Declaraciones del detenido Reynold González González.* MININT Archives, Havana, October 18, 1961.

———. *Expediente de Alfredo Izaguirre de la Riva.* MININT Archives, Havana, 1994.

———. *Expediente de Higinio Díaz Ane.* MININT Archives, Havana, n.d.

———. *Expediente de la Operación Ópera.* MININT Archives, Havana, March 17, 1960.

———. *Expediente de Manuel Artime Buesa: Informe de Rodrigo Rivas Vega, delegado del Buró Agrario de Manzanillo.* MININT Archives, Manzanillo, June 15, 1959.

———. *Expediente de Manuel Artime Buesa: Informe relacionado con la actuación del Teniente Manuel Artime Buesa en la región de Manzanillo,* MININT Archives, Manzanillo, November 19, 1959.

———. *Expediente de Manuel Artime Buesa: Informe sobre Manuel Artime.* MININT Archives, Havana, January 25, 1960.

———. *Historia en prisión de las organizaciones contrarrevolucionarias.* MININT Archives, Havana, n.d.

———. *Informe al Jefe de la Sección Q sobre planes de sabotajes.* MININT Archives, Havana, August 15, 1961.

———. *Informe referente a la Operación Candela.* MININT Archives, Havana, June 8, 1961.

———. *Informe sobre la creación del MRP por el traidor Manuel Ray Rivero.* MININT Archives, Havana, September 20, 1961.

———. *Informe sobre la organización contrarrevolucionaria MRR, Operación América.* MININT Archives, Havana, November 28, 1961.

———. *Informe sobre Manuel Artime.* MININT Archives, Havana, January 25, 1960.

———. *Resolución del Tribunal Superior Electoral del 14 de octubre de 1957 reconociendo vigencia como Partido Político y existencia legal al Partido de Liberación Radical con el carácter de Partido Nacional.* MININT Archives, Havana, 1957.

———. *Resumen sobre el caso Operación Santa Clara.* MININT Archives, Havana, February 18, 1965.

Ministerio del Interior. Departamento de Seguridad del Estado. *Declaraciones de Reynold González.* MININT Archives, Havana, January 5, 1977.

Ministerio de Relaciones Exteriores and Centro Félix Varela. *El conflicto de baja intensidad y el carril dos de Torricelli.* Document, Havana, August 1995.

Miranda, Olga. "Nacionalizaciones cubanas acorde a las leyes internacionales." In *Aquí no queremos amos* (Editora Política, Havana) May 3, 1995.

Miyar, María Teresa. "La comunidad cubana y el tema de las relaciones Cuba–Estados Unidos." In *Temas de estudio.* Havana: CESEU, 1989.

Mohl, Raymond A. *Cubans in Miami: A Preliminary Bibliography.* Boca Raton: Florida Atlantic University, n.d.

Montaner, Carlos Alberto. "Cuba: How, When and Who Could Accomplish a Peaceful Solution." Conference on the Caribbean, Miami, 1992.

Morales, María A. "Comienza campaña, para naturalizar a inmigrantes." *Nuevo herald* (Miami), April 12, 1995.

Movimiento de Recuperación Revolucionaria. "Informe del Movimiento de Recuperación Revolucionaria (MRR) a la opición pública de América y el mundo." Costa Rica, June 8, 1960.

National Security Archive. Cuba Documentation Project. "United States–Cuba Détente: The 1974–75 Initiative and Angolan Interventions." National Security Archive, Washington, D.C., 1993.

Newhouse, John. "A Reporter at Large: A Second Havana." *New Yorker,* May 19, 1987.

———. "A Reporter at Large: Socialism or Death." *New Yorker,* April 27, 1992.

"The 1995 Hispanic Business Rich List." *Hispanic Business,* March 1995.

Núñez Jiménez, Antonio. *En marcha con Fidel.* Havana: Editorial Letras Cubanas, 1982.

Olson, James S., and Judith E. Olson. *Cuban-Americans: From Trauma to Triumph.* New York: Twayne Publishers, 1995.

Orihuela, Roberto. *Nunca fui un traidor: Retrato de un farsante.* Havana: Editorial Capitán San Luis, 1991.

Ornstein, Norman J., and Shirley Elder. *Interest Groups, Lobbying, and Policymaking.* Washington, D.C.: Congressional Quarterly Press, 1978.

Ortiz, Fernando. *Contrapunteo cubano del tabaco y el azúcar.* Havana: Editorial de Ciencias Sociales, 1983.

Osa, José de la. "Califica Alarcón de importancia apreciable acuerdo entre Cuba y Estados Unidos." *Granma* (Havana), September 10, 1994.

Padrón Larrazábal, Roberto, ed. *Manifiestos de Cuba.* Seville: Universidad de Sevilla, 1975.

Panetta, Leon. "Declaraciones a la prensa." Agence France Presse (Washington, D.C.), August 8, 1994.

"Para todos los cubanos una propuesta real del Comité Cubano para la Democracia." *Nuevo herald* (Miami), August 22, 1993.

Partido Republicano de Estados Unidos. "Selección de la plataforma del Partido Republicano." *Cuadernos semestrales* (CIDE, Mexico City), 1981.

Pastor, Robert A. "The Latin American Option." *Foreign Policy,* Fall 1992.

Paterson, Thomas G. *Contesting Castro: The United States and the Triumph of the Cuban Revolution.* New York: Oxford University Press, 1994.

"El pensamiento vivo de Fidel: Frases de un discurso para los trabajadores azucareros." *Bohemia* (Havana), February 21, 1959.

Pérez, Lisandro. "Cubans." In *Harvard Encyclopedia of American Ethnic Groups.* Cambridge, Mass.: Belknap Press, 1980.

Pérez, Louis A. "Cuba and the U.S.: Origins and Antecedents of Relations, 1760s–1860s." *Cuban Studies* (University of Pittsburgh Press) 21 (1991).

Pérez-Stable, Marifeli. *The Cuban Revolution.* New York: Oxford University Press, 1993.

Pérez-Stable, Marifeli, and Miren Uriarte. *Cubans in the Changing Economy of Miami.* Boston: Interuniversity Program of Latino Research, University of Massachusetts, 1991.

Pichardo, Hortensia. *Documentos para la historia de Cuba.* 3 vols. Havana: Editorial de Ciencias Sociales, 1963.

Pino Machado, Quintín. *La batalla de Girón: Razones de una victoria.* Havana: Editorial de Ciencias Sociales, 1984.

Pino Santos, Oscar. *El asalto a Cuba por la oligarquía financiera yanqui.* Havana: Casa de las Américas, 1973.

———. *Historia de Cuba: Aspectos fundamentales.* Havana: Consejo Nacional de Universidades, 1964.

Plataforma Democrática Cubana. Made in USA. Havana: Ediciones Tiempo, 1992.

Poppe, David. "Mas." *Florida Trend,* November 1994.

Portantiero, Juan Carlos. *Los usos de Gramsci.* Mexico City: Folios Ediciones, 1981.

Portelli, Hugues. *Gramsci y el bloque histórico.* Mexico City: Editorial Siglo Veintiuno, 1973.

Portes, Alejandro, and Rafael Mozo. *Patterns of Naturalization and Voting in the Cuban Community.* Boston: Center for the Study of the Cuban Community, 1984.

Portes, Alejandro, and Rubén Rumbaut. *Immigrant America.* Berkeley: University of California Press, 1990.

Portes, Alejandro, Juan Clark, and Manuel López. "The Enclave and the Entrants: Patterns of Ethnic Enterprise in Miami before and after Mariel." *American Sociological Review* 54 (December 1989).

Portes, Alejandro, et al. "The Qualitatively Different and Massive Nature of the Cuban Outflow after Castro's Revolution." *Minorías e inmigrantes.* Los Angeles, 1991.

Portuondo, Fernando. *Historia de Cuba.* 6th ed. Havana: Editorial Universitaria, 1965.

Powers, Thomas. *The Man Who Kept the Secrets: Richard Helms and the CIA.* New York: Knopf, 1979.

Poyo, Gerald E. *The Cuban Community in the United States: Toward Another Overview of the Nineteenth-Century Experience.* Boston: Center for the Study of the Cuban Community, 1984.

———. "The Cuban Experience in the United States, 1865–1940: Migration, Community, and Identity." *Cuban Studies* (University of Pittsburgh Press) 21 (1991).

Prieto, Abel. "Cultura, cubanidad, cubanía." Paper presented to the conference "La nación y la emigración," Havana, April 1994.

Prío, Carlos. "En Cuba" section. *Bohemia* (Havana), November 29, 1959.

Prohías, Rafael, and Lourdes Casal. *The Cuban Minority in the U.S.* Boca Raton: Florida Atlantic University, 1973.

Proyecto de ley Helms-Burton. 104th Cong., 1st sess. Havana: Editora Política, May 1995.

Ramírez, Axel. "Los cubano-americanos en el tratado de libre comercio." *Uno Más Uno* (Mexico City), October 13, 1992.

Rasco, José Ignacio. "El Quinto Congreso Internacional de la Democracia Cristiana." *Bohemia* (Havana), December 6, 1959.

Reyes, Jannice, and Alfonso Chardy. "Estudio: Dade no se gana sin el voto cubano." *Nuevo herald* (Miami), February 6, 1993.

Rivero Collado, Carlos. *Los sobrinos del Tío Sam.* Havana: Editorial de Ciencias Sociales, 1976.

Roa, Raúl. *Retorno a la alborada.* 2 vols. Santa Clara: Universidad Central de las Villas, 1964.

Robaina, Roberto. "Discurso de apertura de la conferencia 'La nación y la emigración.'" Havana, April 1994.

Robbins, Carla Anne. "CIA Tells Clinton He Could Face a Crisis in Cuba If Serious Instability Develops." *Wall Street Journal,* November 2, 1993.

———. "Dateline Washington: Cuban-American Clout." *Foreign Policy,* Fall 1992.

Robinson, William. "El rol de la democracia en la política exterior norteamericana en el caso de Cuba." In *La democracia en Cuba y el diferendo con los Estados Unidos.* Havana: CEA, 1995.

Rodríguez, Carlos Rafael. *Cuba en el tránsito al socialismo.* Havana: Editorial de Ciencias Sociales, 1985.

Rodríguez, Ernesto. *Sobre la ciudadanía norteamericana: Análisis estadístico preliminar.* Havana: CEA, 1995.

Rodríguez, Félix, and John Weisman. *The Shadow Warrior.* New York: Simon and Schuster, 1989.

Roig de Leuchsenring, Emilio. *Historia de la Enmienda Platt: Una interpretación de la realidad cubana.* Havana: Editorial de Ciencias Sociales, 1973.

———. *Tres estudios martianos.* Havana: Editorial de Ciencias Sociales, 1984.

Ros, Enrique. *Playa Girón: La verdadera historia.* Miami: Ediciones Universal, 1994.

"Santana, Maydel. "Encuesta: Cubano-americanos rechazan envíos a Guantánamo." *Nuevo herald* (Miami), August 21, 1994.

Santiago, Ana. "Ni dólares ni vuelos." *Nuevo herald* (Miami), August 21, 1994.

Santoro, Carlos M. "Crisis y recomposición capitalista de Estados Unidos." *Cuadernos semestrales* (CIDE, Mexico City) 8 (1980).

Sartre, Jean Paul. "Huracán sobre el azúcar." In *Sartre visita a Cuba.* Havana: Edición Revolucionaria, 1960.

Scheer, Robert, and Maurice Zeitlin. *Cuba, an American Tragedy.* Harmondsworth: Penguin, 1964.

Schlesinger, Arthur. *Los mil días de Kennedy.* Havana: Editorial de Ciencias Sociales, 1970.

"Segunda Ley de Reforma Agraria." *Gaceta oficial de la República de Cuba,* Havana, October 3, 1963.

Sherman, Wendy R. Assistant Secretary of State to the Chairman of the Foreign Relations Commitee of the U.S. House of Representatives. Washington, D.C., April 28, 1995.

Shultz, Donald E. *The United States and Cuba: From a Strategy of Conflict to Constructive Engagement.* Strategy Studies Institute, U.S. Army War College, Carlisle Barracks, Pa., May 12, 1993.

Sklar, Holly, ed. *Trilateralism: The Trilateral Commission and Elite Planning for World Management.* Boston: South End Press, 1980.

Slevin, Peter. "Mas Canosa traza el futuro de Cuba." *Nuevo herald* (Miami), October 11, 1992.

Smith, Hedrick. *Reagan: The Man, the President.* New York: Macmillan, New York, 1980.

Sociedad Cubana de Derecho Internacional. *Agresiones de Estados Unidos a Cuba revolucionaria.* Havana: Editorial de Ciencias Sociales, 1989.

Stavenhagen, Rodolfo. *The Ethnic Question: Conflicts, Development, and Human Rights.* Tokyo: United Nations University Press, 1990.

Stein, Jeff. "Face to Face with Omega 7." *Cuba Times* (New York), Spring 1980.

Szulc, Tad. *Fidel: A Critical Portrait.* New York: Morrow, 1986.

Taladrid, Reinaldo, and Lázaro Barredo. *El Chairman soy yo: La "verdadera" historia de Jorge Mas Canosa.* Havana: Ediciones Trébol, 1994.

Taylor, Jay. "Playing into Castro's Hands." *Guardian* (London), August 9, 1994.

Torricelli, Robert. "Carta al Miami Herald." *Nuevo herald* (Miami), January 5, 1994.

U.S. Central Intelligence Agency. "Memorandum of Conference with the President." Declassified document. Washington, D.C.: GPO, March 18, 1960.

———. "A Program of Covert Action against the Castro Regime." Declassified document. Washington, D.C.: GPO, March 15, 1960.

———. "Spontaneous Revolts in Cuba: Contingency Planning." Declassified document. Washington, D.C.: GPO, January 5, 1989.

U.S. Department of Commerce. Bureau of the Census. *Persons of Hispanic Origins in the United States, March 1979–October 1980.* Population Characteristics Series P–20, no. 354. Washington, D.C.: GPO, 1981.

U.S. Department of Justice. Immigration and Naturalization Service. *1990 Statistical Yearbook of the Immigration and Naturalization Service.* Washington, D.C.: GPO, 1991.

U.S. Department of the Treasury. Office of Foreign Assets Control. *New Regulations on Cuba Affecting Mailing of Gift Packages, Travel, and Remittances of Funds to Cuba.* Washington, D.C.: GPO, August 26, 1994.

U.S. House of Representatives. Judiciary Committee. *Immigration and Naturalization Act with Amendments and Notes on Related Laws.* Spanish translation. Washington, D.C.: GPO, 1980.

U.S. House of Representatives. Select Committee for the Investigation of Assassinations. *Appendix on Anti-Castro Activities and Organizations.* Washington, D.C.: GPO, March 1979.

U.S. Senate. "Cuban Democracy Act." *Congressional Record,* title 17, 1992.

U.S. Senate. Judiciary Committee. *Terrorist Activity: Terrorism in the Miami Area.* 94th Cong., 2d sess. Washington, D.C.: GPO, 1976.

U.S. Senate. Select Committee to Study Governmental Operations with Respect to Intelligence Activities. *Alleged Assassination Plots Involving Foreign Leaders.* Senate Report 94–465, November 20, 1975.

Universidad de La Habana. *Latin Media USA, 1993.* Havana: Universidad de La Habana, 1993.

Universidad de La Habana. Facultad de Filosofía e Historia. *Selecciónes de lecturas del pensamiento político cubano.* Havana: Universidad de La Habana, 1985.

Varela, Félix. *Obras de Félix Varela.* Ed. Eduardo Torres-Cuevas, Jorge Ibarra, and Mercedes García. Havana: Editora Política, 1991.

Viguerie, Richard A. *The New Right: We're Ready to Lead.* Falls Church, Va.: Viguerie Company, 1980.

Villamil, Antonio. "Making Up for Lost Time." *Florida Trend,* April 1994.

Whitefield, Mimi. "Publicidad en español tienta a anunciantes." *Nuevo herald* (Miami), October 30, 1995.

———. "Reclamantes de Estados Unidos opuestos al plan Helms-Burton." *Nuevo herald* (Miami), October 2, 1995.

Whitefield, Mimi, and Mary Beth Sheridan. "Cuba Poll: The Findings." *Miami Herald,* December 18, 1994.

Witcover, Jules. *Marathon: The Pursuit of the Presidency, 1972–1976.* New York: Viking, 1977.

Woldman, Joel M. *The National Endowment for Democracy.* Washington, D.C.: Congressional Research Service, Foreign Affairs and National Defense Division, June 21, 1985.

Woodward, Bob, and Carl Bernstein. *Los días finales.* Barcelona: Editorial Argos, 1976.

The World Almanac of U.S. Politics, 1991–1993. New York: Pharos Books, 1994.

Wyden, Peter. *Bay of Pigs: The Untold Story.* New York: Simon and Schuster, 1979.

Index

26th of July Movement, 27, 28, 29, 30, 31, 32, 34, 35, 57, 72, 94, 95, 183
2506th Brigade, 82, 83, 120, 153, 154, 170

ABC, 16, 17, 223
Acción Cubana, 152
Acción Democrática Revolucionaria, 71
Agramonte, Roberto, 51
Agrarian Reform Law, 45, 118, 266
Agrupación Católica Cubana, 60
Agrupación Católica Universitaria (ACU), 16, 23, 60, 61, 62, 64, 66, 67, 78, 223
Agrupación Juvenil Abdala, 154
Agrupación Montecristi, 35, 70
Aguilar León, Luis, 227
Ala Izquierda Estudiantil, 16, 69
Alianza de Trabajadores de la Comunidad, 276
Allen, Richard, 226, 231
Alliance for Progress, 101
Alliegro, Anselmo, 43
Alpha 66, 121, 130, 142, 144, 154
AMTRUNK, 134
Angola, 128, 141, 149, 154, 165, 226, 236
Areíto, 162, 163, 168
Arocena, Eduardo, 172
Artime, Manuel, 57, 61–65, 68, 76–78, 87–91, 109, 127–29, 214
Artola, Lázaro, 42
Aruca, Francisco González, 234, 282, 283
Asociación de Ganaderos de Cuba, 46
Asociación de Industriales Azucareros y Colonos Cubanos en el Exilio, 264
Asociación de Veteranos de Bahía de Cochinos, 150
Attwood, William, 134, 137

Baloyra, Enrique, 251, 255
Bandín, Carlos, 94, 110
Barquín, Ramón, 35
Barroso, Octavio, 97
Bastarrica, Julián de, 61
Batista, Fulgencio, 16–18, 20, 21, 23–40, 45, 47, 48, 50, 52, 59, 61, 62, 64, 65, 67, 68, 69, 71, 74, 82, 84, 109, 112–14, 117, 118, 120, 156, 161, 170, 183, 185, 230, 255, 266, 269
Batista, Laureano, 85
Bay of Pigs, 41, 43, 60, 66, 74, 80, 84, 92–96, 99, 102, 104, 105, 107, 109, 112, 119, 125, 127, 128, 131, 134, 143, 149, 151, 184, 186, 221, 228, 255, 281
Bay of Pigs Veterans Association, 154
Bender, Frank, 41, 64, 65, 77, 78, 87
Benes, Bernardo, 169
Betancourt, Ernesto, 227
Blue Ribbon Commission, 243
Bosch, Orlando, 151–58
Bosch, Pepín, 143
Brigada Antonio Maceo, 163, 169, 171, 276
Buch, Dr. Luis María, 32, 33, 34
Bundy, McGeorge, 124, 134
Burton, Dan, 264
Bush, George, 157, 214, 227, 238, 247, 250, 256, 258, 261, 263, 273

Calzón, Frank, 200
Cambio Cubano, 249, 250, 251, 252
Cantillo, Eulogio, 33, 35, 84
Carollo, Joe, 229
Carr, Willard, 77, 87
Carretero, Emilio, 118
Carrillo, Justo, 35, 71, 76, 77, 78, 87, 88
Carter, Jimmy, 149, 160, 164–69, 173–75, 189, 221, 254, 258, 293
Casa de las Américas (NY), 145, 246
Casal, Lourdes, 162, 197
Casey, William, 224
Castañeda, Héctor, 245
Castro, Fidel, 22, 26, 27, 28, 35, 36, 39, 41, 43, 60, 66, 74, 80, 84, 92–96, 99, 102, 104, 105, 107, 109, 112, 119, 125, 127,

128, 131, 134, 143, 149, 151, 184, 186, 194, 221, 228, 255, 281
Castro, Frank, 153, 154
Castro, Raúl, 32, 34, 51, 53, 94, 250
Catholic Church, 49, 45, 55, 57, 60, 65, 186, 273
Central de Trabajadores de Cuba, 49, 73
Central Intelligence Agency (CIA), 32, 35, 36, 38, 41, 42, 43, 51, 56, 58, 59, 62, 64, 65, 66, 68–98, 104–11, 115, 119–22, 125–34, 140, 142, 144, 145, 149–51, 153, 154, 156–59, 186, 205, 224–26, 230, 253, 255, 278
Central Nacional Obrera de Cuba, 15
Cernuda, Ramón, 232, 233, 276
Céspedes, Carlos Manuel de, 16
Chibás, Eduardo, 15, 21, 22
Chibás, Raúl, 71
Chiles, Lawton, 145, 193, 233, 238
Chomón, Faure, 29
Church and Tower, Inc., 229–30
Cienfuegos, Camilo, 29, 42, 54–56
Cisneros Díaz, Rogelio, 57, 71, 130
Clinton, William, 191–93, 214, 232, 241, 247, 248, 250, 264, 267, 280, 289
Coalición Democrática Cubana, 244
Codina, Armando, 229
Comando de Organizaciones Revolucionarias Unidas (CORU), 154–56, 159
Comandos 0, 171
Comandos L, 144, 156
Comandos Mambises, 131, 132
Comandos Rurales, 62, 63
Comité Cubano para la Democracia (CCD), 279, 281, 282
Consejo Revolucionario Cubano (CRC), 87–91, 119, 125, 129, 255
Constitution of 1940, 20, 22, 45
Contrapunto, 282, 283
Coordinadora Socialdemócrata, 251, 253, 256
Cruzada Cubana Constitucional, 52
Cuba Project, 32
Cuban Adjustment Act, 192, 196
Cuban-American Committee, 276
Cuban-American National Foundation (CANF), 144, 151, 157, 224, 226–50, 264, 267, 268, 273, 277, 280, 282
Cuban Communist Party. *See* Partido Comunista de Cuba (PCC)
Cuban Democracy Act. *See* Torricelli Act
Cuban Liberty and Democratic Solidarity Act. *See* Helms-Burton Act
Cuban Refugee Program, 182, 195, 196, 205, 212
Cubelas, Rolando, 133, 134
Cuesta, Tony, 144

Daniel, Jean, 134
del Junco, Tirso, 227
Departamento de Investigaciones del Ejército Rebelde (DIER), 57
Dialog with Representative Figures of the Community, 164, 169–75
Díaz, Higinio "Nino," 57, 65, 84, 228
Díaz-Balart, Lincoln, 215
Díaz-Balart, Rafael, 41
Díaz Hanscom, Rafael, 70, 90, 93
Díaz Lanz, Pedro Luis, 51–54
Díaz Tamayo, Martín, 33
Directorio Estudiantil Universitario (DEU), 15–18, 69
Directorio Revolucionario Estudiantil (DRE), 28, 29, 57, 62, 63, 61, 66, 67, 91, 97, 110, 121, 255
Dole, Robert, 129, 238
Doller, Gerry, 41
Donéstevez, Ramón, 170
DRE. *See* Directorio Revolucionario Estudiantil
Dulles, Allen, 59, 80–82
Duque, Evelio, 115
Duque, Félix, 56
Durán, Alfredo, 215, 281

Eagleburger, Lawrence, 140
Echevarría, Oscar, 77
Echeverría, José Antonio, 28, 29
Eisenhower, Dwight D., 33, 39, 40, 75, 76, 80, 101, 184
Ejército de Liberación Nacional (ELN), 115, 117
Elgarresta, Mario, 226
Encuentro Nacional Eclesial Cubano, 273
Espinosa, Rev. Manuel, 166, 167, 169
Estrada Palma, Tomás, 181

Falcón Zammar, Juan, 110–11
Federación Estudiantil Universitaria (FEU), 15, 28, 66
Fernández, Alberto, 70, 90
Fernández, Manuel, 55
Fernández Nuevo, Antonio, 71
Fernández Travieso, Ernesto, 66
Fernández Varela, Angel, 64, 77, 78

Fiallo, Armando, 62, 71, 283, 284
First Cleanup of the Escambray, 115
Fitzgerald, Desmond, 133
Ford, Gerald, 140, 141, 144, 154
Frente Anticomunista de Liberación (FAL), 112
Frente de Liberación Nacional Cubano (FLNC), 153–55
Frente de Unidad Revolucionaria (FUR), 90, 94
Frente Estudiantil Universitario Democrático, 66
Frente Revolucionario Democrático (FRD), 76–78, 82, 86, 87, 89, 114, 255
Frente Unido Occidental (FUO), 109
Freyre, Ernesto, 143
Fundación pro Hombre, 284

González, Reynold, 61, 71, 73, 95, 96, 97
González Corzo, Rogelio, 78, 90, 93, 109
Gorbachev, Mikhail, 241
Government of 100 Days, 17, 20
Graham, Robert, 243
Grau San Martín, Ramón, 17, 18, 20, 21, 68
Grupo Minorista, 15
Guantánamo Naval Base, 34, 70, 84, 94, 95, 112, 113, 131, 192, 193
Guerra, Ramiro, 4
Guevara, Ernesto "Che," 29, 38, 51, 53, 58, 149
Guillot, Juan Manuel, 109–11, 117
Guiteras, Antonio, 15, 17, 18, 20
Gutiérrez Menoyo, Carlos, 28
Gutiérrez Menoyo, Eloy, 29, 37, 38, 69, 70, 119, 120, 126, 249, 250

Helms, Jesse, 114, 264, 267
Helms, Richard, 98
Helms-Burton Act, 264, 265, 267, 268
Hermanos al Rescate, 268
Herrera, María Cristina, 168
Hunt, Howard, 74, 77, 81, 83, 84, 86, 87, 88, 90

Instituto de Estudios Cubanos (IEC), 168
Instituto Nacional de Reforma Agraria (INRA), 50
Inter-American Dialog, 280
INTERPEN, 133
Iran-Contra, 157, 225, 237
Izaguirre, Alfredo, 70, 93, 94, 112, 119

Javits, Jacob, 139–40
Jiménez, Roberto, 97
JM/WAVE, 120–21
Johnson, Lyndon, 134, 136–38, 141, 196
Jorge Díaz, Dalia, 97
Joven Cuba, 162–63
Junta de Gobierno de Cuba en el Exilio, 133
Junta Revolucionaria Cubana (JURE), 128–30, 134, 156
Juventud Cubana Socialista, 162
Juventud de Acción Católica (JAC), 60
Juventud Estudiantil Católica (JEC), 60
Juventud Obrera Católica (JOC), 60–61

Kennedy, John F., 39, 40, 79–81, 86, 88, 91, 92, 95, 99, 100–106, 113, 117, 119, 122–36, 141, 145, 268
Kennedy, Robert, 104, 106, 124, 127, 131, 138
Kirkpatrick, Jeanne, 243
Kirkpatrick, Lyman, 32
Kissinger, Henry, 138–40, 152, 153

Lansdale, Edward, 104, 105, 108
Lansky, Meyer, 25
Latin Builders' Association, 234
Lechuga, Carlos, 134
Legión Anticomunista del Caribe, 40–41
Letelier, Orlando, 150, 156, 232
Llorente, Armando, 61
López Fresquet, Rufo, 30, 46, 71
Lorié, Ricardo, 65, 112
Lugo, Freddy, 156–58

Machado, 14, 15, 16, 18, 19, 69, 223
Mack, Connie, 243
Mañach, Jorge, 16
Mankiewics, Frank, 139
Mariel, 174, 175, 190, 191, 209
Márquez Novo, Esteban, 109
Marquez-Sterling, Carlos, 42–43
Martí, José, 6, 18, 163, 180, 181, 203, 297
Martín Elena, Eduardo, 83, 86
Martínez, Raúl, 194
Martínez Villena, 15, 18
Mas Canosa, Jorge, 143, 144, 157, 193, 194, 226, 228–38, 241, 243–48, 265
Mas Tec, 230
Masferrer, Rolando, 42
Masvidal, Raúl, 226
Matos, Húber, 51–57, 71, 85
McGovern, George, 139, 141, 145
McKinley, William, 9
McNamara, Robert, 102

Mederos, Elena, 51
Mella, Juio Antonio, 15
Mendieta, Carlos, 17
Menendez, Bob, 171, 215
Mikoyan, Anastas, 66
Milián Rodríguez, Ramón, 128
Miró Cardona, José, 36, 50, 87–90, 119, 120, 125, 154, 211
Miyares, Marcelino, 281
Monroe Doctrine, 3, 6, 38, 102, 221, 247, 289
Montaner, Carlos Alberto, 251, 255
Morales, Ricardo "Mono," 151, 153, 158
Moreira, Domingo, 244
Morgan, William, 69
Mosquera, Amancio, 128
Movement of Nonaligned States, 141
Movimiento 30 de Julio, 71, 95
Movimiento 30 de Noviembre (M-30-11), 71–73, 94, 110
Movimiento de Recuperación Revolucionaria (MRR), 61, 62, 64–67, 70, 78, 82, 85, 86, 90, 94, 109–13, 127, 128, 255
Movimiento de Resistencia Cívica (MRC), 30, 71
Movimiento de Veteranos y Patriotas, 15
Movimiento Demócrata Cristiano (MDC), 61, 65, 66, 78, 85, 86, 94, 110, 143
Movimiento Insurreccional de Recuperación Revolucionaria (MIRR), 151, 155
Movimiento Nacionalista Cubano (MNC), 144, 149, 150, 154, 156, 171
Movimiento Revolucionario del Pueblo (MRP), 71–73, 86–88, 94–97, 110, 129
Muller, Alberto, 66, 91
Muñíz Varela, Carlos, 170–71

National Coalition of Cuban-Americans (NCCA), 165–66
National Endowment for Democracy (NED), 225, 226, 233, 253–56, 261, 293
National Security Council, 32, 38, 59
Negrín, Eulalio, 170, 172
New Frontier, 91, 99
New Right, 218, 220, 224, 277, 296
Nieves, Luciano, 170
Nixon, Richard, 39, 137–41, 188
North, Oliver, 237
Novo Sampol, Guillermo, 149, 151, 152, 232

Oliva, Erneido, 143
Omega 7, 171–72
Operación Liborio, 97
Operación Reunificación Cubana, 170
Operation Condor, 150
Operation Mongoose, 92, 98, 104–8, 112, 113, 117–23, 127, 129, 134
Operation Patty, 95–96
Organización Auténtica (OA), 44, 45, 68, 84
Organization of American States (OAS), 101, 104, 139, 140, 174, 268
Orozco Crespo. Miguel, 121
Otero, Rolando, 153–55

Pacheco, "Congo," 116
Partido Comunista de Cuba (PCC), 15, 22, 29, 136, 139, 175
Partido del Pueblo Cubano (Ortodoxo), 21, 23, 27, 29, 30, 142
Partido Protagonista del Pueblo, 158
Partido Revolucionario Cubano (PRC) (Auténtico), 16, 18, 20–23, 28–30, 44, 48, 68–73, 86, 97, 180, 183
Partido Socialista Popular (PSP), 29
Patterson, William E., 32–34
Pazos, Felipe, 30, 51, 71, 87
Pell, Clairborne, 139, 140
Pérez Alamo, Duney, 52–57, 130, 158
Phillips, David, 130
Pinochet, Augusto, 150
Pinto Rodríguez, Mariano, 109
Plataforma Democrática Cubana (PDC), 251–56, 270, 279
Platt Amendment, 9, 17, 18, 202, 280
Playa Girón. *See* Bay of Pigs
Poder Cubano, 151
Posada Carriles, Luis, 144, 156–58, 237
Prío Socarrás, Carlos, 16, 21, 24, 30, 44, 68, 69, 132
Project Cuba, 104, 106
Project Democracy, 224, 225, 293
Puig Miyar, Manuel, 90
Puig Tabares, Luis, 109
Pujals Mederos, José, 94–97

Radio Martí, 233, 236, 244
Radio Progreso Alternativa, 282–83
Ramírez, Osvaldo, 97, 115–17
Rasco, José Ignacio, 65, 66, 68, 77, 78, 85, 251, 255
Ray, Manuel, 30, 55, 57, 71, 73, 87, 88, 94–96, 129, 130
Reagan, Ronald, 214, 217, 220–22, 224, 226, 227, 234, 238, 254, 258, 275, 293

Rebel Army, 28, 29, 32, 33, 34, 35, 36, 51, 52, 57, 62, 65, 84, 112, 114
Reboso, Manolo, 214–15
Reich, Otto, 227
Representación Cubana en el Exilio (RECE), 143–45, 156, 228
Rescate Revolucionarion Democrático, 68–69
Resistencia Cívica Anticomunista, 112
Ricardo, Hernán, 156–58
Ríos, Nicolás, 282–84
Rivero, Felipe, 144, 149, 150
Roa, Raúl, 16, 17
Rodríguez, Carlos Rafael, 7, 31
Rodríguez, Félix, 84, 157, 158, 237
Rodríguez González, Luis David, 112–13
Rogers, WIlliam, 140
Roosevelt, Franklyn D., 16, 20, 21, 103
Ros, Enrique, 78, 85–87
Ros, Ileana, 157, 215, 232, 243
Rosa Blanca, 40–41
Ross, Alvin, 151
Rosselli, John, 132
Rubiera, Vicente, 143
Ruisánchez, Ramón, 78, 90, 114, 115
Ruíz Williams, Enrique "Harry," 131

Saco, José Antonio, 3, 4, 6, 180
Salmán, Carlos, 226, 228
Salvador, David, 72–73
Salvat, Juán Manuel, 66
San Gil, Tomás, 113, 117, 118
San Román, José, 93
Sánchez Arango, Aureliano, 68, 69, 76, 77, 86
Sánchez Parodi, Ramón, 140
Sanjenís, Joaquín, 86
Santa Fe Committee, 221
Sardiñas, Rafael, 77
Sargén, Nazario, 142
Savimbi, Jonas, 237
Schlesinger, Arthur Jr., 88–89
Second Escambray Cleanup, 118
Second National Front of the Escambray, 29, 36, 41, 71, 73, 114, 130, 142
Segundo Frente Nacional del Escambray. *See* Second National Front of the Escambray
Sierra Martínez, Paulino, 132
Smith, Earl T., 33
Sorí Marín, Humberto, 51, 57, 62, 64, 70, 90, 93, 112
Sorzano, José, 227
Soviet Union. *See* USSR
Special Group Augmented (SGA), 104, 106, 120, 124, 125
Special Tasks Group, 125, 133
Spiritus, John Maples, 73
Stone, Richard, 145, 228
Sturgis, Frank, 51–52
Suárez, Dionisio, 152
Suárez, Xavier, 215

Tabernilla, Francisco, 35
Taconal, Luis, 42
Task Force W, 120, 125
Taylor, Maxwell, 79, 85, 94, 103, 104, 106, 119
Torricelli Act, 232, 245–48, 265, 280, 289
Torriente, José Elías de la, 145, 146, 151
Trilateral Commission, 164
Triple A, 68–69
Trujillo, Rafael Leonidas, 40–42
TV Martí, 236

UN Commission on Human Rights, 237
Unidad Cubana, 242
Unidad Revolucionaria (UR), 70, 94, 97
Unión Liberal Cubana, 251, 253
UNITA, 226, 237
Urrutia, Manuel, 33, 50–54
USSR, 37, 59, 99, 107, 123, 134, 138, 141, 165, 219, 221, 222, 240, 241, 246, 248, 250, 257, 262, 286

Valdespino, Andrés, 71
Valladares, Armando, 237
Vallejo, René, 134
Vance, Cyrus, 165, 169
Varela, Félix, 3, 180
Varona, Manuel Antonio "Tony" de, 16, 36, 68, 69, 77, 78, 86–90, 132
Veciana, Antonio, 96, 97, 130, 142
Vera Catalá, Ciro, 116
Vietnam, 102, 103, 123, 136–40, 151, 154, 159, 218
Villafaña, Manuel, 131

War of Independence, 6, 7, 8, 181
Weicha, Robert, 70
Wells, Sumner, 16, 17
Wilson, Edward C., 57

Yabor, Antonio Michel, 65